1990

Conscience

ANTONIO ROSMINI

CONSCIENCE

Translated by
DENIS CLEARY
and
TERENCE WATSON

ROSMINI HOUSE
DURHAM

Translated from
Trattato della Coscienza Morale
Milan, 1844

Cover photo: Lake Matheson & Mt. Cook, New Zealand

Typeset by Litho Link Limited, Welshpool, U.K.
Printed by Courier International Ltd., Tiptree, Essex

ISBN 0 9513211 1 0

Note

Square brackets [ ] indicate an editor's note or addition.

[. . .] indicates an omission from the text.

References to other works of Rosmini are given by paragraph number unless otherwise stated.

Abbreviations used for Rosmini's quoted works are:
  AMS: *Anthropology as an Aid to Moral Science*
  PE: *Principles of Ethics*
  OT: *The Origin of Thought*

Foreword

This book, the fifth* in a series of English translations of Rosmini's philosophical and theological works, offers a detailed examination of the ethical and theological problems connected with conscience. The abundance of detail, which is apparent towards the end of the book, sprang from Rosmini's declared aim of evaluating current problems of conscience, and may at first sight obscure the value of his treatment of fundamental difficulties felt in our own time. This foreword is written, therefore, to help show very schematically how the author deals with matters of conscience which are the explicit object of attention today.

An initial description of the vicissitudes suffered by the two 19th century Italian editions of the book will illustrate what was of particular interest in theological schools at Rosmini's time and during the following century. Without denying the continuing necessity for light on these topics, we can then show the direct relevance of his basic teaching to ourselves, irrespective of our secular or spiritual stance.

The immediate reaction to the first edition (Milan, 1839) included a violent attack on doctrinal aspects of the work. Rosmini, in order to sustain theologically the existence of inadverted morality in the human subject, had referred to Catholic teaching on original sin and in addition developed at length a distinction between 'sin' and 'fault' (cf. chap. 5, art. 1 and 2). He was taken to task, mainly by anonymous authors who considered original sin as *pura privatio gratiae sanctificantis* (a simple privation of sanctifying grace), for maintaining that the will of the newly conceived human subject is involved in each individual's state of original sin. The ensuing polemic gave rise to two more books on Rosmini's part (*Le nozioni di peccato e di colpa illustrate* [*The notions of sin and fault*], Milan, 1843, and *Il razionalismo che tenta insinuarsi nelle scuole teologiche* [*Rationalism, and its attempted entry into the theological schools*], which remained unpublished until 1882), and innumerable replies from his adversaries. Finally, silence was imposed on both sides by a Roman decree of 1843 which Rosmini obeyed scrupulously, suppressing the publication of his work on rationalism and the

---

* The others are: *The Five Wounds of the Church*, Leominster, 1987; *The Origin of Thought*, Leominster, 1987; *The Constitutions of the Society of Charity*, Durham, 1988; *Principles of Ethics*, Leominster, 1988.

schools of theology. In 1854, the work on conscience was subjected, together with all Rosmini's then published volumes, to examination by the Roman consultors of the Index and declared free from error. In 1887-88, thirty-two years after Rosmini's death, the Holy Office decree *Post Obitum* included amongst forty condemned propositions of Rosmini one proposition (XXXV) on original sin taken not from Rosmini's second, corrected edition, but from the first edition of the work on conscience.†

During this controversy, the principal subject of the book had been almost completely lost sight of. Another dispute, which broke out after the publication of the second edition, was more to the point but still touched upon only a part of the work. Rosmini, while respecting and admiring the spirit of St. Alphonsus de Liguori, disagreed with the material application of his teaching on reflective principles as a way of resolving doubt in matters of conscience. In particular, he opposed the application to the natural law of the principle *lex dubia non obligat* (A doubtful law does not oblige). The many exceptions made by de Liguori to his own general theory served, according to Rosmini, to safeguard morality, but were often overlooked in ill-considered works of probabilists inspired by enthusiasm for the Saint's anti-jansenistic teaching.

With the exception of these attacks on *Conscience*, the work did not attract a great deal of attention. This, however, would appear to depend upon extrinsic factors rather than on lack of internal value. The immense problems of conscience with which we are now familiar in daily life as sources of inevitable perplexity for believers and non-believers, for Christians and non-Christians, were to a great extent unknown not long ago. Only in our own time have moral problems about basic human actions come to be considered as normal matter for considerations of conscience. Although the hearts of previous generations may have been as hard as our own, people were confident enough to assert a categorical difference between right and wrong, however badly they might have chosen between the two. In present-day secular or spiritual life, we lack their confidence and need some direction about the use and formation of conscience. Rosmini's work can contribute to satisfying this need.

Of immediate concern is the relationship between morality and conscience. For Rosmini, conscience can never be the sole, fundamental criterion of morality. As a human act, conscience, according

† For the texts, and a recent theological examination of the proposition cf. Giorgio Giannini, *Esame delle Quaranta proposizioni rosminiane*, pp., 124–128, Genoa/Stresa, 1985.

to which we judge the moral value of actions we are about to do, is itself subject to moral requirements, the chief of which demands that our judgment, by indicating the exact moral state of our actions, should accord with truth. In a word, we must not lie to ourselves about the morality or immorality of the action we are undertaking.

Our actions, therefore, possess moral quality prior to the development of conscience. As a result, although knowledge and will are essential for the existence of morality in the human subject, *ac*knowledgement, *re*cognition or awareness of such morality may often be lacking. On the other hand conscience, when it is present, may be mistaken. I may judge wrongly, and through my own fault, of the moral value of my action.

Has conscience, therefore, no absolute value? It has, but only in a negative sense. That is, while it is never morally lawful for us to act against our conscience, we cannot conclude from such a negative obligation that it is morally necessary and good to follow our conscience, when it has been badly formed. There will be occasions, normally connected with rational rather than positive law, when conscience, which should clarify our view of the moral state of determined actions, becomes a false guide through our own fault. In such a case, the human dilemma is intensified to the point of tragedy. On the one hand, we can never act against our conscience; on the other, we cannot rightly follow the deceitful directions we have set out for ourselves. Yet there is a way to escape the dilemma; we can and must rectify our false conscience. How this can be done is a problem faced squarely by Rosmini, and resolved chiefly by his insistence on the unending presence in human beings of the innate light of truth as the first, unshakeable moral principle. Conscience has only to reflect this light, or at least not obscure it by wilful error. It is indeed possible either to come to the right conclusion or, if a correct solution is impossible for us, at least to admit our ignorance about the moral state of our action.

Acknowledgment of our ignorance in this case means, however, that we have not formed a conscience. Uncertain of the morality of our actions, we suspend our judgment about their moral quality. At this point, rules for the formation of conscience are needed, especially in the case of doubt about intrinsic moral evil in our actions. Rosmini deals with the difficulty at length before considering the question of probabilism, a source of heated debate in his day and later, but now overshadowed to a great extent by more basic questions.

Rosmini's insistence, in the latter part of the book, on the arguments for and against probabilism makes for hard and sometimes wearisome reading. Nevertheless, the temptation to exclude the relevant articles was resisted on the grounds that Rosmini's constant return to principles throws further light on matters he has already examined. In addition, he takes the opportunity of illustrating at length the confessor's duty on the delicate subject of the formation of conscience in his penitents.

Another reason for retaining the last part of Rosmini's treatise is to present his positive view of the moral teaching of St. Alphonsus de Liguori, the bicentenary of whose death (†1787) has led to renewed interest in his work.

This very brief description of Rosmini's work on conscience must be supplemented by mention of two other difficulties arising from his methodology. First, Rosmini's documentation of his own research is extensive, as a glance at the footnotes will show. The immense labour entailed in checking all his references would require the facilities normally available for preparation of a critical edition of the work.‡ Indications of sources have, therefore, been reproduced from the second edition (Milan, 1844), revised by Rosmini himself. Second, some footnotes are extremely long, and stand as essays in their own right rather than as immediate illustrations of the text. These have been collected and printed as an *Appendix* to the work with indications of their place in the original. We hope that in doing this we have not betrayed Rosmini's thought, but made it more accessible.

Denis Cleary
Terence Watson

Durham.
February 1989.

‡ 17 of the projected 80 volumes have appeared in the critical edition (1979–) of Rosmini's works, published as a joint venture between the *Istituto di Studi Filosofici* (Rome), *Centro Internazionale di Studi Rosminiani* (Stresa) and *Città Nuova Editrice* (Rome).

Contents

BOOK 2

MORALITY RESULTING FROM CONSCIENCE

BOOK 3

RULES OF CONSCIENCE

SECTION ONE

RULES FOR A FORMED CONSCIENCE

SECTION TWO

RULES TO BE FOLLOWED
WHEN WE HAVE STILL NOT FORMED OUR CONSCIENCE

Introduction

1. An orderly exposition of moral teaching must begin by establishing a *principle of morality* from which all moral responsibilities can be derived. This has been our aim in the two works forming the first volume of *Moral Philosophy*.[1]

The principle of morality must then be applied to *human beings* whose responsibilities and obligations must be deduced from it. This cannot be done, however, without a prior study of human beings themselves and the elements constituting their intelligent, moral nature. In particular, the relationship between human nature, morality and the supreme principle of morality has to be clarified. We have described the human being as the subject of morality in *Anthropology as an Aid to Moral Science*, the second volume in our series on moral philosophy.

After considering the *principle of morality* and the *human being* to whom it must be applied, we should now apply the principle to its subject in order to set out human moral responsibilities, precepts and laws in an orderly system of ethics. But this will be carried out, we hope, by others. We need to note, however, that such an application cannot be carried out safely, without danger of error, unless great care is taken to follow the rules of reasoning arising from rigorous logic. This is especially true in the many difficult cases we shall meet.

2. We have seen that, in addition to *general logic*, a *logic of ethics* is possible, just as every other discipline can have its special rules of logic.[2] These particular bodies of logic are the dictates of general logic as applied to individual disciplines. Through this application, the dictates become more appropriate for determined circumstances, and more manageable.

[1] The two books are entitled *Principles of Ethics* [PE, Leominster 1988, ISBN 0-85244-148-7], and *Storia comparativa e critica de' sistemi intorno al principio della morale* [Intra 1867].

[2] See the *Preface to the Works of Moral Philosophy* [PE, 12 ss.].

They are now *mediate propositions*, as the classical authors called them, and as such serve to guide our reasoning more closely in particular disciplines.

The principles of general logic, which does not concern itself with individual classes of things, cannot of themselves take cognisance of actual natures; special logic, on the other hand, takes from actual natures the data for determining general principles. An architect, for example, will not roof many buildings if he uses as his sole principle: 'The means must be proportioned to the end.' Nevertheless, when he has worked out the different special rules needed for roofing in arctic or equatorial regions, he will find that his work consists in determining this principle according to circumstances, and that his special rules, for example about the pitch of roofs in regions with heavy snowfall, depend upon this principle for their truth and force.

In the same way, the special rules that together form the *logic of ethics* depend upon the application of the general rules of thought to moral matters. The moralist uses these rules when, through his application of the supreme principle of morals to human beings, he deduces their moral precepts and responsibilities.

Our present work will examine some of the rules proper to the logic of ethics, which we cannot consider here in all its extension. We must begin, therefore, by setting out the necessary limits to our study.

3. By applying the supreme law or moral principle to human beings, it is possible to deduce more or less general laws according to the different ways of considering human nature. For example, if I apply the supreme principle to human beings considered solely from the point of view of their human nature, without considering any relationship or determination in this nature, I will conclude rather generally that 'I must respect this intelligent nature.' If, however, I take into consideration not only human nature as common to all individuals in the species, but also the relationships between parents and their children, my conclusions will be concerned with the less general laws expressing the responsibilities between parents and children. I may then go on to think of more restricted relationships, such as those between sick

parents and their children and, as a result, consider the responsibilities now owed by the children, and so on. This will become clear when we have occasion to speak about it later in this work. Finally, if I am asked what are the most particular laws and moral precepts that can be deduced from the supreme principle, I would have to say that they regard the individual actions which a given person is about to carry out. These most particular laws would tell us how this person is obliged to act *here and now*. But in every case, whether the laws, precepts and obligations deduced from the supreme principle and applied to human beings be general, special or particular, it is always necessary for this deduction to be directed according to the rules provided by good logic. It is clear, therefore, that the *logic of ethics* extends to govern and direct all the deductions, general and particular, made from the principle of morality.

Our study cannot embrace the total extent of the logic of ethics. We intend to set out the *logical rules* restricted to directing the deduction of the most determined of all particular obligations. Our work is concerned with the final step in the application of the supreme principle to human beings and their actions, that is, with the deduced precept which has as its object an *individual action* accompanied by all its circumstances and subjective relationships.

Thus, not all individual actions are taken into consideration in this book. We shall deal only with those actions which are a person's *own*. We shall restrict our investigation to the logical rules according to which a person has to make a judgment about the goodness or malice of his own actions, and about the freedom or obligation he has to carry them out or omit them if he wishes to avoid uncertainty and error in a matter of such importance.

But when a person has judged that an action of his conforms or not to the law, he necessarily becomes *conscious* of the moral nature of what he is doing. Because of this, the rules we intend to examine in this book are rightly called *rules of conscience*.

4. The study of conscience is of its nature philosophical. It is in fact a part of the special logic of ethics. Nevertheless it has been carried out entirely by Christian theologians

without much assistance from philosophers.

It may seem strange that philosophers have consistently neglected the study of the rules directing human moral conscience. But because abstractions and generalities are their preoccupation, it is not easy to bring philosophers down to earth. Christian theology, on the other hand, is exclusively concerned with the moral reform of humanity. It came into being in order effectively to guide the human race to virtue; it did not originate for the sake of offering pronouncements in pompous language or for showing off its logical capacities.

Christian theology has to weigh the very smallest human action on the scales of perfect justice, and offer human beings rules for doing good in every circumstance and condition in which they may find themselves spiritually engaged. The responsibility incumbent on Christian theologians is more than human; they have to look to God, the divine Judge, and obtain from him the moral decisions and rulings to be taught to human beings. God is not like a human judge, nor does he speak simply for the sake of speaking; he pronounces his verdict on the real actions of all people according to the fullness of truth. Rulers and citizens, the learned and the unlearned, have all alike to render him an account according to the principles which have guided their lives. For this reason, Christian law has compelled everyone to take seriously, not academically or theoretically, the sure, certain rules indicating the moral life obligatory on every human being. The learned and ignorant, the intelligent and non-intelligent, all need the practical rules isolating and dividing the moral element from other circumstances in such a way that it stands independent of every exterior accident and of every non-moral condition of mind and soul in the person who acts. Only in this way can we all avoid condemnation by the universal Judge.

Christian teachers, who are in everyone's debt because they are sent to attract all to what is good and upright, had necessarily to investigate the norms according to which all would be judged. In other words, they had to investigate the *obligatory force of the law* according to individual consciences, and give each concience its own rules. As a result, teaching about conscience, although it belongs *per se* to philosophy, has a divine origin, divine content and a divine aim. Its purpose, which has consistently escaped the attention of philosophers, is to render all human beings morally good. And this is God's purpose.

The Saviour, Redeemer and Master of the world sent scribes to co-operate in his work by teaching us to direct our lives according to truth and justice. Their doctrine was not intended simply to satisfy our curiosity. These scribes have provided modern times with studies about conscience and its rules. Consequently, there is a great deal of learning which, although philosophical of its nature and within the possibilities of natural reason, has to be hailed justly as a benefit of revelation, not because revelation has expressly declared it, but because revelation strengthened by grace has stimulated the human heart to undertake studies that would otherwise have been totally neglected.

Later in this work we shall explain why Christian theologians themselves came only very late to study *ex professo* the rules of moral science.

5. For the moment, I need only note that the discussion on conscience has continually increased in importance since it was first proposed publicly by certain theologians in the 16th century. Today the study of conscience is generally accepted as the principal and most difficult part of the whole of moral science.

It is the *principal* part because the right understanding and use of all ethical laws and teaching depends upon the rules of conscience. This is true for simple Christians who need these rules in order to walk through life securely according to moral goodness, and for confessors and spiritual directors who have to make judgments about the good and evil of others' actions and suggest to souls the paths of goodness along which they can safely venture without adding to the difficulties they may find there.

6. Conscience is also the most *difficult* part of moral science. This can be seen by glancing at the innumerable works written on the subject in the last three centuries, or by noting the heated controversies still dividing theological schools on the matter. The difficulties experienced by those wishing to give a proven, coherent and universal solution to

the problem of conscience is a further indication of the intricate labyrinth presented by the question.

7. For myself, my own efforts at understanding the nature and state of this question have convinced me that the greatest obstacle to a clear, satisfying solution lies in the lack of suitable language for establishing unequivocally and exactly ideas that will remain stable throughout the discussion. We need ideas that will compel, as it were, the listener's mind to think the very concept the speaker thinks and wishes to express. Too often, adversaries are talking about different things while using the same words, and continue their discussion without ever being able to agree or even understand one another. The major work on this problem, as on many others, has been done, I think, when the nature of the question has been clearly and manifestly established.

8. Consequently, I am entering the field with the intention of endeavouring above all to provide a precise way of speaking, proper to the argument. I trust that the wise will be indulgent to me, if I stray from the mark, especially in view of the intricate difficulties of the subject, and that followers of any particular school of thought will not hold it against me if I disagree in part with what they hold. My state of life, my way of conducting myself and my manner of writing are completely alien to controversy with any school. My longing is for immortal truth which I am happy either to teach others in so far as I know it or to learn from others when they teach me. If anyone is displeased by the ardour with which truth draws me to write, I now offer that person my hand as friend and comrade; and I know I shall feel pain if anyone tries to disturb with even a touch of agitation the peaceful atmosphere in which love and truth offer only warmth and light.

Book 1

MORALITY PRIOR TO CONSCIENCE

1

DEFINITION OF CONSCIENCE

9. Conscience means consciousness; moral conscience [which in English we normally call 'conscience'] means moral consciousness.

Properly speaking, we *know* other things but are *conscious* of what we ourselves do and of what takes place at the level of our interior feeling. We take the word *conscience* in this sense, and use it to indicate knowledge of ourselves.

Etymology provides the same meaning for *conscience*. The prefix *con* denotes union or conjunction, and tells us of knowledge we have *with* ourselves, knowledge furnished by our inner feeling. We may notice in passing that etymology, especially if it still governs words in use, shows us the concept that ordinary people possess of the thing signified by a word. This is of considerable importance because ordinary usage is almost the sole authority we have for deciding the meaning of words.

10. However, we must subject the word *conscience* to a careful analysis in order to clarify its meaning more surely. And to do this, we first recall the distinction between direct and reflective knowledge which we encountered when we studied the foundations of epistemology.[3]

When we carry out any first intellective act, we do not know the act itself although it is the means by which we know the object of our knowledge. This first knowledge, in which we know immediately the object of our act but not the act itself of our spirit (*means of knowledge*), is called *direct knowledge*.

After direct knowledge has been acquired, *reflection* takes place. But reflection is of two kinds. We can either reflect upon the *objects* of direct knowledge, or we can reflect upon the *act* of the spirit by which the spirit knows. If we reflect only upon the objects of knowledge, we acquire *reflective knowledge* of the objects of our knowledge, but not of the act of the spirit which is the *means of knowledge*. If we reflect

---

[3] *Certainty*, 1258–1263.

upon both the object of knowledge and the act of our spirit (the *means of knowledge*), we acquire *consciousness*, that is, a general conscience of our intellective act in relationship with the object to which it refers.

11. We must note that this consciousness or general conscience is the effect of reflection which terminates simultaneously in the cognitive *act* of the spirit and in the first *object* of that act. As far as the object is concerned, our resulting knowledge is certainly reflective, but the same cannot be said, strictly speaking, about the act of our spirit, of which we knew nothing prior to the act itself. We come to know the act only as a result of our reflection.[4]

12. We should also note in passing that our distinction between reflecting only upon the objects of knowledge and reflecting upon the act of the spirit (which thus becomes an object itself) is extremely important and provides an explanation of a great number of otherwise inexplicable psychological facts. In particular, it throws light upon the difficulty experienced by the spirit in reflecting upon its own *feelings* — a difficulty rarely experienced when it reflects upon its own *ideas*.

13. Certainly, transient feelings occur in us without our reflecting upon them in any way, and very great care is needed if we are to succeed in paying proper attention to them.

But attending to feelings which remain constantly present to us is even more difficult than grasping transient feelings. Lasting feelings are connatural and intimate; they form our nature and constitute our being. But that which is most natural in us and most consistent with our nature is least easy to observe. Our attention is attracted rather by what is novel and unusual, not by what is customary, innate and constant. Our ideas, moreover, in so far as almost all of them are

---

[4] It must be noted that when I assert our ignorance of the cognitive act of the spirit prior to reflection upon the act, I am not denying to our spirit a *feeling* of the cognitive act. On the contrary I admit that our spirit, which is essentially sensitive, has a *feeling* of each of its acts. But it has no knowledge of them until, reflecting upon them, it makes them the *object* of its knowledge. Denying that the spirit has a feeling of its acts would render reflection on the acts inexplicable because the spirit would have no object on which to fix its attention.

acquired, add something new to our nature and more easily become objects of our reflection.

14. If we now ask ourselves which of our ideas we reflect upon most easily, we soon see that reflection becomes more difficult as the distance between ideas and their first, natural source increases. The first principles of reason, for instance, which are the nearest to the common fount of our ideas, are almost the last to enter our sphere of reflection. On the other hand, *perceptions* and *specific ideas*, which are the furthest from their natural source, possess the greatest freshness and are most foreign to our nature, but are the easiest to reflect upon.

This law also explains why reflection upon the idea of being, the source of all other ideas, is difficult in the extreme. Instead of constituting the immediate object of our reflection, this idea is considered reflectively only after it has been separated from partial ideas.

15. We said that *conscience*, in the general sense, is a reflection. But it is not any kind of reflection. It is not that which takes place simply on our ideas or concepts and constitutes *reflective knowledge* properly so-called; it is reflection turned upon ourselves, making us know what we do or what is done in us. Nevertheless, even this is not sufficient to give us a full, clear concept of *conscience* in the *moral* sense of the word.

We act with our understanding, with our affectivity and with our body, and can become conscious of all these different activities.

But our conscience, in so far as it tells us only what we do historically, is not yet *moral*. Rather, it is what we may call *historical conscience*.

When does moral conscience begin in us?

In my opinion moral conscience is not restricted to making us conscious of what we do, and nothing more. It also offers a *judgment* about our actions which makes us conscious of their quality.

We can go further. Interior judgments about our actions can vary enormously according to the rule that we use in formulating them. For example, if I judge that a certain action is going to be economically harmful to me, I have judged it according to economic standards; if I judge that an action is going to diminish my political influence, I have judged this action by a political norm; and so on for every judgment according to the *norms* I use in qualitatively assessing actions.

Moreover, these norms can be classified. By gradually reducing them to their most general classifications, we find that we can allocate them to two supreme *genera* formed by the *utility* and *rectitude* of the action under consideration.

If we judge our action according to the norm of utility, in so far as it brings us nearer to or distances us from happiness, we say that we have made a *eudaimonological* judgment.

If we judge our action according to the norm of rectitude, in so far as it makes us virtuous or evil by conforming to or differing from the law, we say that we have made a *moral* judgment.

These two kinds of judgment, to which we can submit all our actions, allow us to acquire two types of consciousness. We can become conscious of having posited either a *utilitarian* or an *upright* action.

Consequently, there are two kinds of conscience: *eudaimonological* conscience and *moral* conscience.

16. We are now in a position to view the entire concept of moral conscience. By summarising the elements we have seen to be included in it, we find that they can be reduced to the following:

    1. an intellectual, affective or external action of our own;

    2. historical consciousness of this action;

    3. direct knowledge of the moral law;

    4. simultaneous reflection upon the law and upon our action for the sake of comparing one with the other;

    5. the comparision between the action and the law;

    6. the conclusion we draw from this comparison. This conclusion consists in the judgment we make about the uprightness of the action whether it is done or not.

17. At this point we have to add another observation. *Moral conscience* is formed in us only when we are doing, or have already done, an action. If the action has not been done, or is not yet started, we can know it, but we cannot be conscious of it (cf. 9). It follows that a conscience *concomitant* with and *subsequent* to an action can be formed, but not

properly speaking a conscience *antecedent* to an action, or at least antecedent to a projected action.

Nevertheless we have to remember that before the action is done or even before deliberation about actually carrying it out, we have normally thought about it and made a judgment concerning its uprightness. Although we have not yet decided whether to carry it out or not, we have made the action seem our very own by representing it as a possibility open to our deliberation. We then say, improperly, that we have a conscience about the action. This is the conscience theologians call *antecedent*.

2

IS CONSCIENCE A PRACTICAL JUDGMENT?

18. What we have said will enable us to decide if conscience is indeed a practical judgment, as it is usually called. Our decision will depend upon the meaning given to the word *practical*. Πραξις, *practice*, is a Greek word meaning *action*. Strictly speaking, therefore a *practical judgment* means an operative, efficacious, *active judgment*. But a truly efficacious, active judgment must be the root and starting point of our action. In a word, such a judgment must necessarily result in action, unless impeded by a contrary, practical judgment. We must note carefully that the operation of an intelligent being is always physically *begun* and determined by a judgment. When I, as an intelligent being, decide to act, I first say to myself: 'Such an action will help me', and I act immediately on this interior word. The judgment with which I recognise that an action is good for me here and now is the first movement leading me inevitably to what I actually do.

Is this practical judgment moral conscience? Is conscience of its nature an efficacious, active judgment resulting in action?

It is already clear that conscience is entirely separate from action, and that we can act even against the dictate of conscience.

Conscience, therefore, does not necessarily lead to action;

it is not a judgment on which action depends, or to which action is physically joined. Conscience is not an *operative* judgment, and properly speaking cannot be called a *practical* judgment.

19. The *practical judgment*, the effective root of our actions, can be morally good or bad in so far as it rests upon motives conforming to, or in opposition to, the moral law. When a person is mugged and killed, the murderer acts because he has said to himself: 'This will help me.' He would certainly not have acted in this way without making such a practical judgment. But the motive drawing him to judge that the mugging will help him is solely economic; it is unjust, and contrary to the law. The murderer's practical judgment, therefore, is wicked. Moreover, it has nothing to do with his conscience. If anything, his conscience is directly opposed to his practical judgment and condemns it as immoral. Conscience, therefore, is a judgment over and above the practical judgment and as such was defined by me elsewhere as, 'a speculative judgment that a person makes about the morality of his practical judgment.'[5]

20. But if conscience is merely a *speculative judgment* about the morality of our own particular actions, why has it generally come to be known as a practical judgment?

It has been called a *practical judgment* because the word *practical* has been taken in a broad sense. Instead of being understood solely of something active or pertaining to action (its true meaning), *practical* now indicates something referring to, or ordered to, action.

This last meaning is also used when *moral* philosophy is called *practical* philosophy in order to show that the dictates of moral philosophy refer to and regulate human actions.[6] But it is clear that no teaching contained in moral philosophy exceeds the bounds of speculative truth because such teaching has nothing to do with the reality of actions. Like all other ideas, moral philosophy belongs to the order of *ideas*; actions on the other hand belong to the order of real things, not to the order of ideas. Because this has been overlooked and attention concentrated on the ideas which help to regulate our

[5] *PE*, 191.
[6] *Preface to the Works of Moral Philosophy* [*PE*, 1 ss.].

actions, such ideas have been improperly called 'practical', despite their speculative or theoretical status.

21. It seems to me time to restore the proper use of language[7] both for the sake of dealing with the intricate problems of conscience, and in order to eliminate the innumerable, useless distinctions and complicated phraseology needed to express ideas.

An example of the difficulties which may occur is found in the definition of conscience used by certain writers.

Because the word *practical* came to be applied to whatever refers to actions, *moral* philosophy, which refers to actions in so far as it offers rules for action, became *practical* philosophy, and conscience, which judges our own past, present or future actions, became a *practical judgment*. But it was soon observed that moral philosophy does not refer to actions as immediately as conscience does. Moral philosophy indicates only in general terms which actions are to be done and which are to be avoided; only conscience immediately applies the dictates of moral philosophy to present or past actions. It became clear, therefore, that a distinction was necessary to show how conscience was more directly concerned than moral philosophy with action, and barbarous neologisms were invented to provide such a distinction. Moral philosophy was called 'speculatively practical' and conscience 'practically practical'. As Billuart writes: 'The

---

[7] It is worthwhile examining the use made of the word *practical* by our classical writers, who consistently employ it in its exact sense. Villani and others use it as the opposite of *knowledge*, *reason*, and *speculation*. 'Great people, wise in *thought* and *practice*' (Villani, bk. 10, 50); 'Understanding is a true gift when it is related both to *thought* and *practice*' (Man. *Dictionary* 30); 'Practice and age teach a great deal' (Alammani, *Gir.*, 22, 80). *Essays on Natural Experiences* states: 'The rule for making them is acquired only through *practice*.' In all these examples the word *practice* is used in its first, proper meaning. It is then used to indicate 'the habit of action acquired through action itself, and therefore a principle of action.' Berni used it with this meaning: 'His people, prompt, ready and practical, tempered in fact and in war' (*Orl.*, II, 1, 47). Finally, the word is used, with less propriety, about knowledge related to action. But we have to notice that *practical* knowledge, strictly speaking, entails a contradiction. We would be speaking of *knowledge-not-knowledge*, *knowledge-action*. We have to interpret the expression, *practical knowledge*, therefore, as a convenient abbreviation employed in everyday language. We speak of 'practical knowledge' instead of 'knowledge that teaches how practice should be carried out.'

[21]

understanding is said to be *speculatively practical* when, by means of moral philosophy, it reaches general conclusions about good and evil relative to human actions; it is said to be *practically practical* when, by means of conscience, it reaches particular conclusions about good or evil relative to a single act.'[8]

It is clear that the same kind of reasoning will eventually force us to recognise the need of more outrageous jargon. If the word *practical* has to be employed to indicate various degrees of nearness to action in different branches of moral philosophy, conscience can only be called 'practical' through continual repetition of the word. Moral dictates begin in fact with our obligation to acknowledge universal being. This is the *supreme moral law*,[9] and its obligation is very distant from actions, which are approached gradually first through *generic*, then through more *special laws* until conscience indicates the final, particular command.

For example, the first law states: 'Acknowledge being (with your practical judgment) for what it is.' This law is very far from determining, by prohibition or positive command, any particular action. If I apply this law to human nature, I deduce another law: 'Acknowledge human beings (with your practical judgment) as intelligent beings, that is, as beings who possess an end in themselves and cannot be considered as means for your use.' I have now come a little nearer to action in so far as I can determine more closely the respect I should have for human beings.

If I apply this law to slavery, taken in its strict sense, I deduce another, more particular law: 'Slavery in the strict sense is unlawful because by it one human being uses another as a means, without respecting the other as an end.' This third norm is nearer to action than either of the other two because it prohibits that kind of activity which constitutes slavery taken in its strict sense. But we have not yet reached conscience.

For instance, what would Pollio's conscience have told him when he wanted to feed his fish with the carcasses of his slaves? His conscience would have disapproved. It would

[8] *Summa summae etc.*, t. 1, *De actibus humanis*, Diss. 5, art. 1.
[9] The supreme law of morality has been established in *PE*, and in *Storia comparativa e critica de' sistemi intorno al principio della morale* [cf. fn. 1].

have applied the third norm more or less as follows: 'Feeding your fish with human flesh is unlawful because it is an act of slavery in the strict sense, and therefore unjust because it uses human beings without respecting them as having an end in themselves.' This final norm, or judgment of conscience, is nearer to action than any of the three already stated.

If we wanted to express the nearness of moral laws to action, we would have to call the supreme law *practical*, the second law (deduced from the supreme law) *practically-practical*, the third *practically-practically-practical*, and finally conscience *practically-practically-practically-practical*. This kind of semantic barbarism would produce endless confusion of ideas, and would still not express what was required — the four steps I have indicated from the supreme law to action could be multiplied indefinitely, with even greater detriment to language.

22. The truth is that moral teachings, whatever their nearness to action, cannot rightly be called *practical*. They are all *speculative* because they are all contained in the order of ideas, although they do indeed regulate practice, that is, real actions. *Practice*, however, is *action* itself, and once accepted as such gives the lie to its use in any description of moral teaching.

3

THE FACULTY TO WHICH CONSCIENCE BELONGS

23. Because conscience is a moral judgment (cf. 19, 20), it belongs to *moral reason*,[10] the faculty for deducing all laws from the first law.[11]

[10] In *PE* (cf. 184, 185) I distinguished *moral reason* from both *eudaimonological* and *practical reason*. I pointed out that reason is a single power. However, when judging moral matters it is called 'moral'; when judging useful things, it is called 'eudaimonological'; when judging with *effective energy* what should be done here and now, all things being considered, it is called 'practical', and as such is the true beginning of human actions.

[11] The faculty of the first law is the *moral intellect*. Cf. *PE*, 183.

24. The *faculty* of moral reason has different *functions*, but what has been said indicates that conscience belongs to *reflection*. Conscience is a judgment about the morality of our actions, that is, about the morality of our practical judgment which is their foundation. Clearly, therefore, we have to *reflect* upon this practical judgment in order to evaluate its morality.

25. It is more difficult, however, to determine the *level of reflection* to which moral conscience belongs. We know that the theory of knowledge assigns different levels to reflections. The first level is the reflection on our direct knowledge, but we can in turn reflect on this level itself, thus producing a second level. We can then reflect on this second level and arrive at a third level with new information, a process that can be continued indefinitely.[12] To which of these levels, therefore, does conscience belong?

To answer clearly, we must review the successive steps which lead to *morality* in human acts and to our *conscience about this morality*. If we are able to view the whole process generating the quality which makes our acts moral and known to be moral, we will be able to note precisely where and how the interior act of conscience properly originates.

Article 1.
The origin of morality in human beings

26. The process by which morality comes about in human actions has been described in *Principles of Ethics*. Our description, which faithfully observes and follows nature, has prepared the way for us. The process, as described in the book, is:

1. We possess the *supreme Law*, which is *ideal-indeterminate being*, the measure of all *determinate* and *real* beings [*App*. no. 1].

2. As soon as we experience sensible impressions, we apprehend real beings intellectively, as beings. This first *apprehension* is entirely spontaneous, lacking any deliberation and constituting *direct knowledge*. As yet there is

[12] Cf. *Certainty*, 1149–1157.

nothing moral in human acts; at this stage they are purely intellective because they are spontaneous, necessary products of the understanding, not of the will.

3. We reflect upon the beings apprehended. As long as this reflection is merely speculative, it does not generate any morality. But if the *practical energy* with which the will is endowed (cf. 18) is associated with it, there takes place what I call the *willed, practical acknowledgement of beings*. This is the source of *morality*.

27. In our willed acknowledgement we can be just or unjust (cf. 19). If we acknowledge the perceived beings simply for what they are, that is, according to the precise level of good each has (a level equal to the grade of their being), then we are just. Otherwise, we willingly err and contradict the truth, or direct knowledge, in us. It is in this first practical, willed reflection that the morality of our actions begins and defines itself; their morality, in its origin and essence, consists precisely 'in the rectitude and truthfulness which the human being places in the willed acknowledgement we are speaking of.' In this acknowledgement the value of the things conceived in their idea is not dissimulated, nor is a value invented for them (the value of things is expressed generally as a *quantity of being* because the quantity of being consti-tutes the quantity of good in everything).[13]

28. It has been shown[14] that all human morality takes its origin from our first willed judgment on the value of what is perceived, in other words from the first practical reflection on our direct knowledge. We saw that *intellective, affective* and *external* actions in human beings are interconnected as links of a chain and have for their point of reference the willed, reflective judgment which esteems known objects. The source of human morality, therefore, is to be found solely in this first *esteem*, the effect of the first *reflective judgment*, an essentially moral act, generating affections and movements which, together with the actions that follow affections and movements, share in its morality. Hence sacred scripture says: 'Let an UPRIGHT WORD go before all your works.'[15] This word is internal, an acknowledgement of the truth (that is, of the direct knowledge), a willed judgment we pronounce to

[13] *PE*, 20–45.   [14] *op. cit.*, 114–181.   [15] Eccl 37: 20.

ourselves before positing an act. Clearly then *morality* belongs to the *first reflection*. A personal, actual morality, beginning at the level of our first reflections, is possible in every human being.

29. In passing, we may note that we commonly say a person has attained the use of reason when his actions indicate morality. Hence we generally call it the age of 'discretion' of good and evil. Reason does of course begin to develop in us from the first moments of our existence, but only gradually. It first has to acquire perceptions of feelable things, from which it must then separate ideas and eventually form the idea of *intelligent being* to which moral value refers (cf. 28).[16] Because seven years are normally allowed for this, we say that human beings reach the use of reason at seven years of age. But we then explain this by adding that the child at that age can discern good and evil.

Article 2.
The origin of conscience

30. *Morality* begins at the first level of practical reflections (cf. 26). To establish the level at which *conscience* originates, we recall that 'conscience is a judgment on the morality of our actions' or 'a speculative judgment on the morality of our practical judgment.' But if the *morality* of actions is based in the practical judgment, which belongs to the first level of reflections, *conscience*, in order to judge about *morality*, must reflect on the first level of reflections, to which morality belongs. The judgment, then made by conscience, is a later reflection than that of morality; it is *at least a second-level reflection*. Conscience, therefore, cannot begin before we have reached at least the second level of reflections in our development.

31. I say at least the second level because, although actual morality begins at the first level of reflections, it can take place just as easily at all higher levels. Thus, conscience, although it begins with the second level of reflections, belongs equally to the third, fourth, or any higher level.

[16] *PE*, 101–105.

4

THE RELATIONSHIP BETWEEN MORALITY AND CONSCIENCE

32. What has been said shows clearly that in the first development of human beings *morality* precedes *conscience*, because morality belongs to the first order of reflections while conscience belongs to the second. A singular but irrefutable consequence of this truth is that a state can exist where morality is really present in human beings without their being conscious of it. This fact demands our careful attention.

33. We wish to know whether conscience is present in the act of practical acknowledgement, the foundation of moral action. Conscience, we have said, is a judgment the individual makes on his practical judgment; it is a decision whether this practical judgment conforms to the law or not. When I make a practical judgment, therefore, must I at the same time make a speculative judgment on its morality?

The problem may at first seem simple but is in fact complex, because it consists of three different questions:

Does conscience, as a speculative judgment, form part of the *concept* of a moral act?

If indeed a moral act can be considered abstractly as different from conscience, can it be really posited without the accompanying act of conscience?

Finally, does conscience always accompany a moral act, not because of some intrinsic necessity but accidently, because of some cause external to the nature of morality?

We must now answer these questions.

Article 1.
Can we conceive a moral act without being conscious of it?

34. I begin with a concrete case. A child at the age of reflection has already perceived human nature (direct knowledge), and is on the point of judging the worth of a human being, for example, an employee of the house. The child has a choice. Using the rule for measuring himself, he must either judge the

other person to be like himself, that is, worthy of the same respect, and consequently not to be used as an instrument for his own ends, or he must judge and regard the other person simply as an instrument of his will, to be made use of, like his dog or one of his toys. In this case the child makes himself the sole end and the employee merely a means.

As long as the child, this human being, remains on the point of committing himself to one or other of the two opposing practical judgments, he has not posited a moral act. He sees the two judgments as possible, one corresponding to the truth (direct knowledge), the other contradicting and opposing it. We must therefore ask ourselves: before the child pronounces one or other judgment does he, in order to effect a moral act, have to judge the judgments themselves, that is, judge the first in conformity with the law and the second opposed to it? In other words, for the practical judgment he is about to make (but has not yet made) to be morally good or bad, must he have formed a *moral conscience* about it, in such a way that without conscience, his practical judgment would be devoid of morality?

35. We might answer immediately that the child's practical judgment cannot be morally good or bad until he himself judges it so. But such a reply does not do full justice to the question, which is: does the concept of conscience form part of the concept of a moral act?

An exact reply requires us to start from what we have already seen, namely, that the *function of morality* and the *function of conscience* are different functions of *moral reason*. They are two *reflections at different levels*, one higher than the other, since the function of morality naturally precedes that of conscience. Their acts therefore are considered separately and as independent of each other (cf. 23–31). Consequently, in the order of concepts the act of conscience essentially presupposes that of morality and not viceversa.

36. I say *in the order of concepts*, because our discussion is about concepts. In the *order of reality* my conscience could certainly precede my moral action. In fact, this is what normally happens in developed human beings, who judge their actions before positing them. The moral action is first present in me as *conceived*, not posited (together with the

practical judgment it is thought of as possible). Then I make a speculative judgment on the mentally conceived moral action; this is an antecedent conscience. Thirdly, I perform the action to which I have committed myself. The last act in this sequence is, as the Scholastics say, the first to be conceived; the conscience which is posterior to the conceived moral act is anterior to the real act.

Article 2.
Must conscience be formed before a moral act can be posited?

37. In the order of concepts what is judged is always presupposed by the judgment about it. Is the opposite true in the real order? If the moral act, conceived only in the mind, precedes conscience, what is the order of *conscience* and *morality* when the act is really posited and not simply conceived?

We must not confuse this second question with the third, which is to be discussed later and asks whether the moral act is in *fact* always accompanied by a moral conscience. It may perhaps be true that someone acting morally is always conscious of his moral act, but it could equally be true that this consciousness or conscience, which constantly accompanies the moral act, does not influence the formation of that act.

The answer to the question is implicit in what has been said. The nature of a moral act is different from an act of conscience. Moreover, a moral act belongs to a function of moral reason, while an act of conscience belongs to some other function. Furthermore, a moral act is an act of first reflection while conscience is never less than second reflection. Consequently, a moral act need not always and *necessarily* be joined to an act of conscience, which does not have to begin before the moral act is completed. A moral act, therefore, can really subsist without being preceded by an act of conscience.

38. However, as we have said, the real acts are in fact often preceded by conscience. If not, they easily escape our observation. For this reason we have difficulty in understanding

the problem. We judge our future action good or, more often, malicious, and we act with this conscience, which determines the merit attributed to us.

This may be the present state of our developed humanity, which is able to reflect at a very high level. But was it always and necessarily so? The real problem is whether an act of whose morality we are not conscious is moral or not. Such a problem can be solved by concentrating only on what *necessarily* happens, not on what simply happens.

39. What I have written about the morality of human actions will be of great help in solving the problem. A clear concept of rational law (the source of all law) is necessary to understand my meaning correctly.

The essence of natural law can be summed up as follows: 'A human being acts justly when he acknowledges and esteems the beings he has perceived for what they are.' We do not need the abstract concept of law to be able to function morally, nor do we need to know explicitly how to state, for example, the principle that we must give all beings their due. In order to act justly and therefore morally, it is enough for us to give to the beings we conceive what is theirs, without considering anything else. Such an acknowledgement, which accords with truth, that is, with the entity of the perceived being, can be natural and instinctive; we can do it without thinking of anything else, in such a way that every time we act, we simply say to ourselves: 'This being has this amount of beingness; I esteem it as such.' Without needing anything else, we have 1. acted intellectively, 2. with our will, 3. and according to the rule of what is just, that is, according to the *entity* we have perceived. We have therefore acted in a human, moral way. We may not yet be able to talk about law or utter the word 'obligation'; we may not reflect on what we do, but we act according to the movement of our good nature, according to the natural, rational order which indicates the way we should act. This is morality in human beings prior to the formation of conscience. It is a state which justly demands the attention and consideration of philosophers.

Article 3.
Is the moral act, when posited,
always joined in fact to an act of conscience?

40. The answer to the second question helps us to solve the third, which is: 'If the act of conscience is not part of the moral act nor *necessarily* present in the real production of a moral act, does it *in fact* always accompany a moral act for some *accidental* reason?' We believe the answer is negative for the following reasons.

41. Analysis of a practical judgment invariably indicates that it is composed of only two elements: 1. *direct knowledge of intelligent beings*, in whom our moral acts terminate (rule, law, truth); 2. *practical reflection* on the beings conceived in direct knowledge (adhesion to the rule, law, truth). Nothing more seems required for this judgment.

42. If a moral act needs only these two elements, we cannot affirm that it is always accompanied by conscience (which is a third element) unless we have a sufficient reason for explaining the formation of an act of conscience along with a moral act.

This sufficient reason is even more necessary if we are to affirm confidently that we are always aware of the morality of what we do. Such an awareness would require an altogether special explanation because it militates against the general law that 'our acts can exist in us without our being aware of them' or, as I have often noted about this fact of nature, 'each of our acts is unknown to itself.'

Only a sufficient reason could show that morality is always accompanied by awareness and explain this constant union of morality and conscience, which are *per se* two different things, as we have seen.

§1. Observation and experience indicate
that we are not always aware of our moral actions

43. Observation of each moral act would help little, because observation would apply only to the particular cases observed. But by analogy, observation of a great number of

cases would indicate some probability concerning those unobserved cases.[17] However, accurate observation of individual cases is difficult. If there are moral acts in us of whose morality we are unaware, it must be difficult to observe them. The fact that we lack awareness of their morality is a clear indication that we reflected very little upon them when we did them. They have not, as it were, escaped our thought and will; they have escaped our deliberate reflection. Furthermore, acts that take place in us with little or no reflection[18] leave in our memory very weak and easily erased traces, if indeed they leave anything observable.

In addition, as adults, or when our faculties have been activated, we are ceaselessly stimulated by the goad of innumerable sensations, and have continually before us the purpose of our actions, which keeps all our powers ceaselessly alert and active. This allows us to perform a quantity of moral acts with reflection, deliberation, and an acute conscience, which serves as their proximate rule. These actions, splendidly illuminated for our spirit by the light of reflection and conscience, attract our full attention and prevent the spirit from observing the weaker, less important actions which escape both general reflection and the moral reflection suitable for constituting conscience. The eye of our spirit has an experience similar to that of our natural eye when it passes from a brightly lit room to one poorly lit: it has the impression of being in total darkness, unable to see objects, which, although not totally dark, are barely visible.

44. Experience, if it has anything to offer, supports the opinion that moral acts take place in us without our being aware of them. As we have said, it is a constant law that our

---

[17] Experience and observation certainly guide us in these investigations. But I distinguish the experience of *particulars* from that of *universals*. The former reveals little of itself but can, however, be of use when helped by the law of analogy, which is the foundation of induction and belongs to what I call the experience of universals. People satisfied solely with the observation of particulars deceive themselves about what they are doing. If they limited themselves only to particulars, as they claim, science would be impossible for them and their spirit would be reduced to the animal level.

[18] In ordinary speech, 'reflection' means any use of the mind. But I use it in its proper sense of that special function by which the mind turns back on itself and its cognitions (cf. 10–12).

[44]

acts are *per se* unknown to themselves and independent of our awareness of them (cf. 42). Furthermore, as we see when we deliberately examine our actions, we often say to ourselves: 'I have made a mistake; I can see it now', and we try to determine how much harm we have done. We reproach ourselves for not having thought about it previously, and gradually discover the harm present but not adverted to when we did the action. We were too busy causing the damage to think about it.

45. This point is further strengthened by the common opinion of the learned that no human action is indifferent; all actions are either morally good or bad (when I have the opportunity, I shall examine possible exceptions to this opinion, but it is certainly true generally speaking).

But can we in fact pass a moral judgment on every action we do? The smallest actions in our life are linked together, are rational and willed; they are therefore human, and consequently just or unjust. But can we say that they are always accompanied by judgments about their morality, especially when our reason and will perform them more through habit than through deliberate act? Little thought is required to see that we do a great many things without comparing them with the law in order to discover, with yet another act, whether they conform to or deviate from the law. Nevertheless conformity or deviance are present because they form part of the nature of our willed action, from which however they have not been separated and abstracted, nor become abstractly known.

§2. The first, essential concept of human law
indicates that moral acts can exist without conscience

46. The abstract state of law, which is our subject, and the moral quality of actions demand our most careful attention, if we are not to fall into error.

The ideas we each possess have become highly developed, distilled and refined, and we have no difficulty in believing they have always been so. When we meet people who do not share similar ideas, we think they have no ideas at all. But this is a mistake. Sufficient attention has never been given to the initial state of the human heart and mind, and to the first stages of its development. Naturally we cannot observe ourselves directly because the first moments of our development have passed forever. Nor can we focus fully on infants, on the uneducated and on similar people unless we have an extraordinarily acute observation and an unrelenting application to experiment. We can only observe ideas, noting their essential elements and isolating them from our own state of mind which gives ideas a purely accidental mode.

47. If we do this, we are aware that the abstract idea of law, as society now sees it, is not necessary for the formation of the *morality of actions*. Law is now understood as an entity of its own, a being formed by reason, an independent principle directing actions. As a result it seems there can be no morality before we have compared our action with the mental abstract rule called law, which appears to have acquired a body, so to speak, by being spoken and expressed in words, propositions and the formulas of natural or positive precepts.

48. But relative to morality, the primitive state of the human race was quite different. At that time human beings did not need an abstract form of law to act justly or unjustly. It was sufficient to know *intelligent beings*, relative to whom they had to act and exercise morality, which always consists in a relationship between ourselves and the intelligent beings (cf. 29) we know. For example, as soon as we know someone like ourselves, the rule for our treatment of that person lies in the knowledge itself. We may not have heard the word 'law', or cannot say it because we do not have the least abstract, general idea of it. But someone like ourselves, that is, human nature perceived in someone like ourselves, is sufficient law for us. Simply by the perception of someone like us, we are in a position to exercise our will and freedom: we can give to that being an esteem and affection equal to that which we give ourselves, or we can do the contrary. We are therefore free to be good or evil, just or unjust, to that being. Acting like this implies no further reflection nor comparison of our action with the law, which as yet is not conceived separately. In a word conscience is absent.

§3. Is there a sufficient reason to prove that conscience must in reality precede the moral act; if so, when is it operative?

49. Our enquiries can, therefore, be reduced to considering whether the moral act is always related to a reason sufficient to produce an act of conscience along with the moral act itself. We have already seen that conscience is not intrinsically necessary to the moral act.

Because this sufficient reason must be a stimulus capable of prompting a person to reflect upon the morality of what he does, the question can be formulated in the following terms: 'Can it be proved that the moral act produces as its consequence a stimulus causing a person to reflect upon his own act, judging it lawful or unlawful? That is, does the stimulus cause him to form a conscience?'

50. Our answer requires us to distinguish between human beings in a state of totally good and incorrupt nature, unaffected by serious temptations against morality, and human beings in a disordered state where virtue cannot be attained without a struggle.

51. *A*. I cannot conceive that anyone in a naturally good state, and operating uprightly, would simultaneously be stimulated to form a conscience for himself. On the other hand, I cannot conceive that he could carry out an immoral act without feeling some stimulus prompting him to judge his act as guilty and blameworthy. In other words, he would in these circumstances form a conscience.

52. My conclusion depends upon the fact that good acts are spontaneous and in harmony with nature. They are required and demanded by the laws constituting rational, human nature which, when not deformed and disordered, has an innate inclination towards them. Acknowledging willingly what we know necessarily, affirming the truth, telling ourselves that we know simply what we know, and accepting that we have perceived in beings the grades of entity that we have in fact perceived in them, is so natural, easy and simple that an evil act can be explained only by some power at enmity with our nature. When we give our willing assent to what is good in the beings we know and thus acknowledge

[49-52]

them in practice, everything within us is tranquilly ordered and is as it should be; we suffer no disorder, disharmony or interior contradiction.

53. The opposite is true if an evil act is committed. When we do not want to acknowledge what we know necessarily, there is an inevitable struggle within us between *what is willed* and *what is necessary*. The will combats the truth in an interior, irreconcilable conflict: the truth can neither surrender nor change, although the will refuses to recognise and submit to it. Such a struggle must prompt human beings to reflect upon what they have done, or tried to do (evil is a confrontation with the truth rather than an attack upon it — truth is immune from violence and attack).

If humans follow their direct knowledge and simply acknowledge willingly the beings they know, adhering to them according to the quantity of goodness found in them, their action accords with the nature of things and reaches its term without producing any new movement in the agents themselves who simply rest in what they have done because their act of will has reached its term. There is no *internal* cause drawing their attention to reflect upon such an orderly, tranquil act, free from disquiet.

54. It is true that good will, acknowledgement of truth, and love corresponding to what is good bestow an agreeable feeling upon us. It is a law of our nature, or rather a universal law of all intelligent natures, that being, willingly acknowledged, is good for the person acknowledging it, and produces joy proportioned to its quantity. The act of recognition posits or completes order in the nature responsible for the act; it arouses a feeling of peace and pleasant harmony. This, we may think, should also prompt reflection.

But this is not the case. The pleasing feeling — and its displeasing, painful opposite — contains a *moral sense* which must not be confused with *knowledge*. *Sense, feeling* is one thing; *knowledge* is another. The distinction is highly important, and accepted by all, but understood by few.[19] *Conscience*, moreover, is not simply a feeling, but knowledge, true judgment about the morality of our act. Hence, although every good action of ours is accompanied by a feeling of pure

[19] *PE*, 71–75.

[53-4]

moral pleasure (because it belongs to our faculty of *moral feeling*,[20]) not all our moral acts are accompanied by awareness. A good feeling is tranquil and restful; it possesses no extraordinary or adversarial qualifications. It is according to nature. And as we said, only what is extraordinary and novel excites our attention.

Why should we reflect in this case? We feel no disturbance from which we need to free ourselves through reflection. On the contrary, we prefer not to be distracted from our enjoyment by other thoughts. We are like people walking quietly along a road, free to devote ourselves to whatever comes into our mind, without paying attention to ourselves or anything around us. But if we tread unexpectedly on something sharp, we begin to think of ourselves and our pain, and how to stop or prevent it in future. It is always a need, or pain, or contradiction that distracts our attention from external objects, to which our faculties are naturally attracted, and makes us turn back upon what we are doing. In this way we are brought to judge ourselves and our acts. But if we had never experienced any difficulty, need or damage, we would never, of ourselves,[21] have turned to look at ourselves. We would have forgotten ourselves completely. Difficulties and sufferings confer at least this benefit upon us: they draw us back to ourselves and enable us to develop those human powers that have such a bearing on the events and fortune of mankind.

55. This phenomenon is explained by the way in which the pain felt by any part of us is somehow experienced by all our other parts and powers. Our perfect unity as subjects brings this about inevitably. The subject as such endeavours to rid himself of the disturbance by activating all his faculties, animal and intellective, and in particular rouses his reflection to help him in his pain. We may note, for instance, that bodily pain, although it has no direct effect on the under-

---

[20] This faculty consists in feeling pleasure in moral good, and pain in moral evil.

[21] We say 'of ourselves' because we can easily be brought to reflect upon ourselves through speech in the company of mature people. However, even here we are assisted at least by our needs, interpreted by speech, if not by severe pain and discomfort.

standing, becomes an occasion for bringing to bear intellectual action in defence of the whole suffering subject.[22]

56. But we must return to our main point. We lack a reason or necessity for reflection if we have a feeling only of natural, tranquil pleasure. This is the case when we act uprightly. Upright action does not cause disquiet or disorder in well-ordered human nature. The opposite is true of sin. Sin breaks the natural, normal order of human life; and the resultant disorder is always extraordinary, whatever its frequency. And as it is impossible for us to judge ourselves on each of the innumerable, continuous occasions when we act uprightly, so it is impossible not to feel some reproof, and turn back upon ourselves, when we offend against our direct knowledge, the natural rule governing our actions.

57. If all went well in us, we would not even take the trouble to think abstractly about the law; direct knowledge of beings would be sufficient for the presence of law. Sin, however, forces us to think of law in the abstract because we realise that we are doing wrong when we oppose the truth of direct knowledge with the energy of our evil will. Our intelligence focuses necessarily on the duty we infringe, and consequently on a moral necessity (that is, on a law) obliging us to do the opposite. Mankind had never experienced the force of such law until it found the law in opposition to its desires, as the Apostle says: 'The law is not laid down for the just man but for the unjust and disobedient.'[23] 'The just person' is in full accord with the law, in which his will rests as if the law were one with him, not different from him; he has no need to consider the constituent elements of his nature. The unjust, however, cannot act wickedly without some internal, self-imposed admonition and reproof: 'For the evil man will question his own thoughts.'[24]

This characteristic of an evil will, in contradistinction to a good will, draws us to reflect on the relationship between what we do and what we should do. On the one hand we find an unassailable law; on the other, a vain effort on our part to violate the law and contradict nature. The matter is aptly described in the words of Genesis when the serpent tempts

[22] On the unity of the human subject cf. *AMS*, bk. 4.
[23] 1 Tim 1: 9.　　　　　　　　　　　　[24] Wis 1: 9.

[56-7]

Eve to sin by promising her an increase in knowledge: 'Your eyes will be opened, and you will be like God, knowing good and evil.' The seducer kept his promise as the victims fell, but not in the way they expected: 'Then the eyes of both were opened.' The same point is made when God forbids them to eat of the fruit of a tree which he calls 'the tree of the knowledge of good and evil,'[25] that is, of moral good and evil. As they eat, they realise they have sinned; the tree is the tree of conscience.[26]

58. There is nothing repugnant or even improbable in the notion that innocent mankind, prompted by a healthy instinct, can make upright, practical judgments which bring contentment in their wake, without reflecting on the uprightness of the judgments themselves. In our initial state there seems no sufficient reason for innocent, contented mankind, prompted by right instinct, to be brought by some sufficient reason to reflect immediately on what has been done. In this state, mankind could go on acting virtuously in a pure and simple way without the reflective knowledge of which we are speaking; we could be good without realising it: we could feel the benefit of being good and enjoy it without pride because the human subject would not seek to know or say how good he was. His virtue, the result of moral spontaneity, would be perfectly simple. The power of free will becomes apparent only when it contradicts, not when it seconds, spontaneity. Hence Bede and other Fathers and writers understood the tree of the knowledge of good and evil as a symbol of free will because it reveals itself more in evil than in good.[27]

[25] Gen 3: [5: 7; 2: 17].

[26] I do not mean that mankind would not have felt some natural inclination at the sight of the beautiful fruit on the tree of good and evil. This desire, however, was initially prevented from exceeding its limits by the prevalent force of the beauty of order and duty. Perhaps no temptation could have put such beauty in our way if we had not willed it; of itself, beauty's power to tempt was infinitely small, incipient and scarcely perceptible.

[27] 'The tree of knowledge of good or evil is our own power of voluntary discernment, placed in our midst to distinguish good and evil. If anyone, abandoning the grace of God, tastes it, he shall die' (Bede, *Gen.* c. 2). 'As the tree of good and evil was present in paradise, so free will, which enables us to do good and evil, is present in the holy soul' (Egidius Romanus, *Tract. de Paradiso*, c. 5).

[58]

59. *B*. We have shown so far that when a person has acquired ideas of God, of himself and other intelligent beings that serve as the rule and measure of his esteem and love, there is no contradiction in the thought of such a person freely following the exigencies of these ideas by acting truthfully, that is, with uprightness and justice, towards what he knows. This can all be done without any need of reflection on his own actions in order to judge their morality and form a conscience about them. This state, in which we simply do good, without conscience, belongs to an upright nature which does good spontaneously, without effort or violence.

60. This explains why scripture often uses the phrase *to judge* in the sense of *to condemn* or *to condemn evil* without further qualification. For example: 'Judge not, that you may not be judged';[28] 'For God sent not his Son into the world, to judge the world, but that the world may be saved through him.'[29] And although 'to judge' is used here and elsewhere for 'to condemn', the opposite is not true: there is possibly not a single example in scripture where 'to judge' is used in the sense of 'to approve of.' I shall add one more example from the many which could be found: 'He who believes in him is not judged',[30] that is, not condemned.

I would insist that what I have said explains this use by showing that upright actions in conformity with nature do not require any explicit judgment distinct from the actions themselves. But wrong acts, out of harmony with nature, inevitably cause opposition and conflict, and lead to judgment. Division and duplicity spring from evil; union and harmony go hand in hand with doing good.

61. As we know, courts of law exist to try unlawful actions and settle conflicts. The same happens in the internal forum. We establish a tribunal in our heart to judge unlawful, not lawful actions. Our conscience first comes into existence to judge bad, not good acts.

62. But this is no longer true of humanity in its present, disordered condition, as experience shows, sacred tradition teaches and even pagan thinkers lamented. Although a good, upright nature loves to act consonantly with its inclinations, a nature already inclined to evil can do good only with

[28] Matt 7: 1.   [29] Jn 3: 17.   [30] Jn 3: 18.

difficulty, and often at the cost of overcoming the obstacles caused by its own passions. As we have seen, mankind, when innocent, has to choose between opposing forces in order to desire evil. On the one hand, innocent human nature is motivated through the clarity of the idea of the being which exercises its moral action upon human beings; on the other, innocent humanity itself invents its own false good. A similar situation prevails when people are deceived by their own concupiscence and attracted to act in defiance of the law. In this case, an obstacle, their own evil instinct, impedes their acting in conformity with the law, and draws them to reflect upon themselves. From within they must now find the mental energy to struggle and choose between the idea presented to them and the evil inclination. And here we can discern a reason sufficient to move a person to form a conscience about his action.

63. Summarising our position, let us list the different situations in which we can find ourselves when we act:

1. Naturally good humanity possesses an animal instinct that either accords with the rational instinct or is easily conquered by it[31] because the beauty of the moral order (the exigency of *ideas*) has more power over innocent mankind than the sensation received passively from what is external.[32] In this case humanity acts spontaneously to second the known truth, without reflection and consequently without conscience.

2. If human beings are drawn to fix their attention enjoyably on a pleasant sensation opposed to the truth of what they know (and they can only be attracted by the word of someone else), they begin to weaken in their attitude towards the demands of truth. Their will is already at risk,

[31] I mean *accords with natural law* because human beings, in their first, perfect state, were guided by the Creator in such a way that happiness and uprightness were always in harmony. There could, however, have been some opposition between *positive law* and animal instinct, although good will would have conquered the latter without difficulty.

[32] Every sensation is a principle of *instinct*. If a person receives a sensation passively without adding anything of his own to it, the sensation produces a very slight or inchoate instinct. Only through repetition of the sensation, and the assenting activity of the feeling subject, are the sensation and image reinforced to produce an *affection* that strengthens the instinct.

and their inborn inclination strengthened. Having given their attention to what they have heard, they have mentally conceived the possibility of acting against the law and, as *temptation* begins to make itself felt, form a *conscience*.

3. When they deliberate about giving their willing consent to the specious good they have formed by arousing their imagination, they feel their error more strongly, and conscience becomes more insistent in them.

4. After their fall, *concupiscence* is generated in their heart. The inclination to evil becomes constant and habitual;[33] natural instincts are undermined and left to themselves as they are withdrawn from the supernatural influences of God to whom human beings were first bound by the tie of *grace*.

64. In this new state of humanity, *concupiscence* (the name we give today to all spontaneity and natural instinct damaged by sin) is subject to the same law of development as that which governed natural instinct in its pristine state. The first movements of concupiscence, therefore, are weak, but gain strength through repetition and the addition of free activity, which at first is passive related to concupiscence.

65. Besides the general rule governing its increase, concupiscence is found in everyone in infinite varieties, which cannot be foreseen or calculated but depend upon age and circumstances. As far as I can see, such subspecies of concupiscence, which sometimes flares up suddenly only to fade away almost to nothing, are not governed by any law.

66. We can, however, attempt to classify these 'outbursts' of evil concupiscence.

I. Sometimes concupiscence lies dormant. During these periods of tranquillity, we can consent to the demands of our ideas by means of the good, rational instinct[34] which,

[33] This applies not only to inclinations of the flesh, but also to inclinations of the person as a whole, that is, to self-love. The twofold tendency is indicated by St. John in the words 'not of the will of the flesh nor of the will of man' (1: 13).

[34] Three feelings, and hence three instincts, *animal, rational* and *moral*, can be distinguished in human beings. The animal instinct is ordered to the conservation and perfection of animality; rational instinct aims at intellectual perfection; and moral instinct tends to produce moral perfection. Not every rational instinct, therefore, is moral; and moral instinct is more noble and sublime than rational instinct.

because it depends upon the truth of what is already known, is never absent in fallen human beings. This truth never fails, and never ceases to appeal to us — if it were to perish, we would understand nothing and would cease to exist as intelligent beings. Our quiet moments are those in which we can sometimes do good without reflection, and hence without conscience, even in our present state.[35]

67. II. At certain instances and in different circumstances, concupiscence increases to make temptations much more acute and overbearing, but not to the extent that it removes our capacity and power[36] for knowing the exigency of ideas (which constitutes our natural law) and consenting to them if we wish. This embattled state gives rise to the development of human *freedom* and to the extraordinary energy freedom shows in choosing which of two contraries pleases it more. The choice cannot be made, however, without reflection upon the opposing acts forming the choice, and hence cannot be actuated without a judgment about our actions, that is, without conscience.

68. III. Finally, concupiscence acts at certain moments with such rapidity and independence that it forestalls reflection, especially if this is generally slow to come into being. Sometimes the effects of concupiscence begin and end before reflection can come to the rescue, or at least before it has been

[35] This state is found most often amongst still incorrupt, developing peoples. [. . .]

[36] There is in each human being a unique, basic force of a certain quantity. I call *basic force* the power in which all our faculties are based, and which begins, exercises and exhausts itself in them. The more one faculty draws on this force, the less remains available for other faculties and acts. A person activated and intent upon one thing will necessarily lack energy for other things, and may even be lifeless in their regard. I say 'lifeless' because the full development of a single capacity within us would absorb and demand our entire, primal basic force, and leave the other faculties totally inactive. Excessive pain, for instance, deprives a person of the use of his understanding and other faculties, just as intense intellective contemplation also withdraws him from pain, or from advertence to pain. The quantity of individual basic force appears, however, to differ from one person to another, and even to ebb and flow in the same individual according to remarkable laws which it is impossible to indicate in a footnote. The attentive reader will understand, however, that the study of these laws is a subject worthy of philosophers.

able to draw from the contemplation of the exigencies of ideas the feeling of esteem and affection that can arm it against unjust desire.[37]

69. Such an occurrence may take place in two ways.

I. The movement of unjust desire[38] totally precedes the action of reason. In this case, it also forestalls the action of the will which co-operates only negatively by not rousing itself in time to prevent the impetus of desire. This is certainly a defect because no act naturally subject to the rule of will in a reasonable being should be withdrawn from this subjection. The will must rule; it must foresee, permit and approve, at least as basic cause, that which the animal part of the human being does. But the opposite takes place in fallen humanity which has lost its pristine state of well-being, and finds the various parts of its nature at loggerheads with one another. The organic unity humanity once enjoyed has been replaced by a double or triple partition in its being. Its animal part acts without reference to human nature even when this should intervene.

In this case, a human being's act is not necessarily provided with conscience, and may even be *amoral* if it is not of such a kind that the will could or should have foreseen, dominated, refrained from or modified it. I think it highly probable that animal instinct can act alone in the human being without the positive concurrence of the will. Observation does in fact show that animal instinct is a perfect power capable by itself of putting the animal in movement and action. And human beings, as animals, do not differ from brute creatures in whom instinct can be seen as an effective power or full cause moving the animal to act without any need for recourse to

[37] This may be an animal appetite, or the appetite that draws a human being to make himself his own end.
[38] The *unjust desire* of which I am speaking is one destined to be subject to the command of the will. In a state of perfect nature, the will's command probably extended even to animal acts, at least negatively, in the sense that although not commanded, they were conceded and licensed by the will which, however, could not interfere with certain laws of animality. For example, the will could either allow the individual to sleep, or not. But once he had begun to sleep, it does not seem that the will could suspend or interrupt sleep. The extent to which the will is of its nature conditioned by animal laws has been discussed in *AMS*.

reason or will. It seems reasonable to conclude, therefore, that instinct alone is of its nature sufficient to activate the animal, that is, to bring all its acts into being, and it is not absurd to think that human beings also are capable, without the intervention of the will, of every act that does not exceed the sphere of animality.[39]

70. II. Sometimes, in moving the feelings, the desire acts with greater rapidity and violence on human beings than does the morally necessitating truth of ideas, which acquires its operative force only much later. In this case the will is under pressure and surrenders necessarily to the attraction of the apparent good. Weakened by the violence of the unruly desire and by its own weakness and slowness, the will has no time to suspend its assent (the will, too, depends upon laws of time for its operation).[40] Attracted by the movement of instinct towards some present good, the will accompanies the instinct in such a way as to be brought without express deliberation to its own practical judgment. More from inertia than from malice, it cedes to an unjust judgment almost forced upon it by deplorable seduction. In such circumstances the will, already inclined to specious good by a radical defect, feels little or no pleasure from the truth which it disregards for the sake of the seductive pleasure of concupiscence. Blindly, without deliberation, the will abandons itself to the pleasure available to it, and acts almost like the instinct. In this way, it can act without conscience, and even without fault, if necessity impels it.

This is what happens in children. But what I shall say later should help to clarify this teaching.

71. For the time being we can conclude that a morally good or evil act, in order to lack conscience, must be done instinctively, without deliberation, or under spontaneous motivation, when an act of different moral quality has so little force

[39]. For the distinction between will and instinct, and a description of the laws with which they act, cf. *OT*, and more detailed treatment in *AMS*.

[40] Several conditions are required for the will to attain free activity. As I have shown, one of these conditions is the formation of *abstract ideas* and of *speech*, the means by which we acquire abstract ideas. We are born with a *will*, that is, with an interior power of acting according to motives and reason, but we have to acquire dominion over this power in order to manage it as we will. In a word, we are not born *free*. Cf. *OT*, *AMS*.

[70-1]

of attraction that it can be considered outside our powers of advertence. But although the moral act *can* lack conscience, it does not follow that it *must* do so. The force of *wayward* instinct and the habitual love of truth (of being) have many gradations. Conscience is lacking in the disordered act only when *habitual love* is reduced almost to nothing, and the *wayward instinct* is most assertive.

5

THE RELATIONSHIP BETWEEN DELIBERATE AND INDELIBERATE MORALITY

72. But is it possible to posit a human, moral act which, although in opposition to the rule of truth, is nevertheless without *fault*? We cannot answer this question without discussing habitual morality in human beings.

Habit is also a principle of action, and we are sometimes directed in what we do as a result of movements communicated to us through habit. If, therefore, a morally disordered habit can be found, but without fault in the strict sense, the movements and actions dependent upon this habit as necessary effects would have to be considered free of fault, in the strict sense of the word.

We have already seen that it is possible for morality to be imputable as fault without any antecedent conscience. Here we wish to go further and investigate the possibility of positing *disordered*, but not strictly *culpable morality*.

73. Does an *habitual morality* exist prior to our moral acts? If so, can it be *disordered* without express *fault*? It is clear that such a question deals with the most intimate aspects of human nature, and cannot be faced adequately without profound consideration of the notions of *fault*, *will* and *freedom*. Difficult problems cannot be avoided, however, if our study is to be of some assistance to our readers, whose help and patience we seek as all of us turn to good use the gifts of intelligence we have received from God's goodness.

First, we must examine the concepts of *morality*, *sin* and *fault*.

[72-3]

Article 1.
The concepts of
MORALITY, SIN and FAULT

74. As we have seen, the concept of morality lies in the relationship between will and law.[41] Whenever the two extremes of *law* and *will* are related to one another so that the will is in a given state relative to the law, morality is present. Morality is the state of the will relative to the law. But the law, as manifested to us when we first act, is not something abstract. The *beings* we conceive mentally become laws for us, requiring our practical reflection, and our willed, effective acknowledgement. Provided we have some mental conception of an (intellective) being, and some movement or inclination of will towards practical acknowledgement of what we know, morality is present in us. The practical acknowledgement of which we are speaking can, however, be an assent to or dissent from truth. In the case of dissent, the will is in a morally defective state because it stands in opposition to the nature of the conceived being.

75. The will can find itself opposed to the law in two ways, *necessarily*[42] or *freely*. This is the basis of the distinction St. Thomas was obliged to make between the concepts of *sin* and *fault*. For St. Thomas, the concept of *sin* consists in an act of will that departs from the rectitude of the law, although it may not be acting freely, while the concept of *fault* lies in a will which does evil, but by free choice. This is an admirable distinction. It means that the will, if it departs *necessarily* from the law, posits an immoral act and hence a *sin* because in

---

[41] *PE*, 193, 194.

[42] We must note carefully that this *necessity* does not contradict the nature of *will*. If this were the case, the will would be under constraint despite itself — a genuine absurdity, because a will under restraint is not a will. In this sense the will is essentially free. But there is also a necessity dependent upon the will's being determined either because it has reached its term, as in heaven or hell, or because its own internal laws leave it without alternatives — when, for instance, only one good stands before it. In this case, it spontaneously follows that good because it has nothing with which to compare it. In a word, the will is obliged to operate according to its nature. But here what appears as a kind of necessity is simply the spontaneity of the will itself.

such conditions will and law are in opposition. Nevertheless this act could not be imputed to fault in the person who did it because his will, although weak and defective, was not free. St. Thomas says: 'As the notion of *evil* is more comprehensive than that of *sin*, so the notion of *sin* is more comprehensive than that of *fault*. An act is said to be blameworthy or praiseworthy when it is imputed to the person who does it. But *to praise* or *to blame* simply means to impute the goodness or malice of an action to the person who does it. The act is imputed to the agent when he is able to control it; this happens in every willed[43] act because human beings control their actions by means of the will . . . therefore only willed (*free*) acts of good and evil are subject to praise or blame; and in them *evil*, *sin* and *fault* are the same.'[44]

Elsewhere St. Thomas teaches that if the act of will has not been preceded by deliberating reason, a sin cannot be imputed to *mortal fault*, although the will is engaged. 'Mortal sin' (that is, what is imputed as mortal sin) 'consists in aversion from the final end, which is God. This aversion appertains to *deliberating reason* whose function is to direct things to their end. Only when the *deliberating reason* has been unable to intervene, can the inclination of the soul towards something contrary to the final end not be mortal sin. This is the case in sudden movements.'[45]

Article 2.
The possibility of a state of sin
not imputable to the person's own fault

76. According to Catholic teaching, there can be and there is in human beings a defective state of will containing the notion of sin, but not of fault.

Given the notion of fault, which consists in a defective act of *free* will relative to the law, we may ask whether our will may turn from the law through necessity, without being free to do the contrary. In other words, can *sin* exist in a person without its being the *fault* of that person?

[43] St. Thomas is speaking of *free will*, as the context shows.
[44] *S.T.*, I-II, q. 21, art. 2.   [45] *S.T.*, I-II, q. 77, art. 8.

This is a difficult question for natural reasoning alone, but it can be reduced to another: can the will, the human operative principle, be so influenced by the action of some other force as to be *necessarily* inclined or determined to one or other part? We must note that we are not asking if the will can be *violated*, but if it can be *determined necessarily*. *Will* and *violence* are contradictory and mutually exclude one another; it is certain that the will always moves *spontaneously*. But does spontaneous movement exclude *necessity*? Can one conceive of an agent acting upon the will in such a way as to produce spontaneous movement in the will without the involvement of freedom?[46]

77. Natural reason finds no contradiction in the notion of such an agent. Careful observation shows, moreover, that the will is sometimes passive in its own way, and even necessitated. But to surprise our will in this state, and affirm the existence of such a state without danger of error, requires profound and extremely attentive observation that exceeds normal powers. Revelation, however, removes the doubt decisively by indicating the actual existence of such a state, above all in the great fact of original sin.

§1. Application to original sin

78. According to revealed doctrine, the sin in which we are all born is a true sin and a true fault. But if we consider it in the person sharing in it at the moment of his conception, without reference to the free will of its first author, it loses the notion of *fault* and simply retains that of *sin*.

Aquinas teaches: 'What depends upon one's origin cannot be imputed to fault if we consider only the new-born individual in himself; but if we consider him relative to the principle from which he originated (that is, his first parent), then it can be imputable to fault.'[47]

[46] The will is simply the faculty which operates by following knowledge. This constitutive element does not require the will to be free, that is to say, it does not require the will to be able to operate or not, or to operate immediately in a contrary sense. Nevertheless, the human being never lacks *potential* or *conditional freedom*, that is, the will *can* operate freely, given certain conditions.   [47] *S.T.*, I-II, q. 81, art. 1, ad 5.

Again: 'The many human beings born of Adam are like the multiple parts of a single body. Now the action of one part of the body, of the hand for instance, is willed not by the hand, but by the soul, which first moves the different parts. A murder carried out by the hand is not imputed to the hand considered in itself and separate from the body; it is imputed to it as the part which is moved by the first principle in the person. In the same way the disorder in human beings generated from Adam is voluntary (*free*) in respect of the will of our first parent who, with his act of generation, moves all those originating and deriving from him, just as the soul's will moves all the corporeal parts to action. Hence the sin transmitted from our first parent is called *original* sin in his descendants, in contradistinction to the sin passed from the soul into the parts of the body, which is called *actual* sin. And as actual sin committed by a part of the body is only sin in that part in so far as the part belongs to the person himself (and can thus be called human sin), so original sin is not (culpable) sin in this person except in so far as he receives his nature from our first parent. Original sin, therefore, is called a "sin of *nature*", as St. Paul says: "We were by nature children of wrath".'[48]

§2. Application to the demerit of the damned

79. This teaching is wholly in agreement with what St. Thomas says about the demerit of the damned. He maintains: 'The damned are not excused from demerit because they are under necessity to sin, but only because they have reached the depth of evil.' He continues: 'Nevertheless, the necessity of sinning excuses them from *fault* in so far as sin is necessary because every sin (*in order to be fault*) must be voluntary (*free*). But they are not excused in so far as their state depends upon a previous act of will. To this extent, the demerit of the subsequent sin would seem to belong to the previous fault.'[49]

80. I conclude from the teaching of this passage that there is a reason which excuses the damned from *sin* and another which excuses them from *fault*. Because their will has already

[48] *S.T.*, I-II, q. 81, art. 1, in corp.
[49] *S.T.*, Suppl., q. 98, art. 6, ad 3, see also in corp.

reached the depth of evil and they can go no further they do
not incur new *sins*. And they do not demerit through new
faults because they adhere necessarily to what is evil. This
necessity causes what theologians call 'a willed but non-free
act', that is to say, the necessity takes away *free will*.[50]
Consequently, if the damned had not reached the lowest
point of evil, but were inclined to continual new crimes
through unhappy necessity, they would go on sinning. Their
sins, however, would not be fault in themselves but only
relative to their cause.

§3. Application to certain actual sins

81. As we have said, two conditions are needed for an
immoral act: 1. that it be contrary to the law; 2. that it originate from the will. But the will moves itself towards its object
either *through necessity* or *freely*. Sometimes it is subject
necessarily to evil because of some previous fault which leaves
the will so badly and habitually inclined that under certain
circumstances it falls into evil. St. Augustine says: 'An evil
will gives rise to evil desire; surrender to desire causes habit;
and unresisted habit produces necessity.'[51]

---

[50] Some theologians employ the word *voluntary* ambiguously. At times
they use it in the broad sense of *willed*, at other times, in the sense of *willed
freely*, as in this case. This has provoked innumerable disputes. We should
be prepared now to abandon all ambiguous expressions for the sake of
precise, clear language.

[51] *Confessions*, bk. 8, chap. 5. Sometimes *will* and *concupiscence* wage
war on one another. This seems perhaps to contradict what has already
been said about the will's not suffering violence (cf. 76). But even after a
long struggle, the will, if it sins, does so spontaneously, not as a result of
violence. Careful consideration of the will in its different periods of struggle, of sin and of post-sin helps to clarify the matter. After sin, when
temptation has ceased and mental tranquillity has returned, the will is truly
sorry for the evil it has committed; but in the second period, when the will
gives in, it is the will itself which spontaneously consents to sin. Before sin,
a mixture of good and bad motives can present themselves to the will. They
do not force the will, but *persuade* or seduce it. The will is not moved
except by a force which conspires with and conquers the will through a
kind of association and befriending, and does so more easily by entering the
will and uniting with it interiorly. God's activity is such a force: it creates

[81]

82. In this state, the will is unable to *deliberate*. Already inclined to evil, it has in fact deliberated some time before the present, actual deliberation. Now it falls into evil through some blind instinct. Its act, however, is not done unknowingly; it apprehends intellectually the being in whose regard it sins, although passion prevents it from shaking off the unjust esteem that it habitually renders this being. When an occasion arises, the will, without having time for consideration, precipitates an actual unjust judgment, as if consideration had already been given to the matter. The faculty has indeed been suspended, but its general inclination prompts it towards evil as soon as opportunity offers.

83. This habitual evil inclination of the will, in so far as it is a consequence of Adam's sin, is the innate *concupiscence* which completes the notion of original sin.[52] We should note that although all the powers of human nature were wounded by the first fault, the major wound was inflicted on the will, the seat of morality. This wound in the will has also been inherited by posterity along with wounds in the other faculties. And with the wound in the will, that is, the highest power of human nature, sin has been inherited.

84. Our hereditary sin, because it is a defect in the human being's supreme principle (the natural will) makes the whole person defective and subjects him to *damnation*. We could say that this damnation is also *imputation*, but not without

the will, working in and with it. But these forces which insinuate themselves in the will can oppose one another in the same way as motives which draw the will in different directions. Hence the struggle we so often experience. The combat, however, is not between the will and something other than the will. The struggle takes place between two principles in the will where two motives try to attract its attention. The will then increases the force of attraction of one or the other through its own intrinsic energy (freedom).

[52] Aquinas posits the essence of original sin in aversion from God. But this must not be understood as though original sin were a simple negation. A pure negation of grace would be present in a person created by God in natural conditions. In this state the creature would not be positively *averse* from God, but simply *not turned to God* and, as Bellarmine says, *deprived* of supernatural union with him. We must note that the first human being, created with supernatural grace, turned away from God with a positive act of will. This evil act must necessarily have left in the human will an attitude averse from good and from God, and inclined to evil.

impropriety of language. It is certainly not imputation in the strict sense in which we attribute deliberate actions to a person. Nor can it constitute a *personal fault* (the only fault worthy of the name), although again we may say in a broad sense that it is a *natural fault*.

85. Following revealed doctrine, we see that the Saviour's baptism removes the damnation of original sin, or *fault of nature* as it may be called, by introducing into human beings another active, supernatural principle, superior to the natural will. This superior principle now becomes the seat of morality in human beings and, because it is holy, the seat of the holiness and salvation that depends totally upon the supreme principle.

86. Nevertheless the natural will, inclined to evil (concupiscence), remains along with the infused principle of holiness. But it is no longer the seat of original sin, nor through original sin the cause of damnation in human beings, because it no longer constitutes the *supreme active principle*. From now on, because it is subordinate to the supreme principle and dependent upon it, it can be governed and corrected by the supreme principle.[53]

87. 'Original sin,' says St. Thomas, 'is removed relative to its crime (that is, relative to sin and consequent damnation) because the soul once more receives *grace* (the new principle) which enriches the mind. Nevertheless original sin remains in act, not relative to the mind but relative to the fomes, which is a disorder in the inferior parts of the soul, and of the body in so far as human beings generate although not in so far as they understand. Baptised persons transmit original sin to their offspring, therefore, because parents generate not in so far as they are renewed by baptism, but in so far as they still retain something from the first sin.'[54]

88. Hence what remains of original sin is still the source of many moral disorders even after baptism. These unavoidable disorders, however, cannot be imputed to fault, nor are they sins; they do not have their source in the human being's

---

[53] Cf. *AMS*, bk 4, where we have discussed *personality* and shown that it has its base in the supreme principle of the human being.

[54] *S.T.*, I-II, q. 82, art. 3, ad 2 [q. 81, art. 4, ad 2].

supreme principle, where alone sin is truly found, nor do they depend upon free will.

89. The *fomes*, mentioned by St. Thomas and the Council of Trent, which remains in us even after baptism, must not be understood of our vitiated *animal instinct* alone. In addition, we have to take into account the weakness and bad inclination of the *will*, which easily surrenders to the animal instinct. The fomes is not sin, because it has no place in the new, superior will acquired by us in baptism. It does, however, affect the old, and now lower, will still present after baptism. Because of its origin in sin, and its inclination to sin, this fomes is a *moral defect*, and remains in us until death. In this sense, the Apostle rightly extends the word *sin* to mean a *defect in the order of moral matters* when he speaks of 'sin which dwells within me.'[55]

The word 'sin' could not in fact refer to *animal instinct* alone, without relationship to the will, because animal instinct exists in beasts who have no will.[56] Damaged, defective animal instinct, considered without reference to the will, could rightly be called *disordered*, but never *sin* or immorality, which always implies relationship with the intellective power of will. When St. John rightly spoke of 'the will of the flesh,'[57] he was not referring simply to *carnal instinct*, but to the *will* as ceding to this instinct; the *will of man*, also mentioned by the evangelist, has to be interpreted in the sense of a *will* that surrenders to illusions of human happiness and greatness by excluding and opposing justice. It would be rash to affirm that Paul and St. John departed from the proper use of language without evident reason and necessity. The Apostle, speaking of himself after receiving justification,

---

[55] Rom 7: 20.

[56] The word *will* is often used of *animal instinct*, and in this sense generates confusion in philosophical and theological studies. The same confusion arises when the word *knowledge* is applied to pure *sensations*. Although certain respectable authors follow this metaphorical usage and apply to human sensitivity words properly used for human intellection, I think our modern age calls for greater exactness in language. Those wishing to examine more closely the difference between *animal instinct* and *will* which assents to or dissents from this instinct, will find more detailed discussion in *Certainty*, 1285–1300, and in *AMS*.

[57] 'Nor of the will of the flesh nor of the will of man' (Jn 1: 13).

writes of 'the sin which dwells within me.' He means that he bears within himself a will inclined to second the suggestions of his weak flesh which, however, are conquered by the new will placed in us by grace. The Apostle possesses this will, which is at war with his old will although it does not destroy it as long as we walk in what St. Paul calls our 'body of death'.

90. Our interpretation of St. Paul's words is confirmed by the context. 'So then it is no longer I that do it, but *sin* that dwells within me. For I know that nothing good dwells within me.'[58] He says that he acts, but that it is not he who acts; the *sin* within him acts. He means that his supreme will, which now constitutes within him the personal element born of grace, no longer wishes to do evil; the defect is to be found in his natural will which, no longer personal, is unable to restrain the movements of the flesh.

91. We may note here that there are two ways in which a sin that is not free, and hence not imputable, can be present in the human being. They depend upon negative or positive defect in the will.

Negative defect is found in the will's non-intervention, when it should intervene; *positive* defect, when the will intervenes by assenting to the bad instinct. In both cases the disorder is related to the defective will, and can be called *sin* in a more or less extended sense.

92. In the passages quoted, as I understand them, St. Paul is speaking of the *negative* defect of the will. His words could be paraphrased as follows: 'Many movements in my flesh would of their nature be subject to, and governed by, the power of my will if my nature were as it should be. But these movements arise in me of themselves and against my will because through rebellion they have been subtracted from the will's dominion which is now so weak, relative to the overwhelming power of these movements, that they originate in my flesh despite the will and without its permission.'

93. This *negative* defect of the will's power over the flesh means that *sin* can be said to dwell in us even after baptism, provided we understand 'sin' to indicate a simple *moral defect*. But the nature of this defect of will may be understood

[58] Rom 7: 17, 18.

better if we remember that the will has two strictly connected functions. One of them is simply to will (acts of choice); the other to command and govern our lower faculties (acts of command). We may usefully call the first function *superior will*, and the second *lower will*. Our will is shown at its weakest in the second function, where its effective dominion over the lower powers is decisively poor. As the Apostle says: 'I do not understand my own actions. For I do not do what I want, but I do the very thing I hate.'[59] In other words, although I choose with my superior will to rule and hold in order my lower powers, I do the contrary because my weak will is unable to command the subject-powers which act independently. This impotence could result in damnation if the supreme principle or superior will of a person were to surrender and consent to the disorder. The superior will has, however, been healed (it would be better to say that a new will has been created) through baptism so that the insubordination of the lower powers is no longer imputable, but free from damnation. Renewed by grace, the person of the new human being is on a higher level and immune from such corruption. With a simple act of his superior will, he can disapprove of what takes place in the lower will, but cannot always prevent what happens. Nevertheless, this is sufficient for us to be able to say that fault and sin, in their strict sense, have been avoided. St. Paul expresses the matter in this way: 'I of myself serve the law of God with my mind, but with my flesh I serve the law of sin.'[60] *Mind* here is the superior part of the will, the simple act of willing, which is however incapable of suppressing movements of animal instinct; *flesh* is the unbridled instinct.

94. Justification, which God brings about in us here on earth through baptism, takes place in the essence of the soul. Within the soul, now restored to its former beauty through grace, justification creates a supernatural instinct, a power to will divine things. Our co-operation with this justification in the present life is carried out in the higher part of the renewed will within us, although concupiscence continues to oppose the divine law and rebel against it. But human salvation is assured as grace enters the essence of the soul and our will

[59] Rom 7: 15.   [60] Rom 7: 25.

reaches out to collaborate with it (as in the case of infants). St. Paul says: 'If God is for us, who is against us? . . . Who shall bring any charge against God's elect? It is God who justifies.'[61] He goes on to indicate the stability of this justification, and the firmness of the superior will: 'For I am sure that neither death, nor life . . . will be able to separate me from the love of God in Christ Jesus our Lord.'[62] Nothing can conquer the person incorporated in Christ if he does not cede of his own free will.

95. Such is the order of human justification. Christ, by inserting a new, active, holy and divine principle in our spirit, has revitalized what was once subject to death while leaving the initial disorder in our flesh. This new principle is the germ of salvation for the whole human being, a germ destined to flower and, at a suitable time and in a suitable way, to bring salvation to the body also. The Apostle says once more: 'So, then, brethren, we are debtors, not to the flesh, to live according to the flesh — for if you live according to the flesh, you shall die, but if by the Spirit you put to death the deeds of the body you will live.'[63]

96. The flesh, therefore, remains infected and subject to death. But the infection will be destroyed by death itself which becomes as it were another baptism. The New Testament continually warns us to regard the flesh as something dead and to await the salvation of the whole human being in the justice that death will bring to the flesh. This mystery is grounded in fact in the suffering of Christ. 'Do you not know

---

[61] Rom 8: 31, 33.   [62] Rom 8: 38, 39.

[63] Rom 8: 12, 13. In scripture the words *flesh* and *concupiscence* have a very broad meaning. The disorder they indicate is present not only in the *desire* from which *concupiscence* springs, but also in all the lower powers of the soul. Such disorder forms the *matter* of original sin. St. Paul sometimes speaks of this disorder in the plural, for example when he says: 'When we were in the flesh, THE PASSIONS OF SIN, which were by the law, did work in our members, to bring forth fruit unto death' (Rom 7: 5). St. Thomas explains why *concupiscence* is used in preference to other words to indicate every disorder in our lower parts: 'All the passions of anger are reduced to passions of concupiscence because the latter are the principal passions, amongst which *concupiscence* has freer rein and is felt more acutely . . . consequently, all passions are attributed to concupiscence as the principal passion in which all others are somehow included' (*S.T.*, I-II, q. 82, art. 3, ad 2).

[95-6]

that all of us who have been baptized into Christ Jesus were baptized into his death? We were buried therefore with him by baptism into death, so that as Christ was raised from the dead by the glory of the Father, we too might walk in newness of life . . . So you also must consider yourselves dead to sin and alive to God in Christ Jesus.'[64] Again: 'If the Spirit of him who raised Jesus from the dead dwells in you, he who raised Christ Jesus from the dead will give life to your mortal bodies also through his Spirit which dwells in you,'[65] that is, dwells in the essence of your soul.

97. But this is still not sufficient. The will not only plays a *negative*, but also a *positive* part in some sins — in the sense used by St. Paul — which are not imputed to fault in baptized persons.

Concupiscence and other passions appertaining to sins arouse spurious instincts and needs within us with great urgency and impetuosity. A human physical law then brings into play all the powers which can contribute to satisfying these needs; the human being uses his subjective unity to activate the powers that can help him quieten his instincts. Thus, even bodily needs stimulate the intellect to find a way by which the subject may satisfy these needs. The will, however, as the power which operates spontaneously with the understanding, moves more or less rapidly with the intellect according to the urgency of the stimuli and needs. In these circumstances the weak will cannot always use its power of freedom to suspend its practical judgment, which it pronounces without delay. Haste and precipitation cause a willing, effective error in which, as we have seen, the principle of all immorality consists.[66] The will can suspend the judgment only if it has a reason for doing so. But if the reason for pronouncing judgment is pressing, the will has no time to rise above itself and find a good reason for suspending its verdict. As St. Thomas says, the reason remains almost bound in this case. In these circumstances, when suspension of judgment is impossible, the reason proceeds to judge the

---

[64] Rom 6: 3, 4, 11. [65] Rom 8: 11.
[66] Haste in judging as one of the causes of error was examined in *Certainty*, 1331–1334. Moral error, as the principle of all immorality, was examined in *PE*, 114–181.

satisfaction of its immediate need by considering what is *useful* rather than what is *true*. It deceives itself, although its consequent immorality cannot be imputed to personal fault because it arose without the use of freedom. It is imputed rather to the fault of human nature. In other words, it would incur the damnation proper to original sin, to which it would be reduced, had not baptism removed such imputation or damnation.[67]

98. A distinction certainly has to be made between perceiving intellectually a particular act we are about to do, and having sufficient time to recollect ourselves, compare the act with the law, consider the incongruity of the act, and vividly sense its waywardness. If this can be done, and is done, the obligating force of the law, strengthened by our thoughtfulness and by a well-disposed spirit, acquires enough energy to prevail over passion and the disordered instinct. If, however, the urgency of passion and of instinctive need eliminates time, and the person under pressure has not attained the habitual dominion over his will that can only be obtained through constant practice, there will be nothing to prevent the will itself from consenting to the passion, whose satisfaction will be the sole object of willed attention.

99. Such actions, which include first movements,[68] must be considered human actions (although they arise spontaneously or rather slip out of us) because the person is carrying out what he *knows*. They are also *moral* actions because of the intervention of the will, although they are done without

[67] St. Thomas uses these terms in stating the principle: 'The notion of fault cannot exist without the inclusion of the notion of something willed. But as there is a certain good relative to nature, and a certain good relative to person, so we have to distinguish between what we may call FAULT IN NATURE and FAULT IN A PERSON. For fault in a person, the WILL OF THE PERSON has to be present, as we can see clearly in an actual fault committed by a person. But only the will in a given nature is necessary for a fault of nature.'

[68] Although the will sometimes concurs *positively* in first movements, it does not act with advertence to the law, or at least not with clear advertence. The person knows the movement and wants it, but does not reflect clearly that it is opposed to the law. However, the will takes part in the physical, rather than the moral entity of the act. To this extent it can be said that often the will's defect is negative. Although it concurs in the act, it does not do so fully because what it wants is simply the act, not the act clothed, as it were, in its relationship with the law.

deliberation or hesitation as a result of the speed with which the will acts. However, despite the rapid conquests made by the bad instinct in these moments of surprise, negligence is often present in the person who acts. In such a case, at least *venial sin* is committed. If there is no negligence, these acts in the baptised person are merely *moral defects*, not *sins* properly speaking because there has been no co-operation in the act nor turning away from God on the part of the supreme principle. And because freedom is lacking they are not *faults*. But in those not baptized, similar failings have their source in the fault of original sin, which is their ultimate cause and origin, and together with the original sin of which they form part are imputed to human nature, their proximate cause.

100. These non-imputable sins, in which original sin is at work, allow us to explain why our original defect is sometimes called *sins* in scripture rather than *sin*. For example: 'And in sins did my mother conceive me.'[69] Original sin, although one in its root, produces a great many sins in the course of human life.

101. These moral imperfections are found especially in infancy, before we have learnt the free use of our own will. Although the power of will is present at our birth, the use of this power is not attained easily. We must first acquire the notions of the things about which we have to deliberate, and then the abstract notions of the things which we need, in order to choose whether to suspend or put into effect our act of will. In our infancy, therefore, we continuously obey our instincts and passions indifferently. Sensitively, and in its animality, the baby is highly active; its intellect, however, is without sufficient information and its intellective will almost blind as a consequence. At first, freedom is totally lacking; later it is still very weak. The human being as a baby appears little different from a beast, although its understanding is very alert and intent on everything it perceives. When a baby

---

[69] Ps 50: 7 [51: 7]. To say that original sin is a true fault in the strict sense, without considering it in relationship with the free will of Adam, is to fall into Baianism. Baius spoke of original sin as imputable, that is, a fault, and the following proposition was rightly condemned: 'Original sin is truly sin without any relationship or regard to the will of him from whom it originated' (Prop. 47).

perceives something pleasant, it wants it with its natural will; and it rejects what is unpleasant. Understanding and will are constantly at work, but the will obeys carnal motives alone. Spiritual stimuli are unknown; the baby cannot oppose with sufficient rapidity the impetus drawing it to obey sensitive nature; its practical, free energy is still undeveloped.

102. St. Augustine's acute observations on childhood should be recalled here. He indicates clearly the sins (in the sense we have been using the word) of infancy: 'Who will remind me of the sins committed when I was a child? For indeed, there is no one in the world without sin, not even a day-old child . . . How could I sin at that time? Was I too eager for my mother's breast? . . . If I were as eager now, not for milk of course but grown-up food, I would rightly be mocked and reproved. So I was acting reprehensibly. But because, at that age, I was incapable of understanding reproof, neither custom nor reason allowed me to be reproved' (personal imputability is excluded). 'But we gradually reject this waywardness — which proves that it is waywardness because I have never met anyone yet who rejects what he has come to recognise as good.' He goes on to describe other actions that he considers sins of his infancy: 'Can I say that I was doing good when I cried for what I could not have without harm to myself? Or when I was bitterly angry with servants and adult freemen alike? Or when I twisted and turned as babies do, trying as much as possible to hurt even my parents, and those wiser than myself, when they did not do what I wanted, even though they could not have done it without harming me?' And he concludes: 'The baby's bodily weakness is innocent, but not the weakness of his soul,'[70] a distinction that strengthens what we hinted earlier when we said that sin does not reside in the animal part alone, but in the *spirit*, that is, in the will, which allows itself to be guided by the animal element even against all reason until we have attained either dominion over self or at least the free use of our will. St. Augustine would never have considered animal movements in themselves as sins without any relationship to an intelligent spirit. He did see, however, that in human beings such movements become the

[70] *Confessions*, 1, 7.

matter of sin because they receive from the will the *form* of sin either in so far as they lack due subjection to the will — which would be present in an integral human nature — or in so far as the will positively consents to these movements, as in the case of children and of rapid movements, which in certain habits draw us inevitably to sin.

St. Augustine reaffirms his teaching with an observation on a child sucking the breast: 'I saw and sensed the jealousy of that baby. It could not talk, but it was pale with envy at the other baby sucking at the same time.' And he is not afraid to add: 'We accept these things tolerantly, but only because they will pass as the child grows — not because they count for nothing or very little.' Finally he exclaims: 'Lord, it pains me to have to write about this part of my life, the life I lead in this world . . . But if I was conceived in iniquity, and in sins nourished by my mother in the womb, tell me, O my God, I beg you, tell me, Lord, where and when was I ever innocent?'[71]

103. Nevertheless, St. Augustine himself acknowledges that in such acts, although moral, and although called sins by him, there cannot be personal fault because they are not done freely. The great bishop of Hippo takes as an unshakeable principle that sin, 'when it cannot in any way be avoided,' is never committed with personal fault: 'Who sins when his act can in no way be avoided?'[72] St. Thomas affirms the same truth when he makes culpable sin consist essentially in an act of free will: 'Sin consists essentially in an act of free will.'[73]

6

OUR TEACHING CONFIRMED
ON THE AUTHORITY OF SACRED SACRIPTURE

Article 1.
Epilogue

104. We can now summarise what has been explained so far.

[71] *Confessions*, 1, 7.   [72] *De lib. arbitrio*, bk. 3, chap 18, n. 40.
[73] *S.T.*, I-II, art. 6, ad 7.

We have distinguished various *states* in which human beings can be found relative to morality before the formation of conscience.

Morality, we said, consists in the state in which the will is found relative to the law.

We spoke briefly about the will in so far as it conforms to the law, and more at length about the different *states* of the will when it is at odds with the law.

In general we said that when the supreme will clashes with the law it is in a state of *sin*, a state or act of the supreme will contrary to the law.

105. *Sin*, therefore, is for us the genus *immorality*. It has two species, to which a third can be added according to St. Paul's way of speaking when he calls *sin* the *moral defect* remaining in the baptised person after baptism (although properly speaking it is not sin).

The first species of sin is a simple moral defect: it is *sin* lacking damnation and imputation. In the baptized person, this sin consists in the will's retention of an inclination to moral evil and a certain opposition to the law. It does not, however, lead the person to damnation because salvation or damnation depends upon the *supreme* will which is not in question here. This evil inclination of the lower will is nevertheless the cause of temptation and brings in its wake the penalty of temporal affliction and death.

The second species of sin is sin accompanied by *damnation*. This sin consists in the state of the *supreme* will in opposition to the law. As long as the supreme will remains in this state, the person cannot attain salvation. In this case sin is imputed to *nature*, as it were, rather than to the *person* himself.

The third species of sin is sin accompanied by *damnation* and *personal imputation*. This sin is rightly called *fault*. It consists in a supreme *will* not only contrary to the law, but *freely* contrary to it. In the first two species the will is *necessarily* contrary to the law.

106. Normally speaking, the word 'sin' is used to indicate the third species of sin, and especially actual, rather than habitual, sin.

107. Applying these notions to Catholic doctrine about *sins*, and in particular to original sin, we noted that:

1. In the baptized person only the first species of sin is present, that is, sin without any damnation, because the supreme will of the human being is saved through the infusion of grace and the character. Only the *lower will*, called *concupiscence*, is defective. This in turn is destroyed with death and regenerated in the resurrection. Acts which unavoidably arise from the fomes of original concupiscence belong to this class of sin. An example of these *acts* are the first movements springing from our original, *habitual sin*, with which they form a single entity.

2. The *second* species of sin exists in the non-baptized human being whose *supreme* will is inclined to evil, but not freely. This malfunctioning of the will causes human downfall because it is present in the supreme will. In this way, damnation is the consequence of original sin. Actual sins arising unavoidably in a person not washed from original sin in baptism belong to this class because they form a single entity with original sin.

3. Finally, the third species of sin is present in the person who acts against the law with full knowledge and freedom. This sin gives rise to *damnation* and *personal imputation*, that is, to a positive sentence of condemnation.

Article 2.
The authority of sacred scripture

108. We now have to show that this way of speaking is found in the Church's sacred scripture.

Our original stain is called *sin*. We are said to be conceived in sin;[74] to be sinners before we have lived a single day on earth.[75] The whole world is said to be subject to sin;[76] all have sinned, children not excepted.[77] A disorder, therefore, is present in the human spirit. In the language rightly used by

---

[74] Ps 50 [51]: 7.
[75] Job 14: 4. In the Septuagint, according to St. Leo, Serm. 1, *De Nativitate Dom.*, and according to St. Augustine, *Confessions*, bk. 1, chap. 7.
[76] John the Baptist speaks of the *sin of the world* (Jn 1: 29).
[77] 'All have sinned and fall short of the glory of God' (Rom 3: 23); cf. Job 14: 4.

scripture and the Church this disorder merits the name of *sin*, although it is committed necessarily, without any trace of freedom. The notion of *sin* in general, as it is presented in scripture and by the Church, does not contain any element of freedom, although *will* must be present. Without will our state would be one of physical defect, never of moral evil.

Moreover, although original sin does not spring from our freedom, but from that of our first parent, it brings *damnation* in its wake. The damnation we are speaking of does not result, however, from any personal *fault* of ours. It is a consequence of the fault of our first parent by which human beings in their entirety and in their highest principle of action are now damaged and lost. St. Paul says: 'We were by nature *children of wrath*';[78] he does not say that we were *children of judgment*. He does not speak of a judge who pronounces sentence, but of an angry master (with a truly just anger) whose servant has become odious. Again, St. Paul says: 'All who have sinned without the law will also *perish* without the law, and all who have sinned under the law will be *judged* by the law.'[79] *Perdition* is the lot of those without the law, and *judgment* of those with the law. Thus St. Paul distinguished between *damnation* (perdition) and *imputation*, properly so-called. Although people perished even without the law, and hence before the law, St. Paul says explicitly that before the law sin was not *imputed*. 'For until the law sin was in the world: but sin was not *imputed*, when the law was not.'[80] According to the Apostle's way of speaking there was no *imputation*, although *damnation* and *perdition* were present. He goes on: 'Yet death *reigned* from Adam to Moses, even over those whose sins were not like the transgression of Adam'[81] whose fault was free and actual. An *original, habitual sin* was present which brought *damnation* but not, strictly speaking, *imputation* which requires the free will that develops especially through knowledge of positive law. All human beings, therefore, exist with a malfunctioning will. There is no need to condemn them; it is sufficient to leave them in the grip of their disorder. No wrong is done to them;

[78] Eph 2: 3.   [79] Rom 2: 12.
[80] Rom 5: 13. Cf. St. Augustine, *De Nuptiis et concup.*, bk. 2, chap. 28.
[81] Rom 5: 14.

they are simply left with what is their own. The damage they suffer is like a *physical* evil, an unavoidable consequence of the fault of our first parent which only Christ can remedy.[82]

109. Another principle is indeed introduced into human nature, not through the work of *free will*, but of *necessity*, when the grace of our Redeemer is infused into us. Damnation is immediately removed; we are saved. Although a wound remains in our lower powers and in our *natural will*, the new principle — the new *supernatural will* — is whole and entire and, as the superior power, governs the natural will. Moral defect still exists in this state, but it does not merit the name *sin* in the previous exact sense because it does not bring damnation in its wake. In other words, an inclination to evil is present in the *natural will*, but it does not damn human beings in whom is found the saving power of the *supernatural will*. St. Paul says: 'Since, therefore, we are now justified by his blood, much more shall we be saved by him from the *wrath* of God.'[83] Nevertheless, the Apostle does say that sin still dwells in us, although it cannot harm us. Continuing with his explanation of this singular teaching on sin, which dwells in us without leading to our damnation, he says that the law has power over us as long as we live; but that when we die, the law can no longer be applied to us. We are like a married woman who is bound to her husband as long as he lives, but free after his death. In the same way the law of sin is bound to the 'old man' as long as he lives, but cannot be applied to him after his death; the 'new man' is free from sin.[84]

---

[82] 'What shall we say? That God is unjust to inflict wrath on us . . .? By no means!' (Rom 3: 5).

[83] Rom 5: 9. But when original sin is considered relative to Adam who committed it freely, it is imputed to him as the head of the human family: 'For JUDGMENT indeed was BY ONE unto condemnation.' Judgment is 'by one'; condemnation is common to all, 'unto condemnation' (Rom 5: 16 [Douai]).

[84] 'Do you not know, brethren — for I am speaking to those who know the law — that the law is binding on a person only during his life? Thus a married woman is bound by law to her husband as long as he lives; but if her husband dies she is discharged from the law concerning the husband. Accordingly, she will be called an adulteress if she lives with another man while her husband is alive. But if her husband dies she is free from that law, and if she marries another man she is not an adulteress. Likewise, my brethren, you have died to the law through the body of Christ, so that you

What are the *old man* and the *new man* according to St. Paul? They are the two personal wills, natural and super-natural. As long as the natural will alone is present in the human being, it is that person's superior and personal will which, if disordered, brings perdition in its wake. When the supernatural will appears in us, however, it subjects and governs the natural will. The supernatural will is now the unique, personal will in us, and because it is good, it saves us.

It is true that the supernatural will cannot prevent the disorder in the lower powers; its *acts of choice*, although good and holy, will not always have the strength to ensure obedi-ence to its commands from the lower powers. This is a disorder that only death can take away.

All this is taught by St. Paul where he says: 'I do not under-stand my own actions' (the actions of my lower powers). 'For I do not do what I want, but I do the very thing I hate . . .' (he cannot command his lower powers). 'So then it is no longer I' (personal pronoun, it is no longer myself as a person) 'that do it, but sin which dwells within me' (that is: MYSELF is constituted by the supernatural will that desires what is good; but there is also within me a natural will that tends to evil, although this is no longer me, but sin, the moral defect remaining after my rebirth and dwelling in me without me). He goes on: 'For I know that nothing good dwells within me, that is, in my flesh' (he says: 'in his flesh,' because the disorder in the will comes from the infirm flesh). 'I can will what is right,' (with his acts of *choice*) 'but I cannot do it' (with the acts *commanding his lower powers*). 'For I do not do the good I want, but the evil I do not want is what I do.' And he shows that this tendency to evil does not constitute his personality by adding: 'Now if I do what I do not want, it is no longer I' (my person) 'that do it, but sin which dwells within me. So I find it to be a law that when I want to do right, evil lies close at hand. For I delight in the law of God,

may belong to another, to him who has been raised from the dead in order that we may bear fruit for God. While we were living in the flesh, our sinful passions were at work in our members to bear fruit for death. But now we are discharged from the law, dead to that which held us captive, so that we serve not under the old written code but in the new life of the Spirit' (Rom 7: 1–6).

[109]

in my inmost self,' (the *supernatural will*) 'but I see in my members another law at war with the law of my mind and making me captive to the law of sin which dwells in my members. Wretched man that I am! Who will deliver me from this body of death? Thanks be to God, through Jesus Christ our Lord! So then, I of myself serve the law of God with my *mind*, but with my *flesh*, I serve the law of sin.'[85]

Therefore, through faith in Christ and through baptism, our higher part is renewed, although our lower part, called *flesh* or even *body* in scripture, remains disordered. It is in fact the flesh, or the body, that imparts the evil twist, or sin, to our natural will. When the flesh has been removed through death, we are completely purified: 'If Christ is in you, although your *bodies* are dead because of sin, your spirits are alive because of righteousness.'[86]

110. The more we consider this order of justification in us, the more apt we shall find scripture's way of saying that God *covers* certain sins, without *imputing* them. Baptism does not destroy the evil *natural will*, but adds a *supernatural will* to it. This 'covers', as it were, the natural will, preventing it from damning us by the way in which the supernatural principle has changed the nature of our original disorder. Sin and consequent damnation are present in us no longer. As the Psalmist says:

'Blessed is he whose *transgression* is *forgiven*,
whose *sin* is *covered*.'

Transgression is *forgiven*, but *sin* is *covered*, where perhaps transgressions are free, actual sins, and sins are non-free defects, leaving unharmed the persons who belong to the people of God.

'Blessed is the man to whom the Lord imputes no iniquity.'[87]

Here perhaps the Psalmist refers to non-imputed sins. In this case his meaning would be: Blessed is the man who, although he cannot avoid in his human weakness all clashes with the law, commits only those sins that God does not impute to him, that is, sins in which knowledge and deliberate will are not sufficient for imputation. This, I think, is the

---

[85] Rom 7: 15, 17–25.   [86] Rom 8: 10.   [87] Ps 31 [32]: 1, 2.

interpretation given to the passage by St. Paul when he uses it
to prove that we are not justified before God through *works*,
because each of us is full of sin, children not excepted; we are
justified through the act of divine mercy which renews us in
virtue of the merits of our Redeemer.[88]

---

[88] 'I have already charged that all men, both Jews and Greeks, are under
the power of sin, as it is written:
> "None is righteous, no, not one;
> no one *understands*"'

(that is, no one possesses an *upright practical judgment*). In scripture an
intelligent person is held to be upright because the principle of morality
consists in a will that understands uprightly, as I showed in *PE*:
> 'No one seeks for God.
> All have turned aside, together they have gone wrong.'

The Jews themselves could not claim exemption from the universal corruption of the sin infecting human nature as the Apostle observes: 'Whatever
the law' (that is, holy scripture) 'says it speaks to those who are under the
law' (the Jews), 'so that "every mouth may be stopped, and the whole
world may be held accountable to God"' (Rom 3: 9–12, 19).

[110]

Book 2

MORALITY RESULTING FROM CONSCIENCE

111. So far we have spoken about morality which precedes the formation of conscience in the human being, a morality not generally observed. Having determined its existence and examined its nature, we must now consider the more widely known morality resulting from the formation of conscience. Its existence needs no demonstration because people generally accept that all good and evil in the human being is caused by conscience, although this opinion agrees neither with reason nor with the dogmatic teachings of Christianity, as we have seen (cf. 32–71).

112. It is true that once moral conscience has been formed, we possess a new principle of morality. Anyone who judges as evil an action he is about to do, and does it, undoubtedly sins — which indicates how we are obliged to follow conscience, the moral judgment we make about our actions (cf. 15).

113. This truth — that we are obliged to follow conscience as soon as it is formed in our spirit — is taught in scripture. St. Paul says: 'Whatever does not proceed from faith' (that is, from conscience, from the sincere persuasion of doing good), 'is sin.'[89]

114. We must first examine, therefore, how we pass from not having to having a conscience about our acts. This will indicate the way for solving other difficulties. We cannot form a clear concept of the different kinds of moral conscience and their obligating force unless we carefully investigate the origin of conscience and gradually examine all the modifications it undergoes in the human spirit.

1

THE ORIGIN OF CONSCIENCE

115. The problem of the origin of conscience involves:

1. An investigation of the stimuli that lead us to form the judgment called moral conscience before we act;

2. An investigation of the difference between the human spirit devoid of conscience and the human spirit which

---

[89] Rom 14: 23. The Greek word 'πιστις' means both *faith* and *persuasion*.

possesses and uses conscience as a proximate rule of its actions.

Article 1.
Stimuli to the formation of conscience

116. We have already dealt with the first of the two investigations (cf. 49–71). We noted that one of the first stimuli, perhaps the first to move us to make a definite judgment about our actions, is our perverse will. Because we are inclined to evil, we do not follow the spontaneous movement of nature (for which conscience is not required). We act against nature and place ourselves in opposition to the law by determining our free will through a *practical judgment*. We judge it good to act against the law. Such a *judgment* necessarily includes the *ethical judgment* that our act is contrary to the law: and this judgment is *conscience*.

117. We have noted that two circumstances accompanied the first example of sin in Genesis: 1. the evil action done by the first human beings was not against *natural law* but against *positive* law; and 2. they were moved to perform it by the seductive words of the demon.

These circumstances are very important. In a good nature, subject to a loving providence, no reason could be found obliging human beings to decide to sin against the natural law. It is difficult enough to believe that they could be induced to sin even against the positive law if an external being had not moved them to do so through speech, and persuaded them to think they would obtain some mysterious good by violating the law. The natural law itself directed them to the observance of the positive law, because it is a precept of natural law to obey the one who has the right to command.

The first sin, when analysed, reveals: 1. a positive law; 2. an external temptation; 3. speech, that is, a means of communication by which the human mind was able to conceive the positive law and to receive the temptation through belief in the false good deceptively offered to the imagination by violation of the law. Here are found all the elements that explain how the human race passed from a state without conscience to the state of conscience.

It will not be a waste of time if we consider these two *states of the human spirit* so as to explain clearly what we are saying and avoid misunderstanding.

Article 2.
The difference between
the human spirit before the formation of conscience
and the human spirit using conscience
as the proximate rule of its actions

118. The will is the principle of moral actions. Thus, in order to indicate the different *moral states* of the human being and the different kinds of morality he acquires, we must determine and describe the various states of the human will.

119. The will is defined as a principle which acts in accordance with what we know.

120. Its different states cannot be described, therefore. without a prior description of the different *states of the mind*. In our case, this simply means defining the ways in which the mind conceives the law, the norm of the will.

121. Each of the different ways in which knowledge of the law presents itself to the understanding can be a basis for the will's moral action. More importantly, the different ways can be present simultaneously in the same mind, and so the will can have different foundations for its actions. As we shall see, all the difficulties concerning conscience come from this last fact.

122. Let us see, therefore, amongst the different ways in which the law can be present in the human mind, those to which no conscience corresponds, and those with corresponding consciences. We will then examine how the states with corresponding consciences differ from each other, and thus determine the different states of conscience. This will allow us to investigate the logical *rules* for solving the difficulties found in those states.

123. At first, the human being lacks all determined ideas, which are acquired only at a later stage. But he perceives

beings, and notices among them not only those like himself, endowed with feeling, intelligence and the desire for a pleasant existence, but also those lacking all feeling, or which, having feeling, lack intelligence and will. Here, I am not concerned whether such a person sometimes wrongly attributes intelligence and will (qualities proper to him) to beings that do not have them. Even if mistaken, he still conceives beings like himself, and distinguishes them from those without his own endowments.

124. The spontaneous movement of his own nature (granted that it is not damaged) is to *acknowledge* these beings in practice for what they are, according to his mental conception of them. This means giving them the same value he gives himself, and results in an equivalent affection. But to acknowledge spontaneously these beings conceived in his mind, in the way he conceives them, requires no other law or norm than the beings themselves as determined by the judgment made at the time of their perception. All that is required, is 1. the perception of the beings (direct knowledge), and 2. the spontaneous movement of the will, which adheres to the entire conceived entity (practical, reflective-willed knowledge).

125. These are the first moral acts of a human being. They precede the formation of moral norms and precepts, but their morality is undeniable because the will acts in conformity with the exigency of beings. They also precede the formation of all *moral, abstract norms* because the first moral acts require only the mental conception of the beings towards whom they are directed, and the spontaneous movement of the will.

In these first moments when the human being begins to act morally, he has not formed any *science of morality*, nor could he answer questions on the matter; he could not state any precept or law externally with words or even internally in his mind, because a *precept* or law, whether spoken or thought, is something abstracted from beings, a general concept. At this stage the human being has only the perception and conception of individual beings without any reflection.

126. Comparing our *actions* with the law to discover whether they conform to it or not, requires a judgment of

conscience. Neither a mental conception of individual beings, by itself, nor the spontaneous movement of the will determining our actions, is sufficient. An abstract, general norm is necessary, to act as *mediator* for the comparison between actions to be done and conceived beings. The analysis of any comparison clearly demonstrates this need, and I have shown that no *comparison* could be made if only two real terms were present, for example, two sensations of a similar white colour. To be able to compare these two kinds of whiteness, we need the abstract concept of *whiteness in general*. In the comparison, we are simply applying the axiom: two things equal to a third are equal to each other.[90]

127. Thus, in our case, each action must be judged either right and good or evil. Or to keep the expression that first comes to mind, we must judge whether the *esteem* we give to each being is equal or not to the exigency of its mentally conceived being. And we cannot make this judgment unless we have previously abstracted from the being the concept of its *exigency*, that is, the force of obligation, the rule, precept and law.

128. A study of knowledge shows that an abstract idea is formed only with the help of speech.[91] Consequently, in order to have conscience, we must live in *society*, and receive from the *speech* preserved by the society the development necessary for us to form the abstract concept of obligation. We will reach the same conclusion if we recall that conscience is a judgment at the second level of reflection at least (cf. 30, 31), and that we do not move to this level except by means of speech obtained by our association with other intelligent beings.

129. Furthermore, if we find in society someone to teach or state for us the formula containing the abstract law, our understanding carries out the abstraction much more quickly. And this is what usually takes place, especially if we are in contact with a higher, intelligent being from the beginning of our development, as happened with the first father of the human race, to whom God himself spoke.

In fact, people often say to children: 'You must do this;

[90] *Nuovo Saggio sull'origine delle Idee*, Intra, 1885, vol. 1, sect. 3, c. 4, art. 20.   [91] *OT*, 514.

you must not do that' or 'Don't do that; it is wrong.' In this
way they communicate the idea of duty, obligation and law,
an idea or mental being, abstracted from perceived beings.
Such instructions have an extraordinary way of moving the
child's attention (which is concentrated naturally and totally
on understanding the words it hears) to determine abstrac-
tedly the idea of law, duty and obligation.

130. If we are stimulated to form this abstraction by
speech, and by society's use of speech, we must also admit
that the abstract idea of law becomes even more distinct and
separate from perceived beings if we are victims of temptation, that is, if some evil being proposes and persuades us to
do evil, or act contrary to our duty. The reason for this, as I
have already explained, is that on the one hand we feel the
exigency of the being against whom we are being induced to
sin, while on the other we are aware that the suggestion itself
is contrary to the exigency. Because of this opposition, the
obligation we are tempted to violate presents itself more
urgently to our mind and is felt more acutely in our spirit.
This is the normal way in which human intelligence perfects
its knowledge; it notes differences when faced with compari-
sons and contraries.[92]

131. Finally, the greatest help we have in fixing our attention on our obligation and on the law abstracted from beings
is the imposition of a positive law, which also requires
speech.

A precept or positive law is simply the will, expressed in
signs, of a being who has the right to command. The expression is itself something abstracted from the beings to which it
applies. For example, the concept contained in the formula:

---

[92] It will be helpful to quote St. Augustine who, after mentioning certain
passages of the letter to the Romans that deal with the law as the occasion of
sin, adds that if the law produced sin, sin then gave human beings
knowledge of themselves and awareness of their own weakness. 'Well then,
can it be doubted that the law was given for us to *find* ourselves? As long as
God did not prohibit evil, we were hidden from ourselves; we did not
discover how weak we were until we received the prohibiting law. It was
then we found ourselves, found ourselves acting evilly. Where could we
flee? Wherever we went, our very self followed us. And what use was the
knowledge of ourselves as refound, if we were reproached by conscience?'
(St. Aug., *Serm. 154, de verb. Apost.*, Rom 7, c. 1, 1).

'You shall not eat of the tree of knowledge of good and evil' differs so much from the concept of the tree itself that a human being would never have obtained it from the perception of the tree. But once the law was stated, two things were present: the perceived tree, object of the law, and the law itself. This indicates an important difference between *positive law* and *rational law*. In positive law two things are always distinguished, the object of the law and the law itself; in rational law this is not necessarily so. As we develop, rational law is present in us in two successive states corresponding to the levels of development. In the first state, there is no law differing from mentally conceived beings; they are themselves laws. Their quantity of being shows the amount of action we need towards them and also manifests their exigency, which is felt not in the abstract but in their perception. The second state follows on the first: moved by some stimulus, we abstract this exigency and, separating it from the subsistent beings, express it in some way, giving it a condition similar to that of the positive law. It becomes a *mental entity* formulated in words, independent of any being and applicable to every being of the same species or genus.

132. Only when law has acquired its own mental existence in human understanding, can it be called 'law'. Because of this, I have made the essence of law consist in a *notion of the mind*, according to which we must act.[93] This does not exclude the existence of the force of law and obligation prior to the notion in its abstract form. In fact we have seen that this force is the *exigency* in beings to be spontaneously and rationally acknowledged for what they are as soon as they are perceived. The exigency has no name because it has no mode of being of its own, a state required for anything to be named. However it receives such a mode of being of its own when it is abstracted as a mental being from beings and becomes applicable to them as their measure.

133. This change of the *exigency* of beings into a true *law* expressed like positive law is mentioned by St. Paul when he is speaking about the pagans' lack of the positive law of Moses: 'When Gentiles who have not the law do by nature what the law requires, they are a law to themselves, even

[93] *PE*, 1, 2.

though they do not have the law. They show that what the law requires is written on their hearts, while their conscience also bears witness and their conflicting thoughts accuse or perhaps excuse them.'[94] He says the Gentiles have no law. This refers to an early stage of humanity, when positive law, such as the law of the Hebrews, did not exist. Secondly, he says that, although they did not have a law, they did *by nature* what belongs to the law.[95] This is a second stage of humanity: because intellectual and moral faculties have their own instinctive action, people act naturally and spontaneously according to the exigency of beings. Thirdly, he says the Gentiles are a law to themselves, conscious of doing good and evil, accusing and defending themselves. This is a third stage: humans have noticed within themselves the exigency of beings (through conscience, with its remorse and approval) and have expressed the exigency in words, demonstrated by their mutual accusations and defence.

134. Hence, as soon as human beings acquire in their spirit the abstract, formulated notion called 'law', they are able to use it as rule and norm of their actions, and are forbidden to act against it.

135. In fact the formed law becomes our rule of action because it is extremely helpful, is clearly present to our minds and attracts our free, personal attention much more than the felt exigency of beings which, in its non-abstracted state, is one with our perception.

[94] Rom 2: 14, 15.
[95] The scientific precision of St. Paul's words needs to be noted. In several places he implicitly refers to the *acknowledgement*-principle that we accept as the essence of morality. He says that although the Gentiles '*knew* God they did not *honour* him as God'. Here we find direct knowledge of God, which requires as a consequence that God be honoured, that is, acknowledged in practice. He goes on: 'and they exchanged the glory of the immortal God for images resembling mortal man or birds, or animals or reptiles.' Here he indicates the efficacy of a corrupt will to transform one being into another by attributing to it what belongs to the other, despite what is known about the perceived being. Thus, he says: 'They exchanged the truth about God' (direct knowledge, in which the true concept of God is found) 'for a lie', that is, for a fiction of their imagination. That we must act according to the *knowledge of being* is wonderfully expressed in the words about the Gentiles: 'They did not see fit to acknowledge God' (Rom 1: 21, 23, 25, 28).

136. However, we must not think that when we possess the law, we no longer feel the *exigency* of the perceived beings which beforehand we felt directly without the mediation of formulated law. Perceived beings continue to make their exigency felt directly in us,[96] although the exigency is of things that take place in us without their being noticed by ourselves or even by philosophers. First, as we have often said, our spontaneous action is always difficult to observe and analyse because it contains nothing new and extraordinary to engage our powers of attention and reflection. Second, formulated law, which has become the clear, general rule of our activity, is nearly always associated with the exigency of perceived beings, and demands our full attention in such a way that we persuade ourselves that we follow no other principle of action. In reality, however, things are often very different: two principles controlling our actions are at work simultaneously, namely, the exigency of perceived beings, inseparable from beings, and formulated law. When we act in accordance with the exigency of beings we act immediately and spontaneously, and although we operate rationally, our actions are very similar to those produced by feeling — so much so that the effect produced in us by the exigency of beings can be called feeling. When we act in accordance with formulated law, however, we usually pay attention to what we are doing, make a choice, and even deliberate.

137. But even more thought needs to be given to the fact that these two principles not only move us simultaneously to action but draw us in opposite directions. This explains the state of *perplexity* in which we sometimes find ourselves.

138. All this will be clear from what has been said. When we act according to formulated law, as we do in a developed state, the *application of the law* must be made to the act we wish to posit, because formulated law is not a part of beings,

[96] For this reason the law inscribed in us is fittingly called both 'natural' and 'rational'. It is *natural* in so far as the intellectually conceived *nature* of beings is a law or rule for our actions; it is *rational* in so far as it is reason which first *conceives* beings and then abstracts their *exigency* and formula. Thus the term 'natural law' is appropriate for the law's first appearance, when it is still part of the *natures* of beings; 'rational law' is much better adapted to describe the law's second appearance, when it has been *abstracted* and becomes a being of our reason.

[136-8]

as we have seen, but something separate and abstract, a mental being on its own. It is impossible for us, therefore, to use it as a norm of our actions if we do not first apply it to beings and to the actions we intend to do, when we judge them in conformity or not with the law. However, we can err in making this *application*, and often do so without noticing what we have done. We make a false judgment, pronouncing as right an action that is wrong, or viceversa. Our judgment now contradicts the judgment we have called moral sense or feeling produced in the perception of beings. Thus there are two conflicting rules of action in us.

139. And here indeed we see clearly how we cannot act in accord with formulated law if we have not first formed a *conscience* about our actions. As we have said, formulated law cannot be used as a norm for our actions until it is *applied* because, by means of this application, our actions are judged right or wrong, in conformity with the law or not. This judgment on actions we intend to do is precisely conscience.

140. Conscience therefore is the proximate rule for human actions, but it is not the only rule. There are two proximate rules: 1. the *moral sense* or non-formulated law, which guides human beings to moral actions without conscience and needs no application, since it applies itself and 'adheres' to perceived beings; and 2. *conscience*, which is the application of formulated law to the individual actions each person is about to do.

2

MORALITY CONSEQUENT ON CONSCIENCE

141. It seems certain that when we possess formulated law and by its means form a moral conscience about our actions, these actions take on a greater degree of morality because the rule governing them becomes clearer, more distinct and personal. Our will is able to desire good more purely, attentively and deliberately.

142. But I think the main reason for growth in morality, which comes to us with the birth of conscience, must be sought in the state of human decadence after sin. Wounded in

all our faculties, *moral sense* is no longer capable of giving us clear, effective guidance. Perceived intelligent beings continue to stimulate a corresponding moral affection but the stimulus is weak in comparison with other, depraved, tendencies of our spirit that slavishly drag us along, preventing us from gently following the rational light of perceived beings.

143. Hence, for St. Paul, the gravity of the Hebrews' sin was increased because they had received the positive law enabling them to form a clear, certain conscience of their actions: 'Since through the law comes knowledge of sin'[97] — 'For the law brings wrath, but where there is no law there is no transgression.'[98] Again, 'Sin indeed was in the world before the law was given but sin is not counted where there is no law . . . Law came in, to increase the trespass.'[99] And 'What then shall we say? That the law is sin? By no means! Yet, if it had not been for the law, I should not have known sin. I should not have known what it is to covet if the law had not said, "You shall not covet." But sin' (that is, original sin, present in a baby as well), 'finding opportunity in the commandment, wrought in me all kinds of covetousness. Apart from the law sin lies dead. I was once alive apart from the law' (that is, when I was a baby), 'but when the commandment came' (when, by means of reflection, I acquired knowledge of formulated law), 'sin revived.'[100] He says he did not know concupiscence, meaning he was totally ignorant of the fact that actions resulting from concupiscence were sin. Human beings not instructed in formulated law follow impulses of nature without reflection; they are moved by the force of the impulses, which engage them and draw them more strongly than the gentle light of reason. This allows some excuse for the sin of human beings, and although the total, original disorder, without faith in Christ, leads of its nature to damnation, it does not merit any special, particular imputation.

144. For this reason the Apostle condemns the Gentiles, even though they did not have the Mosaic law. There was clear evidence that they had progressed to a formulated

---

[97] Rom 3: 20.   [99] Rom 5: 13, 20.
[98] Rom 4: 15.   [100] Rom 7: 7–9.

natural law, according to which they formed a conscience about their actions.

His proof lies in the judgments by which they condemned or pardoned themselves. Such judgments are the application of formulated law, and could not be made without it: 'Therefore you have no excuse, O man, whoever you are, when you judge another; for in passing judgment upon him you condemn yourself, because you, the judge, are doing the very same things.'[101] These words agree with those of Jesus Christ which command us not to judge in order not to be judged.[102] He also says: 'If I had not come and spoken to them' (this is the language formulating the law), 'they would not have sin; but now they have no excuse for their sin.'[103] This means: 'If I had not given them my law, they would have contracted original sin and its consequences, but would have been excused because of the ignorance and mental blindness resulting from the passion of concupiscence. But I have made the truth clear by what I have said, and have given them the power to see and follow it. Therefore, all the consequences of the original sin fall again upon their head.' Christ also says: 'If you were blind, you would have no guilt; but now that you say, "We see"' (proving that you have a conscience), 'your guilt remains.'[104] Once a formulated law is posited, its application, which consists in a judgment, must follow, as we have seen. Consequently, Christ, the preacher of the new law, says: 'For judgment I came into this world, that those who do not see may see, and that those who see may become blind.'[105] Those who did not see were simple people, not instructed in positive law, who, because they generally used moral instinct as their rule, were not so guilty, and were easily enlightened. Those who saw, however, were educated in the Mosaic law, but were content to know it rather than observe it.

[101] Rom 2: 1. [104] Jn 9: 41.
[102] Mt 7: 1. [105] Jn 9: 39.
[103] Jn 15: 22.

3

THE ORIGIN AND DEVELOPMENT OF
MORAL SCIENCE IN HUMAN BEINGS

145. We have seen that *conscience* necessarily begins in human beings when they are in possession of abstract, formulated law, which they must follow when they act (cf. 139, 143, 144). They are therefore obliged to apply the law to the particular action they are performing by making a judgment on it, and thus forming a conscience about it. But abstract, formulated law, which we simply call *law*,[106] acquires different states in the human mind, giving rise to different kinds of conscience.

146. In addition we do not always *apply the law* immediately to what we are about to do, or at least not always in the same way. As a result, the various ways of applying the law give rise to different judgments about our actions and therefore different kinds of conscience.

147. The different kinds of conscience originate from:

1. the different states that the law, applied to our actions, assumes in our mind;

2. the different ways the law is applied in the judgments we make about our actions.

In this chapter I shall discuss the different states of the law as they vary with the progressive development of the human mind. In the following chapter I shall discuss the different ways of applying the law to particular human actions, of

---

[106] This appropriate use of the term conforms to St. Paul's use of it (Rom 1), as we can see from Tertullian's commentary on the Apostle's words: 'If God is to judge the hidden things of those who have offended either with or without the law — those ignorant of the law naturally do what is under the law — he will certainly judge those who are under the LAW and also subject to NATURE, which serves as law for the uninstructed' (L. 5, *contr. Marcionem*, c. 13). We note: 1. *nature* took the place of *law* for the Gentiles. This is precisely what I say: *beings* themselves, that is, the *nature* of conceived beings, are from the start the norm for human beings, from which only later is the formula of law derived. 2. In this first state, the human being is said to be without *law* because moral obligation, despite its efficacy and obligation in its first unabstracted condition, does not merit the name 'law' as we commonly use the word.

judging these actions and of forming a moral conscience about them.

148. An investigation into the different states assumed by the law in the human mind according to the stages of human development concerns the origin, growth and perfecting of *moral science*. This science is simply the complex of all moral laws in their respective order, that is, of all the obligatory formulas that constitute the moral rules of human actions.

Hence, the investigation entails a philosophical survey of the development of the human spirit relative to moral notions. It is not a survey of contingent facts but, given certain positive conditions, of necessary facts. We can therefore ignore any accidental development of the mind dependent upon positive, accidental factors. For instance, it is certain that if our predecessors of two thousand years ago were to speak to primitive people living today in order to give them moral instruction, they would use language quite different from ours. Their logic would correspond to a level of development lower than our own and their teaching would involve ideas less abstract and less clear than ours. Thus, their way and ours of instructing these primitive people would produce different thought processes. In both cases, however, the development of mind and spirit would be subject to the same logical and psychological laws; only the accidental circumstances in which these laws operate would be different.

149. Accidental circumstances must, therefore, be ignored. Our investigation must deal only with the constant effects of the understanding's development relative to moral concepts.

Article 1.
SPECIFIC MORAL formulas are formed before GENERIC MORAL formulas

150. We must first establish the general principle that human beings, when forming abstract notions to serve as the moral rule of their actions, obey the logical and psychological laws governing the formation of all abstracts.

The study of knowledge shows that abstracts in the human

mind have two grades, specific and generic.[107] Because every moral norm is an abstract idea, it must be either specific or generic. This is the first and fundamental division of all formulas expressing obligation, because formulas are stated either in regard to a species of beings or in regard to an entire genus.

Thus, just as beings are classified into species and genera, so formulas expressing obligation (or, if preferred, moral imperatives) are classified into specific and generic.[108] For example, the imperatives that directly apply to the human species constitute *specific* laws. If these specific laws are generalised, they become laws having the genus 'intelligent beings' as their object, and are therefore *generic* laws. 'Do not kill' is a specific imperative because it refers to the human species, but 'Do not hate' is a generic or universal imperative because it refers to all intelligent beings, and in fact to all beings.

151. Anyone seeking to construct a science of ethics should carefully consider the species and genera of beings, and use them as a foundation for dividing the various formulas of obligation into an ordered hierarchy. He should note that every species has three *modes: full[-imperfect], imperfect-abstract* and *full-perfect*,[109] and that genus also is of three kinds: *real, mental* and *nominal*. He must show that a class of moral imperatives corresponds to each of these different forms of *species* and *genera*, and that the imperatives of one class must not be confused with those of another, nor inter-mingled indiscriminately, as commonly occurs in treatises on ethics.

152. The *specific* and *generic imperatives* are subordinate to the *universal, categorical imperative*, which is the principle and source of all imperatives, wonderfully containing and uniting the whole of moral science.

153. If we consider these different imperative formulas relative to the action of the spirit conceiving them, we see that the *specific formulas*, which prescind only from the being's

[107] Cf. my theory of species and genera in *OT*, 646–659.

[108] Above every *species* and *genera*, we posit three CATEGORIES, one of which is universal *moral being*.

[109] Cf. *OT, loc. cit.*

subsistence and from the accidents (which belong to the *abstract species*[110]), are at a lower level of reflection than the generic formulas. The spirit has first to reflect on specific formulas before it can make them generic, at least in the case of *mental genera*. *Real genera*, because they are founded in nature, could be abstracted directly without the use of specific abstractions.

154. The level of reflection required to express the mental genera in words is proportionate to the level and extent of the genera. And because higher reflections cannot be made without lower reflections, we can understand why the *science of morality* begins with specific formulas. Only after a long time do these specific formulas become generalised. Continually expressed in more general propositions, they assume a nobler, more scientific appearance, giving greater satisfaction to the mind, although ever more distant from their practical applications.

155. But it is precisely from the varying condition of these applications that different consciences originate when we act. Each formula, whether specific or generic, can be used as a rule of our actions, although specific formulas are easily (and sometimes immediately) applied to the judgment of actions about to be done, whereas generic formulas are applied only when the specific formula has been deduced from them to serve as mediator in the application.

Thus, the person who follows *generic formulas* in his action will be more liable to error in forming a conscience than the person who forms his conscience by means of *specific formulas*. On the other hand, the former will have a greater appreciation of the dignity of moral virtue than the latter, because generic formulas contain the explanation of specific formulas and are therefore closer to the *categorical imperative*, which is the source of the evidence for obligation. This explains why educated people can speak more eloquently about moral matters; they have a more universal view of

[110] Although formulas belonging to *full-imperfect* species could be verbally expressed if we wished, the exercise would be pointless. In any case, they are so many that we could never express them all. Full-imperfect-specific ideas are not found in books on ethics because they are not expressed in any language. Even philosophers do not generally notice them.

[154-5]

them. However, when acting, and in consequences closer to practice, they are less sure than ordinary people, who simply follow specific precepts. Those who follow universal principles can easily make a mistake, precisely because such principles are so far removed from life itself, and because the mind has to pass through a long succession of intermediate propositions before being able to judge the actions to be done.

156. For example, the moral formula: 'You must help your country' is more generic than: 'Punishment of the guilty must be left to magistrates.' The need for magistrates and judges to judge crimes committed by individual citizens is founded in the necessity to preserve order in the state, if the country is to be helped. But anyone who regulated his actions solely by the more general principle of helping his country, could make a mistake about the respect due to the judiciary more easily than the person following the more specific rule of leaving the treatment of crimes to magistrates; the first would form an erroneous conscience more easily than the second. If the first knew of a depraved, evil man, he might think it lawful to kill him, by reasoning: 'Everyone must help his country. But doing away with the wicked is a great good for one's country. Therefore my act of ridding the country of this criminal is an excellent work.' This application of the principle is wrong. The general principle, when used by itself as a rule for a person who refuses to take specific formulas as a norm, gives rise to pretexts for mistakes, particularly if the person is already blinded by passion. The principle 'You must help your country' does not in itself determine any good and upright way of helping one's country. Consequently, because the means are not determined in reality, anyone following the principle can use apparent rather than true, real means. On the other hand, another person following the more specific formula 'Punishment of the guilty must be left to magistrates' cannot make a mistake, because the formula, being specific, determines the means of attaining real, public utility. But if the first person, instead of immediately applying the general principle, moves to the particular formula and uses it as a means for judging his action, he avoids error.

[156]

Article 2.
We first form moral formulas about beings
considered in themselves and then formulas about beings
in their different relationships

§1. Formulas about beings considered in themselves

157. From what has been said about the laws governing the development of human intelligence, we can conclude that 'as people develop, they first form moral formulas about beings considered in themselves and then formulas about beings in their various relationships.'

158. It is a fact that we first perceive individual beings. We then perceive several beings together, and subsequently distinguish them with their different relationships. We cannot see these relationships before we have perceived the beings as individuals. Knowledge, therefore, of the relationships belongs to the faculty of reflection, and the level of reflection depends on the quality of the individual beings whose relationships are being determined.

Furthermore, just as we cannot know our duties towards a being unless we have first perceived the being, so we cannot know our duties arising from the relationships between beings unless we have first conceived these relationships.

Thus, duties to beings in themselves become known before duties deriving from the relationships between beings. Hence, at the beginning of moral science, imperative formulas which express the first kind of duties are antecedent to those expressing the second kind. For example, we know that in the union of the sexes nothing must be done contrary and harmful to the generation of children; only later do we become aware of the incongruity of polygamy. The first truth is drawn easily from the dignity of a creature that possesses reason, but to know the second, we have first to observe the relationship existing simultaneously between many wives, and then the incongruity present in this simultaneous relationship.

159. But here we must pay careful attention to a kind of exception to the logical law I have posited as controlling the origin of the different moral formulas.

Many relationships between beings are known by us from the beginning because of the synthetical or complex nature of our first perceptions. In fact, at least by means of sight, we perceive the whole universe from the beginning in one single perception. We distinguish beings, noting their differences and relationships. But our knowledge is not perfect, nor do we understand remote, abstract or complex relationships. Relationships like father and mother, brothers and sisters, husband and wife are conceived with almost the first concepts of these beings, but in a confused manner. I say 'confused' because at the beginning, a child sees in his father and mother only other intelligent, good, caring beings with power over him; he loves them naturally, habitually and gratefully but without understanding the notion of parent. We must conclude therefore that we perceive beings by means of our relationship with them, a relationship made up of the action they exercise on us and of the element added by our perceiving understanding. In the first perception of a being, for example, we feel the being as pleasant or unpleasant to our nature. We then see that it is like or unlike ourselves. These relationships are the foundation of the first duties we feel towards beings.

The first relationships that we know, therefore, are: 1. those which beings have directly with us; and 2. those which we suppose or imagine perceived beings have among themselves, as we reason by analogy with ourselves and judge all other beings to have feeling and intelligence as we have.[111]

160. The *first relationships* are not apprehended as relationships; they are the perceived beings themselves apprehended under a particular aspect arising from the special action they exercise on us and we on them. For example, colour is not apprehended in a being as an action of the being on us (in

---

[111] The authoress of *Essai sur l'éducation de l'enfance* (Madame Necker, Geneva, 1837) writes very much to the point: 'It is commonplace to see very young children attributing vital powers to inanimate objects, and this illusion increases their fears or pleasures threefold. A portrait is looking at them; a table suffers when someone hits it. And what about the little finger of their mother or the maid? — what kind of role does that play for a great number of children? This little servant of the secret police is listening, answering, denouncing the guilty ones, who see nothing surprising in so absurd a fact.'

[160]

which the relationship would consist) but as the coloured being itself. Fatherhood is not apprehended as the relationship between the one begetting and the one begotten; what is apprehended is simply a lovable human being called father.

161. The *second relationships* also are not apprehended initially as relationships but as qualities seen in the conceived being. The relationship of equality between a being and us is not apprehended by abstracting the equality but by directly imagining in the being a feeling and intelligence similar to that in us; we imagine ourselves to be in the being. But these relationships are soon abstracted to become true *relationships*, existing as such in the mental concept we have of them,[112] and provide the foundation for other moral formulas.

§2. Formulas concerning beings in their mutual relationships

162. With the exception of the relationships contained in the concept of beings, all other relationships become known later when we have occasion to compare several beings.

If we make a contract or form any kind of association, a pact exists between the contracting parties, and relationships are established between associates. These relationships are foundations for new formulas enjoining obligation. Thus, the formation of civil society would give rise in moral science to a great number of moral formulas.

In the same way, as the uses of things and their effects for the good or evil of humanity become known, the number of moral duties increases proportionately, and obligations arise from the use of natural resources and manufactured goods.

163. If, therefore, we want to know the connection between these formulas and the faculty of reflection in order to distribute the formulas according to the *levels of*

---

[112] The formula, 'A human being must not harm a fellow human being', belongs to the first species, where the *relationship* is not yet separated from the concept 'human'. But the formula, 'You must not harm your like', belongs to the second species, because the *relationship of similarity* is abstracted from what is human, and expressed. The second formula is discovered after the first, which implicitly contains it, and expresses the reason for the first — the reason one human being should not harm another is that the other is his like.

[161-3]

reflections, we must simplify our teaching and look for a principle that will guide us in classifying duties according to the levels of reflections.

The principle is: 'Relationships between beings (the cause of moral obligations) fall under two heads: the *being* and the *action* of things.'

164. The moral formulas, therefore, that spring from these relationships concern either 1. the respective value of things, or 2. their direct and indirect actions with their good or bad effects.

165. In the case of *simple beings*, the first formulas, concerned with the respective value-relationships of things (the respective entity of things) arise, as we said, from the *perception* and *concept* of beings, and are now further distinguished by the differences noted between the beings. In the case, however, of *complex beings*, which like societies and moral bodies are made up of many beings, appropriate formulas come after the first formulas and require a higher level of reflection. Let us take a particular case.

An example of a formula derived from the concept of simple beings is: 'A human being must not be used by another as a means.' But if I consider human beings in their relationship with animals, I discover a second formula: 'A human being is more valuable than an animal which, unlike a human being, can be used as a means.' This formula does not differ essentially from the first, but it is more precise because by means of the *difference* between human beings and animals, it indicates better what is due to human beings. It belongs to the group of formulas founded on the respective value relationships of simple things.

If I now compare a human being with the union called family (a complex being), I form the following formula: 'A family is more valuable than one human being. When conflict arises, I must therefore prefer the preservation of the family to that of the individual human being, all things being equal.' But if I compare a family with a complex of families, I have the formula: 'Many families are worth more than one family, I must therefore prefer the preservation of the many to the one.'

All these formulas are founded on the relationships

between simple and complex beings, or between different complex beings. It is clear that a complex being presupposes the simple beings that form it. It is equally clear that I cannot make a comparison between complex beings except by an act of reflection at a level higher than the level for comparing simple beings. Moreover, complex beings themselves are of different natures, with different levels of complexity and artificiality. Their concepts do not belong to the same level of reflections; some hold a higher and others a lower place in a fixed order.

166. Relationships that have their origin in the *action* of things, that is, in their mutual interactions, are the basis for formulas of obligation according to the *effects* produced by the interaction. Whatever the actions and their order, they must eventually produce a good or bad effect, helpful or harmful to (intelligent) beings, the objects of the action. The universal principle 'You must do good and not evil to all beings', a very general, imperative formula, gives rise to many other, less general and more specific principles. These prohibit certain actions with a bad effect and approve certain others with a good effect.

167. But the final effect of the interaction of beings is not easily perceived; it can be seen only with time and the development of human intellective functions. There are two reasons for this.

1. Sometimes the effect is immediate; at other times it is the result of a series of subordinate causes. Although an *immediate effect* can be judged easily, it is not easy to judge the usefulness or harm of an ultimate, *indirect* effect. The difficulty is increased in proportion to the distance of the effect from its first cause, often resulting in a conflict of judgments: one person judges a certain action as good because his attention is fixed on the immediate, advantageous effect, while another person judges the same action as wrong because he considers a complex of distant, indirect effects, which he finds harmful.

168. This gives rise to different consciences. Moreover a person's conscience can sometimes be uncertain and doubtful because he sees how difficult it is to calculate all the effects, including the remote effects of an action. Another person,

however, forms a certain conscience without difficulty because his vision of the series of effects is restricted. He thinks his calculation is complete because it includes the effects he sees; and he does not suspect the existence of more remote effects.

169. Once again, it is easy to note that if the judgment on the immediate effect of any action belongs to a certain level of reflection, the complete, indirect effect cannot be calculated without reflection at a higher level, which, of course, is proportionate to the length and number of the series of causes and effects. In this respect moral science starts from the discovery of formulas concerning the immediate effects of actions of things, and moves on to the discovery of formulas concerning ever more complete, indirect effects.

170. In the same way, it is possible to calculate how varying numbers of people acting simultaneously produce different effects. The calculation required for many agents belongs to a higher reflection than that required for a few. Consequently, moral formulas dealing with many agents are discovered after those dealing with few.

171. 2. The second reason for the progress of moral science is the discovery of formulas of obligation regarding the *action* of things.

I can know the effect, considered in itself, of one or many actions and causes, but to know the real value of the effect I must sometimes judge it in relationship to all its circumstances. Let us suppose that an effect takes place in part of a complex, physical or moral body, and that it is beneficial to this part. It does not follow, however, that it will be beneficial to the whole body. For example, I can take some wine for the sake of my stomach, which produces a good effect. But the overall effect is worse because some other part of my body is diseased. In which case I have done more harm than good.

The part therefore must fit the whole. For example, I could misjudge the beauty of an ornament by not considering it in relationship to its setting, just as I could misjudge the usefulness of some part of a mechanism if I were unaware of its relationship to the whole device. What is good or bad in an effect, therefore, is not found simply in the effect but also in its relationship to all the circumstances around it. The history of moral science shows that this truth had been noticed by the human mind. The Stoics understood it as the foundation of the whole of moral science; for them, *that which is fitting* became the principle of ethics.[113]

172. However, this principle, a very general one, is not yet universal, although it does embrace less general formulas, and progressively developing specific formulas. This development depends upon the way in which we extend the judgment we make about the goodness of an effect not only to the accompanying circumstances but also to many other circumstances, both close and remote, as we continue to consider new relationships. In a word, we do not judge the effect alone; we judge it as part of a larger physical or moral body, and finally as part of a greater complex concept. The moral formulas develop *pari passu* with the levels of reflection to which they belong.

173. We have seen that there are as many consciences as there are imperative moral formulas. Conscience is always formed according to a norm applied for the purpose of judging an intended action. Human conscience, therefore, is subject to the modifications of *moral opinions*. As moral science progresses, imperative formulas are continually discovered. The result is new and different consciences in people and humanity as a whole.

174. Furthermore, as imperative formulas increase in number, conscience easily becomes doubtful or perplexed, and subject to other modifications. It is therefore understandable that when we use different formulas or norms to make the proximate judgment of our actions, we obtain different results and make conflicting decisions. This can happen in the same person, and the result is a perplexed, uncertain, doubtful conscience.

[113] In order to arrive at a very general formula the understanding does not have to pass through all the less general or specific formulas. It need only reflect on, and then abstract from, one of them. For example, we do not need to observe different cases of the following truth: 'A part of a whole cannot be judged good or bad except in relationship to the whole', in order to abstract from it the general imperative of Stoic *fittingness*, that is, 'nothing may be done that is not in keeping with everything else with which it forms at least a mental whole.'

§3. Positive laws are deduced from rational laws

175. *Positive law is founded in rational law*. To understand this clearly, we must determine what we understand by positive law.

I define *positive law* as the will of a being made known to other beings so that they can carry it out. The obligation to execute the will of the being depends solely upon the will itself of the being communicating the law.

176. Hence positive law first differs from rational law because rational law, which has its own reason independent of the legislator's will, is founded, as we have seen, in fittingness or usefulness (considered in the *object* of the duty, not the *subject* performing the duty). The reason for the positive law, on the other hand, is simply the will of a respected and honoured legislator, and the *fittingness* of carrying out that will.

177. Second, there is in fact a reason for positive law, a reason which lies solely in the eminence of the will constituting the law. This reason does not spring from the *real form of being* (usefulness) or the *ideal form* (necessary fittingness) but from the *moral form* (hypothetical or arbitrary fittingness).

178. Third, the source of all positive laws, strictly speaking, can only be the will of God, because this will alone is good in itself, lovable and observable. Its sublime dignity makes it equal to divine reason, so that St. Augustine makes both the reason and will of God the source of law: *the reason or will of God*.

179. Fourth, if God were to give the human race a law identical with the rational law (for instance, the commandment 'Do not kill') such a law, positively promulgated by God, would be true rational law and true divine positive law. It would thus have greater dignity and authority.

180. Fifth, if the rational law were declared by a human being, no matter with what authority — granted the declaration was not made in the name of God, or the common good did not require submission, even to an erroneous will (in which case the reason for the law would be the common good and not the will of a human being) — such a law would still be rational law, with the same obligating force. It would be now

understood more clearly, however, and have its own persuas-
ive force rendering its transgressors less excusable. The
degree of its clarity and persuasion would correspond to the
degree of wisdom and authority of the person promulgating
it.

181. Sixth and finally, human authority can, itself, make
positive laws, if such laws are necessary for the better observance of rational laws.

182. Human laws can also have a positive or willed
element, provided they contain an element of rational law
supplemented by positively willed determinations. These
determinations render the execution of the law possible, easy
or complete. For instance, soldiers are to be transported from
one place to another. Obviously the order for their transport
is not given without necessity or utility. The order therefore
is not positive, but rational, and to this extent is independent
of the commander's will. However, there is a choice of roads
and means of transport, and no reason for preferring one of
these to another. Nevertheless a choice has to be made, but
not by the soldiers themselves who would all choose different
roads and different means. The result would be confusion or
worse. One, single will, that of the commanding officer, has
necessarily *to make the choice.*

183. Such are the limits that bind human authority in the
making of positive, willed laws. Determining *ends* is the
function of rational law, not of human authority which at
most can only declare rational law. The true function of
human authority consists in determining the *means* for the
attainment of these ends when the means are not already
determined by some more suitable reason.

184. We must now consider the obligation of subjects to
observe the positive laws of competent human authority. The
foundation of these laws is not *human will* (which is neither
law nor able to make laws), but the need to follow rational
order. We must observe this order, and therefore must use
the means necessary for its observance. One of these means is
that of a single will determining that which of itself is indetermined. We must accept this will and conform to it.

185. For this reason, and within these limits, every will is
subject to a single, individual or collective will.

[181-5]

This subjection may seem to be a kind of contract because an act of will is present in those submitting. It is not, however, an arbitrary contract, since all are morally obliged to submit. If they did not submit, they would sin. It is obvious that this obligation is independent of the question (irrelevant to our discussion): 'Can those who are not united in civil societies be forced to unite?' or 'Is there a case where people can be legitimately compelled to submit to a single will?'[114]

186. We should not infer from what has been said that things determined by rational law cannot be the object of human legislators. The need for order, which authorises the *formation of positive laws* by human legislators, gives the legislators the faculty and duty of *declaring the rational law* in those cases where the people must act in a uniform way for the sake of society — the declaration, of course, does not bind unless it is just or probable. When the rational law is not evident, the competent power must express the declaration so that the people are not divided and split by conflicting opinions (if the law is evident the human authority need not *declare* it but only *sanction* it). In doubtful cases the people must follow the authentic, probable declaration of the rational law because of their obligation to co-operate in social order.

The argument supporting this is exactly the same as for human positive law, which I presented above. If natural order is a duty, the means necessary for it must also be duties. But these means include a declaration (to be accepted by all) about doubtful points of the rational law. Hence a human tribunal declaring the natural law, within these limits, must be recognised.

187. Summing up, we have seen that positive law always has its origin in a will; that this will can be either divine or human; and that the divine will, which constitutes good simply by willing, makes laws of itself without any further reason. We have also seen that the human will does not make laws of itself; its act as such does not constitute good but must

[114] This question can be discussed under either *signorial right* or *social right*, a very important distinction. I refer the reader to my treatment of the matter in *La Società ed il suo fine*.

be rendered good by following the good already constituted by the rational order or the divine will. Nevertheless the human will, in desiring good, often has many ways and means of choosing it and, when unable to discern the best, is left free to choose. We have seen, however, that this faculty to choose freely from equally suitable means cannot belong to each individual where social action is concerned. For the sake of order this action must be unified so that the society as a whole, not the individual, makes the choice. This single and social will, which binds and preserves the people, must be made and declared by an individual or collective person, called the supreme, legislative 'authority'. All the members of the social body obey this authority and in associating renounce both in fact and by right their natural free choice. They submit to the judgment of the single will that has retained all its natural power and become the norm for the whole society. In cases, therefore, where the rational order is indetermined, the people, who are bound to make a choice of some kind, have to follow what the public authority enacts for all.

§4. Supreme formulas

188. In the light of what has been said, we will conclude with some indications about the last period of moral science.

This period can come about only when moral opinions are fully developed, when humanity has passed from infancy to perfect maturity, and when all the imperative formulas rooted in the apprehension of beings and their relationships have been deduced. After that, an attempt must be made to summarise all the moral formulas deduced from universal principles not known by reflection as expressions of universal principles known by reflection. This is the work of the last period of the science.

189. I believe we have already reached this stage in which the most universal formulas of all have been formed by reflection, and include all other formulas. I also believe that these principles are only four in number. The first has *being* as its

object; the other three have the *internal relationships* of being as their object.

190. In fact all possible relationships of beings are reduced to three ultimate *categories* in which all *genera* are found.

191. The first formula, which precedes the other three and is simply *being*, states: 'Acknowledge BEING for what it is.'

192. But BEING has three, supreme *internal relationships*, or forms, *reality*, *ideality* and *morality*, in all of which it must be acknowledged. Hence, three supreme imperative formulas.

Ideal being (*ideality*), which is itself *light*, reveals the other two. Through it we know *real beings*, which indicate in us the first imperative formula: 'Acknowledge real beings for what they are', that is, 'Esteem beings, love them, help them; rejoice in the being they have, and desire for them the being they require according to their nature, and which perfects them.'

When we acknowledge *moral being*, that is, the essentially moral will, the will of God, the second moral imperative reveals itself in our spirit as: 'Make your will one with the essentially moral will.'

After making known *real being* and *moral being*, ideal being finally makes itself known by reflection as *truth* and gives rise to the third imperative which states: 'Acknowledge ideal being,' or 'Esteem the truth unreservedly,' or 'Follow the light of reason.'

193. All four formulas are equally supreme, but the three last are contained in the first, which is perfected by each of them.[115]

194. The last of these supreme formulas comes to be known after the other two because it depends upon a higher level of reflection. However, it contains the others and leads to them, because ideal being extends to all things. For this reason, the command: 'Adhere to the truth' includes: 'Adhere to real being' and 'Adhere to moral being or the divine will.' We could in fact say it is the first imperative taken to a higher level of reflection.

---

[115] The three *moral categories* I have dealt with have their origin in the first formula completed by union with each of the other three formulas.

Article 3.
We first form reflective moral formulas
having EXTERNAL ACTIONS as their object;
then formulas having AFFECTIONS of the spirit as their object,
and finally formulas expressing PRACTICAL ESTEEM

195. Our actions are determined in reality by the *affections* that accompany them. These affections involve a preceding judgment about things, which I have called *practical* because it has power for action (cf. 18–22). Hence, all moral actions can be reduced to *external actions*, to *affections* of the spirit and to *practical judgments* about the goodness of things. All moral formulas must belong to these three classes of moral act.

196. We now have to determine the order in which these formulas were discovered and expressed.

When we perform a moral act we first make a judgment about things. Then, on the basis of our judgment, we adjust our *affections* towards these things, and finally we *act* according to these affections. But the order in which humanity forms and expresses moral formulas is the opposite of this.

The teaching of the earliest moralists dealt in the main with the precepts about *external actions*. Only much later, when ethics is evolving into a science, do we see thinkers concerned with formulating directives that govern the order of our *affections* — and only at this time were these directives willingly accepted by all as something beautiful and new. Finally, moral science reaches perfection with the discovery of the real source of the affections, namely, the *practical judgment*. All moral teaching is now directed to the right formation of this judgment.

197. Thus, moral science duly followed the path indicated for its origin, growth and perfection. As we know, the easiest things for us to observe are *external actions*; they are immediately present to us and directly concern human association. Obviously they were the first to need rules and directions; God himself began his legislation with a command

[195-7]

whose object was external action, that is, the prohibition not to eat the fruit.

People then turned their thoughts to what was happening within them, and they saw that good or evil actions sprang from the right or wrong ordering of *affections*. Only then did moralists examine affections, as civil legislators tried to do also in their own way. Earlier, this would not have been possible.

Finally thinkers, after realising that affections are the result of practical esteem of things, determined the supreme moral imperative: 'Esteem all things in practice according to their worth.'

Article 4.
Summary and classification of all moral formulas

198. In the preceding three articles I presented a *philosophical survey* of the origin and progress of moral science. Because this science is substantially nothing more than a complex of formulated precepts, I tried to show the progressive order in which the formulas have been gradually thought out, and I spoke about them from three different points of view. I considered them: in themselves as *general or specific*; in their origin from the *apprehension of beings* or *apprehension of their more or less close relationships*; and finally, in their object which could be *practical judgment*, or *affection*, or *exterior action*. I must now unify all three points of view, briefly indicating their mutual connection and drawing up a single, simple classification for all the formulas that have been or will be composed in works on ethics.

199. The first and fundamental division of moral formulas must express *acts of morality*. It must therefore originate in the distinction between esteem for things, affections seconding the esteem, and actions following from the affections. Esteem, affections and external actions constitute only one thing, as a human being is one. They are a single moral action with three grades, issuing, as it were, from the human being and attaining its term in three stages. The first stage is suitable esteem, the second the affection following the esteem, and the

third, which completes the moral act, the external action caused by the affection.

The second division, adhering to and continuous with the first, arises from beings and their relationships as the *objective cause of moral acts*. In fact, all the preceding formulas, whether they determine esteem, affections or external actions, can be subdivided and classified according to the cause determining the degree of esteem and affection, and the quality and quantity of external action. A being, or a relationship between beings, obliges me to make a determined value judgment, to have a determined affection and to posit a determined action.

Finally, the basis for a subordinate classification is *the logical form of the more or less general formulas*, or even the universal formulas we have discussed (the principle of morality and the three imperative categories). The entire classification of possible imperative formulas in ethics would then be determined according to the table on the next page:

CLASSIFICATION TABLE
OF ALL POSSIBLE MORAL FORMULAS

200. I. Imperative formulas for a just *practical esteem*.

1. Imperative formulas for a just practical esteem according to the truth (ideal being) of beings *considered in themselves*.

A. THE UNIVERSAL FORMULA, PRINCIPLE OF MORALITY.

B. General formulas.

C. Specific formulas.

2. Imperative formulas for a just practical esteem according to the truth of beings *considered in their relationships*.

A. Relationships between *real beings*.

I. FIRST CATEGORICAL FORMULA.

II. Formulas drawn from relationships between real beings (series of beings). Such relationships are generally close, multiple (between varying numbers of beings), and belong to a more or less complex body (determined by its circumstances and the number of parts). Each relationship is

a) general,

b) specific.

B. Relationships between *moral beings* (subordinations of will, positive laws).

I. SECOND CATEGORICAL FORMULA.

II. General formulas.

III. Specific formulas.

C. Relationships between *ideal beings* (the logic of duties).

I. THIRD CATEGORICAL FORMULA.

II. Rules of conscience.

II. Imperative formulas regarding *affection*, necessarily derived from the *practical esteem*. (The same subdivision).

III. Imperative formulas regarding *external action*, necessarily derived (given the required circumstance) from preceding *affection*. (The same subdivision).

4

THE DIFFERENT STATES AND ACCIDENTS OF CONSCIENCE

201. So far, I have presented a *philosophical survey* of moral science and shown that the formulation of moral obligation and its conversion into express precept came about in step with the development of the human intellective faculties. Imperative formulas increased in number, and progressively changed in accordance with the invariable laws of understanding itself.

The purpose of the discussion was to make possible a demonstration of the various ways of applying the law to our actions (cf. 147) and so give a satisfactory explanation of the different states and accidents of conscience. I indicated the process by which we form, or try to form, conscience in our spirit. I did this in order to determine the *rules of conscience*, the purpose of this book. I showed how any moral formula can generate a conscience when the formula is applied to the judgment of a particular action we are about to perform. Consequently there are, or can be, as many causes of conscience as there are, or can be, moral formulas, and as many consciences as there are causes producing them, although these consciences are sometimes identical and sometimes different.

Article 1.
Why questions on conscience have been discussed
in the Church for three hundred years only

202. Before we investigate the rules of conscience we must consider the important fact that the state of conscience in individuals and in the whole human race, which is composed of individuals, varies according to the times.

We must note that the *moral law*, which is everlasting, does not change substantially. What alters is the *mode of*

discovering and determining the obligation, that is, the way
we apply the law to the judgment of our actions.

A judgment about our actions always requires a syllogism,
whose major is an *imperative formula*. These formulas are
innumerable; we do not know them all, and they are not
continually present to our spirit. As we have seen, we
discover and form them successively, relative to the development of our faculties which takes place in three ways:
according to the degrees of universality of the formulas,
according to the kinds of relationships on which the formulas
are founded, and according to the three stages of human
action (esteem, affections, external acts).

203. Hence, Prospero Fagnani should not be surprised at
finding that the question of *probabilism* has been raised only
in recent times. He admits that it is a 'difficult, dangerous'
question, and accepts it is a matter of fact, but he is not
justified in saying that 'the teaching is suspect for the sole
reason that it is new and a break from Church custom.' He
adds: 'We cannot believe that so many enlightened men, of
great intelligence, who have made it their chosen work to
investigate human acts and moral virtues, did not recognise
the force of probability.'[116] He would not have said this if he
had known our theory about the different levels of reflection
into which human thoughts are successively divided.

204. These levels cannot be ignored by anyone, however
intelligent; they must be considered in their order because
each level is the matter and object of the one above it. Because
we are all subject to the psychological law according to which
the mind operates only step by step, we require time to move
through succeeding levels of reflection to higher thoughts.
This is true for each of us, and if it is true for each, it is true
for the human race, and for the large or small societies into
which the human race is divided. All require lengthy periods
of time to move to a higher level of reflection from any level
other than the first. Furthermore, thoughts belonging to a
high level of reflection do not become *ordinary*, and hence
interesting, enlightening and worthy of our attention and
discussion, except with the passage of time.

[116] In I lib. *Decretalium.*

205. This fact should be borne in mind when we are dealing with the history of different sciences, and is especially important in the history of literature. If we neglect the fact in the study of literature, we shall have only imperfect sketches and learned dissertations, but never true history.

206. But granted a study of moral questions in the light of this principle revealed by true philosophy, we could indicate with historical sources the evolution of moral science as we have described it. At certain periods new, unheard-of questions would arise to herald a new epoch in which human understanding would pass from or arrive at a higher level of reflection.

This is not the place for us to deal with this very important but neglected area of research, although we would like to point out that when barbarism ceased and great thinkers appeared in the 13th century (thanks mainly to the religious orders founded by St. Francis and St. Dominic), new questions in moral matters soon arose. St. Thomas, who lived at the time, makes the same observation: 'In our time we have heard among experts many new controversies about both natural and moral matters.'[117]

207. We should not wonder that in the intellectual splendour of the 16th century, questions on conscience appeared under a new guise. A consideration of these questions, stated clearly only by theologians of the last three centuries, shows that the problems belong to a very high level of reflection.

In a period when the law is considered directly, we can concern ourselves only with the law and the absolute respect it merits. Decisions in cases of doubt are quite naturally made

---

[117] *Opusc. 73, de Usuris in Proemio.* The following is correct, if understood within certain limits: 'Experts engage in contemporary problems. A person who can solve the modern difficulties about simony, irregularity, etc. with St. Augustine's teaching, and settle the question of contracts with the principles used by Gregory of Nyssa and of Nazianzen, is indeed a fine judge.' The limits are: 1. the experts must themselves be true and sound, not people who have the temerity to write nonsense and call themselves 'experts'; 2. being *sound* does not depend upon finding detailed answers in St. Augustine and other Fathers, where such answers are often non-existent, but in deducing answers from the same more or less proximate principles and with the same iron logic used by St. Augustine and the other Fathers.

in favour of the law, and give rise to the principle: 'in doubt, the safer part is to be chosen.'

But let us suppose that instead of the law alone, we consider, by a further reflection, our spirit in relationship to the law. As the object of special attention, this new *relationship* changes the question. When human beings gave their attention directly to the law, only the authority of the law had to be considered together with its sacred right of imposing obligation. But when people reflectively consider themselves in relationship to the law, and ponder the uncertain state of their spirit, wondering whether the law obliges in such a state, they no longer think of the law alone, but ask whether the law binds them here and now; they consider the law in the force it exercises over human beings. In the first period, only the law was considered, and its effective bond was accepted as certain; in the second period, the question falls on this bond itself. In the first period the obligation was examined relative to the law; in the second it was examined relative to human freedom as well, that is, to the person, the subject of the obligation. Thus, a new factor had to be considered, not clearly noted beforehand, because reflection had not yet progressed to such heights or at least had not been strengthened enough to include and calculate simultaneously both elements constituting the bond, that is, the law that binds and the subject capable of being bound.

It is not my intention in the above observation to express any opinion or declare defective the principle mentioned, which would be untimely. I simply wish to explain the reason why, for three centuries, debate about probable opinion has continued in the Church. For many years the authority of the law and the conclusion that it must be observed even in doubt had been the centre of attention. In a succeeding period, when the human spirit was the centre of attention, it was thought the principle could be submitted once more to examination, and be doubted. This may or may not have been a correct conclusion, but we should not be surprised that modern authors believed themselves authorised to depart from the opinion of earlier thinkers; their argument was now based on a new element, on a relationship scarcely considered by their predecessors.

[207]

208. Consideration of the nature of all the principal questions concerning probable opinion would show that only at a late stage could these questions be raised in the Church and the world. The world first had to have books, and different opinions had to be debated. It should not surprise us that only when the world had reached this stage did people begin to ask questions about the opinion to be followed. Thus, for a person to act safely, was it sufficient that the chosen opinion could rely upon the authority of one, two, three, or even more moral theologians? And if the authority was sufficient, could the opinion be followed with peace of mind, even if unfavourable to the law and opposed by an equal number of equally authoritative teachers, or even by a greater number with greater authority? Could one at least follow the majority opinion that favoured freedom and declared the action lawful, when no contrary argument was known?

These questions are at the centre of the whole debate about probable opinion. They all presuppose a relationship between our conscience and the authority of moral theologians. They also presuppose reflection upon the opinion of many moral theologians, a reflection impossible for the theologians themselves to make at the time; they had to decide by other arguments whether an action was lawful or not. Thus, when we hear: 'Follow the authority of moral theologians', or: 'If you have the support of sound moral theologians, you can safely follow them' (this second formula limits the first), and form our conscience accordingly, we act differently from our predecessors. They formed their conscience either according to the most immediate formula, which is 'Follow the light of reason', or the formula: 'Follow the word of God in the divine scriptures', or similar moral formulas, which all existed prior to writers of moral theology and disputes about their authority.

209. It is foolish, therefore, and unjust to use certain generally accepted views to block discussion of the new questions as though modern problems constituted an unlawful departure from tradition. Such a mistaken attitude has no bearing on the questions, and offers no help in solving them. We should keep in mind the words of Jesus Christ who, in his wisdom, foresaw that the divine truths he had consigned to

the human race would necessarily undergo development in
the course of time without losing anything of their validity.
The immense possibilities of his heavenly teaching would be
shown by constantly renewed applications of the same truths,
and through insistent reflection. As Jesus said: 'Every scribe
who has been trained for the kingdom of heaven is like a
householder who brings out of his treasure what is new and
what is old.'[118]

210. Nevertheless it would be seriously wrong to try to
solve new problems by new principles irreducible to earlier
principles. Such solutions would be fully refuted by showing
that the principles used in the solution were not to be found,
even implicitly, in Christian tradition. On the other hand,
when those who propose and resolve new questions can
demonstrate that they are using the earlier, unchangeable
principles, or principles logically reducible to these, the new
form of the questions and their solution cannot harm the
researchers, who are praised by Christ for being 'scribes
trained for the kingdom of heaven.'

211. There is only one way, therefore, to refute new
solutions, when they have indeed been shown to be founded
on the earlier, perpetual principles. Granted the reasonable-
ness of the questions, it must be demonstrated that the error
of modern moralists lies in the application of the principles. If
this is not shown, it is useless to object that the questions and
their solutions are new. A new, correctly reasoned solution
does not change old teaching; it enriches it.

212. This is the teaching of the Fathers, one example of
which will suffice. Vincent of Lérins proposed a question that
has become extremely important in modern times: 'Can
religion progress?'[119] He replies: 'Certainly it can, and
greatly. What can be more invidious to human beings, and
hateful to God himself, than attempting to forbid progress?
But it must be true progress of faith, not an alteration of faith.
Progress is present when a thing grows of its nature; change
transmutes one thing into another. Intelligence, knowledge
and wisdom must increase and make solid progress in each

---

[118] Mt 13: 52.
[119] 'But someone might ask: "Is there no progress of religion in the
Church of Christ?"' (*Commonit.* n. 23).

[210-2]

individual and in mankind as a whole, in each person and in the whole Church, through different ages and centuries, but always consistently, that is, according to the same teaching, sense and opinion. Religion in our souls imitates the body. The parts of the body grow and take shape as the years pass, but they still remain what they were before.'[120] Could there be a better solution in our days to questions concerning the *progress* of religion?

213. It is, therefore, neither completely true nor completely false to say, as some probabilists do that 'in difficulties about faith, recourse must be had to the earlier authorities, but in difficulties about morals, to modern teaching.'[121] No modern teaching about morals or faith can be accepted unless it is a legitimate *conclusion* from earlier principles as old as the gospel and reason. The conclusion must be tied to these eternal principles, whether the arguments connecting it to the principles are long or short; what matters is the final connection with the irrefutable principles. Granted this connection, the *conclusion*, resulting from new circumstances, new positive laws, and new relationships discovered by the mind, can be as *new* as we wish. In short, it is drawn from a *new level of reflections*.

214. What we have said complies with the method which, with God's help, we have constantly followed in this work: 'We will start with self-evident principles continually taught in the Church. From them we shall deduce by logical necessity the solutions we seek.' Whether these are new or old does not interest us; in the end they will always be old if they are seen to be virtually contained in the old principles, despite their new appearance or expression.

If we have erred, anyone who has received a greater light from God can correct us, but only on condition that he uses the principle of method we have proposed for ourselves. He must show that in our reasoning we have either lost sight of the earlier principles, or not deduced our opinions directly from them. If he does this he will finish our work for us; he will accomplish what we have tried to do, and what we believe we have done. But because we are not infallible, our

---

[120] *Commonit.* n. 23.
[121] [Rosmini provides no reference]

persuasion of success (in good faith) may have deceived us. We have only one desire in this and all other writings: to uphold firmly the constant principles of faith and morals in the Church, teacher of all who are willing to listen to her; and by strict logic to deduce our teaching from these principles. If we have inadvertently departed from these principles, we have done the opposite of what we wish; and anyone who points this out to us, will be doing what we desire and ask him to do.

Article 2.
States of conscience, and states of the spirit when trying to form conscience

215. To sum up. Our intention was first to describe the origin and the different states and accidents of conscience, and of the spirit that tries to form conscience, so that we could investigate the rule of action applicable to each state and accident. We could not fully describe these states without first observing the diversity of the *moral formulas* according to which we form conscience. We therefore traced the history of these formulas and their different classes. We said that consciences vary according to the nature of the formulas producing them. We then distinguished and classified consciences according to the distinction and classification of the formulas.

216. We must note, however, that besides distinguishing consciences according to their *causes*, which are the moral formulas used to produce them, they must also be distinguished according to certain characteristics they have. These characteristics are the *effect* of the moral formulas themselves and of their different application. We must list them carefully, together with the various states of conscience they constitute.

217. First, because conscience is a moral judgment about our actions, the judgment has either been made and completed or does not yet exist. If it does not exist, we have not formed any conscience about the moral value of our actions. Thus, relative to conscience, there are *two states of*

our spirit: the state when our spirit has *formed a conscience* and the state when it has *not formed a conscience*.

218. It is clear that as long as we doubt whether our action is lawful or not, we have not yet pronounced a definite judgment on its moral value; we still have no conscience about the action. This obviously contradicts the commonly used term *doubtful conscience*. A doubtful conscience in fact is not a conscience, because anyone who doubts has not yet made a judgment.[122]

219. On the other hand, a *formed conscience* with its different kinds is a judgment, and will therefore have the same accidents as other judgments. But every judgment is true or false. Therefore any conscience is *true* or *false*.

Article 3.
Questions on conscience

220. The different states of conscience we have listed present certain questions relative to our actions. Ethics has to solve these questions, which can be reduced to the following:

When conscience is *not yet formed*, can we act licitly before forming a conscience about our action? When we are obliged to form it, what are the rules governing its formation?

When conscience is *already formed*, how must we act if it is *a true conscience*? How must we act if it is *an erroneous conscience*?

These four general questions will form the subject of the next book.

221. However, before applying ourselves to the task, we must again point out (cf. 217) that both true and erroneous

[122] It is not correct to say that anyone with a so-called doubtful conscience *judges* that he doubts. Judgment about the doubt, if formed at all, is not conscience, which is a judgment about the morality of an action. Nor is it sufficient to say we judge that the morality of the action is doubtful. Such a judgment is impossible because the morality of the action in itself can be only good or bad. Consequently, to speak about an action of doubtful morality affirms nothing whatsoever about the action but only that *we are doubtful* about its morality; we still do not have reasons for making a certain judgment about it. It is exactly the same as saying that we have not yet formed a conscience.

[218-21]

conscience, as well as the suspension of our judgment which prevents us from forming a conscience, are:

    1. the effect of one or more of the moral formulas we have noted;

    2. the effect of the different way we apply the formulas to our conscience.

Because formulas are the major of a syllogism, whose conclusion is conscience, conclusions will vary according to the nature of the major proposition and the way it is applied.

Moreover, because the state of our conscience changes according to the *variety* and multiplicity *of the formulas* and the *different ways of applying them* (and the ways are partly dependent on the moral state of our will), we can now identify various subdivisions of conscience. However, such modifications are closely connected with the rules of conscience, and it will be more appropriate to discuss them when we set out these rules.

Article 4.
Rules of conscience are also moral formulas
— their classification

222. The *rules of conscience* are themselves *moral formulas*, and we have distinguished moral formulas into classes. If we wish to know the class to which the rules belong, it is easy to see they belong to the highest order of reflection, and bring moral science to completion, as shown in the 'Classification Table' (cf. 200). A work on conscience, therefore, should conclude ethics, not begin it.

223. This will be clear if we consider that the formulas which direct our conscience presuppose already determined formulas so that the formulas of conscience are founded in the relationship of the determined formulas with the subject they bind, that is, the human being.

In fact all the formulas constituting moral science can be divided into two classes: 1. those determining the *actuality of the law* (these are more or less abstract in form, and include a greater or smaller number of beings and their relationships); 2. those determining the *bond of obligation* produced by the law in each person (these are mainly the formulas of conscience). The second group presupposes the first, and therefore has to be determined last. This explains why this work on conscience, as we have said, could not have been written earlier: moral science was not yet sufficiently developed.

Book 3

RULES OF CONSCIENCE

224. The two preceding books serve as an introduction to this third book devoted to answering very serious questions on conscience which have been discussed in the Church only in recent times, and to which solutions that command the full agreement of modern moralists and Catholic schools of thought have yet to be found. Before any review of problems and conclusions of such importance for the Christian people, some attempt had to be made to indicate preliminary notions which would help to clarify the subject matter of the discussion and remove all ambiguity about its content. This we think we have achieved.

We also saw that the solution of these questions depends upon discovering certain *rules* or principles by means of which we can safely know how to carry out every one of our actions without failing in our duty. These rules will have to be valid whether we have formed a conscience or not, or having formed it, whether it is true or erroneous.

225. When the understanding is sufficiently developed, we become used to acting only after judging whether our actions are licit or illicit, good or evil. This judgment, or conscience, becomes the necessary norm of our behaviour (cf. 118–140).

Sometimes, however, we are unable to form this judgment with certainty. In such a case, our spirit lacks a norm necessary to its action (cf. 201–225 [205]).

Nevertheless, whether we have been successful or not in completing our judgment and thus forming a conscience, we have to act, and in acting be guided by some rule. We ask therefore what are the special rules to be followed in our various states of judgment on the morality of the actions we are about to do. Whatever form these norms take, they are what we call *rules of conscience*.

226. Having established what we understand by rules of conscience, we now have to formulate them, and in doing so rely upon sure guides. As we have said, these guides cannot be other than the principles accepted by the Church from the beginning. We have to show that the rules of conscience are logically connected with principles as true as the Church herself is true (cf. 210–214). This is not a question of *prudence*, as some authors suggest, but of *truth*.

In fact, it seems to me that the search for what is *prudent* instead of what is *true* explains why this extremely relevant study of rules of conscience remains confused and undeveloped.

227. Authors who follow the more benign opinion offer a clear example of this wrong approach to difficulties when they defend their doctrine on the basis of effects desired from their teaching. According to them, proposing the rigid opinion would have the effect of alienating and frightening people, who could not be persuaded to undertake such a burden. 'The world has little desire to change,' says Fr. Paolo Segneri, an author of some prestige. 'If you attempted to confine it to the limits just described, the world would not be satisfied with showing that painting or dancing or racing or going to the theatre on days of obligation was a sound opinion. It would go on to show that such an opinion was sounder than its opposite. The effect would undoubtedly be a laxer attitude amongst Christians. Great numbers, who now abstain from following such teaching because it is less probable than its opposite, would follow it without difficulty when they heard that it was more probable.'[123]

It is sad to find such a person writing like this. Whatever his views, it is not right that he should search for a moral rule on the basis of 'The world has little desire to change', or go on to say that if the more probable opinion were proposed as a rule of action, people would soon come to take the laxer opinion as the more probable. They would do this, he affirms, not because 'they were deficient in the fear of God, but because, being human beings like everyone else, and strongly inclined to what is less upright, they would have no difficulty (and this is especially true of educated people) in persuading themselves about the uprightness of their own opposite opinion. "Each easily believes according to his desires," says St. Thomas very clearly.'[124] But if 'each easily believes according to his desires', does this justify people before God in their erroneous belief that what pleases them is to be preferred to the truth? If, because I am inclined to what is less upright, I persuade myself that wrong is right, can I be said to do this with an upright conscience? Scripture declares

[123] *Lettere del P. Paolo Segneri sulla materia del probabile*, 1, §2 (W. Metternich, Cologne 1732, reprinted at Benevento).   [124] *ibid.*

[227]

blessed the person who speaks truth in his heart,[125] and can we, as teachers of the gospel, connive with our own wrong desires? My true responsibility is to shake off my deception and view things rightly.

We are not surprised to find pagan philosophers, who also knew that 'the world has little desire to change', hesitating to proclaim the more difficult aspects of truth. Pagan thinkers have always suppressed the truth about God by their wickedness.[126] Terrified by the inclination to evil which they saw in human beings, and despairing of making their voices heard and their example followed if they promulgated virtue in its entirety and truth unmixed with falsehood, they compromised with the vice present in corrupt humanity. They preached virtue, but simultaneously fawned over and flattered human passions. Lacking generosity and moral strength themselves, they despaired of imparting it to others.

This is not the case with Jesus Christ, nor with those who are prepared to learn from the only-begotten Son who came down from the Father in order to save Adam's children. Human timidity, vileness and lying are unknown to the one Teacher who has no part in human weakness. Our divine Master, and all those sent by him, proffer truth in all its purity, just as it is.[127] The Lord is fully aware of his power to make the truth he proclaims the ruler of souls. 'The world has little desire to change' is certainly not the starting point of his reasoning. The Master of the universe, and his representatives, know that once the world has heard the word of God it will want to change a great deal and become what it never desired to be. This has happened, and continues to happen every day. Only overwhelming ignorance and error can make us think that the present world is what it always has been. Christianity has overthrown from the foundations the world that once was, and renewed it in the depths of its being. Adam's offspring, buried in the blood of Christ, has risen as the offspring of God, who lives and reigns for ever.

We cannot imitate the pagan philosophers and ask ourselves whether people will listen to us or not. Our

---

[125] 'Who speaks truth from his heart' (Ps 14 [15]: 3).
[126] 'That detain the truth of God in injustice' (Rom 1: 18 [Douai]).
[127] 'All the truth' (Jn 16: 13).

business is simply to ensure, with all our strength, that we speak the truth. We need not trouble about the consequences which God has foreseen from all eternity, and in which he finds his good pleasure.

As Christian philosophers or, more appropriately, theologians, we should think it unworthy to propose as the sole aim of our teaching rules of conduct that help people simply to quieten their conscience. What would be the consequence of false rules of conscience? We would have formed human beings who, while they do what is wrong, blindly believe that they are doing good. But to be far from the truth and yet at peace, without making any serious attempt to amend, is the greatest of all deceptions. Such a state is reproved in words similar to those with which Christ condemned the sin against the Holy Spirit, and the condemnation is frequently repeated in scripture. For example:

'There is a way which seems right to a man,
     but its end is the way to death.'[128]

We are not helped if we imagine we are doing what is right, but form a confused, false conscience that betrays us. There was a time, unfortunately, when outward religious conventions were the order of the day, and we can only hope that in those times God did not take too different a view from that of the world. Let us hope that God did not see, deep in the heart, vice that appeared to the rest of us as virtue, disguised even under ecclesiastical dress and religious habits, and shielded from condemnation by the subtleties of human theology.

228. I am not alluding in any way to the worthy person who has prompted these remarks of mine, but I am sure that they are true and can be seen to be true. What I am affirming is that an investigation into the rules of conscience cannot fittingly begin by deciding what is *useful* or not, in its effects. We can search only for what is *true*, because this is a question of truth and falsehood alone. If we find the *truth* through living faith in God who, loving us and wishing us to be saved, saves by giving us his truth, we shall most certainly have found what is *useful*, whether we have looked for it or not.

[128] Prov 14: 12.

[228]

Rules for a Formed Conscience

229. We have seen that there are only two states of the human spirit relative to conscience: *formed* and *unformed* conscience (cf. 215–218). Formed conscience, we said, can be either *true* or *erroneous* (cf. 220).

We shall first present the rules for a *true* conscience, then those for an *erroneous* conscience. Finally we shall investigate how we move from unformed to formed conscience.

1

TRUE CONSCIENCE

230. It is always unlawful to act against a true conscience when it declares an act[129] sinful. This is an obvious, well-known rule, needing no demonstration. Clearly, to desire an act which we have truthfully judged unlawful, is to desire what is unlawful, that is, to sin.

2

ERRONEOUS CONSCIENCE

Article 1.
Different kinds of erroneous conscience

231. The rules for an erroneous conscience are more difficult to determine and must be deduced more carefully.

We should note that error in conscience can happen in three ways:

1. we can be mistaken about the *law*, that is, about the moral formula applied in the judgment of conscience;

[129] Whatever can be said about *action* can be said equally about *omission*: if conscience *prohibits*, action is blameworthy; if conscience *commands*, omission is blameworthy. To choose either is to choose sin.

[229-31]

2. we can be mistaken in our way of *applying the law* or formula to our actions;

3. we can be mistaken about *some factual circumstance* when applying the law.

232. An error therefore can concern either *law*, or an *application* of the law, or a *fact*. An example will illustrate the three kinds of mistake.

At the beginning of Christianity, some Jews believed that the law of circumcision and other ancient ceremonies were still obligatory. Hence they formed an erroneous conscience about the necessity of maintaining the Mosaic law. This erroneous conscience was caused by an error regarding the *law*.

The Pharisees formed an erroneous conscience about the sanctification of the Sabbath: they forbade certain minute actions as if they were prohibited by the law which obliged the sanctification of the seventh day of the week. Their conscience was erroneous because it came from an error about the *application* of the Sabbath law to minute actions.

Jacob formed an erroneous conscience when he believed it was lawful for him to sleep with the woman in whose company he found himself on the first night of his marriage; he thought Lia was his wife Rachel. This erroneous conscience was due to an error about *fact*.

233. These examples, however, are not sufficient to classify the various errors possible in forming the judgment. Each example is only a particular case of the three kinds of erroneous conscience we have distinguished. But we can in fact err in many ways not only about the law, but also about its application and about fact. Discussion about conscience would receive much light if we could carefully enumerate all these ways, but to avoid prolonging the argument, we shall deal with the distinctions as they arise.

Article 2.
Invincibly erroneous conscience in general

RULE

234. 'It is always unlawful to act against an invincibly erroneous conscience.'

[232-4]

Explanation

Whether the error is due to a *preceding* error about the law or about fact, or due to an error *concomitant* with the application of the law, is indifferent. If at the time the conscience is formed the error is truly *invincible* so that the conscience is formed without any hesitation or doubt whatever, it obliges; to act against the dictate of such a conscience is unlawful. This obvious truth is accepted by all. If a person is persuaded *without any hesitation* — this proviso must be carefully noted — that an action or its omission is a sin, he cannot desire the action or omission without desiring the sin and performing a reprehensible act.

235. This fault, depending entirely on the false persuasion of the subject, belongs to *subjective morality*.

Article 3.
Vincibly erroneous conscience in general

236. Before we determine how a person with a vincibly erroneous conscience is obliged to act, we must describe what constitutes *vincible* error and distinguish it from *invincible* error. Without an accurate concept of vincible error, no obligation can be safely determined.

§1. Explanation of vincibly erroneous conscience

237. Vincible error is usually defined as 'that which can and must be avoided'. Although this definition is sufficient, an important question has to be solved: *When* can and must we avoid error?

238. First, the expression, 'an error that *can* be avoided', certainly has different meanings. If it meant absolute possibility, no error could be avoided because every error is of its nature contingent and not necessary. Moralists therefore are not speaking about this kind of possibility.

239. I have shown in *Certainty* that there are only two causes of human error: *human will* and *a false datum supposed true*.[130]

[130] *Certainty*, 1279–1334.

Is every willed error *vincible*? Can all *willed* errors be avoided? If somebody chose to follow an opinion known to be erroneous, it is clear that the error would not only be vincible but also a free aversion from the truth.

240. To speak about 'willed errors', however, means to refer to cases where the will is involved but, because of a hurried and immature judgment, does not know that error is present. Are all such errors invincible and inevitable?

We must distinguish three cases. The will can be moved to an erroneous conclusion by three causes: 1. evil disposition, which induces the will to see as true the erroneous conclusion favourable to its yearning and urges it to a precipitate judgment; 2. natural instinct; 3. the need to act, which obliges the human being to make a practical decision in favour of one side or the other.

241. If the will is ensnared by evil disposition, the culpability of the error conforms with the cause. Thus if the evil disposition as cause of the error was free, the error was free and vincible. If it was not free, the error is a necessary moral evil (cf. 81–110).[131]

242. If the error has its cause in *natural instinct*, as in the case of thinking the sun revolves around the earth, the error is innocent, provided it is, as we have said, *provisional*, and rejected as soon as the light of truth presents itself.[132]

243. Finally, if the cause is the need to act, the error is innocent provided the person makes a simple *practical* assertion of his own choice, without adding absolute certainty, and is ready to change his opinion once the truth is made known.

244. If the error is caused by some false datum supposed true, it can be simply material and entirely innocent, provided it is not produced by any evil disposition of the will, in which case the error would be willed because of its cause.

We must now examine whether material error can occur *relative to the law*, or *to the way the law is applied* or *to some fact or circumstance serving as the occasion for applying the law*.

[131] I have shown in *AMS* that errors can be willed without being free [738–744].
[132] *Certainty*, 1302–1306.

[240-4]

245. If we consider the *application of the law to a particular action* (the judgment of conscience is formed by means of such an application), we see that every error is always willed and very often vincible. The application is a judgment, an action, by which we affirm the harmony or disharmony of two terms. Now either we see this relationship of harmony or disharmony between the two terms and affirm it, committing no error; or we do not see it, or doubt we see it and are unable to make ourselves fully aware of what we see. In this case only an evil energy of the will influenced by passion can force us to affirm, not merely *provisionally* and practically (cf. 242, 243) but absolutely, that we do see it. In other words, only an evil will can force us to lie to ourselves, producing a spurious persuasion about something we do not actually see. This is a formal error and cannot be called invincible in our sense of the word.

246. Invincible error must be sought either in an *opinion about the law* or in a *presumed datum or fact*, that provides an occasion for applying the law.

In the case of truly invincible error about the law, we must distinguish *rational* from *positive* law. We must further distinguish in *rational* law between *our own cognitions* and cognitions received on *another's authority*.

247. A necessary error regarding our own cognitions in rational law is impossible if we exclude the cases already discussed of provisional, practical conclusions (cf. 246). We cannot be forced to deceive ourselves if our will sincerely desires to follow only the truth. Because the first principles of natural law are placed in us by nature, nature does not deceive us. The deductions, however, that we make from these principles of the law in order to arrive at specific formulas, can only result from reasoning. But as we have said, there can be no definite, firm, entirely unwilled error, in our reasoning. No one can force us to draw consequences from premises unconnected with the consequences, or to see a connection which does not exist. If we persuade ourselves that we see some connection when we do not, there is disorder within us in the form of a precipitate will which prefers illusion rather than truth — an illusion which cannot deceive without the support of the will. This is not a truly unwilled, invincible, and inevitable error; it is an error certainly avoidable by a

simple, true will, which affirms only what the intellect sees.

248. This does not mean that we deny the debility of *our reason* or its incapacity for making remote deductions from the natural law. It means that we are not *constrained* to make the deductions; we can either suspend our judgment, or at most and if necessary make a *provisional* or *probable* judgment, or, if we have to act, a judgment in the form of a *supposition*. In this case we are *ignorant*, but not *mistaken*. If we are ignorant, the natural law, in respect of the deductions we are incapable of making, can be given us on another's authority. The natural law then becomes known positively, and takes on the character of positive law, which is susceptible to *invincible* error.

249. But if the deduction of the natural law is not given us on another's authority, we remain ignorant. Such ignorance can truly be unavoidable and entirely inculpable precisely because it is necessary. Consequently, when we apply the law to our actions, this ignorance gives rise to a directive which in itself is erroneous but without fault and moral defect, because it comes from *weakness in our reasoning*, not from a *distortion of the will*. For example, a simple, virtuous person may so weaken himself in his pursuit of some virtue that he shortens his life. If he had *reflected* on the harm caused to his bodily health by his fervour, and on the duty of conserving his health while not neglecting other duties, he would have moderated his excessive external effort for the love of good without diminishing that love. But he never reached this height of reflection, and so could not deduce the moral formula prescribing greater discernment in his behaviour. He therefore devoted himself totally to the duty and virtue he had in mind, fulfilling the former and sacrificing himself for sake of possessing the latter.[133]

250. Invincible error therefore must be sought:

1. in *positive law*;
2. in *natural law*, *a*) which is received as positive law

---

[133] The same limited reasoning applies to the difficulty of the first Jewish converts to the Christian faith: they could not understand the abrogation of the ceremonial law of Moses by the new law of Jesus Christ. It also explains the forebearance shown them by the Apostles who understood their ignorance. Cf. the letter of St. Paul to the Romans, chapter 14, and the First to the Corinthians, chapter 8.

on another's authority, and is relative to consequences a person cannot deduce for himself from the principles; *b*) in remote deductions (of the natural law) which are either not deduced because of weakness in reasoning or are assumed as probable, provisional judgments because of the need to act; *c*) in a particular directive we have formed in invincible ignorance of a remote deduction of the natural law;

3. in a *fact*, occasioning the application of the law.[134]

251. Everything we have said accords with the principles of the science of knowledge. I have shown that 'material errors have two causes: 1. a judgment based on a *datum* produced by a blind power; 2. a judgment based on a fallible authority.'[135]

252. In the case of human positive laws or opinions of experts about the natural law, unwilled and entirely invincible errors can easily arise because it is not our *reason* that acts, but our *faith* in another's authority. Thus, to assume a conclusion as certain because of our need to act, although we are unable to judge it as absolutely certain, is the action of a blind power in that we choose to *suppose* the conclusion as certain without any cogent reason. In the same way, we can either know a contingent fact on another's authority or, basing ourselves on certain probabilities, assume it as true. We may need to believe the authority, or accept the probable fact by supposing it hypothetically true. For example, if during a journey a priest tells me it is a fast day in the region, I must believe him if I have no contrary reason. If he tells me it is a non-fast day and I eat accordingly, my error is material, not willed, and therefore invincible. Absolutely speaking, I could have avoided the error, of course; I could have asked someone else. But relatively to my circumstances, I neither could do so nor needed to do so because: 1. I suspected no deception; and 2. I had no reason to suspect deception (I was reasonably bound to suppose that what the priest affirmed was true).

The same can be said about errors of *fact*. Absolutely speaking, Jacob could have verified whether the woman with

---

[134] This is true even though we are dealing with natural law, as in the case of Jacob taking Lia for Rachel — the law is not formally involved in the error.   [135] *Certainty*, 1309–1314.

[251-2]

him was Lia or Rachel. But relative to his circumstances he neither could nor needed to. It was impossible and unbecoming to think that his father-in-law had betrayed him: impossible, because a reason is required for thinking of such a possibility; unbecoming, because if he had thought about it, he would have to reject it as inopportune, and harmful to Laban.

We can conclude by saying that if error in conscience arises solely from a preceding error about positive law or fact, it can be entirely unwilled and completely invincible.

253. But errors about the law and about fact can come also from rash and formally erroneous judgments. We must therefore investigate the characteristics that determine these errors and make them truly *invincible*, in the moralists' sense of this word.

I can make a mistake about the law because I am ignorant of it, or believe it to exist when it does not, or do not recognise its extent, and I can do so either through negligence or imprudence or my evil disposition, or without fault if I have diligently and attentively informed myself of the law, performing the act circumspectly and wisely.

Similarly I can be culpably or innocently mistaken about fact. If I have committed no fault and suspect no error, my ignorance is truly *invincible*. But if the ignorance and error are my fault, my ignorance is *vincible*, according to my use of the word in this book.

254. Before continuing, we must note the characteristics we assign to *invincible* and *vincible* conscience. Conscience is *invincible* not when it contains an error which can be avoided absolutely, but when the error is such that: 1. it cannot be avoided by its perpetrator, who has no reasonable suspicion of its existence; and 2. is either independent of any distortion of will, or 3. is present in a person with some evil, habitual and necessary disposition of will which however produces no actual effect and is not consented to. In these conditions, the will, despite its error, seeks only the truth in the judgment which it made. It has no intention of detracting from truth through love of falsehood. On the other hand, I call an erroneous conscience *vincible* when one of these three conditions is absent.

255. A human being may be moved to a rash, erroneous

judgment solely by the evil disposition of will that comes from original, not actual sin. The erroneous judgment is not imputable as fault because the judgment is necessary (cf. 83–110) and in fact forms one thing with original sin, just as a branch and tree are one thing. However, the distortion of the will is certainly not good or meritorious, and could be called *vincible* in the sense that it can be corrected, if not immediately, at least by a constant study of divine law,[136] by prayer which increases grace, and by our co-operation — as scripture says:

'How can a young man keep his way pure?
By guarding it according to thy word.'[137]

256. But if the evil disposition urging us to error is the effect of preceding actual sins, it is also one with them in such a way that whenever we repent of our sins and our will is opposed to subsequent misdeeds, the error is free of fault and does not harm the spirit. Nevertheless it is not good and can still be called *vincible* through the formation of better habits, continual vigilance of spirit and holy practices.

257. Moreover we must carefully note that the guilt attached to the evil actions of a vincible erroneous conscience is of the same kind and amount as the guilt of the error causing them. In fact their guilt is identical with the guilt of the cause itself, that is, of the erroneous conscience which produced them. Hence, if the error was only a venial sin, the actions can only be venial sins.

§2. Summary of the different kinds of vincibly erroneous conscience

258. I shall summarise the different cases of error of conscience in order to establish clearly when error is invincible and when vincible:

1. If error is about the rational law and its *rationally* deduced consequences, it can never be truly invincible in the

---

[136] St. Thomas defines invincible ignorance as that 'which cannot be removed by study' (*S.T.*, I-II, q. 76, art. 2).
[137] Ps 119: 9.

full sense of the word, because this kind of error[138] presupposes a distortion of will which in misleading the understanding's judgment makes it act rashly.

2. The distortion of will which causes the rash, precipitate judgment can be either free and culpable, or necessary and therefore inculpable.

3. Certain propositions and opinions, accepted instinctively as true by a provisional but not absolute judgment, cannot be called errors. This is also true of propositions taken as rules of conduct when action is necessary and no definite, theoretical judgment is formed about the matter.

4. If error affecting conscience concerns positive law, or rational law positively received, or concerns fact occasioning the application of the law, it can be either *vincible* or *invincible*.

5. If error *about the law* is not caused by lack of respect for the law or by culpable neglect, and if error *about fact* is not the result of culpable imprudence, error is *invincible*. Otherwise it is *vincible*.

6. Finally, error can come from simple, unwilled ignorance of some rational deduction of the law which we do not suspect and which our weak reason is unable to make. Error of this kind is completely invincible.

§3. Questions about erroneous conscience

259. Clearly, what has been said raises the following questions about erroneous conscience. Concerning *vincibly* erroneous conscience we ask:

1. Must we follow a conscience that is mistaken about the rational law or the rational application of law when the error is willed and free? What is the morality of an action carried out in conformity with or against such a conscience?

2. Must we follow a conscience that is mistaken about the rational law or the rational application of the law when the error is *willed* but not free in itself although free in its

---

[138] It should be noted that we are talking here about *error* committed when deducing consequences from principles of rational law, not about *ignorance* concerning these consequences.

cause, that is, when the will's evil tendency drawing us necessarily into error is the effect of preceding, actual faults? What
is the morality of an action carried out in conformity with or
against this conscience?

3. Can error about the law or its rational application
be the necessary effect of original sin?

4. Must we follow an erroneous conscience about
positive law or law positively received, or about fact, when
the error, although unavoidable, was free in its cause, because
culpably we did not verify the law or fact as we were bound?
What is the morality of an action carried out in conformity
with or against this conscience?

As regards *invincible* or unwilled erroneous conscience we
ask:

5. Must we follow an inculpable, unwilled erroneous
conscience coming from error about the positive law, or the
law positively received, or from error about a fact occasioning
the law's application? What is the morality of an action in
conformity or not with this conscience?

6. Must we follow an inculpable, unwilled erroneous
conscience which is not caused by *error* but by *ignorance* of
some rational deduction of the law? What is the morality of
this conscience?

7. Can we act according to erroneous persuasions
which we form by natural instinct without evil intent or
suspicion of error?

8. Can we act according to opinions which we suppose
true because we need to act in conformity with them or their
opposites? What is the morality of this conscience?

§4. *Upright* and *non-upright* conscience,
to be distinguished respectively from
true and *false* conscience

260. The final question is proper to our state of soul when
we have not yet formed our conscience. We note, however,
that the practical propositions used when we have to act are
rules that stand in place of conscience, and will therefore be
discussed when we speak about the formation of conscience.

[260]

261. The seventh question deals with factual error, not with an error of reason.

262. The fifth and sixth questions were dealt with when we showed that *inculpable, unwilled* erroneous *conscience* can and must be followed because error, when conditioned by inculpability and absence of will, is *invincible* (cf. 234).

Here we need only add, as confirmation of teaching commonly accepted by moralists, that this kind of conscience, although erroneous, does not lose its uprightness because of error. The mistake is not found in conscience properly speaking; it precedes conscience, and is supposed, but not formed, by conscience.

263. Cardinal Gerdil, following Aquinas on this subject, expresses the matter very clearly. He says: 'When *synderesis*[139] is applied to what we do (this is the principal element in *conscience*), two judgments can be distinguished. In the first, we decide what kind of action we are dealing with: theft, murder, adultery, a lie, or their contraries. In the second, we judge that the action we have considered is lawful or unlawful, just or unjust, and hence to be done or to be abandoned. The first judgment is not conscience, but is presuppposed by conscience . . . A hunter, for example, judges that the object before him is a human being or an animal, and decides accordingly whether the decision to shoot is homicide or simply the slaying of a beast. But in discerning only the material object of his act he still has to pronounce on its morality or immorality . . . It is true, of course, that before he fires, the hunter has to be careful about the object of his aim, and cannot shoot without due precautions. Nevertheless, judging that his prey is a human being rather than a beast is not an act falling within the ambit of morality, and hence cannot in itself be a judgment of conscience, although it is presupposed in the formation of conscience . . .

'This opinion can be explained fairly briefly. I think that when we accept in a particular proposition some error eliminating knowledge of our act or of what we are about to

[139] *Synderesis* comes from Συντερεω, *I keep*. Salvini says elegantly that this word 'serves simply to preserve and guard the first notions, that is, those rational, natural lights that are the soul's heritage. Synderesis is our rule of action.'

do, the error itself is absolutely unwilled and inculpable, and does no harm to uprightness of conscience. But when our error is such that we think an act is lawful, although we know it to be murder or lying because it is in fact opposed to moral norms, we *unlawfully apply* the moral norms. In this case, our judgement is totally incompatible with an upright conscience . . .

'We have no difficulty in granting to those who defend the first opinion (invincible ignorance does not destroy uprightness of conscience) that if a person adoring the Blessed Sacrament publicly exposed is invincibly ignorant of the non-consecration of the wafer, he acts nevertheless with an *upright* conscience, and in a good, praiseworthy manner. Relative to the norms of morality, the incorrect judgment about Christ's being present in the wafer is in itself neutral. If we add to this judgment the dictate of reason which prescribes that Christ be worshipped under the appearances of bread, the dictate, which is wholly in conformity with the norms of morality, forms our judgment of conscience which, in this case, is wholly upright . . .

'But we can also support strongly those defending the second opinion (an invincible error lessens uprightness of conscience) to this extent: if the error is present through an unwarranted *application* of the principles of synderesis — when, for example, it is thought that lying for the sake of religion is good — then this error is incompatible with upright conscience.'[140]

264. This fine passage shows that error does not detract from uprightness of conscience if it is concerned with some *fact*, such as the consecration of the wafer exposed for public adoration; but it does render conscience less upright when it is concerned with the *application* of the rational law to some fact, that is to say, with the *deduction* of conscience from such a law.[141]

---

[140] *Tractatus de actibus humanis*, III, q. 1. c. 2. We shall continue later our analysis of the act by which we form an erroneous conscience.

[141] Cardinal Gerdil gives the following reason for this conclusion: 'Conscience is said to be the law of our intellect. St. Thomas explains this in the passage we have already admired. He says that IT IS A JUDGMENT OF REASON DEDUCED FROM NATURAL LAW. According to St. Thomas, therefore, conscience

265. But we also observed that error would be foreign to the judgment of conscience, and consequently not affect its uprightness, if it were concerned with *positive law*, which can be ignored in an entirely inculpable and unwilled way — if, for example, I were deceived on the authority of a person worthy of trust from whom I had asked some information, or were misled by some responsible book about which I could have no reasonable suspicion.

We also observed that the same could be said about an error concerned with moral formulas which, although deduced of their nature from principles of natural law, take on the nature of positive law. This would happen in the case of a person incapable of deducing the law himself and, as a consequence, receiving it on another's authority, and accepting it solely on that authority.

The same can be said in so far as a person deduces some consequence from the rational law not on the basis of an absolute judgment, but as a *practical assumption* stimulated by his need to deliberate or act.

Finally, we observed that error dependent on simple ignorance of some distant deduction from natural principles does not affect *uprightness* of conscience or our merit in following it, provided that the mistake springs not from a defective will but from an inactive reason.

These are material, unwilled errors, and do no harm to *uprightness* of conscience.

266. Error in these cases may be compared with the defects present in a block of marble worked by a truly great sculptor whose masterpiece will lose none of its value because of some faulty vein in the marble. If in judging some proximate action of ours, we apply a law with good will and then act according to our upright application of the law, we lose no merit although our error may unwittingly depend, without any fault or will on our part, upon some false presupposition (as in the case of the consecrated wafer or, relative to positive law, when we eat meat after being told by someone worthy of

is a law, and consequently upright in so far as a judgment of reason deduced from the natural law. But a judgment which concludes, for any reason whatsoever, that a lie is a worthy act, is not a judgment of reason deduced from the natural law. Therefore, etc.' (*Tractatus de act. hum.*, III, q. 1, c. 1).

trust that we are not obliged to abstinence) or be the necessary consequence of incupable ignorance on our part.

267. *Upright* and *true* conscience are not the same. Upright
conscience has a greater extension than true conscience.
Conscience may be both *erroneous* and *upright*, although a
non-upright conscience is always erroneous.

268. *Upright* conscience, whether true or erroneous, must
always be followed. This rule corresponds to the last four
questions we have proposed (cf. 259).

269. This teaching allows us to see clearly the reason for the
common opinion that uprightness of conscience depends
upon its conformity with *eternal law*. Conscience could not
be upright unless it applied eternal law adequately to what is
being done. Applying the law adequately means judging and
acting without malice, in complete good faith. Eternal law is
law purged of every positive and material element, and is
expressed in the duty which obliges us always 'to act without
malice.' If our error of conscience is without malice of any
kind it leaves uprightness of conscience intact.

§5. Non-upright conscience in general

270. We are left with the other four questions (cf. 259), all
of which refer to non-upright conscience. Each of them
presupposes a willed, vincible error which can be corrected,
at least given time. The error is found in opinions formed
about the dictates of the rational law, or in the law's rational
application to what we are about to do. In other words, the
error, which is present in conscience itself, is always either a
rash judgment or a *gratuitous persuasion* contrary to what has
been inscribed deep in our understanding. We refuse to read
what is there in order to deceive ourselves freely.

271. A *non-upright* conscience, therefore, is *vincibly
erroneous* because it results either from our freedom or from
our disordered passion. St. Thomas speaks about this in the
following way: 'Good intention is not the entire cause of [an
act of] will,'[142] and 'malice in the intention is of itself sufficient
to vitiate [an act of] will, but the opposite is not true if we are

---

[142] I-II, q. 19, art. 8, ad 2.

dealing with what makes the will good.'[143]   St. Thomas reasons: 'Evil arises from each single defect; good requires the cause as a whole. The will, therefore, is always evil when a person wants either what is evil under the appearance of good, or what is good under the appearance of evil. Contrariwise if the will is to be good, it must have good as its object under the appearance of good, that is, it must want good and want it because it is good.'[144] Gerdil concludes: 'Willing to lie for a good end means willing something evil in itself although under the appearance of good. But this is not sufficient to make the will good (the whole cause must be good for the will to be good), nor is it sufficient for forming an upright conscience in practice.'[145]

St. Thomas repeats his reasons, confirming them on the authority of the author of *The Divine Names*: 'Therefore, in order that the object of the will be evil it is sufficient that it be evil of its nature, or that it be thought to be evil; but for the object of the will to be good, it must be good under both respects.'[146]

St. Augustine expresses the same opinion: 'Everything done is a sin if it is not *rightly* done. Nor can it be rightly done in any way if it does not arise from right reason. Right reason is virtue itself.'[147]

All this shows, according to the mind of St. Thomas and St. Augustine, that a person acting with a non-upright conscience — in the way we have defined it, that is, with an erroneous moral persuasion caused by an evil disposition of the will — cannot be said to act uprightly. Even a good end referred to an evil object, thought to be good, cannot prevent the action from being evil.

272. But we ought to note that in this case the spirit, if it truly abhors sin and would not want to commit any sin it knew of, cannot sin mortally even if the animal instincts and affections remaining from previous cancelled sins trivialise

[143] *ibid.*, ad 3.
[144] I-II, q. 19, art. 8, ad 3.
[145] [Gerdil, *Tractatus de actibus humanis*, 3, c. 2, *Opere edite e inedite*, Naples 1856, vol. 6, p. 89]
[146] *S.T.*, I-II, q. 19, art 6, ad 1.
[147] *De utilitate credendi*, c. 12, 27.

and darken the mind, and prevent its judging with total clarity and uprightness.

§6. Does a non-upright conscience have to be followed?

273. Before answering our four separate questions about vincibly erroneous or *non-upright* conscience, I would like to comment on a common teaching about this kind of conscience. The teaching needs to be upheld, and I would not want to be thought opposed to it. What I am about to say is simply intended to put the teaching in its proper light in order to prevent its being misunderstood and used as a basis for false conclusions.

It is commonly held that any erroneous conscience, whether it commands or gravely prohibits an action, must be followed. The reason for this is clear: 'If anyone decides to act against such a conscience as long as it exists, that person, as far as he is concerned, has the intention of not observing the law of God, that is, he sins mortally (if the matter is serious).'[148] The person wishing to sin, sins. If I firmly believe that my action is a sin, and I do it, I sin. This is indubitable.

274. But this is the case only on the following conditions:

1. If someone thinks he sins either in acting or not acting, his belief must be *sincere*. He must not deceive himself by imagining he believes what he does not believe. If this were the case he would not have an erroneous conscience, but only suppose he had it. Hence St. Thomas' phrase: 'as long as such conscience exists.'

2. The action must be truly opposed to such a conscience; the person must want to sin. In fact, an erroneous conscience which declares an action or omission to be sinful could be accompanied by a contrary conscience. In this case, the person would vacillate from moment to moment as one or other conscience dominated in his spirit, and would not sin if he acted against the erroneous, non-upright conscience at the moment when the true, upright conscience took control. The immediate return of the other conscience, which could seem

[148] St. Thomas, *De Veritate*, q. 17, art. 4.

never to have left him, would not then influence the morality of what he had done.

Because of the speed with which these consciences succeed one another, they are often confused. It is then very difficult to discern which conscience has been followed.

275. It may be objected that by following a non-upright conscience, we posit a morally defective, and even culpable act. How can we be obliged under pain of sin to commit sin?

We preface our reply by noting that many of our acts, which appear *simple* at first sight, are in fact *multiple*. Let us say, for example, that someone thinks he is obliged to tell a lie in order to save another's life. Here, two judgments are made, and both of them judgments of conscience. Gerdil is of the opinion that only the second is a judgment of conscience, but a careful examination of the case shows the contrary. One judgment tells the person in this situation that the words he is going to utter are a lie; the other judgment tells him that he is obliged to tell this lie in order to save a human life. Error is certainly present in the second judgment while the first judgment is correct. I maintain that conscience is found not only in the second, but also in the first because the first, as far as I can see, is not a judgment in which only the physical existence of the act is apprehended; its moral existence is also grasped. The words to be spoken are not considered simply as words, but are judged as true or lying words. In judging that the words are lies, as in our case, the person already discerns their moral quality, constituted by their being lying words.

But we must note here an extremely dangerous and facile illusion which deceives many.

The words 'moral good' and 'moral evil' signify abstract and generic ideas. To say *moral evil* or *moral good* (or to say *sin* or *fault*) is to indicate something in an abstract way because the kind of moral good or evil has not yet been denoted. But have we an absolute need of this abstraction in order to begin acting morally? I do not think so. As I have already shown, we could indeed undertake moral good or evil before the formation of this very general notion, cut off as it is from every particular good or bad action. If, as my understanding develops, I am able to abstract from my very own actions the general notion of moral good and evil, my actions must already have been moral and immoral, good and evil. Otherwise, I could not have abstracted such a notion from them.

We have to keep in mind these two moral states, and the two forms which the moral law takes in successive moments (cf. 32–71). In its first form, the law is simply 'perceived beings' themselves, which require from us a willing acknowledgement proportioned to their entity; in its second form, the law is an abstraction, the exigency of the perceived beings, but now abstracted from them and formulated and expressed in more or less general ways. *Moral law*, for example, expresses the force of obligation, while *moral good* and *moral evil* express the *relationship* between acts of will and the law. Both expressions are phrased in the most general way.

If we apply this teaching to our present case, we see that in saying 'The words I am about to say are a lie', we indicate their immorality under a *specific* form. If I say 'These words are obligatory for me because they are a means of saving human life', I indicate their morality under a *general* form. In both cases, I attribute to them without distinction a *moral quality* entailing obligation. But in the first case, it is a quality obliging me not to say them; in the second case, a quality obliging me to say them.

Because the obligation and the exigency are not something different from the concept of lying speech, it is impossible for me to conceive the words as a lie without my knowing that I cannot utter them, although the exigency as such will only be expressed in other words and judged by other acts appertaining to a higher level of reflection. When I say 'These words are a lie', I conceive and pronounce the evil present in the words in a less abstract way than saying 'I am obliged to avoid these words'. But in both cases I mentally conceive the malice of the action. If I say 'I am obliged to avoid it', I use the universal idea of obligation, or obligating force; if I say 'This is a lie', I express the same obligating force, but in act, that is, as adhering to the thing, not as abstracted from it.[149] In both cases, I have fully experienced the obligation incumbent upon me, and I am *aware of the immorality of these words*.

[149] See my *Storia comparativa e critica de' sistemi morali*, c. 8, art. 8, for a clearer exposition of the teaching on titles of obligation.

It is now possible to see how confusion, and hence contradiction, between ideas sometimes arises in the human spirit. I can certainly know through a natural, direct judgment that certain words are immoral because they contain a lie. At the same time, I form another reflective, willed judgment overlaying the first. With the second judgment I tell myself that I am obliged to utter these words for the sake of saving human life. We note, however, that the second judgment, precisely because it is reflective, prevails over and obscures the first, but without destroying it. Finding myself in this state, at two levels of reflection, I have two moral formulas before me. One of them tells me that I must not lie, the other tells me that I must lie in order to save human life. The first persuades me that lying is immoral; the second, that lying is necessary if I am to obtain the end for which I have to lie. The first formula leads me to think that I sin by uttering the lying words; the second formula, that I sin by not saving human life. In the first case, I find myself obliged not to use an unlawful means; in the second case, I am obliged to obtain an end.

The conscience which obliges me, therefore, in this contradictory state, is not a simple formula telling me to lie (I cannot be obliged to commit sin). It is a formula telling me to save someone from imminent death and simultaneously persuading me to shut out what conscience itself is telling me about the unlawfulness of the means which I have to use to save the person.

If I do not save the person's life when I believe I am obliged by God's law, I sin. But I do not sin by omitting to tell the lie (the only means of saving that life); this would be absurd. I sin because I refuse to save a human life which I firmly believe I am obliged to save under pain of grave sin. But if in saving the person by means of the lie, I do not sin against the conscience commanding me to save life, I sin nevertheless against the conscience indicating moral improbity in the lie.[150]

---

[150] It may be objected that the second conscience prevails over the first and destroys it; in other words: 'When a person thinks of saving life, he judges it licit for him to lie.' I would answer that the concept of *lying* and *immorality* include one another, as we have seen. One necessarily implies the other. The 'prevailing' conscience, therefore, would be a judgment

276. The thought of two contemporaneous consciences, one included in the other, leading us to sin whether we act or abstain from acting, may occasion some surprise. St. Thomas, however, has a very appropriate comment on the matter. 'Given one mistake in a syllogism, other mistakes will follow. In the same way, if one mistake is posited in moral matters, others will necessarily follow. For example, if a person does his duty out of vainglory, he will sin if he does his duty, or if he does not . . . In the same way, if an error of reason or of conscience is posited, evil follows in the will.' 'Nevertheless,' adds St. Thomas, 'the person is not perplexed. He can abandon his error because his ignorance is vincible and willed.'[151]

277. The same teaching is confirmed by other authorities, and in particular by St. Bernard in a remarkable passage answering the question: 'Why does the erring conscience not change evil into good as it changes good into evil?'[152] The question itself shows St. Bernard has no doubt that conscience changed good into evil by thinking good evil, but does not change evil into good by thinking evil good. The saint replies: 'You think it strange and unjust that in human intention what a person thinks has more power relative to evil than to good. If I replied that this occurred justly in evil matters because the eye was evil, you would ask why the same should not be true, relative to what is good, when the eye is simple. He who said that the darkness of the body was dependent upon a defective eye, also maintained that light in the body was dependent upon a simple eye.' St. Bernard goes on: 'But be careful. If the eye deceives, it is perhaps not truly simple. Both the person who thinks good evil, and the one who

stating: 'When it is a case of saving life, I can commit sin.' Such a conscience contains knowledge of the commission of sin; the person knows he sins although on reflection he excuses himself, and scarcely adverts to it. Contradiction is present in this conscience which includes another, contrary conscience. Finally, I point out that the example I have adopted presupposes that lying is intrinsically evil. Consequently, the example would not be valid in the opinion of those defending the morality of 'lies of necessity'. But it is impossible to say in a note all that I think of such a relevant question, and I would refer the reader to *Filosofia del Diritto*, D. 1.

[151] *S.T.*, I-II, q. 19, art. 6, ad 3.
[152] *Lib. de Praecept. et Dispensat.*, c. 14.

thinks evil good, are deceived. WOE is prophesized of each of them: "WOE TO THOSE WHO CALL EVIL GOOD AND GOOD EVIL" . . . As far as I am concerned, I BELIEVE THAT TWO THINGS ARE NEEDED for simplicity in the interior eye: CHARITY IN OUR INTENTION AND TRUTH IN OUR CHOICE.'[153]

St. Bernard's way of indicating that the eye of the intention may not be truly simple where the intention is erroneous seems to me both beautiful and profound. Certainly neither the intention nor conscience is simple in the case we examined above. Such a case is present, however, only when truly rational law, or rational law reasonably deduced, is in question. St. Thomas seems to be speaking about this when he says: 'If a person knew that human reason commanded something against God's precept, he would not be held to follow reason; but in this case reason would not be totally mistaken.'[154] The last phrase would mean that conscience, in order to be truly erroneous, should have no suspicion of erring relative to the law of God (the same can also be said relative to the rational law) because a conscience that perceives an act to be against the law of God or the rational law cannot in good faith believe the act good. This is equivalent to saying that the person's conscience cannot be totally and simply mistaken.

278. St. Thomas seems to say the same when he comments: 'If a person's conscience tells him to avoid adultery, he cannot set aside this conscience without committing grave sin.'[155] I think we can infer from this that a conscience which errs about the rational law (for example, one declaring adultery to be lawful or praiseworthy) is by that very fact sinful. But if deceiving oneself about a dictate of the rational law is sinful, the erroneous conscience responsible for the deception is not altogether sincere nor truly invincible. If it were, it would not be sinful. Just as a person perceiving a horse cannot be forced to tell himself that he has perceived a cow, a person conceiving an intrinsically disordered action — a lie, for example — cannot tell himself that he has conceived a good, well-ordered action. Moral disorder in the actions of which we are

[153] *Lib. de Praecept. et Dispensat.*, c. 14, nn. 34, 35.
[154] *S.T.*, I-II, q. 19, art. 5, ad 2.
[155] *De Veritate*, q. 17, *De Conscientia*, art. 4.

speaking is inherent in the actions themselves and necessarily conceived together with these actions.[156]

§7. *Ignorance* and *invincible inadvertence*, but not *invincible error*, are possible relative to the rational law

279. We have proved there cannot be a totally *invincible* and unwilled *error* relative to the rational law rationally conceived except in cases where the need to act impels us to judge (cf. 242, 243) (which means, of course, that the rational law has not been rationally conceived). Consequently, such an error cannot give rise to an altogether sincere, simple, erroneous conscience without fault, or sin, or some moral defect.

There can, however, be *ignorance* about the remote deductions from the natural law; not everyone is capable of drawing distant conclusions from basic principles. Such ignorance, if it results from natural debility of *understanding*,[157] and not from a defect in the *will*, does not make conscience less upright, nor diminish merit in the act. This is especially the case when a person, who may know the value of *beings*, is incapable of calculating *relationships between them*.[158] However, the act remains materially good, taken as a whole, while its material defect consists in the absence of certain refinements that would render it morally perfect.

280. In addition to *ignorance* about a part of the rational law, there may also be unwilled *inadvertence*[159] about certain

---

[156] St. John Chrysostom says: 'No one can offer the absence of a teacher or of some guide along the right path as an excuse for neglecting virtue. Conscience is a sufficient guide, and *no one can lack such help within*' (*Gen.*, Hom. 54). This passage can be understood only of *direct knowledge*, which is always present in us and can be considered as a *kind of potential first conscience*.

[157] St. Thomas says: 'Blindness excusing from sin depends upon a natural defect in the person who cannot see' (*S.T.*, II-II, q. 15, art. 1, ad 1).

[158] St. Thomas comments very subtly: 'The special ignorance which totally excuses is ignorance of SOME CIRCUMSTANCES which the person cannot know, even granted due care on his part' (*S.T.*, I-II, q. 77, art. 7, ad 2).

[159] We have to distinguish, therefore: 1. error, 2. ignorance, 3. inadvertence. *Error* is present when I affirm something contrary to the natural law,

more remote or minute dictates of this law at the moment when a person acts. Such inadvertence does not arise from any defect in the will, but from some limitation of physical or intellective forces which renders a person incapable of observing all the circumstances of his action and of applying the law completely.

281. *Error*, however, cannot be considered in this way. As we said, no one can force another to assent to what is false; only his own will, inclined to what is false, can do this.

'Error', says St. Thomas, 'means approving what is false as though it were true, and consequently adds some kind of action to ignorance. Simple ignorance is present when a person passes no opinion on what he does not know; in this case he is *ignorant*, but not *mistaken*. On the other hand, when he pronounces judgment on things he does not know, he errs properly speaking. Because sin consists in an act, error obviously takes on the notion of sin. It is indeed presumptuous to pronounce about what is unknown, especially in dangerous matters.'[160]

282. Many authors, unaware of this important truth, have been led to support very strange opinions. They have even concluded that invincibly erroneous conscience could be extended to the natural law and convert what is essentially evil into good.

Daniel Concina argues strongly against this position, which would destroy all morality, and is particularly vehement against the absurdities of Claude La Croix and Antonio Tirillo who taught that erroneous conscience even had the power to make lying good. He shows the extremes inherent in such a system: 'Tirillo and La Croix, who state that lying is morally good if conscience errs invincibly, must

either by denying the principles, or deducing pretended consequences on the basis of defective reasoning. *Ignorance* is present when I have no knowledge about some consequence of the principles of the natural law. In this case I err simply because I judge and act as though the consequence did not exist. *Inadvertence* is present when in theory I know a consequence of the principles of the rational law, but in acting do not reflect or pay attention to what I am doing, and have no intention of opposing the law.

[160] *De Malo*, q. 3, art. 7. Nevertheless, although I accept that formal error is the work of the will, I believe that the will can, in certain cases, be drawn *necessarily* into error, as I have said.

necessarily say the same about every other kind of wickedness, however abhorrent. Atheism, idolatry, heresy, masturba-
tion, and theft will all be good and meritorious because,
according to these authors, there can be invincible ignorance
in their regard.' Concina rightly continues: 'If invincible
conscience is possible in matters of natural law, an invincible,
erroneous conscience can certainly be present relative to
divine, positive law and, consequently, to true religion . . .
Granted this, willed unbelief and pagan, Islamic, Arian,
Macedonian, Lutheran and Calvinistic teachings could come
from God because the will of people holding such doctrines
may be the result of invincible ignorance. At least by
accident, therefore, the Priscillian, Lutheran and Calvinistic
heresies could be founded in God. Even atheism will depend
upon God if, as Molina and Arriaga maintain, it is possible to
be invincibly ignorant of God himself. Finally, according to
our opponents, fornication, sodomy and other crimes can
spring from an invincible, erroneous conscience. So I would
have to conclude: lies declared lawful by an invincibly erroneous conscience are good and meritorious; and the same
applies to every other horrible sin about which invincible
error is possible.

'Instruction, preaching, admonitions and missions would
all be superfluous if an erroneous persuasion were capable of
infusing goodness into an evil action, as true knowledge can
into a moral action . . . What better theology could be found
than this modern teaching which places on a par with virtue
all kinds of immorality carried out under the veil of ignorance?

'Father La Croix asks what difficulty prevents these horrible acts from being good and meritorious. If they are evil in
themselves, he says, as lying and other sins are, they can still
be represented as good; the will, in fact, does not receive its
species from objects as they are in themselves, but as they are
presented by the intellect.'[161]

283. La Croix's objection, or the objection attributed to
him, would indicate a lack of sound philosophy. It would
show that La Croix and those like him were ignorant that the

---

[161] *De Conscientia*, diss. 1, c. 4.

intellect in its first operation conceives things as they are[162] —
a most important philosophical truth. Lying is necessarily
conceived as the opposite of truth and, therefore, as dishonest. 'Opposed to truth' and 'being dishonest' are synonymous.[163] Hence, a formal lie can never appear necessarily as
something good. On the contrary, it is necessarily conceived
as something evil by the intellect (conceiving something as
evil means conceiving it in its nature as evil; it does not mean
that we apply the word *evil* to it). But the intellect, after
conceiving something as evil in itself, can reflect upon it and,
through the reflection, either judge it as evil by acknowledging reflectively the direct knowledge that the intellect has or,
contrariwise, judge it as good (for whatever motive). Because
this second intellectual operation is always directed by the
will, it is possible for us to accept what is evil as good, and
what is good as evil — just as it is in our power to accept as
good what we have conceived as good, and as evil what we
have conceived as evil.

The objection would also show that La Croix and those
like him were ignorant both of the great principle of all
goodness in human beings, which consists in *willed, practical
acknowledgement* of what we have directly apprehended and
known, and of the great principle of evil which consists in our
refusal to acknowledge what we know, and in the internal,
willing distortion of what our intellect has necessarily

---

[162] Prospero Fagnani is not altogether accurate when he writes: 'The intellect is not free to think the less probable opinion; it has to follow the
stronger motives of the more probable opinion. As scales inevitably drop
on the side of the heavier weight, the intellect weighing dispassionately the
reasons for both opinions is necessarily drawn to the side where stronger
motives are to be found' (*Comment. in I lib. Decretalium*). The intellect has
to act when it is moved by *nature*. This happens in its first operation when
it apprehends things. But the intellect, which should here be called *reason*,
is free to draw its conclusions when it is moved by the *will*. This takes place
in reflective, practical judgments in which we estimate the value of things as
we please. This is the great source of human errors, precisely because 'each
easily believes what he desires', as St. Thomas says (*S.T.*, II-II, q. 6, art 3,
ad 4).

I wished to draw attention to Fagnani's inaccuracy because of its multiple consequences which merit attentive observation.

[163] Opinions may vary about the moral duty of expressing the truth in
words, but what we affirm here about a *formal* lie cannot be gainsaid.

received and conceived. The Holy Spirit says: 'Woe to those who call evil good and good evil,'[164] and Christ wants our eye to be simple, that is, he wants us to behold in simplicity what we have conceived mentally, without alteration or forgery. An inflamed, diseased eye impresses its colour and defect on what it sees. This explains why those who do not affirm to themselves interiorly in their willed, practical judgment what they have seen in their direct, natural, mental conception do not affirm the truth: 'they do not obey the truth, but obey wickedness.'[165]

284. Father La Croix, and others holding the same opinion, start from a false premise; 'evil objects can present themselves as good to our understanding without the intervention of our will.' The true teaching, however, is this:

1. Essentially evil objects cannot present themselves as good to the understanding. Hence, the direct knowledge we have of them is always in conformity with the truth.

2. Our will, by means of reflection which could and should conform to direct knowledge, may alter what we know, and utter an interior lie, the true source of all human iniquity.

§8. The accidental differences
between the first three questions on vincible error

285. We must return to our questions (cf. 259) about what we have called *vincible* error.

The first three differ only in the cause of the error, or more precisely in the condition of the cause. The error is always caused by the will which is inclined to lie to itself, calling good evil and viceversa. It does this either through some necessity or through an entirely *free act*. In both cases the mind, while reflecting, is directed by a distorted, defective will. Consequently an upright conscience is unobtainable. As theologians correctly say: 'An upright conscience conforms to upright desire.'[166]

---

[164] Is 5: 20.　　　　　　　　　　　　　　　　　[165] Rom 2: 8.
[166] 'An upright conscience conforms to upright desire. Theologians

286. St. Basil himself notes the practical energy we have for making internal judgments, and how our will esteems the value of things we conceive. He says: 'Because we possess a natural energy for judging (κριτηριον φυσικον) and distinguishing good from evil, we have to discern justly in the choice of what we must do, seconding virtue and condemning what is wrong, in the way that a fair-minded, unbiased judge pronounces sentence on contrary claims.'[167] He says again: 'With all diligence we should interiorly, in the hidden forum of our thoughts (note these words carefully), make upright judgments about things. Our spirit should be like scales which weigh unbiasedly what is to be done, and give the victory to God's law against sin.'[168] It is always true, therefore, that in these three cases, in which the will causes error in our conscience, immorality is present because the will is distorted and defective.

287. But each case can be subdivided because the error can consist either in judging as good what is evil, or judging as evil what is good. Furthermore, when we judge as good an action that in itself is evil, we can judge it in three ways: as *lawful*, as *meritorious* and supererogatory (in addition to being lawful), or as *obligatory*.

288. Moreover, the three erroneous judgments can be made for different reasons:

1. From a passionate, unjust love of an evil action, when we desire to form a conscience that will allow us to do the action. In this case the evil is clearly evident and deeply rooted. The Holy Spirit is speaking principally of this ugly lie that we pronounce in our hearts, when he says: 'Woe to those who call evil good and good evil'[169] and also: 'There is a way which seems right to a man, but its end is the way to death.'[170]

2. We make erroneous judgments, not for a disordinate love of some action, but for love of something to which the action is a means. This kind of judgment also has a triple morality; the thing we desire can of its nature be *lawful*, commonly teach that upright desire, which follows upright reason, leaves no room for doubt' (Gerdil, *Tractatus de act. hum.*, III, q. 1, c. 2).

[167] St. Basil, *Hom. in principium Proverb.*, n. 9.
[168] St. Basil, *ibid.*, n. 10.
[169] Is 5: 20.
[170] Prov 14: 12.

meritorious (as well as lawful), or *evil*. For example, if I judge that I can tell a lie to obtain some advantage which in itself is just, what I desire is not evil in itself. If, however, I judge I can tell a lie for some unjust advantage, the case would be different. Finally, if I thought I could lie to obtain an alms for some poor person, my purpose would be of its nature *meritorious*.

These distinctions must be made if we wish to determine as well as we can the moral state of the less than upright, erroneous consciences we are discussing.

289. The same kind of distinctions must be made when we judge something good as evil. The good in the thing can be simply *lawful*, or *meritorious* (as well as lawful), or *obligatory*. Moreover I can judge the good to be evil because of my hatred for the action; in this case the hatred is as immoral as the action is holy and obligatory. Or I can hate the action and desire not to do it because of my attachment to something which the action prevents me from obtaining; and again, the thing itself can be lawful, meritorious or evil.

The same applies in both cases (that is, whether we judge good evil, or evil good) if, by omitting an action, I am able to avoid either an evil or something I detest. The same three situations would be possible: I could judge such an action either simply lawful or meritorious (as well as lawful) or obligatory.

290. We see, therefore, that the accidents affecting erroneous conscience are many and various. Every accident changes the moral state of a conscience at least in degree if not in its nature. Anyone wishing to determine the moral defect affecting a vincible, erroneous conscience must therefore carefully distinguish each case and form a particular opinion about each. On the other hand, anyone wanting to give a general opinion about vincibly erroneous consciences would be acting too vaguely, and confusing very different concepts.

Reverting to our three questions, therefore, let us note the two things we asked in each of them:

1. Must we or must we not follow this erroneous conscience?

2. What is the morality of an action performed according to such a conscience?

We shall answer by taking each of the three questions, and first examine what each requires of us, and then the moral value of actions regulated by the consciences in question.

§9. The first question

291. Is it possible for error about the rational law or the rational application of law to follow necessarily from original sin?

The *concupiscence* that remains in us after baptism, is certainly not *sin* or *fault* (cf. 105); it is an impetuous inclination to false, natural good, continually tempting the will, urging it to consent to evil. The following question therefore presents itself: 'Can the will sometimes be so necessarily inclined that it cannot avoid forming one of those false, secret, interior judgments which constitute a false conscience and are a false rule of action?' For example, would a child attracted by the love of food necessarily judge the food (compared to other things) a greater good than it is? And as a consequence of this practical, erroneous judgment, would the child internally consent to the sin of greed, or hatred of companions?

292. I make the two following observations about the question: first, we must distinguish between the child's *conscience* and his false, interior judgment about the food. To value mistakenly the pleasure of the food more than it merits is a disorder, but this is not conscience. A false conscience would be the child's judgment that he can lawfully esteem the food more than it merits.

I am convinced that after baptism, as long as we are not harmed by actual sins, we cannot be necessitated to form such a conscience. Forming a conscience is the function of the personal principle, which is sound after baptism — only the power of our free will can harm us. Therefore we cannot be necessitated to commit such an error.

Moreover, I am certain that consent to evil by a practical judgment cannot be necessitated after baptism; we need to have lost grace through free, actual sins and become once again servants of sin. The redemptive effect of baptism, which

[291-2]

renews us, would evidently not be full and perfect if there still remained in us a principle so dominant that it made us desire evil.

I think therefore that the two hypotheses given above offend against the grace of baptism and cannot be reconciled with Christian faith. In particular, it seems obvious and in keeping with God's goodness, that a soul having God as its master and protector is never abandoned and left in such desperate straits except through its own fault — as St. Paul says: 'God is faithful, who will not suffer you to be tempted above that which you are able.'[171]

Nevertheless the Apostle clearly admits by these words the possibility *per se* of human nature being tempted beyond its strength, a possibility, however, that is not actuated because of God's provident care. God governs external circumstances so that they do not exercise an attraction and excitement to evil stronger than our powers.

293. What remains after baptism, besides the fomes of concupiscence, is *ignorance* of the consequences of the supreme principle of the natural law. But because this ignorance is independent of our will, it is not sin, as we have said and St. Augustine teaches.[172]

294. *Sluggishness* of mind also remains. Our mind moves slowly to deduce moral formulas derived from the supreme principle of the law impressed in our soul. This sluggishness is the origin of the mind's ignorance and of its absorption in feelable objects, but it remains outside the sphere of morality as long as it does not depend on the will.

295. We think these observations answer the question by showing it to be without foundation. We must add, however, that although the will of a baptised person, free of new sins, is safe from temptation beyond its power, there is no doubt it can be tempted by concupiscence and, as it were, charmed into evil. Furthermore, we certainly have a duty to be vigilant against this propensity of the will which frequently leads the intellect into false judgments and even to the formation of a false conscience. We must heed the words of Christ: 'What I

[171] 1 Cor 10: 13.
[172] *Contra Jul.*, bk. 6, c. 16.

say to you, I say to all: Watch',[173] and invoke divine help: 'Watch and pray',[174] using all means to deprive our passions of their power: 'Be sober be watchful.'[175] Above all, the eye of our mind must accustom itself to rectitude by loving and contemplating truth with sincerity and clarity.

§10. The second question

296. We must now examine the second question: must we follow an erroneous conscience concerning the rational law or the rational application of law when the error is in itself willed and free? We cannot omit the question without causing confusion in the development of the argument. Moreover, an actually free, formal error of conscience (the kind of erroneous conscience referred to in the question) is one that can and must be avoided without delay.

297. But we either advert to the error or not. If, when forming a conscience, we are aware of being deceived but want our error and fully consent to it, we advert to it. For example, a person who loves money makes a contract. If necessary, he can reveal to friends and relatives certain details of the contract which make him appear more generous than the other party. In the depths of his heart, however, he knows something seen only by God, that is, that the contract contains an injustice. If he were the other party, he would certainly know how to exploit the knowledge to his own advantage. His conscience is not *sincere* and, properly speaking, is not a conscience. Hence he is not obliged to follow it because he has not yet formed it; in fact he must follow the opposite conscience that lies deep in his heart, a reflective, vivid conscience easily available to him, if he wishes.

298. The degrees of advertence, however, can vary a great deal and thus cause the degree of fault to vary. Only God can measure these differences but whatever their degree, the person by deceiving himself betrays his own soul.

299. But a formal error of conscience which is free but not

[173] Mk 13: 37.
[174] Mt 26: 41; Mk 13: 33.
[175] 1 Pet 5: 8.

adverted to can also exist. For example, a person is suddenly
overcome by a raging passion which limits his right use of
reason; unaware of his self-deception, he can at that moment
persuade himself that he is able without sin to perform some
reprehensible action. However, he was free not to surrender
to the passion diverting his attention of mind. If he had
maintained his calm of spirit and mind, he would not have
had to make the false judgment of conscience, which was free
because the preceding or accompanying act that produced it
was free.

The rule, therefore, to be followed in this case is evident::
'No one must allow a passion to change the state of his spirit.
When disturbed, he must avoid any disorder by doing
nothing until he has regained the calm lost through his fault.'

§11. The third question

300. Must we follow an erroneous conscience about the
rational law or the rational application of the law, when this
error, although willed, is not free in itself but free in its cause,
because the evil inclination of the will which necessarily
attracts us towards error is the effect of previous actual faults?

For the sake of clarity we shall summarise what we have
already said in a series of propositions, to each of which we
shall add some explanation or proof. We shall then move
from proposition to proposition until we find the correct
answer to our initial question.

1. 'The *formal, vincible error of conscience* we are
speaking of, which does not excuse people from sin, differs
from simple *ignorance* of certain deductions from moral
principles, and differs from natural mental *sluggishness* in
making these deductions.'

Only the will is the seat of moral good and evil. Neither
good nor evil morality is present if there is no question of will
but only of an understanding incapable of foreseeing the
consequences of moral principles. St. Thomas shows that this
kind of ignorance is possible: 'Every judgment of speculative
reason comes from the natural knowledge of first principles.
In the same way every natural judgment of practical reason

comes from certain natural known principles . . . But there are different ways of moving from these principles in judging different things. Some things are so explicit in human acts that they can easily be approved or disapproved on the basis of common, first principles. Other matters, however, can only be judged after careful consideration of their various circumstances. Not everyone is capable of doing this; only wise people can carry it through, just as philosophers alone can examine the particular conclusions of scientific matters.'[176]

301. Nor is *sluggishness* of understanding, upon which such ignorance normally depends, to be confused with formal error. A person is incapable of deducing remote consequences from the principles of natural law, not because the eye of his intellect is inept at seeing them, but because he is slow in using and focusing his mental vision on the consequences. If he could fix his eye upon them, he would undoubtedly see their splendour in the principles. But if this sluggishness is unwilled, and natural, it has no good or bad moral character-istics because it is extraneous to the will. This would not be so if the sluggishness were willed by the supreme will (cf. 89). In this case, sin would be present, as St. Thomas affirms in speaking about mental *debility* which differs little from the mental *sluggishness* that we are examining. 'A person is said to be sharp, intellectually speaking, when he can apprehend what is proper to a thing, or even some effect of it, and immediately grasp its nature and succeed in considering its least conditions. Contrariwise, a person is said to be intellec-tually *weak* when he can arrive at the truth he is dealing with only after lengthy explanations. Even then he does not grasp perfectly all that can be found in the concept of the thing. *Debility* of intellectual feeling implies a definite mental weakness in considering spiritual matters; but mental *blind-ness* indicates total privation of knowledge of these matters. Both weakness and blindess are impediments to the gift of understanding by which a person comes to know intimately the spiritual matters he grasps, but they entail the *notion of sin* only in so far as they are willed. This is clear in the case of a

---

[176] *S.T.*, I-II, q. 3, art. 1.

[301]

person who is bored with spiritual matters and neglects to examine them with care because of his love for carnal things.'[177]

302. 2. 'Willed and sinful false consciences exist.'

This is shown by the previous quotation from St. Thomas. We need note only that although sinful *false consciences* can spring from two causes, *ignorance* and *mental sluggishness* or *weakness* together with real *error*, we are not dealing here with consciences dependent upon *ignorance* and *mental weakness*. We shall deal with them more extensively under the heading 'positive law'. At the moment our concern is consciences containing a true, actual, willed *error*. We can however corroborate our general proposition on the basis of certain authorities.

First, we have the theological and legal adage: 'Ignorance of the law does not excuse.' If legal theorists alone used this phrase it could perhaps be understood in the sense that ignorance of the law does not excuse in the external forum. Theologians, however, also use it and apply it expressly to the internal forum. Here, however, it has to be restricted for the most part to ignorance of the *rational law* — ignorance of the positive law can easily be present without sin. But even related to the rational law, the adage is restricted to cases in which ignorance itself is willed in some way.

303. St. Thomas says: 'A person can be unaware of his sin in two ways. In one of them, he is at fault either because through ignorance of the law, which does not excuse, he thinks something not to be a sin which is sin (someone who commits fornication may think that simple fornication is not a mortal sin) or because he neglects to examine himself . . . Hence a sinner, although he may not be aware of his sin, sins in receiving the body of Christ because in this case the ignorance itself is sin.'[178]

Here St. Thomas distinguishes two cases in which a person is not aware of the sin he commits. In one, examination of self is neglected; in the other, a false dictate springs from ignorance of the rational law which does not excuse from sin.

St. Antoninus has the same comment: 'In evil matters,

[177] *S.T.*, II-II, q. 15, art. 2 [*App.* no. 2].
[178] *S.T.*, III, q. 80, art. 4, ad 5.

ignorance can be twofold: ignorance of the law and ignorance of fact. If ignorance of the law, divine or natural, is in question, or ignorance of matters that a person is bound to know because of his state, the evil action done through such ignorance does not excuse from all, but only from part of the fault.'[179]

304. 3. 'Willed, sinful consciences exist which depend not only on previous culpable ignorance, but on error which itself is an evil act of the will.'

It is easy to understand the existence of sinful, erroneous consciences dependent upon previous culpable ignorance. If we willingly neglect to instruct ourselves about our duties, we are obviously in a state of culpable ignorance.

305. If this were the only kind of erroneous conscience, the Fathers of the Church would not have attached any particular difficulty to explaining the sins of ignorance indicated in sacred scripture. In fact, these sins are considered so difficult to understand that according to the Fathers it is better simply to accept what the scriptures say about them than to try to explain them.

In the dialogues of St. Jerome against the Pelagians, Chrisobalus makes the following objection against sins of ignorance: 'Tell me, is it just for me to be bound by sin relative to an error of which I am not aware?' St. Jerome makes no attempt to explain the matter: 'Are you asking me about God's decision and disposition? You will find the answer to your foolish question in the book of Wisdom: "Seek not what is too difficult for you"[180] . . . Listen to the Apostle who sounds the gospel trumpet with the words: "O the depth of the riches and wisdom and knowledge of God!

---

[179] Part I, tit. 4, c. 14, §3. The wise reader will notice immediately that my principle aim in citing theological authorities and holy scripture is to indicate how these authorities are to be understood and interpreted. The chief reason for the interminable discussions provoked by the use of authority in difficult questions is lack of care in obtaining a well-balanced understanding of the authorities quoted. Conscientious understanding sometimes indicates that certain general propositions are to be restricted to the object under examination; that other, apparently opposite, propositions are to be reconciled; and that finally the solid meaning of the authors' fundamental opinions is to be given more attention than the slippery sands of their material words.   [180] Sir 3: [21].

How unsearchable are his judgments and how inscrutable his ways!'"[181] For St. Jerome, as we can see, sins of ignorance, so frequently mentioned in divine scripture, were especially difficult to explain.

Concina, an excellent theologian, rightly says: 'It is extemely difficult to explain how we can sin in ignorance.'[182] And Francisco Suarez was right to be suspicious when he saw how easily sins of ignorance were explained by modern moral theologians who maintained that no sin could be committed inadvertently, and that sins of ignorance were only present through negligence in instructing oneself. For the writers criticised by Suarez there was no sin in the actual error sometimes committed without advertence by the will, which would however itself be present with a less than upright act. Suarez saw this easy explanation as an open contradiction of the teaching of the greatest of the Fathers, who themselves confessed the difficulty of the problem. He commented: 'Precisely because this opinion solves the difficulties in such a subject, I doubt the explanation, which I am not prepared to accept' [*App.* no. 3].

306. It is quite certain that very careful attention is needed if we are going to understand how the human will can move the reason to decide on a false judgment by uttering an interior lie. We have to observe what takes place within us, and not allow ourselves to be led astray by imagination, fantasy or preconceived common opinion. As far as I can, I have tried to contribute to the progress of philosophy by faithful adherence to what interior observation reveals, and hope that it is now possible to understand the nature of sins of ignorance which until the present has necessarily remained a mystery.

This philosophy has produced the following results. It has

---

[181] *Advers. Pelag.*, bk. 1, c. 10, Dialog.

[182] D. Concina, bk. 2, *De Consc.*, c. 1, §3. Suarez asks: 'Does actual inattention make unwilled an act whose condition is unknown?' He says that the question is difficult, and still scarcely discussed amongst writers on morals. 'There is not much to be found directly on this question in the authors . . . and the question is PARTICULARLY DIFFICULT' (*Tract. de Voluntar. et Involuntar.*, Disp. 4, sect. 3). And the question proposed by Suarez is only a branch of the whole question about sins of ignorance and inadvertence.

[306]

shown that the will has an extraordinary efficacy in determining our faculty of judgment, especially when we make decisions about the value of things; it has allowed us to understand how the will, affected by passion, corrupts the judgment by drawing it to pronounce in the way the will wants rather than as things are; it has affirmed that the inevitable consequence of an unjust judgment by the will, which persuades us that the unlawful is lawful and the bad good, is an intrinsically and inexcusably erroneous, evil conscience, and itself a sin; it has also affirmed that we do not have to reflect when we make a judgment, and that advertence to a judgment is not a necessary element of its immorality. Such immorality is constituted when we are capable of speaking the truth to ourselves interiorly, but wish to lie, simply because it pleases us to do so. Whenever we are in possession of direct knowledge, we can tell ourselves the truth if we wish to do so. And this is the case relative to rational law in so far as it is present to the human mind, and therefore known to us directly.

307. Ecclesiasticus puts the matter very plainly:
> 'He who seeks the law will be filled with it,
>   but the hypocrite will stumble at it.'

The sacred author says that 'he who seeks the law will be filled with it' because, if we wish, we can draw many conclusions from the principles of rational law, which is present to us all. He goes on: 'but the hypocrite will stumble at it' because in forming a non-upright, insincere conscience for himself his cunning will not pass unpunished.

He continues:
> 'Those who fear the Lord shall find *just judgment*
>   and shall kindle justice like a light.'

Fear of the Lord, and a spirit unaffected by passions and sins, enables us to pass *just judgment*.[183] Those who fear the Lord form a just judgment, that is, an upright conscience, because they judge uprightly, without passion. They kindle justice like a light because an upright conscience is a *light*; as we form it we become like persons who kindle a light in themselves. Forming an upright conscience is an act of justice which truly

---

[183] Sir 32: 19, 20 [32: 15, 16].

[307]

entitles the upright consciences we make for ourselves to be called *resplendent justices*.

308. By following disordered passion, we form erroneous consciences for ourselves which tell us that something is lawful when it is not. Our situation is now very serious. St. John says: 'He who says he is in the light and hates his brother is in the darkness still.'[184] The Evangelist is writing about people who deceive themselves by thinking they are just in carrying out a part of the law while neglecting, without scruple, love of their neighbour by subtly dispensing themselves from their duties of charity. In other words, they are forming an erroneous conscience that condemns rather than excuses them.

309. Jesus Christ was more indignant about the *false consciences* of the Pharisees than about any other sin. Our Saviour had to use violence almost to uproot false conscience and reveal hidden corruption; this kind of conscience is in fact the most *hidden* sin, and the true root of innumerable other sins. Jesus calls the Pharisees *blind* on account of the *false consciences* they form for themselves. They were 'spent lamps' not because they did not know the law,[185] but because they did not want to know it and erred in applying it.

He said to them: 'But woe to you, scribes and Pharisees, hypocrites! because you shut the kingdom of heaven against men; for you neither enter yourselves, nor allow those who would enter to go in' with your false ways of applying the law and judging what should be done.[186] 'Woe to you, scribes and Pharisees, hypocrites! for you devour widows' houses and for a pretence you make long prayers; therefore you will receive

---

[184] 1 Jn 2: 9.

[185] At the beginning of his discourse Christ clearly stated that the Pharisees knew the law only too well: 'The scribes and the Pharisees sit on Moses' seat; so practise and observe whatever they tell you' (Mt 23: 2–3).

[186] Elsewhere he says of the lawyers: 'Woe to you, lawyers! for you have taken away the key of knowledge; you did not enter yourselves and you hindered those who were entering.' (Lk 11: 52). With these words Christ indicates two errors. The first lies in the pretentious presumption of the lawyers that they alone understood the law; the second lies in their interpreting and applying the law according to their own passions — the cause of perdition for themselves and their disciples.

the greater condemnation.' They thought that virtue consisted in long prayers, and blinded by self-interest thought it lawful to get rich at the expense of poor widows . . . 'Woe to you, blind guides, who say, "If any one swears by the temple, it is nothing; but if any one swears by the gold of the temple, he is bound by his oath".' This false application of the law about oath-taking enables them to form a *false conscience* which would lawfully free them from the oath made by the temple. Christ goes on: 'You blind fools! For which is the greater, the gold or the temple that has made the gold sacred? And you say, "If any one swears by the altar, it is nothing, but if anyone swears by the gift that is on the altar, he is bound by his oath".' This is another example of false conscience by which they hoped to free themselves from their obligation to maintain the promises sworn by the altar. 'You blind men! For which is greater, the gift or the altar that makes the gift sacred? Woe to you, scribes and Pharisees, hypocrites! for you tithe mint and dill and cummin, and have neglected the weightier matters of the law, justice and mercy and faith; these you ought to have done, without neglecting the others.' This is yet another example of *erroneous conscience* which made them rigid upholders of certain things appertaining to the positive law, and excused their laxity, as they thought, in matters regarding the natural law. 'You blind guides, straining out a gnat and swallowing a camel!' (that is, you are subtle and scrupulous about certain matters that leave your passions unhindered, and even augmented; but when your vices are in question, you show extraordinary elasticity of conscience). 'woe to you, scribes and Pharisees, hypocrites! for you cleanse the outside of the cup and of the plate, but inside they are full of extortion and rapacity. You blind Pharisee! first cleanse the inside of the cup and of the plate, that the outside also may be clean,' that is, first make clean the internal injustice which causes false consciences, each of which is itself an injustice. Then alone will your external works be upright and innocent. The *foolishness* and *blindness* attributed to the Pharisees by Christ is found in the formation of *false consciences* which instead of acting as lighted lamps to the soul are smoking wicks that make the darkness more intense and suffocating.[187] These false consciences and this darkness are the work of cunning, blatant malice, and account for Christ's description of the scribes and Pharisees as 'serpents and brood of vipers.'[188]

310. It will be helpful now, after indicating willed, false conscience as the seat of *spiritual blindness*, if we speak more at length about this blindness.

Our divine Master uses the metaphor of leaven to illustrate how this spiritual blindness originates in previous malice obscuring the light of truth: 'Beware of the leaven of the Pharisees.'[189] By 'leaven' Jesus means the teaching of the Pharisees, as the sacred text explains. In other words, as leaven alters the nature and the condition of flour by making it first ferment, then rise, and finally corrupt, so passion serves to ferment teaching, knowledge and opinion by changing it from what it was and subjecting it to interior alteration and upheaval in all its elements. There can be no better illustration of the power of a perverse will to change direct knowledge and distort judgment by making it apply the law in a way altogether different from sincere, natural uprightness.

311. We can be sure, therefore, that it is an evil disposition of spirit which produces in the mind the teaching called 'leaven' by Christ. If we want to examine the way in which this false teaching is produced by human self-deception (as scripture says: 'Iniquity has lied to itself'[190]), we find that a person in the grip of passion sees in a distorted fashion not because he lacks an intelligent principle (which he cannot lose), but because 1. the light of grace does not guide him away from such vision; and 2. he is impeded by his passions[191] from *acknowledging* the truth which is in him (his direct knowledge), but from which he flees.

---

[187] Christ reproves the Pharisees for neglecting '*justice* and *love*' (Lk 11: 42). Because they were dominated by blameworthy, internal affections, they were incapable of making upright *judgments*, the foundation of all morality. As a result, they judged badly the importance of *love*.

[188] Mt 23.   [189] Mt 16: 11; Lk 12: 1.   [190] Ps 26: 12 [Douai].

[191] St. Thomas, speaking of the blindness of mind produced by sensual pleasures, says: 'The flesh acts in the intellective part not by changing it, but by impeding its action' (*S.T.*, II-II, q. 15, art. 3, ad 2).

[310-1]

312. St. Thomas, speaking of truth, the final principle of natural vision, says: 'The human mind can either understand or not understand by means of this intelligible principle. Non-understanding takes place in two ways. Sometimes the person's will spontaneously withdraws from considering the principle. As the Psalmist says: "He did not want to understand in order to avoid doing good."[192] At other times the person's mind is so taken up with things he loves that it is distracted from the principle. As the Psalmist says: "Fire has fallen on them, and they shall not see the sun."[193] In both cases, this mental blindness is a sin.'[194]

313. This distinction between those who reject the truth because they cannot be bothered to conform to it in their actions, and those who turn away from contemplating it through the force of passion, should be noted very carefully. Those under the pressure of passion are much less guilty than the others.

The Fathers of the Church often spoke about these varieties of ignorance. Isidore says: 'There are those who sin from ignorance and those who sin knowingly. There are others who do not want to know in order to excuse their ignorance. These however deceive rather than defend themselves. Not knowing is simply ignorance; not wanting to know is stubborn pride. Not wanting to know the will of one's Lord can only mean despising the Lord out of pride. Let no one excuse himself through ignorance, therefore. The Lord judges both those who turn away from knowing him, and those who do not know him.'[195]

Bernard says: 'Malice generates ignorance, and ignorance conceals malice in such a way that often a person who does not know, either does not do some evil he would want to do, or does some good he would not want to do. The heart of such an unwise person is darkened. As the prey of wayward understanding, he reaches a point where he is totally unable to love or discern what is good.'[196]

---

[192] Ps 35: 4 [Douai].
[193] Ps 57: 9 [Douai].
[194] *S.T.*, II-II, q. 15, art 1.
[195] *Levit.*, bk 2, c. 17.
[196] *Lib. de Praecept. et Dispensat.*, c. 14, n. 39.

314. 4. 'Culpable, erroneous consciences are principally connected with the rational law or the rational application of the law.'

We have seen that the erroneous consciences of the Pharisees consisted in:

a) neglecting the rational law despite their exaggerated care about certain parts of the positive law;

b) badly applying the positive law to their actions.

If we now examine the general tenor of the chief places in which ecclesiastical writers speak about willed, erroneous consciences, we will see that they refer for the most part to the *rational* law, or to the way in which this law, or any other law, is *rationally applied* to action. Let us consider some of these references.

Tertullian says: 'Everyone grants that what is against nature is monstrous; amongst us it is also termed "sacrilege" because it is against God, the Lord and Creator of nature. Are you searching for the law of God? You will find it as the common law of the open universe, written into nature, to which the Apostle appeals when he speaks of women's veils: "Does not nature itself teach you?" or says to the Romans: the "Gentiles do by nature what the law requires". He is indicating both natural law and lawful nature.'[197]

Augustine says: 'The person who sins *without knowing* could suitably be said to sin *without willing*, although that which he does without knowledge he does in fact with his will because even this person's sin cannot be void of will . . . He does it, therefore, because he wills to do it; he sins although he does not know that it is a sin. The sin, therefore, cannot be void of will: the fact is willed, although the sin is not, and the fact is a sin. It is the fact itself that should not be done.'[198] These words would have no force if they were applied to some fact which was not intrinsically evil. But in the case of an intrinsically evil act, to will the fact is to sin because the fact itself is sin.

Again: 'Sins committed in ignorance or by people under pressure are said to be involuntary, but cannot be said to be done without the intervention of the will. Even people who

---

[197] *Lib. de Coron. Militis*, c. 5, 6.
[198] *Retract.*, bk. 1, c. 15.

sin through ignorance act of their own will in judging that
they should do what ought not to be done.'[199] In this passage
St. Augustine presupposes that the will has the power to
judge uprightly or evilly about the probity of an action. This
is true in the case of the rational law, or the rational application of the law.

St. Thomas, commenting on Romans, where the Apostle
teaches that the use of certain foods becomes sinful if they are
eaten against conscience, but not sinful if conscience does not
disapprove,[200] says: 'You have to understand the meaning as:
"if a person judges with upright faith that this can be done."
But if he decides on the basis of false belief that something has
to be done — if, for instance, he thinks that he honours God
by killing the disciples of Christ — he is not excused because
he has judged himself irreprehensible, as John says, 16: 2. He
would, in fact, be in a happier state if his conscience pricked
him because he would be drawn away from evil. What the
Apostle says here[201] must be understood in reference to
LAWFUL matters alone. In this case, a person's glory consists
in not being reproved by conscience.'[202]

315. 5. Erroneous consciences are inexcusable related to the
rational law because we possess by nature the principle of
law, that is, the *conception of the entities of things*. This is a
norm of action. In addition we have the faculty of deducing
natural laws in an upright way and applying them rightly to
our actions within certain limits. And beyond the limits of
this faculty, it is impossible for a sound will to be forced to
consent to error. This is true also of *rational application* to
our actions of natural and positive law.

We can prove this on the authority of divine scripture also,
upon which ecclesiastical writers depend. In Deuteronomy,
God stimulated the Hebrews to keep the natural law of love
of God and neighbour, which he had promulgated positively,
by reminding them of its natural presence in intelligent
spirits. He says to Israel: 'For this commandment which I

---

[199] *Retract.*, bk. 1, c. 15.
[200] 'Happy is he who has no reason to judge himself in what he approves'
(Rom 14: 22).
[201] 2 Cor 1: 12.
[202] *In Ep. ad Rom.*, c. 14, 22.

command you this day is not too hard for you, neither is it far off. It is not in heaven, that you should say, "Who will go up for us to heaven, and bring it to us, that we may hear it and do it?" Neither is it beyond the sea, that you should say, "Who will go over the sea for us, and bring it to us, that we may hear it and do it?" But the word is very near you; it is in your mouth and in your heart, so that you can do it. See, I have set before you this day life and good, death and evil. If you obey the commandments of the Lord your God, by walking in his ways, and by keeping his commandments . . . then you shall live.'[203] It is clear that those failing to keep the natural law on the pretext of an erroneous conscience are inexcusable. They should be told to reject their substitute conscience in order to find beneath it a better norm of wisdom. They will find the truth close at hand in their heart.

316. This truth or law, when loved, is called *wisdom* (it is always present to our intelligence because it is in its essence the first concepts we have of things).

The holy scriptures speak of wisdom in the following terms:

'Wisdom is radiant and unfading
and she is easily discerned by those who love her
and she is found by those who seek her.
She hastens to make herself known to those who desire her . . .
To fix one's thought on her is perfect understanding
and he who is vigilant on her account will soon be free from care.'[204]

In affirming that 'wisdom is easily discerned by those who love her', the text reaffirms that when love of what is good and love of truth move the will, the will in turn directs the eye of the understanding which sees and acknowledges the object of its direct cognition. This object is clear and unfading because the conceived entities of things cannot be falsified. Willingly thinking of truth, instead of fictions created by our passions, and of the true worth of things, rather than of what we invent about them, is 'perfect understanding'. Our conscience is upright and secure when we are really diligent in

[203] Deut 30: [11–16].
[204] Wis 6: 13–16 [12–13, 15].

[316]

reflecting in this way in order not to deceive ourselves. As scripture says, we are then *vigilant*, and *he who is vigilant on her account will soon be free from care*.

317. The Gentiles had formed many false consciences for themselves: they thought fornication was lawful, and idolatry an act of piety. But the blindness of their erroneous consciences did not excuse them. St. Paul says they were altogether without excuse: 'So they are without excuse'. But why were they without excuse? Were they not obliged to follow their erroneous consciences?

They were not, and could not be obliged to do what was intrinsically evil; nothing can oblige a person to do this. They were, however, obliged to set aside such consciences, just as they were obliged not to form them in the first place.

But was it possible for them not to form false consciences? Yes, says St. Paul; this is why they are without excuse. It was enough for them to have adhered with their will to the *notion* of divinity undoubtedly present in their first, natural, direct knowledge. This notion should have been the sole norm of their actions.

The Apostle describes how the pure, true notion of God was to be found in the depth of their spirits, and how they had distanced themselves from it by following reflection based upon imagination. 'For what can be known about God' (that is, what can be known about him naturally speaking) 'is plain to them, because God has shown it to them. Ever since the creation of the world his invisible nature, namely, his eternal power and divinity, has been clearly perceived in the things that have been made.'[205] By means of what we have called (in the *Origin of Thought* [*fn. 14*, 623, 624]) the *integrating function*, they passed from created things to the notion of the uncreated principle, the Author of the universe. This was *direct knowledge*, according to which they were held to act in their relations with God. Because they possessed this norm, says St. Paul, they were able to follow it. But they behaved very differently. 'For although they *knew* God, they did not honour him as God':[206] they did not *acknowledge* him; they did not cling lovingly to this divinity which they had known. And this precisely is their sin.

[205] Rom 1: 19, 20.   [206] Rom 1: 21.

Its effect was mental blindness. The vision which they had now willingly made for themselves was no longer that of the God whose notion resided in their soul, but of an idol created by their passions. This was the source of their erroneous consciences; their depravity of will made its influence felt in their understanding. 'They became futile in their thinking,' says St. Paul.

As long as willed thought remains based on direct knowledge, which is always true, it has a sure foundation. But when, instead of referring to the content of direct knowledge, it affirms what is not present to the intelligence, or denies what is present, the thrust of such thoughts ends in pointless nothingness: they become *futile* indeed.

He goes on: 'Their foolish heart was darkened.' The heart is the reflective will, that is, the willed reflection. This *willed reflection* is obscured if it does not receive the light of truth found in the notion of direct knowledge — and the will does not receive it if, instead of gazing at the light, it is taken up with its own fantasies.

'Claiming to be wise, they became foolish.' This is a third grade of human corruption. The first is sin; the second, willed, erroneous conscience; the third, glorying in this erroneous conscience, as if it were the repository of wisdom.

318. The nature and source of what St. James calls, 'earthly, unspiritual, devilish *wisdom*'[207] is found here. It is the deceitful wisdom so frequently mentioned in holy scripture. St. Paul says of its admirers: 'They glory in their shame, with minds set on earthly things,'[208] and of their knowledge: 'The Lord knows that the thoughts of the wise are futile.'[209] St. Paul's description of true wisdom is very different: 'But we impart a secret and hidden wisdom of God . . . none of the rulers of this age understood this; for if they had, they would not have crucified the Lord of glory.'[210] St. Paul attributes the crucifixion of Christ to a false conscience, and hence to a false wisdom.[211] Christ had pointed to the same cause of his death

---

[207] Jas 3: 15.   [208] Phil 3: 19.
[209] 1 Cor 3: 19.   [210] 1 Cor 2: 18 [7, 8].
[211] The Pharisees were ambitious to be called teachers and to sit in the chairs of learning (cf. Mt 23: 6), and showed their monstrous pride in saying to the man born blind: 'You were born in utter sin, and would you teach us?' (Jn 9: 34).

[318]

when he said: 'Father, forgive them, for they do not know what they do.'[212] This kind of wisdom and false conscience could never save the world, as scripture says:

'"I will destroy the wisdom of the wise,
and the cleverness of the clever I will thwart."

Where is the wise man? Where is the scribe? Where is the debater of this age? Has not God made foolish the wisdom of the world?'[213]

319. What are the special, characteristic effects of this erroneous conscience in which humanity treasures its wisdom? St. Paul in describing the Gentiles indicates two of these effects, *idolatry* and *lust*. Of idolatry he says: 'they exchanged the glory of the immortal God for images resembling mortal man or birds or animals or reptiles.'[214] The word 'exchanged' is admirably suitable for showing how such a change in the notion of God depended upon the work of their own will. They exchanged it, says St. Paul; hence they must have possessed the notion of God ('what can be known about God is plain in them').[215] They changed their right notion of God's glory and his surpassing divine nature by refusing to acknowledge it; they substituted vain appearances in its place; and they turned their practical reflection from the notion of God to vanity. The effect was foreseeable and inevitable. The vile, vicious false gods they had made were a prelude to unbridled licence.

The notion of the true God, pure spirit, all truth and holiness, requires pure and holy worship. But guilty human nature did not want purity and holiness; uncleanness was its aim. It was more useful, therefore, to alter the notion of true divinity, which could not be *acknowledged* without the profession of a pure life, and to substitute in its place a false notion, the *acknowledgment* of which would permit subjection to the desires of passion. In desiring this impurity, humanity also wanted a false notion of God. This, according to St. Paul, explains the origin of idolatry: 'Therefore' (that is, as a result of idolatry) 'God gave them up in the lusts of their heart to impurity, to the dishonouring of their bodies among themselves, because they *exchanged* the truth about

---

[212] Lk 23: 34.   [213] 1 Cor 1: 19, 20.
[214] Rom 1: 23.   [215] Rom 1: 19.

God' (that is, the true, divine nature which shone in their direct knowledge) 'for a lie and worshipped and served the creature rather than the Creator, who is blessed forever!'[216] St. Paul continues with a long description of the wickedness prevalent amongst the Gentiles.

320. The Gentiles were guilty of all this wickedness, and without excuse, although they had acted with an erroneous conscience, which was in fact the chief sin and root of all their other sins. Let us conclude with a passage about the natural law from St. Thomas which confirms our thesis in its entirety. 'This *law* is simply the *intellectual light* placed in us by God, through which we know what has to be done and left undone. God gave this light and this law to mankind at the moment of creation. Nevertheless, many think they can excuse themselves from the observance of such a law on the grounds of ignorance. But the prophet addresses them in the psalm: "Many say: Who shows us good things!", as if they did not know what to do. But the prophet replies: "The light of your countenance, O Lord, is signed upon us," that is, the light of the intellect through which we know what has to be done.'[217]

We have shown on the authority of St. Paul, who speaks of the notion of God, that there is present in us a living, resplendent principle of law, together with the incorrupt notions of beings; we also have the faculty of applying uprightly, if we wish to do so, the law known to us,[218] and deriving from it more particular laws. We conclude that we are without excuse in forming erroneous, non-upright consciences for ourselves where upright, true consciences could be formed in their place.

[216] Rom 1: 24 ss.

[217] Opusc. 4, *De praeceptis charitatis, et decem legis praeceptis* (foreword).

[218] According to St. Thomas, 'Certain very common precepts, known to everyone, hold first place relative to the natural law; certain secondary, more particular precepts, hold second place as proximate conclusions from the principles. The natural law cannot be universally erased from human hearts in so far as it is contained in the first, common principles; but it can be erased relative to a given particular action in so far as reason is impeded from *applying* a common principle to the action because of concupiscence or some similar passion' (*S.T.*, I-II, q. 94, art. 6).

[320]

321. 6. 'Because advertence is not necessary in our use of reason and will, we can form erroneous, non-upright consciences without being aware of them.

As we have said,[219] it is possible to sin when following our culpably erroneous conscience. Consequently it is possible to sin without advertence because the possession of an erroneous conscience not only leaves us unaware of the unlawfulness of our action, but makes us believe it lawful.

322. But our proposition goes further. It affirms that we can form erroneous consciences without advertence. This arises because knowing, and willing what we know, does not require advertence. Actions of this nature can be done inadvertently.

We need to ponder what I indicated in *The Origin of Thought* [cf. 927]: *knowing* is not the same as *being aware* that we know; *willing* something as a result of knowledge is not the same as *being aware* that we will. If we are in the habit of observing what takes place within us, we are almost certain to have surprised ourselves now and again in the act of thinking although at the time we were not aware that we were thinking. What we call *distractions* form part of this phenomenon. The culpability of our action, I must insist, requires us to know the action and will it freely, but adverting to it is not necessary. As a result, an erroneous conscience in matters of rational law is intrinsically evil when it springs from error (not of course from mere ignorance). Anyone willing such a conscience sins, although he may not have reflected upon his act of will and become aware of his sin.[220]

323. What I am trying to show here (through careful observation of the way in which our internal operations arise and by an exact distinction between a *moral act* and *a reflection upon it*) has already been demonstrated by moral theologians

---

[219] 'That which is carried out against the law is always evil, nor is it excused because it is according to conscience' (St. Thomas, *Quodlib.*, 8, art. 13).

[220] It will be said that if we do not *advert* to our sin, we cannot avoid it. This is false. It is possible to *know* without *adverting* to the fact that we know. And what can be known can also be wanted or rejected. Freedom therefore is present prior to advertence to our act. It occurs at the level of moral reflection which precedes advertence to this reflection.

through the authority of sacred scripture and the Fathers.[221]
The need for actual advertence in order to sin is an opinion
not found expressly and clearly in the writings of moral
theologians before 1581, when Gabriel Vasquez published his
work.

324. In fact, it is my own opinion that this teaching was
already condemned by the Church in the case of the
Pelagians, as we can see clearly in several places of St. Augustine and St. Jerome who consistently combated this heresy.[222]
The error of the Pelagians is made very clear by my distinction between mere *knowledge* of our moral act, and the
reflection upon it by which we make ourselves *aware* of it.
Only the first act (knowledge) is necessary for sin, not the
second (reflection). This distinction has not been grasped
clearly by Concina or other modern writers.

325. St. Gregory's words, therefore, have the authentic
ring of truth: 'Our "hidden path" has another meaning
because we do not know if the things that seem upright to us
will present the same appearance when subject to examination
by the severe judge. Often what we do, as we said above, is a
cause of damnation to us although we think it an advance in
virtue. Often what we imagine placates the judge rouses him
rather to wrath. As Solomon says: "There is a way which
seems upright to man, but the end thereof is death." Holy
people, even when they overcome evil, fear their good actions
lest while desiring to do good they are deceived by the
appearance of good in what they do.'[223]

326. It will not be out of place to take our analysis of this
mysterious operation a stage further. By coming to know its
nature better, we shall form a firmer persuasion of its
existence. The mystery lies in the nature of *habits* which, as
principles of spontaneous action, are either adverted to with
great difficulty or not at all.

Let us take as an example the condition of a person in
whom an habitual affection to self-interest, or lust or
ambition, is firmly rooted. This affection gives rise in his

[221] Cf. Daniele Concina, bk 2, *De Conscientia*, disc. 2, c. 4, §4–11.
[222] A list of these places may be found in Stefano De Champs and Card.
Noris.
[223] *Moralium*, bk. 5, c. 7.

spirit to a constant reaching-out for possessions or pleasures or praise; it is a *permanent assent* to evil, an immanent act giving rise to adventitious acts. Every time the opportunity offers, he has a constant will to enjoy the satisfaction to which he is addicted. When an occasion of such enjoyment presents itself, therefore, he has no need to deliberate; his mind is already made up. His act flows like water when a valve is opened. The water is already there, continually exerting pressure; all that is needed is to turn the tap.

When a person acts according to wilful passion without need of further deliberation, he does not initiate anything new. His will, which had previously been blocked, now rushes forward in the course opened to it. If he does nothing to impede it, no new act or new state of spirit is found in him; he has no need for consideration in order to act, nor does he have to produce any new energy. He simply has to let himself go by not positing any obstacle to the movement of activity already within him and bursting to expand. Because nothing new takes place within him, he is not roused to reflect on what he is doing. A sensual person, for example, thinks and gives consent to what is impure without any awareness; an avaricious person deceives himself, and without reflecting tells a thousand lies in pursuit of gain. His self-deceit and mendacity are so familiar that he cannot even remember lying. The same can be said about people enslaved by other passions.[224]

327. Nevertheless, a sermon, or some accidental recall of an eternal truth, could occasion disquiet in the lives of those habitually taken up with some vice. Although they do not advert distinctly to many actions in particular, it is difficult for all their actions to remain unobserved. If, on hearing the call, they accept the grace of conversion, they abandon their evil way of life. But if the eternal truth they hear only causes them some natural fright, without arousing a resolution about true conversion, several things happen, one of which is often as follows.

Fear of losing their soul, with all that entails for the future life, causes great anguish, as we would expect in people whose

---

[224] Cf. AMS, 750–763, for a longer treatment of this spontaneous, inadverted action of the will.

sole desire is to be comfortable and satisfy passion. Their will now turns therefore to a new desire, that is, they want to remove from their spirit the trouble caused by remorse and by fear of what is to come in the future life, but without losing the satisfaction of their passions in the present life. This satisfaction is their true end, and it is diminished by any disquiet accompanying it. They now ask themselves how they can continue doing what is wrong and at the same time quieten their interior discomfort of conscience.

This is their great problem, and they turn their energy to solving it in the most subtle ways. Having entangled themselves in the solution, they look for help from friends and flatterers whose advice is acceptable, from other persons and above all from priests whom they call to direct their spirit. They put every effort into using such means and eventually, after untold sophistry, they finally form extremely comforting conclusions which, under the appearance and title of decency and piety, leave the most horrible vices hidden in the depth of their heart. And in talking to God about these matters, they delude themselves even further: 'We shall adopt every appearance of religious behaviour ("I fast twice a week, I give tithes of all that I get"[225]), but you, our Lord, will turn a blind eye in the matter of charity, compassion, temperance, chastity.'

In this way they profit by lax teaching, sophisticated reasoning, badly applied examples, instant answers, and every word of comfort they hear from those with vested interests and affections. They also take advantage of the weakness and ignorance of the sacred ministers they choose and protect, and of the connivance of other sacred ministers as depraved as themselves. There is no room left for truth as they fill their heads with satisfying reasons and authority. Contrary opinions, which they either ridicule or dismiss with specious gravity, weigh nothing in their balance. Remorse, which could devour their heart, is silenced except for an occasional, strangled whimper.

The imprudent person, who with gospel freedom proposes true, frank morality to them, will either be considered an oddity or answered with the kind of nod that indicates how

[225] Lk 18: 12.

foolish he is. If he were to go further and sustain the truth with firm persuasion and good, forceful reasons, he would soon find himself touching some remarkably sensitive areas. Meek, composedly peaceful countenances would rapidly change into the faces of furies, ready to attack and overwhelm the poor soul for the rest of his mortal existence.

False consciences about the rational law, which destroy the very core of humanity, develop in this way. But they still lie crouched and hidden under the appearances of religion and external composure.[226]

328. But because God scrutinises the heart, he knows us in this state and judges us. We may indeed imagine ourselves just and pious by relying to a great extent on certain religious acts or on human good works, and by covering evil actions with the shield of the erroneous consciences we are discussing. But in this miserable condition we can only lead a life of perdition as St. Augustine says: 'It is just punishment of sin for a person to lose what he did not want to put to good use when he could easily have used it if he had wanted. I mean, if someone does not act uprightly when he knows how to, he may lose his *knowledge* of what is upright; and if he does not want to act uprightly when he is able to do so, he may lose the *power* of doing so even when he wants to.'[227]

329. 7. 'The possibility of non-upright, inadvertent consciences in the human spirit was the source of the saints' fear in all that they did.' We read in the book of Job that he feared in all his actions: 'I feared in all my works.'[228] We have already quoted the commentary of Gregory the Great on another phrase of Job, 'To a man whose way is hid',[229] where the holy

---

[226] We fall into the same trap today although passions have changed. Nowadays we quieten our remorse of conscience with acts of beneficence and charity. We say to God: 'I will do these works of charity, but leave me free to satisfy the desires of the flesh, and dispense me from the laws of the Church.' This is the opposite of what was done previously when God was addressed as follows: 'I will observe the laws of the Church, but dispense me from being charitable, and let me be avaricious.' Whichever way we act outwardly, we remain the same internally, although we think we have changed considerably.

[227] *De lib. arb.*, bk. 3, c. 18.

[228] Job 9: 28.

[229] Job 9: 23. Cf. 426 [325].

doctor asserts: 'The just fear even in their good words, and
pray continually, lest through some hidden error they fail in
their very works.'[230] Holy King David felt the same fear, and
prayed to the Lord: 'The sins of my youth and my ignorances,
do not remember.'[231]

St. Augustine, in a letter to Paulinus, shows himself fearful
of the blame that ignorance and non-upright conscience, the
subtle outcome of our secret passions, could bring upon him.
He goes so far as to accuse himself of sin: 'As far as I am
concerned, I confess that I sin in these matters, and do not
know when and how I can fulfil the commandment "In the
presence of all, correct those who sin." Oh, Paulinus, holy
man of God, what terror and darkness envelops these
matters! Surely it is of these things that it is written: "Fear and
trembling are come upon me: and darkness has covered
me".'[232] St. Augustine's words show clearly the danger of
sinning without advertence. Our secret self-love and other
passions easily deceive us, as we said, and either block our
vision by spreading darkness around us, or — and this is
more terrifying still — lead us to form erroneous consciences.[233]

330. 8. 'We are obliged to lay aside our vincible, erroneous
conscience by rectifying our will.'

This follows from what has been said. If the vincible,
erroneous conscience, as we have described it, is itself a sin, it
is clear that we must overcome it and form for ourselves a
true, upright conscience. But how can our evil conscience be
put right? We shall discuss this shortly. For the moment we
may conclude and affirm that:

[230] The text itself reads: 'Holy people . . . fear even their good deeds.
While they desire to do good, they may be deceived by what they see
outwardly. What looks healthy may sometimes disguise a festering sore'
(*Moralium*, bk. 5, c. 7).

[231] Ps 24: 7 [Douai].

[232] Ep. 250, *Ad Paulinum*.

[233] Mortal sin is not present, however, if we are sincere in deploring our
sin, and would rather die than commit it (provided we knew it) (cf. 272),
although we cannot avoid all the *small deceits* interwoven for us by our
passions. The act with which we deplore our sin is at a more elevated level
than the self-deceits into which we fall, and is therefore *personal*. It is the
disposition of the person which renders the human condition morally good
or evil (cf. 85).

[330]

331. 9. 'The teaching we have examined is of great comfort to holy, God-fearing souls; it is frightening only for those who are habitually evil.'

The explanation for this final proposition depends upon what has been said about the nature of moral habits (prop. 6) as principles of inadvertent action. It is clear that if an habitually evil person can commit sins knowingly indeed but without reflection and hence without adverting to his act, so an habitually good person can often do what is good, and do it without in fact reflecting upon what he is doing.

According to this principle, God-fearing souls who abhor sin can be happy because they have every reason for believing: 1. that if they doubt about having assented to sin, they have not in fact given it their assent, and 2. that when they fear they have made little progress in virtue, they have in fact made progress (this is normal in the case of such persons, although they do not notice their daily progress).[234]

Experienced spiritual directors will have observed that the unease suffered by good people comes in great part from their being unaware of following the right path. Good people remain in darkness and uncertainty about their moral state and their salvation. But what has been said above, if it is rightly understood, destroys all foundation for such disquiet by showing that there can be, and certainly is, progress in good even though the subject of this progress cannot always be aware of it.

Opposite reasons should lead those who are habitually evil to find in this teaching solid motives for rousing themselves and for fear about their own state and the outcome of their

---

[234] In his biography of St. Francis de Sales, Canon Gallizia says that the Saint taught his penitents not to be distressed when they could not recall all their faults. He used to say to them: 'You fall frequently without noticing, but you also get up without noticing. The Wise Man did not write that the just realises he falls seven times a day, but that he falls. And if he falls without noticing his fall, he gets up also without reflecting upon it. So do not worry. Confess humbly and frankly what you remember, and leave the rest to the mercy of him who supports those who fall without malice. He ensures that they do not hit the ground, and then raises them so swiftly and gently that they are unaware they have fallen, and equally unaware of their rise. His hand is under them as they fall, and raises them immediately without their realising it' (bk. 3, c. 9).

eternal salvation. Teaching of this kind provokes in those who think about it the states described by St. Paul, 'There will be tribulation and distress for every human being who does evil . . . glory, honour and peace to those who do good.'[235]

§12. The general moral state of an action performed according to a less than upright conscience where error concerns the rational law or the rational application of the law

332. We now come to the second part of our enquiry: 'What is the moral state of an action done with a less than upright conscience concerning the rational law or the rational application of the law.'

I. Moralists first ask whether an evil action following from an evil conscience forms one sin with the sin inherent in the conscience, or whether it is a separate sin.

It is not my intention to discuss the relative importance of this question but to show that knowledge of the presence of one or more sins in a person does not provide knowledge of his true moral state. The moral condition resulting from a single sin could be worse than that resulting from two. In fact, distinguishing two sins implies analysing a moral state already known, which remains the same whether we analyse it or not. I deliberately mention this because some people seemingly place too much importance on defining the number of sins involved in a particular action. Very often they are simply speculating without throwing any light on the sinner's true state of soul.

But I cannot omit the question altogether because I hope it will clarify the teaching about the evil contained in certain erroneous consciences. The more the evil is hidden, the more we should make an effort to reveal it.

333. Moralists are divided by three opinions on the question. Some maintain that a sin committed with a vincibly erroneous conscience does not differ from the sin contained in the conscience. Others say that every time we act with a

[235] Rom 2: 9, 10.

culpable erroneous conscience we commit a new sin, different from the sin inherent in the conscience. The third opinion lies between these two. It says that an erroneous conscience, in itself or as a result of ignorance, either contains a full species of sin (for example, unbelief, heresy, schism) or does not, if the ignorance or error consists simply in neglect to instruct oneself. In the first case, they say, the sin in the conscience is distinct from the particular sins of actions dependent upon the conscience. In the second case, the ignorance, or the erroneous conscience caused by the ignorance, forms one sin with each subsequent blameworthy act.

334. It seems to me that none of these three opinions entirely answers the question. This will be clear if I list the various distinctions which, in my opinion, must first be made in order to give a clear, unequivocal, complete answer to the question.

The first and most important distinction is the distinction I have made between *rational* and *positive* law. Intrinsically evil actions are not the object of positive law as such. To perform actions that are forbidden or to omit actions that are commanded positively is a sin only because of the law or will of the legislator forbidding or commanding the actions. Therefore every time we are ignorant of the law, we do not sin in desiring such actions. The only sin (whose gravity would vary, as I will explain below) would consist in our *culpable*, willed *ignorance* of the law, and our neglect to inform ourselves about it. If the ignorance were sought in order to avoid the obligation of acting in conformity with the law, the sin would be multiple, and its gravity would correspond to the degree of clarity or confusion with which the defects of the action were foreseen. There would also be all the various kinds of evil that are possible in an evil will. Hence, *relative to positive law*, the following words of Fr. La Croix are substantially true: 'Although ignorance and lack of forethought are culpable, a subsequent action has no particular evil except the negligence itself or negligence to recognise or advert to the evil.'[236] His mistake is to give the words too general a meaning by applying them not simply to positive

[236] Bk. 5, n. 16.

[334]

law but to rational law as well.[237] On the other hand, his opponents err in saying that the words apply neither to rational nor positive law.

335. But relative to rational law there is no doubt that an action can be intrinsically evil. To wish such an action is a sin totally independent and separate from the sin inherent in conscience. We want what is intrinsically evil and truly conceived as evil, although we judge it as good through a culpable error of reflection. Every time we perform an action evil in itself, a new sin is committed different from the sin committed when we form our blameworthy conscience.

336. Another distinction we must make, and have already discussed, is whether an erroneous conscience relative to rational law is caused by *ignorance* or by *error*.

If it is caused by *culpable error* in judging lawful what is unlawful and seen by our spirit as intrinsically blameworthy, clearly a sin of rash, unjust judgment is committed in forming our conscience. If we act according to this judgment we commit an altogether different sin, because we desire an act that is intrinsically evil independently of the judgment. The matter is totally different, however, when an erroneous conscience is preceded by ignorance. In this case, as we saw, there may be no moral defect in the erroneous conscience if: 1. the ignorance producing it is an effect of the limited power of our mind in deducing the remote consequences of rational law from its principles; for instance, when a person notably and without necessity hastens his own death because of zeal in doing good works; 2. the ignorance concerns a fact requiring application of the law, for example when Jacob believed he could lawfully live with the woman who was with him the first night of his marriage. But if the ignorance were the effect of freely neglecting to inform oneself, and therefore culpable, the negligence would be sinful although any erroneous conscience resulting from it, and any subsequent action based on the conscience, would not be a new sin. Granted preceding ignorance, the will acts uprightly, having no culpable object in view either when forming the conscience or acting

---

[237] Another error in the quotation makes *advertence* constitute the evil of sin. As we said, *knowledge* is sufficient without any need for *advertence*, that is, knowledge of knowledge.

[335-6]

according to it. Hence subsequent sins do not differ from the first sin.

337. Bearing in mind these two distinctions, it is my opinion that relative to rational law a less than upright conscience which judges lawful what is intrinsically wrong perpetrates three totally distinct sins. They are:

1. the cause of the erroneous conscience, that is, the *disordered tendency* which moves us to the judgment, whether it is avarice or another *capital sin*;

2. the *unjust judgment* we make when forming the conscience; by it we affirm to ourselves the lawfulness to act which we do not truly see or know;

3. the intrinsically evil, *particular action* we do according to the conscience we have formed.

338. These sins differ because they are three different acts of will, but they can also differ *specifically* among themselves. Thus, an unjust, interior judgment is a sin whose object is falsehood and untruth, although the cause of the judgment may be avarice or covetousness. In addition, the intrinsically evil act that is carried out is a new act of will desiring an evil that, although generally belonging to the same genus as the cause of the evil conscience, can sometimes differ in species and genus. For example, a man ruled by ambition may judge it lawful to kill someone who insults him; here the murder would be of a different genus from that of ambition, and only accidentally part of the ambition, that is, because of the purpose for which the murder was committed.

339. I said these sins were *at least* three, because a fourth can easily be added: we can convince ourselves of acting uprightly when we are in fact acting evilly with a false conscience. This was the case of those pagans of whom St. Paul says: 'Claiming to be wise, they became fools,'[238] and also of those Jews about whom Christ said: 'If you were blind, you would have no guilt; but now that you say, "We see", your guilt remains.'[239]

340. On the other hand, we should distinguish *at least* two sins relative to the rational application of positive law which was erroneous because of some sinful affection: 1. the first would be the cause, and would consist in the *sinful affection*,

[238] Rom 1: 22.   [239] Jn 9: 41.

evil from its beginning, which perverts the uprightness of the judgment; 2. the second would be the *distortion of judgment* constituting the erroneous conscience. Because the object of any action done according to this conscience is not evil in itself, the action does not form a distinct sin but is one with its cause.

341. II. After describing the number of sins involved in an erroneous conscience, we must now turn our attention to their level of gravity which must be measured by the norms governing the gravity of other sins. Consequently their matter, and the evil present in the will, can be light. I believe that these slightly culpable, erroneous consciences and their subsequent acts form the larger part of those minor, inadverted faults into which the just fall, as scripture affirms: 'A righteous man falls seven times.'[240] These are much lamented by holy people who apply themselves so diligently to purify themselves of these consciences.

342. An upright conscience is undoubtedly a judgment, but to judge properly is very difficult, as we gather from Christ's great praise of Nathanael: 'Behold, an Israelite indeed, in whom is no guile!'[241] If judging uprightly were easy there would be no real force in David's assertion that he is addressing God with 'lips free of deceit.'[242] Christ's words indicate that guile resides in the spirit where we fabricate our own deceits; and what David says is so true that not even the one who saw the depth of his heart found fault with it. A tiny weight placed on perfect scales will tip them; the same happens on the scales of justice. Anyone making a judgment must be free of any inclination that does not come from sincere truth in his heart. But who can do this with a pure spirit, free of all passion, in the midst of so many attractive pleasures, so many frightening evils, deep emotions and other influences that demand an immediate judgment? Is it possible for the most innocent human mind to be free of the heart's aversion or inclination? What holy person has never offended a hundred times a day against the dictate of justice and truth, and in spirit given more value to things and actions than they really merit? What holy person has never been indulgent to himself, followed his own inclination, or for a moment not

[240] Prov 24: 16.   [241] Jn 1: 47.   [242] Ps 16: 1 [Douai].

[341-2]

shut his ears to the dictate of pure truth? All this is so impossible to human powers that we have to say ceaselessly with St. Augustine: 'What terror! What darkness!'.

I am certain that anyone to whom God might have specially granted the gift of avoiding all sins of erroneous conscience would already be at the summit of perfection and live in pure light. The only sins he could commit would be those which he adverted to and assessed clearly in his interior conscience, and such sins are easily avoided by good and upright people.

343. III. We now consider the role of ignorance and mental darkness (always present in the less than upright conscience we are discussing) in determining the moral state of human beings. Our discussion will demonstrate two things:

    1. that ignorance and darkness greatly multiply our sins;

    2. that they diminish the actual evil of every sin committed with a less than upright conscience.

344. The first proposition needs no special demonstration. It is clear that, if we consider what is unlawful to be lawful, or even meritorious, we act without difficulty; and if the actions are pleasant, we act as often as we can. The proposition, it seems to me, is supported by the following authorities.

St. Bernardine says: 'In the present, wicked world, the devil has no greater friend than ignorance. The minds of Saracens, Turks, Jews and a countless number of Christians are deceived and fettered by ignorance' (deception and error, as well as ignorance, are involved). 'Thus, in a certain sermon, Richard says: "The doors to hell are two, ignorance of what is good, and desire for what is evil"; and again, in distinction 38: "Ignorance is mother of all errors". Isidore says: "Ignorance is mother and nurse of vice; the ignorant person sins every day." Gregory, in his morals, says: "Anyone ignorant of the purity of the light, approves as light what is dark." And St. Augustine, on the psalms, says: "No one is more incurable than the one who thinks himself healthy."'[243] This is what happens to anyone who has a less

---

[243] T. 2, *Feria IV post Dominicam Palmarum*, art. 1, c. 1.

than upright conscience; it is worse if they think themselves informed and just.

St. Laurence Justinian says: 'Which person diligently searching for himself will ever expel from the fount of his intelligence the flood of ignorance within him about good and evil, about true and false, and about what is fitting and unfitting? . . . Lack of virtue indicates either the error of ignorance or abundance of evil, and both are harmful, both hated by God. This is true regarding the good that is virtue, but what about evil? Evil is in itself always sin. Sin is a prevarication of divine law. There is no one without this ignorance' (note carefully this very serious statement). 'Hence the Prophet says: "Who understands crimes? Cleanse me, Lord, from my hidden misdeeds." How often virtue is considered vice, and vice considered virtue!' (this indicates the many erroneous consciences we form). 'Thus, anger is called zeal, presumption authority, voluptuous pleasure brotherly love, gluttony moderation, indolence humility, insensitivity strength, righteousness cruelty, malice wisdom, meekness timidity, audacity freedom, etc.' This is the way the saints speak; whether we like it or not, they have the truth, and their opinions are of great value. We should note carefully what Justinian adds: 'It would be especially noticeable if this ignorance dominated only in sinners . . . But those who call themselves just possess another kind of ignorance of what is true and false, which is no less harmful. Who can ever express the extent of their ignorance? They blindly follow the spirit of error, ensnared by the deceptions of the devil whom they regard as an angel of light. They give their wills full rein and fall into the pit. They are unable to discern or judge anything honestly. They pursue their desires for virtue without any discipline, and believe every spirit.'[244]

This explains why culpable, erroneous consciences are common in people of all conditions, and why, consequently, so many sins are committed inadvertently every day. But the eyes of holy people, enlightened by divine light, see differently from earthly eyes. The saints salutarily advise us to keep watch over ourselves, to scrutinise the depths of our hearts, and to fear and lament.

[244] *De casto connubio Verbi et Animae*, c. 17.

345. Regarding the second proposition — ignorance diminishes fault — we must distinguish carefully.

We have indicated at least three kinds of sin against the rational law dependent upon vincibly erroneous conscience: 1. previous sins that produce a sinful affection in us, obscuring and corrupting our judgment, and causing us to form a false, evil conscience; 2. the unjust act contained in the false judgment which constitutes the blameworthy conscience; 3. the unlawful actions we perpetrate with this conscience.

We must note that anyone burdened by this triple sin is in a much worse state than someone who, with eyes open and against his conscience, perpetrates an unlawful action. The second person would sin, but unlike the first, the sin would not be continually inherent in his erroneous conscience. His spirit would not be held and bound by a hardened affection to evil, which perverts judgment, suppresses remorse and, as it were, envelops the human heart in damnation (to use the psalmist's expression). The person with the vincible erroneous conscience would have festering wounds, the other, bleeding but clean wounds, although we are frequently deceived into thinking that the condition of the second is worse because he commits the act with more actual knowledge and deliberate will.

346. From one point of view, any particular action involved in the triple sin but considered independently of the previous actions connected with it, can certainly be less blameworthy. But unfortunately the action cannot be separated in any way from its previous actions. It can certainly be a lesser evil, but it has deep roots and is the offspring of a greater sin, or more accurately, of a complex or mass of sins. The blameworthy affection which incites the action and gives it *form* is much more culpable than the affection of someone who sins once, even with open eyes.

347. Having clarified these important points, we can say that unlawful actions, such as usury, fornication or any offence whatever, done with an ignorant and mentally blind erroneous conscience, are less intensely evil than actions done with clear, actual knowledge, and still less evil than actions done with full advertence.

The reason is evident. The more clearly we conceive the

guilt of an action, the more our will is determined to evil if we do it. But in the case of blindness of conscience, although truth is present in the depths of our spirit to be followed if we wish, its light is not present to our reflective vision. The intention of our spirit is directed to the concept of probity that we have incorrectly formed about the unlawful action. Hence our act of will cannot be perfectly evil, nor simply have evil as its object. But this does not alter the moral *state* of a person with a culpable, erroneous conscience whose condition remains far worse than that of a person who has a true conscience which he does not follow. I am simply saying that the former's *particular act*, considered in itself, is less blameworthy than the latter's act, because the darkness in which he has enveloped his spirit has removed some of the evil.

348. Thus Jesus Christ could pray for those crucifying him: 'Father, forgive them; for they know not what they do.'[245] Those crucifying Christ did not know what they were doing simply because they were blinded by their own passions. Hence: 1. they seriously and undoubtedly sinned; but 2. their ignorance, although culpable, diminished the fault of the particular act of crucifixion, because it prevented their knowing who it was they were nailing to the cross, and drew them instead to think they were honouring God.

349. Similarly, St. Paul, after saying he had been a contumelious blasphemer and persecutor, adds: 'But I obtained the mercy of God, because I did it ignorantly in unbelief.'[246]

The authority of the Fathers confirms this teaching. St. Basil demonstrates it by quoting Christ: 'God's judgment on those who sin through ignorance is truly clear in the words: "He who did not know, and did what deserved a beating, shall receive a light beating".'[247] In another place he says: 'Christ does not judge as entirely free of retribution the person who sins through ignorance.'[248] St. Augustine says: 'Perhaps there is no sin of ignorance and therefore no need for

---

[245] Lk 23: 34.   [246] 1 Tim 1: 13 [Douai].
[247] *In Reg. brevior., Regul.* 56; Lk 12: 48.
[248] *Orat. 3 de peccato.*

[348-9]

cleansing? But what is the meaning of: do not remember the sins of my youth, and my ignorances? Things knowingly committed are more harmful, but if there were no sin of ignorance we would not read what I have recalled: do not remember the sins of my youth, etc.'[249]

350. Granted that ignorance and darkness of mind, although not free of fault, reduce the evil of an act posited with an erroneous conscience, without entirely destroying the evil, in which part of the act is the evil diminished and in which does it remain entire?

We must first recall that a less than upright conscience presupposes 1. direct knowledge, which is the true norm of action, and 2. reflective, invented, willed knowledge which by overlaying the direct knowledge obscures it and constitutes an erroneous conscience. I concluded that this kind of conscience is not entirely sincere or well-founded, because contradicted by a principle in us that silently appeals against it. This vacillation of erroneous conscience, this lack of sincerity accompanied by the prompting of truth in the depths of our heart, varies in degree, and is seen and measured only by God. It is clear therefore that the amount of fault in an erroneous conscience is proportionate to its lack of sincerity, to the light emitted in the sinner's spirit by the truth he possesses interiorly, and to the vague or distinct, confused or sharp, disquiet it causes him.

351. Moreover, the extent to which ignorance reduces the sin of a particular act done with a less blameworthy erroneous conscience, can be determined only by distinguishing the cause in some way responsible for the ignorance. The cause can be threefold: 1. neglecting to reflect; 2. our own evil affections; 3. the authority or practice of others.

1. *Neglecting to reflect* and to apply the rational law so that a particular dictate is neither applied nor deduced from principles, does not necessarily produce an erroneous judgment in itself. It only brings about a false conclusion due to lack of data or means. Hence negligence to reflect is culpable to the extent it depends upon sluggishness of natural virtue, a given quantity of will, and perhaps previous evil

---

[249] *De peccat. merit.*, bk. 1, 36; Ps 24: 7 [Douai].

passions.[250] In this case these passions would also be sinful. It remains true, however, that where the terms of the judgment have been justly united, although some datum is lacking which causes the conclusion to be erroneous, the sin does not lie in the judgment but in its sinful cause or causes. Nor is there sin in any acts that depend on the judgment, because the immediate object presented to the will's desire by the essentially upright judgment is not intrinsically evil.

352. 2. The other two causes, *evil affection* and *authority* or *common custom*, not only render the conclusion erroneous but distort and harm the judgment itself.

St. Thomas clearly distinguishes and notes both causes: 'First, there are the most general precepts, known to everybody, which belong to the natural law. Then secondary, more particular precepts, which are proximate conclusions to the first. Relative to the general precepts, the natural law cannot in any way be extinguished in the hearts of human beings in general. But it can be obliterated in particular actions if reason is prevented by concupiscence or some other passion from applying the general principle to the particular action. Relative to the secondary precepts, the natural law can be cancelled in the hearts of human beings either by evil persuasions, in the same way as we have errors about necessary conclusions in speculative matters, or by depraved practices and corrupt habits, in so far as robbery and unnatural vices, for example, are not considered sins, as the Apostle tells us.'[251]

353. Amongst the affections which lead to sin, the desire for possessions undoubtedly blinds human beings more than anything else, and perverts their judgment. Scripture calls it 'the root of all evils.'[252] All the saints denounce it as the source of less than upright consciences. St. Bernardine of Siena says: 'Love of temporal things blinds conscience. Today many people think they can make usurious contracts, sell their time, and do similar things with a good conscience!'[253] The

---

[250] St. Thomas writes excellently about this point. I refer the reader to *S.T.*, I-II, q. 77, where he shows how the intellect can be bound and distracted by passion.

[251] *S.T.*, I-II, q. 94, art. 6.   [252] I Tim. 6: 10.

[253] Vol. 2 *Quadrag. post. Domin. palm.*, art. 1, c. 1.

capital sins are called the 'head' and source of other sins precisely because they blind us. Thus, erroneous consciences arising from sinful affections can be divided into seven groups corresponding to the seven capital sins.

354. 3. Authority and custom (the other source of less than upright erroneous consciences) give rise to idolatry, the best example of their evil consequences. Scripture says: 'In the process of time, wicked custom prevailing, this error was kept as a law; and statues were worshipped by the commandment of tyrants.'[254] Inveterate custom furtively insinuated serious error and non-upright consciences amongst the chosen people. So Christ said to the Apostles: 'The hour is coming when whoever kills you will think he is offering service to God.'[255]

Generally speaking, it is certain that, while the culpability of a false conscience increases in proportion to its dependence on depraved affections and previous sins, it decreases in so far as such conscience is influenced by the example and authority of others. For this reason, Christ prayed on the cross particularly for the people who had been deceived and blinded by the authority of the priests and scribes who had urged them to accomplish his death. To this prayer we must undoubtedly attribute the conversion of the many Jews who accepted the grace accompanying the Apostles' preaching.

355. However, if an evil conscience, influenced by authority, custom and example, concerns remote consequences of the rational law not rationally deduced but received solely from such authorities, it becomes, as I have said, a matter of positive law precisely because positively received without any willed error of judgment.

356. IV. But a cause of erroneous consciences exists in us from the beginning, prior to acquired, depraved affections and misleading authority. It is the inclination to evil that comes with original sin. We have already spoken about it but must refer to it again for the sake of good order in our study.

All human, moral evil can be said to begin with this evil tendency which, because it is placed in in us by corrupt nature and does not spring from freedom, can, granted God's goodness, contribute quite considerably to reducing the

[254] Wis 14: 16 [Douai].   [255] Jn 16: 2.

culpability and demerit of our transgressions. For example, in order to move God to compassion and mercy, Job reminds him of the innate misery of human beings conceived in sin;[256] the psalmist shows great confidence in the mercy of the Lord who knows 'our frame';[257] God himself indicates that he takes account of the inborn weakness of human nature when he says after the Flood: 'I will no more curse the earth for the sake of man: for the imagination and thought of man's heart are prone to evil from his youth: therefore I will no more destroy every living soul as I have done';[258] the book of Wisdom testifies that God mitigated the punishment deserved by the Canaanites because the principle of their perverted iniquity lay in their very seed.[259]

Nevertheless, God punishes. For although the natural inclination to evil diminishes the culpability of sin in so far as it diminishes freedom and clarity of understanding, and thus introduces something false into consciences, it does not entirely remove culpability, nor completely cleanse us of our transgressions. In particular cases, the nature and extent of the diminution of culpability is known only to God. But our obligation, as mortal human beings, is to continue, with the power of grace, to oppose and conquer the depraved inclination of our nature.

§13. Particular problems concerning our moral state when we follow a less than upright conscience

357. After the general discussion on the moral state of actions done with a less than upright conscience, we must

---

[256] Job 14.   [257] Ps 102: 14 [Douai].   [258] Gen 8: 21 [Douai].

[259] Here I must quote those fine words in the book of Wisdom which tell us how God punished the inhabitants of Canaan more gently than their actions merited: 'Yet even those you spared AS MEN, and sent wasps, forerunners of your host, to destroy them by little and little. Not that you were unable to bring the wicked under the just by war, or by cruel beasts, or with one rough word to destroy them at once: But executing your judgments by degrees you gave them place of repentance, not being ignorant that they were a wicked generation, and their MALICE NATURAL, and that their thought could never be changed. For it was a cursed seed from the beginning: neither did you for fear of any one give pardon to their sins' (Wis 12: 8–11 [Douai]).

[357]

consider the special accidental qualities that distinguish this state. We listed the principal accidents and their individual problems (cf. 259, 285–290), when we divided all possible erroneous consciences into two groups: those that judge evil good and those that judge good evil. We begin with the first group.

We noted the possibility of three accidental qualities, that is, we could judge what is unlawful

1. *lawful*,
2. *meritorious* or supererogatory (as well as lawful),
3. *obligatory*.

In order to examine the moral state of a person with these consciences we must distinguish two questions:

1. Is it a greater sin to judge an unlawful action *lawful*, or to judge it *meritorious*, or to judge it *obligatory*?
2. What is the different moral state of acts posited according to these three kinds of consciences?

358. Answers to the first question depend upon the certain principle that a fault is as great as the willed error (all things being equal). Consequently, to judge what is unlawful as meritorious and obligatory is more blameworthy than to judge it as simply lawful. For example, it is a more repulsive sin to judge that the divinity could be honoured by prostitution than to believe prostitution is simply lawful.

359. But determining the greater error of the other two judgments, that is, judging the unlawful as meritorious or obligatory, requires consideration of the circumstances, although to judge the unlawful *obligatory* seems of its nature more monstrous than to judge it *meritorious*. 'Meritorious' simply means pleasing to the divinity, whereas 'obligatory' means expressly willed by the divinity, and posits depravity in the concept of the divine nature.[260]

360. But we must judge differently the actions dependent on these consciences. Each action is the result of two acts and has therefore a twofold morality, so to speak. On the one hand, morality comes from the will *terminating in the erroneous conscience* (as we have said, this kind of morality is always to some degree blameworthy); on the other hand, morality

[260] The result is the same whether the depravity is measured according to the violation of the moral law or according to the injury done to God.

[358-60]

comes from the act of our will *terminating in an action* presented by a reflective, false conscience. This morality can vary. If the action is presented as lawful, the will, in so far as it desires what is lawful, neither sins nor merits; if the action is presented as obligatory, the will, in so far as it intends carrying out the law, can (in some way) merit, and merit considerably when the action is difficult, for example, suffering death or some great pain; if the action is presented as supererogatory, the will, when it genuinely desires and apprehends it as such, can (in some way) also merit relative to the action's difficulty. However, there is no merit in these two last cases unless the purpose is truly good and not influenced by a *capital* sin, and provided, therefore, that only *venial* sin, not *mortal sin*, is involved in the formation of the erroneous conscience. Masters of the spiritual life are speaking about this case when they say that even the holiest deeds are not always free from the veniality of false judgment in an erroneous conscience. The same could be said about imprudent zeal: the action may basically be good, despite the veniality of a false conscience urging a person to do more than is appropriate [*App*. no. 4].

361. We now have to consider what causes a less than upright conscience. The stimulus tempting us to deflect our judgment from the right path can, relative to each of the accidental qualities, be a disordered love of what is intrinsically *unlawful*, a disordered love of what is in itself *lawful*, or finally a disordered love of what is *good* and *meritorious*. These three cases of disordered love constitute three degrees of malice, of which the first is much greater than the second, and the second (all things being equal) greater than the third.

362. In the other class of erroneous consciences we judge as evil what is truly good. This judgment can be primarily due to *hatred of good* and to our effort to avoid doing good, granted the passions that enslave us. Here we must recall the nine differences in the first kind of conscience. Any good we wish to do is either lawful, or supererogatory, or obligatory. Malice in the last case is greater than in the other two, and greater in the second than in the first. Moreover each case can have one of three causes: a disordered love for an object that is blameworthy in itself, a disordered love for a lawful object, or a disordered love for an obligatory object. If we omit

disordered love for a lawful object, at least two differences remain, and therefore six cases in all, which are governed by the rules already stated.

363. At this point it will not be out of place to mention what seems to me a strange example of the subtleties which produce laxity in morals.

Certain authors, including Sanchez and Cardenas, ask whether 'a person who intends to commit a fault, fornication for example, but is unable to do so, is excused solely because he mistakenly believes that to intend evil is not sinful if the action does not take place.' They reply that he is more probably excused!

St. Alphonsus comments excellently on the matter: 'I have never considered this opinion probable. I could never understand how those who deliberately wish to do an action they know to be offensive to God could innocently believe that God is not offended by the genuine desire for an action known for certain to alienate a person from God. We may ask how such people sin formally by their desire if they do not know it is evil. They may not know that the internal act is evil, but they certainly know that the external act is. So how can they be excused from sin if they wish to carry out the external act? All human beings know by the light of nature that they are obliged to obey the Creator. If people therefore deliberately wish to carry out what they know is forbidden by God, they also know simultaneously and necessarily that they do evil. They may not sin *reflectively* because they believe that only the external act is a sin, but they sin *in effect* and in fact. They deny the obedience due to God while they are thinking of carrying out the sin.'[261]

We should also note St. Alphonsus' response to the assertion that many ordinary people do not confess evil desires because they think they sin only when performing the sin externally. He says: 'They deceive themselves when they believe they need not confess sins they have not fully carried out. A prudent confessor must judge that in willingly consenting to carry out a sin, they truly and formally sin, alienating themselves from God by their evil will.'[262] In this well-known passage the saint agrees that ordinary people deceive themselves when they believe their evil desire is

[261] *De Consc.*, c. 1, 9.   [262] *De Consc.*, c. 1, 9.

lawful. Nevertheless they sin. Although they have an erroneous conscience, which in itself would seem to be invincible, they have a second erroneous conscience concerning the external act. This conscience gives the lie to the first, which becomes a vincible conscience, as we have called it, although such consciences could perhaps be better described as *non-consciences* or disregardable consciences.

364. When the question is expressed in these terms, dissent amongst moral theologians probably concerns fact rather than theory because both parties admit that theoretically a person can sometimes have two consciences, one true, the other erroneous. Although considered in itself the erroneous conscience seems invincible, a true conscience renders it vincible. Opinion is in fact divided about the number of these cases, but this depends on how shrewdly we observe and discover these double consciences in the depths of the human heart. Unfortunately they seem to me very frequent.

365. Finally, the error of judging what is good as evil can also occur because of a scruple, and disturb peace of mind. I should therefore discuss the scrupulous conscience at this point, but will do so more conveniently at a later stage.

§14. Continuation

366. 'Must we follow an erroneous conscience concerning positive or positively received law, or concerning fact, when the error, although actually invincible, was free in its cause because of culpable failure to verify the law or fact? What is the moral state of an action done with this conscience?' This was our fourth question (cf. 259), and I think it has been sufficiently answered in what has been said. In fact, we saw:

1. that we should follow an erroneous conscience which does not involve an intrinsically evil action, when we cannot actually correct it or know it is erroneous, although it was caused by our neglect to instruct ourselves about the positive law or about a fact requiring the application of natural law;

2. that neglect to acquire necessary knowledge about our duties is culpable; but because the act of the will is

directed to a proximate object good or lawful in itself, an action done with this conscience has no added malice, if the action is not evil in itself;

3. that if we knew, or merely suspected, our conscience were false, we would no longer have a convinced, fully formed and completely safe conscience; our duty would be to abandon or correct it.

367. I will add an observation of some importance for necessary progress in virtue. Erroneous consciences concerning both rational and positive law are frequent in human beings. They are sometimes temporarily invincible, but can be overcome by means of unceasing, general effort. For example, I may not know at any given moment what particular erroneous conscience I have and cannot therefore free myself of it simply by a specific, direct act. But, generally speaking, I know that I probably have many such deceptive consciences. Hence, distrusting myself and with constant love of truth, I will be able, by a careful study of my duties, to free myself from them gradually.

368. We can therefore conclude:

1. There are erroneous consciences that are here and now *vincible*; they can and must be corrected immediately.

2. There are *invincible* erroneous consciences, which cannot be corrected because of the circumstances and the limitations of our reasoning.

3. Finally there are erroneous consciences that are here and now *invincible* but *vincible* by means of constant acts, by study, and by continual endeavour to know the truth; these must gradually be set aside, and their successive abandonment indicates the stages of spiritual and moral progress in our soul.

§15. Continuation: the degree of evil present in culpable ignorance concerning the positive law

369. There are two grades of evil in culpable ignorance about the positive law. They depend on the two kinds of ignorance distinguished by St. Thomas:

'Ignorance is *consequent* upon the will in so far as the

[367-9]

ignorance itself is willed. This happens in two ways . . . First, when the act of the will relates directly to the ignorance, for example, when someone wants to be ignorant in order to have an excuse for unbridled sin, as we read in Job:[263] "We do not desire the knowledge of thy ways." This is called *affected* ignorance. Second, when ignorance concerns something we can and must know.'[264] It is obvious that the first kind of ignorance is worse than the second.

370. The second kind of ignorance is twofold, as St. Thomas tells us immediately afterwards. We are ignorant of what we *ought* and *could* know either because we do not actually attend to what we are doing, or because, through our own neglect, we completely lack the necessary knowledge.[265]

St. Thomas says that we sin in this second case when we fail in our duty to instruct ourselves: 'The sin of ignorance is the same as other sins of omission, that is, we actually sin only at the time an affirmative precept obliges. A person who is ignorant does not sin actually all the time but only when he should acquire the knowledge he must have.'[266]

371. These words of St. Thomas confirm indirectly our own opinion. We maintain that when an action is evil not in itself but only because of the positive law prohibiting it, actual ignorance of the law, although culpable in its cause, does not make the act a new sin. According to Aquinas, the sin of ignorance is committed only when we could and should have instructed ourselves. Consequently if we are truly sorry for our ignorance and justified through confession, the ignorance is considered invincible, and our defects not imputable, even if it remains for a time (because it cannot be banished in an instant) and makes us liable to fall again. This is the common opinion of moral theologians.[267]

[263] 21: 14.

[264] *S.T.*, I-II, q. 6, art. 8.

[265] 'It is said to be this kind of ignorance either when a person does not actually consider what he can and must consider (this kind of ignorance is due to an evil choice, passion or habit), or when a person does not make the effort to acquire the necessary knowledge' (*S.T.*, I-II, q. 6, art. 8).

[266] *S.T.*, I-II, q. 76, art. 2, ad 5.

[267] Concina himself says: 'Personal, vincible and blameworthy ignorance is absolved with other sins by sincere repentance. In the justification of a sinner, known sins or evils cannot be wiped away without the absolution of

372. St. Thomas says of the sin of *inadvertence* in the application of the law, which is the first of the last two cases we distinguished: 'Defect in an upright judgment is a sin of lack of consideration in so far as we contemptuously disregard and neglect to attend to those things on which an upright judgment depends. Hence, lack of consideration is clearly a sin.'[268]

We must, however, note that such a case falls outside our present heading. It belongs rather to the preceding heading where we discussed the erroneous conscience coming from an error in the *rational application* of positive law. An *error* committed in applying the law does not depend solely on previous ignorance but on a true *distortion* of our judgment. Defect and sin are certainly present in this distortion.[269] Whenever we make an error of false judgment, the elements of truth are still in us, enabling us to emend the judgment. Thus, the actions that follow from such a false judgment, although innocent in themselves, cannot always be excused of new sin because the culpably mistaken judgment is renewed in each action.

sins of ignorance. Ignorance therefore remains in a justified Christian (if indeed it remains and there is no infusion of light together with the grace of justification) as a kind of penalty, just as ignorance due to original sin remains in those reborn. If ignorance remains after justification, it is neither sin nor a cause of sin, except material sin only, which is very different from formal sin. In this sense we say it changes from vincible to invincible ignorance' (*Lib. 2 de Consc.* Diss. 3, c. 2, q. 3).

[268] *S.T.*, II-II, q. 53, art. 4, concl.
[269] In the *Summa* (II-II, q. 54, art. 3) St. Thomas asks: 'Can *negligence* be a mortal sin?' He answers: 'Negligence is said to arise from a certain sluggishness of will, such that reason is not stimulated to perceive the things it should, or in the way it should. Hence, negligence can be a mortal sin in two ways. First, concerning what is neglected; if this were something necessary for salvation (whether an action or some circumstance), it would be mortal sin. Second, concerning the cause; if the will is sluggish regarding divine things so that it fails altogether in its love of God, the negligence is mortal sin. This is especially true when the negligence springs from contempt.' In this passage I note that St. Thomas posits two seeds or principles of the morality of actions: 1. the *action* itself, which is the intrinsically moral object; and 2. the *act of will*. This distinction is very important and we will use it often.

Article 4.
Summary of the division of erroneous conscience

373. Let us now summarise the division we have made of erroneous conscience as a further step to identifying its different kinds. The division is founded on the *action of the will* producing the conscience: if an erroneous conscience is produced by the will itself, it is sinful; if it is not produced by the will, there is no moral defect.

The will can cause an erroneous conscience either by *positing the cause* or by *erring* in forming the judgment constituting the conscience. The cause can be either *willed ignorance* or *disordered affections*.

In the case of positive law ignorance is sometimes willed, in two ways: either we do not wish to know the law expressly, or our negligence and indolence prevent us from learning it.

In the case of rational law ignorance can be involuntary relative to the remote consequences of the law, if we lack the necessary degree of intellective power to deduce them or are ignorant about a fact requiring the application of the law. However, ignorance can be willed in the same two ways as in positive law: by express decree of the will wishing to be ignorant 'in order not to do good', or through negligence. In the case of an express decree, the ignorance springs from a previous passion that gives us an aversion to law and truth.

When there is ignorance or invincible doubt about remote consequences of the rational law, and we have to act, we provide an ordinary norm for ourselves which, if followed in good faith, is not a true error and therefore does not involve any sin. This is an example of cases, to be discussed later, when we have not yet formed a conscience.

Sometimes, however, *passions* or *disordered affections* are the direct, willed cause of an erroneous conscience. They cause not only the ignorance which becomes the source of an erroneous conscience, but also and directly the erroneous conscience itself. They pervert and seduce the faculty of judgment, drawing it to make an unjust judgment. These passions, once present in the human spirit, become tyrannical masters of our faculties of judgment and reasoning and, although they vary, can be reduced to their ultimate genera in the seven capital sins.

[373]

374. In the language of divine scripture the different, disordered affections which distort our judgment are aptly called *spirits of error*,[270] in the way that inclinations and habits of behaviour are called *spirits*. Consciences resulting from these spirits of error are called *stained minds* or *stained consciences*.[271]

375. We must, however, take careful note of what has already been stated, namely, that the errors which the will, influenced by some passion, immediately commits in forming a new conscience, are very often venial rather than mortal sins. What we should note here is that all degrees of fault can be present, from the smallest and imperceptible to the greatest and most diabolical. Hence, the greatest circumspection is required for judging interior faults of this kind (cf. 341, 342).[272]

376. We also have to distinguish between an error committed fleetingly by a hasty judgment, and one dependent on the continual pressure in us of a dominating, disordered affection.

377. But a transitory hastiness of judgment can also be due to a disordered affection, which, although slight, may be sufficient to produce a habit of hasty judgment, resulting at times from physical causes and from the original harm suffered by human nature. Thus, if we watch children at play, dashing and dodging about, bumping into each other, tumbling on the ground, hitting their friends and tearing their clothing, then defending them and finally coming to blows, we can see that their ceaseless change of attitudes and gestures is not governed by reason. How is it possible that persons, endowed with reason, are so extraordinarily offended that the light and force of intelligence becomes almost completely incapable of directing them in an orderly way? On the other hand, animal instincts are disproportionately able to attract human activity and, so to speak, make it perform as they please. Just as the movements of the body are outside the reasoning control of the will, so the faculty of judgment itself is largely unbridled because of natural defect, and influenced

---

[270] 1 Tim 4: 1, 'giving heed to spirits of error' [Douai].

[271] 'Their mind and conscience are defiled' (Tit. 1: 15 [Douai]).

[272] St. Thomas himself teaches that 'sins consisting of interior acts are more likely to be hidden' (*S.T.*, II-II, q. 54, art. 3, ad 3).

[374-7]

in its conclusions by instinctive stimuli. This certainly diminishes, although it hardly removes entirely, the moral defect of the error.[273]

378. All these causes produce a conscience made erroneous either by judging as sinful what is not sinful (a *rigid* conscience), or by judging not sinful what is sinful (a *lax* conscience). The norms for judging the degree of moral defect in these two consciences and the presence of such defect can be determined from what has been said earlier.

379. Let me add an observation. It nearly always happens that those who have a rigid conscience about certain matters regarding positive law, are lax in conscience regarding the natural law. This was the case of the Pharisees, who were excessively severe in some positive rulings but very broad-minded on the substance of the law. The substance of law is the natural, immutable part, and people are mistakenly called *rigid* if they are lax in its regard.

380. Sometimes consciences broadly interpret both positive and rational law so that the only difference between these and the first kind of conscience is a broader, more coherent laxism relative to the rational law. Therefore all wrongly formed consciences are lax, and rigorism in cases like these exists at most only as a protective veneer.

381. I would call 'rigid' those whose rigidity is due 1. to their inability to deduce certain ultimate consequences of the law, which would mitigate their moral approach, or 2. to their ignorance of some factual circumstance of human nature, or 3. to a minor but morally defective mistake by which they persuade themselves that they please God more by their inclination to rigidity. This rigidity occurs in good people, who are not without some defect, and sometimes helps greatly to purify them; at other times the rigidity itself is subjectively true holiness.

382. Returning now to the *lax* consciences of people who seem rigid, or seem and are truly lax, I want to affirm that the names given these consciences (*somnolent, dull, cauterised,* or *pharasaical*) were suitable for designating the general state of the consciences but of little use in determining their malice.

---

[273] Cf. *AMS*, 727–744.

[378-82]

383. A *somnolent* conscience is negligent in learning the truth.

384. A *dull* conscience has difficulty in feeling remorse either because the person has a habit of vice, or is ready with subtle excuses, or judges vice lawful and good.

385. These two defects debase the *faculty of conscience* by impeding its development. The faculty is susceptible of progress and education. In fact, we see that in different human beings it has different levels of activity and alertness. But if the restricted development of the faculty does not depend on an evil will, it does not necessarily detract from our moral perfection.

386. Educated people, however, have a moral duty to educate their faculty of conscience; they must not allow it to grow worse and insensitive. Because they already act reflectively, they have a duty to know themselves and to guard their actions which, before being posited, must be weighed in the scales of justice and righteousness.

387. A *dull conscience* is not only *undeveloped*, negligent and *somnolent*; it is also one to which we pay no attention and from which we permit no disturbance despite remorse.

388. These defects of conscience are in contrast to the noble qualities of a keen and truly sensitive conscience, qualities acknowledged by common sense and splendidly illustrated by the author of the *Divine Comedy* where he exclaims in praise of his guide:

'O noble, delicate conscience,
How bitter your remorse for such a petty fault!'[274]

389. A *cauterised* conscience not only judges evil good in practice but makes a maxim of its error for teaching others.

390. Finally, a *pharasaical* conscience delights in teaching error, thinking itself *holy* because it practises this teaching, and *wise* because it teaches error to others. It thus despises other people of sound opinion and pure life, persecuting them and rashly condemning them.

391. Material error, which renders conscience erroneous but leaves it free of moral defect, is known by three names: *simply erroneous*, *perplexed*, and *scrupulous*. We have spoken

[274] *Purg.*, 3: 8, 9.

sufficiently about the simply and invincibly *erroneous* conscience.

392. A *perplexed* conscience is present when we believe we sin by following one of two opposite opinions. Analysis shows that this conscience is not simple but the result of many simultaneous consciences. These can co-exist in a person in the way that different levels of reflection co-exist. We noted, for example, that people who believe that they are obliged to tell a lie to save someone's life and at the same time sin by lying, believe they sin whichever action they follow. They have formed two judgments and so two consciences. With the first judgment, they say they sin by lying; with the second, they say it is sinful not to save a life when they can. They conclude that to save the person's life they are obliged to tell a lie. It is obvious that this second judgment is more reflective than the first, because the first belongs to a lower level of reflection than the second. But both judgments cannot be true; at most only one is true, the other false. To this false judgment we must apply all we have said about erroneous conscience in general.

393. I have said that at most only one of the two contrary judgments can be true. Both could be false if they concerned an action which was simply permitted, and involved no sin whether the action were done or not. This case of two erroneous consciences, one contrary to the other, co-existing in the same person, is rare, but can be solved easily by recourse in the first place to another's authority.

394. When one of the judgments is true, the perplexed conscience can be removed either through the *authority* of a spiritual director or through one's own individual study.

395. Here we can state a very helpful rule, known to sound philosophy: 'Error nearly always lies in the most reflective judgment; truth in the most direct, least reflective judgment.'

396. But not everyone can understand this rule or apply it. To such people we suggest:

    1. They check their certainty that sin is present on both sides of the difficulty. It can happen that they are certain of sin in one respect but feel less certain regarding the other. They should then avoid what they clearly see as sin.

2. If they are unable to decide in this way, and still seem to see certain sin in both cases, they should find out what law on both sides appears to oblige them under sin, and always avoid the possibility of sin against the rational law. If the rational law seems to be broken in both cases, they should investigate which of the two laws obliges more, and avoid the greater sin.[275]

3. But if both laws seem to oblige with equal strictness and force, they should prefer not to act or do anything new, so that if they are on the verge of doing the act, they should continue, and if they have not yet begun the act, they should refrain.

Nevertheless it is better, as I have said, to have recourse to another's counsel, if possible. Failing this, we should examine which of the consciences is more direct and less reflective, that is, which law obliges first and which second, and follow the first.

Article 5.
The scrupulous conscience

397. Finally we must speak about the scrupulous conscience. We will discuss it only briefly because many excellent authors, to whom we refer the reader, have treated the subject fully.

A scrupulous conscience is always at the third level of reflection at least, as follows:

1. The *practical judgment*, basis of morality, which belongs at least to first-level reflection;

2. The *first conscience*, which judges the morality of the practical judgment, and belongs to second-level reflection where scruples never occur;

3. The *scruple*, which is a judgment made about the goodness of the first conscience, and therefore belongs at least to third-level reflection.

398. A scruple is an error; if it were not an error, it would not be a scruple. But a *scruple* does not always form a *scrupulous conscience*. Sometimes it causes only a state of fear in the spirit without involving a true judgment or persuasion that

[275] *Decr. Grat.*, p. 1, dist. 13, c. 1.

the action is lawful or blameworthy. For this reason theologians normally discuss scruples when considering what they call *doubtful conscience*, which in fact is not conscience. Nor is a scruple a *doubt*; it is a *fear* that there is sin where there is none, a vain fear that arises in us without a sound reason.[276]

399. This *fear*, however, can sometimes produce a *persuasion* and judgment that certain or doubtful sin is present. If a firm persuasion arises that there is sin in an action, we must not act before relinquishing the persuasion. We must do the same if we are persuaded of the danger of formal sin, because in this case an *erroneous conscience*, called *scrupulous* from its cause, would be formed on the basis of the scruple.

400. Gerson, therefore, correctly distinguishes *scruple* from *conscience*, stating that we should respect conscience and despise scruples.[277] He says: 'Conscience is *formed* when after discussion and deliberation we finally judge definitively, and firmly establish that we must do or continue something, or not do it but avoid it. To act against a formed but erroneous conscience of this kind is sinful. But *fear* in conscience, or scruple, is present when our judgment after discussion and deliberation is not definitive, and does not establish what is to be done or continued, or not done and avoided. The mind vacillates, not knowing what is best nor what is more to be upheld. At the same time, there is no desire to omit what might be known to be pleasing to the divine will. It is not always sinful to act against this fear or scruple of conscience, although it may be a very dangerous fear which should be banished and eliminated as much as possible.'[278]

401. In my opinion, the *proximate* cause of scruples is always a disturbance in the *imagination* or at least a disturbance in the nerves. Philosophy demonstrates that 'there is a particular bond between mental images, feelings and reasonings', so that certain feelings or phantasms awaken particular ideas, reasonings and persuasions. This means that a physical

---

[276] Silvestro, under the word *scruple*, calls it *pusillanimity of spirit*.

[277] Clearly, Fagnani speaks very imprecisely when he says: 'A person who judges that something is probably lawful but also has a scruple that the opposite is true, acts contrary to the dictate of his conscience and sins' (*Dissert. de opinione probabili*, num. 246).

[278] *De natura et qualitate conscientiae*.

cure for a scrupulous person is very helpful, if carried out prudently and sensibly.

402. The *remote* causes of the nervous disturbance are one or more of the following:

1. The devil.

2. A physical principle, temperament, nervous stimuli, etc.

3. A moral principle, passions of our spirit, fears, etc.

4. Previous vices.

5. Images acquired in our imagination from books, stories, etc.

6. Evil habits, prejudices, resistance of mind, etc.

Each of these has to be opposed by contrary remedies.

403. An important observation, helpful for understanding the nature of scruples as an illness, is that the *fear* or apprehension called *scruples* concerns certain determined matters and not others, or at least only rarely. We would have to examine carefully the objects of *scrupulous fear*, because they could probably reveal the intimate pyschological nature of the illness. The matters most frequently involved regard:

I. The present:

a) fear of not making a proper *intention* in saying Mass, Office, or other prayers;

b) internal *consent*

1. in judging evil of one's neighbour, or

2. in matters of purity, or

3. faith.

II. The past (and this is more common): fear

a) of having given *consent*;

b) of not having said prayers of obligation or carried out other duties satisfactorily, and the desire to continually repeat them;

c) of not having made a good examination of conscience, confession, etc., and the desire to perpetually repeat these exercises;

d) of having incurred ecclesiastical censures.

404. A consideration of these matters, which are the most frequent in cases of scruples, gives the following results:

1. The scruple is nearly always about *internal* things.

2. It mostly concerns things *in the past*.

[402-4]

These two observations involve to some extent the imagination, which easily apprehends the *possibility* of evil and stimulates the consequent anxiety.

3. It springs from a will that wishes not only to do good but *to feel* that it has done good, and to attain certainty and satisfaction about the good it has done. This indicates some attachment to self, an intention that is not entirely pure, and a faith lacking in total abandonment to God.

4. There is always a fixation about certain determined things.

405. These observations indicate that the best remedies for scruples are:

1. Recreation and good, honest distraction so that the mind is obliged to move quickly through many disparate ideas and change its feelings often and rapidly.

2. Solid instruction that teaches scrupulous persons to rid themselves of the will to *feel* good before God. It is sufficient for them to be in a good state although they may not feel it, and to abandon themselves to God with complete confidence, that is, to the supremely good Lord who helps the weak and blesses the good desire even of those who do not achieve all they would like. We could add exercises in detachment, gradual humbling of oneself, etc.

3. Perfect obedience, as taught by all the masters. This demands submission of mind, something that is precisely contrary to the fixation of the scrupulous person, which makes obedience difficult.

3

DUTIES OF A SPIRITUAL DIRECTOR TOWARDS PENITENTS WITH FORMED CONSCIENCES

Article 1.

406. A spiritual director must always keep in mind the sublime purpose of his holy ministry. He must lead those he is directing 1. to purify themselves of all moral defects, and 2. to grow in Christian perfection. If they have a *true conscience*,

it is obvious that he must help them to conform their life completely to it. But what must he do in the case of an *erroneous conscience*? The answer to this question is the subject of this chapter.

407. No one doubts that a director must always speak the *truth*, but he must speak it *prudently*, and it is here that disagreement begins, because what is thought prudent by some, is not by others. Before discussing this problem, let us see in general what must be understood by speaking the truth *prudently*.

408. The prudence in question is obviously not restricted to purely human purposes or secondary interests. It would clearly be wrong for a confessor to take a prudentially softer approach in order to retain a penitent's goodwill or the material benefits dependent upon the favour of some powerful person. We are not dealing with worldly prudence and human aims, but with holy prudence whose purpose is the very end of priestly ministry, namely, the moral good, purification and greater perfection of the person under direction. Clearly the supreme rule of this priestly prudence is 'to speak words of truth and justice in such a way and to such an extent that what is said must be as profitable as possible to the hearer.' Catholic theologians do not dispute this, nor can they.

409. The problem therefore is to know 'how words of truth must be spoken to the penitent so that they are most advantageous to spiritual progress.' The best solution will determine the confessor's or director's *prudence*. However, this problem must be restricted for present purposes.

We are not concerned here with deciding the gentleness, firmness and diligence proper to a confessor. We wish only to investigate 'whether he must dispel any erroneous consciences a penitent may have, and whether he must always do this or can temporarily leave the penitent in error.' It is understood that the intention is always to help the penitent make greater progress in virtue.

410. Before undertaking the enquiry, we must first establish two certain principles.

First: 'When the penitent has sinned *formally*, the confessor must 1. consider the sin and above all judge it correctly before giving or denying absolution, as the case demands: here he acts as *judge*; 2. admonish the penitent about his sin, and instruct him if he does not know it, before giving absolution: here he acts as *teacher*; finally 3. correct him by making him see the gravity of his fault, exhorting him to repentance (with the imposition of relevant satisfaction), and suggesting means to avoid the sin: here he acts as *healer*.'

Second: 'When a penitent has sinned *materially*, the confessor must instruct him only in so far as it is helpful for the penitent's spiritual progress. In order to prevent material sin from becoming formal sin, the confessor must carefully avoid the danger of overburdening the penitent.'

411. These two principles, it seems to me, need no demonstration, and can be applied to our problem about *erroneous consciences* of which we have distinguished two kinds: those containing *formal sin*, and those without formal sin but containing so-called *material* sin, which is not sin.

The first principle must be applied to the first kind of conscience. Further action on the confessor's part must be guided by results. The second principle must be applied to the other kind of conscience. Here the confessor must follow the principle as his rule of conduct.

I think this is clear. But because the matter is important and delicate, many uncertainties can arise, calling for further clarification, which I will now try to present.

Article 2.

412. We have seen that *erroneous consciences* classed as formal sin (considered not in their cause but in themselves, in the judgment constituting them) are those which we form in opposition to the *moral dictate* in the depth of our spirit (direct knowledge) which declares an action unlawful. These consciences spring from irrelevant reflection, dependent either upon simple, hasty judgment[279] or upon disordered affection. They absolve us from sin by declaring as lawful

---

[279] In this case the sin is often light.

actions which we would certainly have considered unlawful if
we had applied upright, dispassionate judgment to them.

413. On the other hand, if the norm or *moral dictate*[280] is
lacking deep in our spirit, there is no formal sin in conscience
itself (although sin may have been present as the cause of the
conscience if our ignorance or lack of a dictate sprang from
negligence or aversion to justice). When forming conscience
in such a case, we have no norm to apply, and hence are not
free to form it in any other way.

414. The *dictate* is not normally lacking in rational law, but
sometimes we do not wish to apply it to a particular action
and use it to form an upright conscience.[281] Instead, we form a
conscience with other reflections and arbitrary principles
(bypassing the true dictate within us), because these give us a
conscience more in keeping with our passions. This is an
unjust, willed judgment, although not always adverted to
because of mental blindness, and hence formal sin. The same
can happen, although infrequently, in the case of positive
law, when we do not wish to apply the law rightly; we find
pretexts or vain reasons to excuse ourselves without any
remorse from its observation.

415. However, it can happen that the dictate is lacking even
in the case of the rational law, if we are dealing with remote

---

[280] This *moral dictate* does not mean any *dictate* whatsoever, but the
proximate dictate which, when present and applied, results in a perfect
conscience. Some moral *dictate* or formula is always present, but not
always the dictate that must be applied. For example, although a person
does not know that today is a fast day, he may certainly understand that we
must eat with sobriety, etc. However such a dictate is not sufficient for him
to form an entirely true conscience which in this case tells him that he must
also fast today, etc. We are speaking therefore of the absence of the dictate
or particular proximate formula which causes error in a conscience.

[281] This explains why we feel no remorse. St. Thomas, in his *Commentary on part two of the Sentences* (dist. 39, q. 3, art. 1, ad 3), explains the sin
of those who persecute the just, although they do not know or feel remorse
for their sin. One reason he gives amongst others is: 'Because those
deprived of the light of faith are blind, their synderesis does not reproach
them for things contrary to faith. Or else we must say that although
synderesis always reproaches evil in general, it does not reproach the
heretic in particular because of his error of reason in applying the universal
principle.' This is the synderesis or *dictate* which we do not apply because
we do not wish to apply it.

[413-5]

consequences of the law. If so, such ignorance may be a fault due either to simple neglect to draw the consequences or to passionate aversion to the law. Nevertheless the conscience itself cannot be at fault, because there was no dictate to be applied, and therefore no freedom to apply it.

416. We have said that 'when the dictate is present but not applied through defect of will, the resulting conscience contains a formal error which, however, is not always mortally sinful.' Consequently, actions which depend on this conscience are also sins; in each of them we posit a new act in which we neglect to apply, as we could and should, the true dictate present in us.

417. I have dealt with this matter in order to answer an objection that can easily arise. The objection is: theologians accept the principle that 'habits neither merit nor demerit.' If an habitual passion has already altered our understanding, and we have an erroneous conscience, the conscience does not apparently increase our demerit, because it is present in us in the same way as habits.

I first reply that when we fall into sin, we place ourselves in a *state* of sin, because our guilt remains as long as we do not obtain remission by a contrary act and opportune means. We cannot say that this state of sin demerits of course, but it is very different from and less harmful than that *state* of sin in which we are not only burdened with *guilt* but also with a *habit of sin* understood as an *inveterate affection and an habitual inclination of the will to renew the sin*. This state is much more blameworthy than the other, and we are certainly obliged to oppose immediately the inclination to which we explicitly consented. The malice of the state corresponds to the length of time we are content to rest in it because, during this time, we delay our opposition to the evil which we could and should oppose promptly and instantly; this is willed inaction, the equivalent of willed action.[282]

418. Secondly, even if living for a long time with a spirit disposed to sin did not (as it in fact does) increase the fault in proportion to the time we obstinately live with such an evil

---

[282] St. Thomas, too, recognises that inaction is willed and sinful when we have an obligation to act (*S.T.*, I-II, q. 6, art. 3, ad 3).

will, and the demerit did not increase as long as a habit[283] of this kind endures, it would be undeniable:

1. that guilt is present in the acts which gave rise to the stable propensity and habitual consent of the spirit to the sin;

2. that whenever, as a result of the habit or of the conscience produced by the habit, another action is posited, demerit is attached to this action, both because it is an act and not a habit, and because the just dictate is once again rejected and error acknowledged in its place.

419. As *judge*, a confessor must obviously assess all the formal sins of his penitent. He must therefore take into account any sins due to false consciences in order to decide whether the penitent merits sacramental absolution, and in order to impose fitting satisfaction.

420. As *teacher*, the confessor must of course admonish the penitent about all formal sins and remove culpably erroneous consciences. However he may doubt whether he can lawfully defer a clear explanation of the penitent's serious, formal sin. In fact, before receiving *absolution*, a penitent must be instructed about any formal, grave sin of which he is ignorant through blindess, and must show clear signs of sorrow. Thus, the confessor may have to defer absolution if he sees the penitent is so badly disposed that he cannot obtain any profit from the truth, especially if the truth were to give occasion for greater evil. In this case charity and prudence allow the confessor to continue the instruction over a period, provided absolution is withheld until the instruction is finished and the penitent has fully acknowledged and repented of his formal sins.[284]

---

[283] 'Habit' implies two things:

1. Something exists in us, preserved within as it were, without actuating our activity. Thoughts which do not actually occupy our attention exist in this way in our memory as *a habit of memory*. The guilt of a sin whose object we no longer think about and which we have perhaps completely forgotten, remains with us in the same way.

2. Some inclination we possess as an incipient action and as a principle of other actions. This inclination can be *habitually consented to* by the guilty will. In this case our sin is continuous.

[284] There can also be the rare case where the prudence of the Christian teacher is guided by the words of Christ: 'Do not give dogs what is holy; and do not throw your pearls before swine' (Mt 7: 6). In this way the

421. Finally, as *healer*, the confessor must give the penitent every help to eradicate these truly fatal consciences. Such assistance will bring him to see his profound illness and the need to eradicate it. If the consciences are embedded in him as they were in the Pharisees, the confessor must bear in mind he is not only a healer but also a surgeon. His strength lies in acting as a priest, the sublime duty of those constituted on the earth as ministers of God and sent by Jesus Christ. He must use the freedom and power of speech that Jesus Christ used when he rebuked the Pharisees. At the same time he must employ all prudence in avoiding rash judgments, and in distinguishing one disease from another. Only extreme cases demand extreme remedies.

Article 3.

422. If, however, the dictate to be applied is lacking in the penitent so that his conscience is *erroneous* through simple ignorance, not evil judgment, no fault is present in the conscience or in actions dependent on it. At most, fault is present in the *cause*, which may depend upon negligence in instructing oneself, or aversion to the law and to the virtue consequent upon the law.

The confessor must investigate these causes. Since there is no aversion to good, he will find that ignorance arising from *simple negligence* depends on *indifference* or *lack of necessary affection*. In this case he must distinguish wisely whether this absence of sufficient affection is due to *simple-mindedness*, as in the case of the uneducated who do not reflect on the importance of moral good and live naturally according to the impression made by sensible things. *Tepidity*, which is much more serious and often conceals its roots in the depths of our

teacher imitates the wisdom and goodness of God who hides many of his mysteries from idolaters. When St. Augustine speaks of the economy of divine providence towards the Gentiles, he says: 'When Christ knew the early world to be full of such unfaithful people, why should we be surprised that he justly did not want to appear and preach to them; he already knew they would not believe his words and miracles?' (*Ep.* 102, 14). Nevertheless, we must not entirely despair of the conversion of the sinner; we must use all the charity we can towards him.

heart, is another cause of insufficient affection. Tepidity can also result from the moral inertia and insensitivity we inherit at birth in common with other evils. The confessor must instruct the *simple-minded* and give them the desire to learn; he must *rouse* the *tepid* from their sleep.

423. But in particular he must not lose sight of anything concerning the rational law which, by coinciding in great part with the divine law, is raised to a level more sublime than natural law.[285] The confessor must provide much more instruction about the rational law than about positive law with due regard, however, for the abilities of his penitents. Indeed instruction about the positive law can sometimes offer the best way to instruction in the rational law, and this is possibly its most important function. Consequently instruction must often begin from the positive part of law but in such a way that everything is finally directed to the rational and eternal in moral law, which is then confirmed and completed by divine positive law. Usually, this is precisely what is neglected.

We have mentioned that necessary, simple instruction enabling the penitent to avoid material sins can in part be deferred till after absolution. The instruction should be given gradually, with prudence as the guide to what promotes the penitent's true good, that is, *moral* not *intellective* good.

424. Here I must make an observation. Anyone who considers the matter carefully will see that inculpable, natural and *intellective limitations* are the foundation of *different spirits* and of the division of graces which God grants in so many different ways. Although the love of good is *one* in all the saints, the practical, proximate concepts of this good differ. Thus the same love is divided and takes on many different forms and, as it were, different colours. The confessor must take careful note of this so that he can distinguish the

---

[285] Christ will judge the world according to rational, divine law, whose dictate, as the law of charity, is present in everybody (Mt 25: 31–45). The confessor must therefore encourage in everyone *charity towards our neighbour*. Origen rightly says: 'We must not be surprised that God has placed in the spirit of all mortal beings the seeds of those things which he taught through the Prophets and the Saviour. In the light of divine judgment, therefore, they are inexcusable, because the mandate of the law is written in their hearts' (bk. 1, *Contr. Cels.*).

[423-4]

intellective limitation, which harms the progress of good and must be gradually removed, from the *limitation* which is of assistance and perhaps natural to us. This last kind of limitation is impossible or at least difficult to remove, for it is sanctified by God himself by means of *good will* which nourishes itself on, and derives merit from, the limitation.

425. But the source of the ignorance can be *aversion* to good from which a passionate spirit, distracted by temporal good, flees. The confessor must prudently reveal this evil cause to the penitent (as we mentioned in the case of a culpably erroneous conscience), and he must require proof of change.

As we said, however, this must be done wisely. The confessor must not invent a cause; it is not for him to penetrate the closed doors of the penitent's heart. He has a sacred duty to presume well of his penitent and, in judging the cause, depend upon external indications which give him moral certainty or great probability about it. As long as he is doubtful, he must be content to investigate and examine the spirit of the penitent by relevant and wise questions. If he does not find any logical reasons for certainty or positive doubt, he must pronounce in favour of the penitent.

Article 4.

426. In order to know better the importance of destroying the false consciences which passions furtively introduce into our hearts, we must consider:

1. that an upright conscience is the first means to virtue;

2. that all vices come from a non-upright conscience, just as all virtues originate from an upright conscience.

427. Hence, there is nothing which scripture inculcates and recommends more than an upright, sincere conscience, a conscience that is not sly and deceitful. We read in Joshua: 'Now therefore fear the Lord, and serve him with a PERFECT and MOST SINCERE heart,'[286] that is, with an upright conscience. St. Paul says: 'Once you were darkness, but now you

[286] Josh 24: [14, Douai].

are light in the Lord.'[287] What is this *light* that Christians are, if not the formed, upright conscience that was absent before the Lord shone in their souls? There is a light that is in the human being, and a light that is the human being: the light in the human being is grace and the law of truth; the light that is the human being is an upright conscience. Indeed, we become light when we share in the light of the law of truth by means of an upright conscience in conformity with the light. The Apostle continues: 'Walk then as children of the light', that is, according to the upright conscience which makes us children of the light. With an upright conscience we ourselves take on the nature of light, participating in the truth which is already light. What will happen if we walk according to an upright conscience? We will acquire virtue, says the Apostle: 'The fruit of the light is in all goodness, and justice and truth.' A little further on he insists again: 'See, therefore, brethren, how you walk circumspectly: not as *unwise* but as *wise*.' The 'wise' are those who, by judging their own actions in the right way, have an upright conscience, the 'unwise' those who judge contrariwise and so form a less than upright conscience. Again he says: 'Become not *unwise*: but *understanding* what is the will of God.'[288] The will of God is not understood by our erroneous conscience, which conceals his will from us. According to St. Paul uprightness of conscience, the root of all virtues, is so important that it is the first thing to be attended to by anyone who wishes to make progress in virtue: 'For the fruit of the light is in all goodness, and justice and truth.'

428. Just as an upright conscience brings with it the fruit of all virtues, so a willed erroneous conscience blinds us, depriving us of all virtues. St. Peter says that those people are blind and groping[289] who do not 'minister in their faith, virtue: and in virtue, knowledge: and in knowledge, abstinence: and in abstinence, patience: and in patience, godliness, and in godliness, love of brotherhood, and in love of brotherhood, charity.'[290] *To minister virtue in faith* means to exercise virtue

[287] Eph 5: [8].   [288] Eph 5: [9, 15, 17 Douai].
[289] 'For he that does not have these things with him is blind and groping' (2 Pet 1: [9, Douai]).
[290] 2 Pet 1: 5–7 [Douai].

as a result of the light of faith, through which we form upright consciences. Consequently, those without this light of faith to make judgments about things cannot form an upright conscience. They stagger about blindly, incapable of being helped by the virtues which accompany the clear vision of an upright, truthful conscience. Thus, when the prophet David ceaselessly cries to the Lord: 'Take away the veil from my eyes', 'Give me understanding', 'Teach me thy justifications',[291] he is asking for a pure, enlightened conscience free from darkness and stubbornness.[292]

We can understand, therefore, that an enlightened confessor must above all dispel the darkness of such false, malicious consciences, which prevent all progress; virtue must be firmly founded on uprightness of consciences.

Article 5.

429. I must now digress to discuss the way God educated the human race in virtue. The digression is not irrelevant because I want to offer the spiritual director God's own example and most wise providence which truly does everything for the salvation of all. Confessors must regard this providence as a true, sublime teacher. They, and all spiritual directors, should look upon it as their pattern for imitation.

After Adam's fault, or after the Flood, human beings formed *erroneous consciences* and thus justified their sin. Sinning is the first step; persuading oneself that evil is good is found as human wickedness develops.

The book of Wisdom tells us that as time passed *idolatry* became custom and finally law, so that not to be an idolater was considered a crime against society (cf. 354).[293] The abominable, unnatural practices of the Canaanites and

---

[291] Ps 118 [18, 34, 26 Douai].

[292] St. Thomas says that one meaning given to the words 'blindness' and 'stubbornness' in scripture 'is the action of the human spirit adhering to evil in opposition to divine light' (*S.T.*, I-II, q. 79, art. 3).

[293] '. . . and he now honoured as a god what was once a dead human being, and handed on to his dependents secret rites and initiations. Then the ungodly custom, grown strong with time, was kept as a law, and at the command of monarchs graven images were worshipped' (Wis 14: 15, 16).

[429]

Egyptians passed into custom, habit and law. Leviticus calls them *their statutes*.[294] Little by little fornication first became lawful,[295] then virtuous, then meritorious and finally sacred and divine.[296] In some places a cleverly devised theft was considered worthy of reward,[297] and was divinised. Murder became a boastful game; vendettas were lawful and praised. Subduing others and lording it over them was thought the greatest of ventures. All these false consciences threw the world into an abyss in which, with all ideas swept away, it could only submerge itself in ever greater darkness. A light from heaven was necessary to dispel these consciences; hence the reason and origin of God's positive promulgation on Sinai of the rational law. This law, implanted in the human spirit, was in danger of being darkened. St. Ambrose says: 'If human beings had been able to preserve the natural law infused in them by God, the law would not have been necessary. The law, written on tablets of stone, bound and restricted human infirmity rather than release and free it.'[298] The Mosaic law was given to human beings, whose minds had been darkened by passions, not so much to help them do good as to know good. It was given not because *direct knowledge* of virtue was absent in the world but because this knowledge no longer became *conscience* for guiding actions. It lay in the depths of the unenlightened heart, badly received, unacknowledged, and unapplied to life's actions.

430. The Mosaic law rectified many opinions and consciences that were either false or becoming irremediably false. But how long did these consciences, rectified and maintained by the new and clearly visible light, endure in their uprightness? If we examine the history of the Hebrew people and of

---

[294] 'You shall not do as they do in the land of Egypt, where you dwelt, and you shall not do as they do in the land of Canaan, to which I am bringing you. You shall not walk in THEIR STATUTES' (Lev 18: 3).

[295] St. Thomas observes: 'Amongst the pagans, fornication was not considered unlawful because of the corruption of natural reason' (*S.T.*, II-II, q. 154, art. 2, ad 1).

[296] The existence of temple prostitution and obscene divinities is well known. Cf. *Frammenti d'una Storia dell' Empietà*, Giuditta Pogliani, publishers, 1834.

[297] Amongst the Spartans.

[298] Ep. 41, *ad Iren.*, n. 1 (in the Paris edition, 1836, Ep. 74).

their malice, we see that with the Mosaic law a new period of wickedness begins which ends with the time of Christ.

By the time of Christ, human malice, which continually advanced even amongst the Hebrew people, was extreme. It had found every means to abuse the law and dim the new light added by God to the light of natural reason. Every erroneous conscience, whether dull, cauterised or pharasaical, had surfaced; erroneous consciences had become erroneous *opinions* which were then formed into *theories*. Jesus Christ wonderfully describes the customs of his time when he says to the crowds gathered around him: 'This generation is an evil generation.' He attacks all his generation, showing how the falsification of consciences had become universal: 'It asks a sign, and a sign shall not be given it, but the sign of Jonah the prophet.' He then indicates the blindness of minds incapable of acknowledging him as Messiah. They could have known him, for he had given them the clearest proofs of his mission, but they did not wish to acknowledge him. 'The queen of the south will rise in the judgment with the men of this genera-tion and shall condemn them: because she came from the ends of the earth to hear the wisdom of Solomon. And behold more than Solomon here. The men of Nineveh shall rise in the judgment with this generation and condemn it; because they did penance at the preaching of Jonah. And behold more than Jonah here.'[299] He condemned them because they behaved like people hiding a light under a bushel, as the Hebrews did with the resplendent light of Christ. They turned their mental gaze elsewhere so as not to see what they hated and did not wish to see. By willing the darkness they hoped to quell the remorse that would have disturbed them so much.

When the world had once again reached this state, Christ was sent upon the earth to rectify erroneous consciences, and to pronounce as foolishness everything the world believed it knew, although its knowledge was nothing more than self-made deception. In this way Christ fulfilled the prophecy of Isaiah: 'And the Lord said: Forasmuch as this people draw near me with their mouth, and with their lips glorify me, but

---

[299] Lk 11: 29, 31, 32 [Douai].

their heart is far from me, and they have feared me with the commandment and doctrines of men: Therefore, behold I will proceed to cause an admiration in this people, by a great and wonderful miracle: for wisdom shall perish from their wise men, and the understanding of their prudent men shall be hid. Woe to you that are deep of heart, to hide your counsel from the Lord.'[300]

People who have formed false consciences are appropriately called *deep of heart* because in the depth of their hearts lies the truth (the norm of uprightness) which they never allow to come to the surface; they bury it under false applications and false judgments. Instead of acknowledging the truth, they affirm the opposite of what it tells them. They are *deep of heart* because their heart is difficult to penetrate; deep in their heart lie iniquity and evil. They reshape the truth with learned opinions, under the pretext of devout, honest excuses. This allows them to avoid knowledge of themselves and to consider themselves just, although they are full of iniquity and deceit. Such was the state of the Hebrews at the time of Christ; they thought they could deceive the Lord and hide from the one from whom nothing is hidden: 'So that you may hide your thoughts from the Lord.'

Humanity could not recover from such an unhappy state with the aid of rational law, nor through the addition of positive law. It had learnt all too well how to abuse both laws, interpreting and applying them to avoid their force and worth. But it was fitting that new help be given, Christ himself, who revealed false judgments, destroyed the cavilling by which people drew a thick veil over their consciences, and demonstrated with the marvellous light of his grace the foolishness of the wise, according to the prophecy: 'For wisdom shall perish from their wise men, and the understanding of their prudent men shall be hid.'

431. This economy exercised by God towards humanity must also be followed by the confessor as minister of Christ. With the light of the law and the unction of the word of grace he must enlighten darkened consciences, where human wickedness continually tries to hide.

---

[300] Is 29: [13–15, Douai].

Article 6.

432. Because the formation of false consciences is subject to the law of progress, we will conclude this chapter with an observation relevant to this law.

The first stage of human corruption was from Adam's sin to the Flood. This *corruption of the external sense* came to an end at the Flood.

The period from the Flood to Abraham comprised the *corruption of the imagination*, of which idolatry was a product. The remedy against this very extensive evil was Abraham's call to save one people from such an incurable disease.

The period from the call of Abraham to Moses was a time of darkness in regard to the natural law, and the first period of the *corruption of reason* (false consciences). The remedy was the new light of the Mosaic law, which is substantially the positive promulgation and declaration of the natural law.

The period from the Mosaic law to the Messiah, a time of darkness in regard to the positive law, was the *second period of the corruption of reason* (false consciences sank lower). Only a supernatural power could remedy this, Christ, the divine Word, and light that enlightens all things, 'and pierces to the division of soul and spirit' [Heb 4: 12].[301]

433. What we see happening in the case of natural and divine legislation as a whole, constantly occurs in particular legislation. For example, as soon as civil law is promulgated,

---

[301] According to divine scripture, God's greatest punishment for human perversity lies in abandoning it to its own blindness. Nothing is more fearsome than Isaiah's prophecy about the Hebrews (29: [10–12]): 'For the Lord has poured out upon you a spirit of deep sleep, and has closed your eyes, the prophets, and covered your heads, the seers. And the vision of all this has become to you like the words of a book that is sealed. When men give it to one who can read, saying, "Read this," he says, "I cannot, for it is sealed." And when they give the book to one who cannot read, saying, "Read this," he says, "I cannot read."' The natural law is a sealed book for evil fabricators of false consciences. If the positive law opens it before them, they do not read because they cannot. Those who are masters in cavilling about the law (theologians should take note) are called by Isaiah 'all who watch to do evil . . ., who by a word make a man out to be an offender' (29: [20, 21]). They *watch* not in order to know the truth, but to know evil. This vigilance is not Christ's but the devil's, for the devil also watches.

the principle of evil seeks to evade it and to interpret and apply it evilly. This continues until the law is rendered useless through false interpretations and artificial decisions clothed in sophisms. This is the meaning of the popular saying: 'A law enacted is evil invented'. Hence the continual need for new written laws and new declarations of old laws, producing an immense volume of legislation, impossible for the human mind to hold.

434. The same observations can be made about legislation in every lesser society. They explain in a wonderful way the decline of religious orders, or at least the different stages of their decline. The holy founders understood their laws to have a sublime power, which was the light of gospel perfection. As time passed, the light was lost. Succeeding generations religiously and carefully retained the same material words of the law, but no longer sought the deep, moral sense given them by the first members, for whom the words, which had been full of fire, were now insipid, ordinary, and troublesome. The words had truly changed their meaning, and the obligation of the rule was now understood differently. Insensibly, the point had been reached where the perfection contained in the noble rule came to be ignored, and, in fact, the contrary of what was expressly found in the rule became the practice. And this happened unnoticed. Perhaps, in the examination of conscience at the end of the day, the religious found nothing with which to accuse himself, because he understood the written rule in the way he saw it carried out or it had been explained to him. Thus, the laws that were divine in origin became, as Isaiah and Christ say, 'doctrines and commandments of men.'[302]

435. An enlightened confessor must bear all these considerations in mind so that his penitents do not remain in the darkness of their own ignorance and malice. Leaving them to

[302] In Isaiah (29: [13]) God says: 'Their fear of me is a commandment of men learned by rote.' He says they feared him, as required by the *divine law*, but they did not fear him by means of this law. They had preserved only the material part of the divine law, which had become truly human law and custom. They feared God because human beings told them they should, and because that was common practice. 'In vain do they worship me,' says Jesus, applying the prophecy to his time, 'teaching as doctrines the precepts of men' (Mt 15: [9]).

sleep peacefully in such darkness means destroying them. He would not be encouraging *virtue* but a false *peace*; he would imitate and minister to Satan, not God and Christ. The solemn words written in the book of Ezekiel are very apposite: 'If I say to the wicked, "You shall surely die," and you give him no warning, nor speak to warn the wicked from his wicked way, in order to save his life, that wicked man shall die in his iniquity; but his blood I will require at your hand. But if you warn the wicked, and he does not turn from his wickedness, or from his wicked way, he shall die in his iniquity; but you will have saved your life. Nevertheless if you warn the righteous man not to sin, and he does not sin, he shall surely live, because he took warning; and you will have saved your life.'[303]

Confessors should consider all these words, and from them learn how much discretion and holy freedom they require in their divine ministry.

4

SOME MEANS FOR PURIFYING OURSELVES
FROM FALSE CONSCIENCES

Article 1.
Means

436. Our need for purification from inadvertent but willed, erroneous consciences is extreme. It will not seem irrelevant, therefore, to indicate the principal means for obtaining such purification. We must free ourselves from evil consciences which would cause us to lose our souls; at the same time, we have to endeavour to cleanse ourselves day by day from false consciences that defile us lightly. The few means that we suggest here will help both those who love virtue and apply the means on their own account, and confessors and spiritual directors whose duty it is to encourage holiness in those entrusted to them by Providence.

[303] Ezek 3: [18, 19, 21].

I

437. The first means is *a sincere desire for good and truth*. We must desire not to deceive ourselves, and go even further by uncovering all our self-deceit. We need to be fully persuaded that *love of truth* is the first, most universal kind of precept, and the source of all others. The spiritual director is therefore obliged to encourage the love of truth in those whom he directs. Whatever the cost, they must want to acknowledge truth practically, that is, to love and desire moral good.[304]

II

438. The second means is to encourage *a reasonable, salutary fear of perhaps not possessing or of losing the treasure that is moral good*. This fear is neither salutary nor holy unless preceded by love of moral good. Only when moral good is looked upon as a priceless treasure which we are afraid of losing can our fear be qualified as salutary and holy. For this reason, love of moral good as a condition for just, salutary fear is given priority amongst the means we are outlining.

439. A fear of losing *one's own happiness*, not *moral good*, would not be holy but only a disposition for holy fear. Fear of punishment can make us resolve to love virtue; love of virtue is succeeded by a holy fear of either not acquiring or of losing virtue. In this way, love of virtue stands between two fears: on the one hand lies fear which, although not yet holy, is often the first cause of virtue; on the other, holy fear, which is the effect of virtue.

440. In order to stimulate this holy fear in souls that love good as their true and only treasure, we can use the admirable

[304] St. Augustine offers a wonderful witness to teachers of Christian doctrine when he urges them to form right intention in their disciples by directing their aim towards *charity* in general, which is indeed moral good: 'In everything we have to keep in mind not only the end of the precept, that is, charity issuing from a pure heart and a good conscience and sincere faith, to which we refer all that we say, but also the end of the person whom we instruct. What we say should move and direct him to the end' (*De catechiz. rudibus*, c. 3, 6).

[437-40]

advice of Cardinal Bellarmine, a great theologian of the Society of Jesus. He says: 'It is very easy for an erroneous conscience to be occasioned by the example of others so that, WITHOUT ANY WARNING FROM CONSCIENCE (that is, without advertence), we descend whither the worm does not die and the fire is not exstinguished.'[305] If we know that culpable, false consciences easily lie hidden in us, we will be encouraged to open our eyes and by scrutinising our hearts discover if any unknown enemy has entered.

441. Our salutary fear will be strengthened if we remember that according to uncontroverted theological teaching no one without a special revelation is absolutely certain of being in God's grace. We may also consider that scripture calls God's judgments *unsearchable*[306] and very different from human judgments.[307] If God's judgments are so different from ours about the morality of actions, it is clear that he will correct our false consciences.

III

442. The third means is *careful search for the truth, and self-examination*. This is a consequence of holy fear.

St. Augustine reproves three classes of ignorant people: those who 1. believe they know, but do not; 2. know they do not know, but take no effective steps towards dispelling their ignorance; 3. know they do not know, and have no desire to take any steps towards dispelling their ignorance.[308]

443. We need to be convinced of the precept obliging us to seek moral truth, that is, our moral duties, and to seek it in the right way. In the old law, sacrifices for sins of ignorance existed to expiate the fault of those failing to observe this

---

[305] *Ep. ad nepotem suum Episc. Them.*

[306] Rom 11: [33].

[307] St. Gregory the Great takes as an example of the difference between our judgment and that of God the sentence God passes on Job and his friends — a sentence which could appear unjust: 'Lord, your decision shows how much our blindness is at odds with the light of your uprightness' (*Moral.* bk. 35, c. 7).

[308] *Liber de util. cred*, 11.

precept.[309] And St. Paul's forceful words apply here: 'If anyone does not recognise this, he is not recognised.'[310] From these words St. Thomas argues that mortal sin can indeed exist under the cloak of ignorance itself. Otherwise St. Paul would not have spoken so strongly.

444. St. John Chrysostom comments at length on the care and vigilance needed in searching for moral truth. 'This life is a stadium, and we need to be able to look in all directions. We must not imagine ourselves excused through ignorance. The time will come when our ignorance will be punished without pardon. The Jews lacked knowledge, but their ignorance did not gain them remission; the Gentiles lacked knowledge, but this was not an excuse.'[311]

445. He goes on to object: 'But how could God reject the sincere, upright Gentile?', and answers: 'First, we cannot know if a person is sincere. Only God who forms each heart individually knows that. And we have to remember that we are often careless and negligent . . . But, you will say, how can that be the case if we are upright? . . . Take a good look at the person you call simple and sincere, and see how he acts in worldly matters. Notice how careful he is about them. Now, if he put the same kind of care into spiritual affairs, there would of course be no trace of neglect. What concerns the truth is brighter than the sun, and wherever we go we can easily take care of our salvation if we want to give it due attention and treat it seriously.'[312] He goes on to show that, however simple and uneducated we may be, we are careful enough in human affairs. This, he says, serves only to

[309] Lev 5: 17, 18. 'If anyone sins though he does not know it . . . he shall bring a ram without blemish'; and 4: 27, 28, 'If any one of the common people sins unwittingly . . . he shall bring for his offering a goat, a female without blemish'; and Num 15: 27, 28, 'If one person sins unwittingly, he shall offer a female goat for a sin offering, and the priest shall make atonement for him.'

[310] An ancient writer comments on the precept of knowledge: 'Although doing the will of God is greater than knowing it, knowing it comes before doing it. This is clearly the order of precedence. As the prophet says: "And you, Israel, be not ignorant," and St. Paul: "If anyone does not recognise this, he is not recognised." And again elsewhere: "Therefore do not be foolish, but understand what the will of the Lord is"' (*Ep. ad Demetriad.*).

[311] Hom. 26, in *Ep. ad Rom.*, n. 3.

[312] Hom. 26, in *Ep. ad Rom.*, n. 3.

condemn us because it throws light on how little we value
heavenly things compared with earthly.

IV

446. The fourth means for rendering the soul free and
sincere in its search for moral truth is *to avoid everything that
can cause prejudice in us* and as a result lessen our impartiality.

447. Prejudices are often inherent in moral bodies. They
consist of judgments or opinions received blindly on the
authority of the societies in which we live. Such prejudices
often form part of opinions called in scripture 'human teaching and commandments.'

448. The golden rule for avoiding this pitfall on the road to
full, unblemished virtue is found in St. Augustine's words,
which can never be sufficiently insisted upon: 'Unity in what
is necessary, freedom in what is doubtful, charity in all
things.'

This rule does not prevent our holding our own views, nor
defending them forcefully, nor demonstrating the blameworthy effects of opposite opinions. This can all be done,
provided we do it logically, not rashly. In other words, it
must not be done from self-love, nor from blind attachment
to a group professing such an opinion when equally respectable groups profess the contrary. Holding firm opinions is
wholly pertinent to individuals, but never to moral bodies
unless they are made up of members who hold those opinions
as individuals and not as members of a body.

449. It is clear, therefore, that I cannot be happy with the
oaths taken to uphold doctrines not defined by the Church in
certain religious bodies, or in centres of study before a doctor-
ate is granted. I consider all these oaths as rash judgments
doing violence to the truth. Those who make them either lack
sufficient reason for unshakeable belief in the teachings they
swear to, or have reasons against these teachings, or finally
see reasons showing that these teachings, affirmed on oath,
are completely true. In the first case, those taking the oath
solemnly affirm that what they are told by fallible, incompet-
ent authority is unshakeably true; in the second case, they

swear to uphold as true what they do not recognise as true, that is, they take an oath against their own persuasion. Finally, although the teachings in question are known to be true, those taking the oath cannot be sure that they themselves will always retain their certainty, or whether after further reflection they may not arrive at conclusions opposite to those which now appear true to them.

In all these cases, such oaths are impossible. Swearing to uphold for the whole of one's life opinions not defined by the Church means swearing to something which clearly cannot be maintained with certainty. In other words, those who take the oath either presume too much on their own account or on account of the body to which they belong, as though their own certainty or that of their group-authority were capable of continually providing a firm, immovable foundation for undefined matters. The custom of swearing 'on the word of the teacher' often produces situations in which persons belonging to different moral bodies swear to uphold different teachings and opinions, some of which, because of their mutual opposition, are inevitably false.

We can only conclude that the Church is extremely wise in maintaining and defending freedom of opinion in all Catholic schools, and in disapproving those who want to censure the opinions of others. In acting like this, the Church is assisting both in the progress and conservation of truth.

I know I shall hear it said: 'The custom of affirming certain teachings on oath has held in check dangerous tendencies in clever people, and kept moral bodies within the limits of Catholicism.' But let us look a little farther afield at the Protestant universities, for example, where the use of such oaths has been of considerable help in maintaining error consistently; this is one effect of oaths made on human authority, *commandments of men*. Again, the very opposite of what is proposed in the objection can often be seen amongst us Catholics. Lively intellects look upon their arbitrary shackles as a genuine injustice, and violently break away from them at the cost of infinite damage and scandal.

Nevertheless, I am prepared to grant that some good comes from these arbitrary restrictions. But even so, as St. Paul says: 'Evil is not to be done so that good may come.'

450. It is therefore extremely important to keep the spirit free from every preconceived notion and unstained by prejudice so that the love of good and truth alone should rule in us. We shall thus be able to consent immediately to every ray of truth that shines before us. All its colours and tints will have an attraction for us; nothing it offers will be repugnant.

V

451. The fifth means is: *to protest frequently, and show through our acts, that we want to love and seek truth alone*, not the deception of self-love.

452. If we recall our teaching about the various levels of reflection and the kinds of volition corresponding to them, we shall be able to grasp that an inadverted, sinful, erroneous conscience can exist in the depths of the human spirit as a judgment at third-level reflection. In the ordinary course of events, a less than upright conscience presupposes a level of reflection additional to that of upright conscience.[313] If the less than upright conscience is not adverted to, granted the blindness caused by passion, then direct, free action against it is not always possible — precisely because it is not adverted to. Nevertheless acts of will can be made by which we protest in general against all possible false consciences hidden deep in our heart, and against the illusions and deceits we have brought upon ourselves through lower-level, partial reflections. These acts of will, which show the effort we are making to purify our spirit from all interior malice and deception, are volitions belonging to a higher-level reflection than that of false consciences in general, and provide great assistance in

[313] For example, a person who judges that stealing is permissible for the sake of giving alms makes a judgment belonging to at least third-level reflection:

1. He perceives stealing as possible in itself (direct knowledge).

2. He conceives it as desired (a practical judgment: first level-reflection).

3. He judges that this practical judgment is evil (an upright conscience: second-level reflection).

4. He judges nevertheless that it can be excused for the sake of almsgiving (a non-upright conscience: third-level reflection).

[450-2]

rectifying false consciences or at least in rendering them no longer gravely imputable (cf. 329).

453. We should note that even one of these general acts, if done perfectly and with all our available energy, is sufficient to purify us. Carried out in this way, it would be a personal act of such efficacy that inferior acts would no longer be personal; they would of course spring from active, interior principles, but as inferior acts would not result from the supreme, active principle of freedom.[314] The perfect act of supreme reflection (especially if it has become a habit and as such remains constantly present in the human spirit) is enough to save the person, provided it is supernatural. This explains why the perfect love of God cures all mortal infirmity.

VI

454, The sixth means, in keeping with the fifth, consists in *taking every care to purify ourselves more and more from adverted sins*.

455. Careful attention to purifying ourselves from adverted sins is carried out by the *personal principle* which, with divine help, succeeds in removing the passions or habits of sin causing our blindness or the withdrawal of divine grace.[315]

Anyone desiring conversion re-acquires grace and with it an ever increasing light and force which grows in proportion to the light and to co-operation with grace. As we cleanse ourselves more thoroughly from *adverted sins*, therefore, we receive more light to perceive our *inadverted sins* and so to cleanse ourselves from them. St. Teresa compares the supernatural light entering the soul to a ray of sun showing up the dust drifting about in a room. Before the sun penetrated the

[314] cf. AMS, 851 ss.

[315] 'Blindness and obduracy imply two things. First, the movement of the human spirit as it adheres to evil and turns away from the divine light; in this sense God is not the cause of the blindness . . . Second, the removal of grace which leaves the mind without the divine light that enables it to see rightly, and leaves the heart without the ability to live rightly; in this sense, God is the cause of our blindess and obduracy' (*S.T.*, I-II, q. 79, c. 3).

room, nothing could be seen, but now the dust is obvious. The same is true of our defects when divine grace has come into our spirit.

VII

456. Finally the seventh and most effective means is *unceasing prayer* that God, who searches minds and hearts, will purify us in the depths of our soul.

457. This was what holy people asked: prophets' lips were purified by the action of lighted coals, a symbol of divine love. David said to the Lord: 'Lord, judge my judgment,'[316] that is, 'Reform my judgments which can be wrong without my knowing it.' Ecclesiasticus also asked that '*his ignorances might not increase* nor *his offences* be multiplied.'[317] Errors increase through the formation of new erroneous consciences which, precisely because they are errors, weaken the truth within us: 'Truths have vanished from among the sons of men.'

458. Christ's promise is certain: 'Every one who asks receives, and he who seeks finds, and to him who knocks it will be opened.'[318] The means to destroy less than upright consciences will never be lacking to the person who desires it with a pure heart. God offers grace to all. Moreover:

> 'Wisdom hastens to make herself known to those who desire her.
> He who rises early to seek her will have no difficulty, for he will find her sitting at his gates.
> To fix one's thought on her is perfect understanding and he that watches for her shall quickly be SECURE.'[319]

Article 2.
The care to be used in avoiding errors of conscience

459. What has been said enables us to evaluate correctly the opinion of some moral theologians who teach: 'The highest care is not required in overcoming the error of an erroneous

[316] Ps 118: 154 [Douai].   [317] Sir 23: 3.
[318] Lk 11: [10].   [319] Wis 6: 13–16.

conscience; moderate care is sufficient.'[320] It is clear that such an opinion is an unqualified pronouncement offered without the necessary distinctions.

460. There cannot be a simple, universal answer to: 'What care is necessary in reforming a vincibly erroneous conscience?' It is absolutely necessary to make some distinctions because every absolute answer is true only in certain cases, and false in others.

We have already distinguished between *upright*, and *less than upright* erroneous consciences. In the class of less than upright consciences we have also distinguished those in which the sin consists of *ignorance* (although culpable), but not in any *formal error* (which is committed in the judgment of conscience despite the just dictate found in the depth of the heart).

It is certain that only moderate care is required in avoiding *erroneous* but *upright* consciences, and equally certain that there is no precept entailing the highest care, which would humanly speaking be impossible.

461. In dealing with *non-upright, erroneous* consciences, on the other hand, which have their initial origin in simple carelessness and haste or in some habitual disordered affection, as much care must be used in avoiding them as in avoiding sin. In other words, because sin has to be avoided absolutely, the care we need must be increased to the point where simple *rashness* in judging or *disordered affections* are removed and sin is avoided. If such an aim can be achieved only through maximum care, maximum care must certainly be employed.

462. The penalty of not using the required care in avoiding non-upright, erroneous consciences lies in incurring whatever degree of sin is present in the malice leading to rashness in judging[321] or in the disordered affection. While, therefore, we

[320] 'The Salmaticensians (Tract. 20, c. 14, n. 9), Castro Palao (Tract. 2, *De Pecc.*, d. 1, p. 15, n. 6), Azorio, Suarez, Vasquez, Bonacina, etc., and Wignandt (*De Consc.*, ex. 1, q. 3, n. 7) note that the care required for removing error need not be the greatest; normal, ordinary care is sufficient' (Liguori, *Theol. Mor.*, *De Consc.* c. 1, 3).

[321] Rash judgment is present whenever we pronounce absolutely on the harmony or disharmony of the terms in our judgments before it truly forms part of our mental vision.

must not judge too soon nor too easily that any fault is a mortal sin, we must also be careful not to deny the presence of all fault if we have not employed all the care required to avoid willed, distorted consciences. We may add, however, that when the *protests of our personal principle* against the distortion produced by lower-level reflection are sincere and valid, they suffice to remove the gravity of such sins (cf. 452).

SCHEMA OF MORAL CONSCIENCE

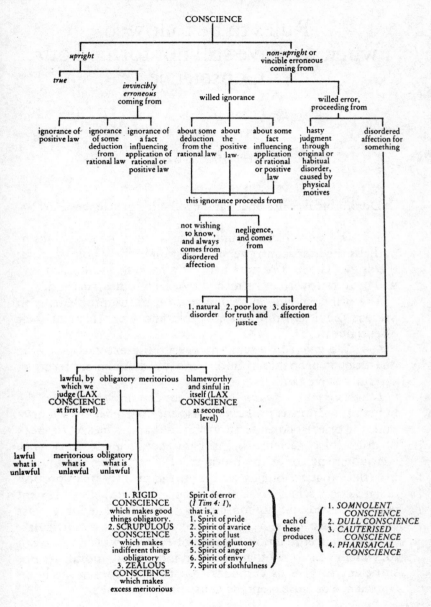

SECTION TWO

Rules to be followed when we have still not formed our Conscience

1

THE PROBLEM

Article 1.
Do doubtful consciences and probable consciences exist?

463. We now have to undertake a study of probabilism, perhaps the most controversial question in the whole of moral theology. The first requirement, if we want to walk securely, will be to follow rules furnished by exact, logical method.

The principal rule in dealing with intricate problems is to present them as simply as possible and view them in their essential features.

464. We begin by excluding everything extraneous to the question of probable opinion, and by defining its terms as carefully as we can.

Doubtful and *probable opinion* are certainly present in the human mind but is *probable conscience* present? As we have said, the briefest consideration shows that it is inexact to speak of doubtful conscience or probable conscience. Conscience is a judgment about the morality of a particular action, and it is clear that as long as we doubt the probity or improbity of an action which we are about to perform, no judgment is pronounced and no conscience is formed. The same must be said if we do not reach a decision about a particular, probably upright action because of reasons which, although they incline us to say that an action is probably moral, are not sufficient to give us certainty. A probable conscience is no conscience because it entails a suspended judgment.[322]

---

[322] How often what we say makes a mockery of our mental judgment! For example, 'I judge this action doubtfully or probably moral. I am

465. In speaking about *doubtful conscience* or *probable conscience* moralists attribute to conscience descriptions that belong properly speaking to *opinions*, that is, to *reasons* determining the spirit to hold its judgment suspended or inclined to one side without the full weight of a final decision. They do this, I believe, for the sake of brevity.[323] But my opinion is that we have to renounce brevity for the sake of clear ideas and follow Horace's advice, especially in complicated questions: 'I try to be brief, but I become obscure.'

466. If we wish to speak accurately, therefore, we have to say that doubtful consciences and probable consciences do not exist. What they refer to is a *state of our spirit* in which we have not yet formed a conscience, but remain hesitant and suspended between judging an action moral or immoral because there are equal reasons for both sides or because the weight of reason inclining us to one side rather than the other is insufficient for a final decision.

Our heading: 'Do doubtful consciences and probable consciences exist?', can therefore be changed to: 'What are the rules according to which we must act when we have not yet formed a conscience about the rectitude of some action, and are still uncertain whether it is upright or not?' Hence the title we have given to this whole section: 'Rules to be followed when we have still not formed our conscience.'[324]

making a judgment about the morality of the action and therefore form a conscience.' It is true, of course, that our words express a judgment, but we must not be satisfied with what we hear: we have to ponder what is expressed by our words. If we consider what we are referring to, we will see that our words do not indicate any judgment constituting a conscience. To judge that an action is doubtfully or probably moral is equivalent to judging its probity as uncertain from our point of view and this, in turn, means that we have not yet formed a definitive judgment about it. The real meaning of a judgment declaring an action doubtfully or probably moral is that we have decided to suspend our definitive judgment on its morality because our reasons for pronouncing it are insufficient. Our judgment simply tells us that we do not, and cannot as yet, form a conscience about that action.

[323] Some moralists are conscious of this impropriety of language, but they lack the courage to avoid it. Paul Gabriel Antoine, for example, speaks of perplexed and doubtful conscience, but then adds 'although this is not truly conscience' (*De Consc.*, in princ.).

[324] Theologians give the following definition of doubtful conscience: 'Doubtful conscience is that which, suspending its assent about a doubt, remains unresolved and hesitant' (Liguori, *De Consc.*, c. 2, n. 20). But if

[465-6]

Article 2.
The possibility of practically and speculatively doubtful consciences

467. The non-existence of doubtful conscience destroys the distinction between *speculatively and practically doubtful* consciences. This distinction should, however, be considered from another point of view. Because theologians usually define conscience as a *practical judgment* we now have a *practical judgment* which is divided into speculative conscience and practical conscience. Most modern moral theologians have in fact lost sight of their original definition when they go on to divide conscience in this way. Their negligence and mental limitations show up badly in comparison with the extreme care taken by the Fathers of the Church in their use of words.[325]

According to the moralists, the question under discussion concerns doubtful conscience and practical conscience; according to us, it concerns the state of our spirit when it is uncertain about the rectitude of an action. We are concerned with so-called practical doubt, which is in no way related to speculative doubt. In other words, we are asking: 'What must we do when our spirit is uncertain about the morality of an action?', not: 'What are the motives or reasons that make our

conscience is a judgment, we can only conclude from this definition that it is a judgment where assent is suspended, that is, an unjudging judgment, a judgment that is not a judgment.

[325] Speculative doubt is sometimes defined by moralists in this way: 'Speculative doubt is present when we doubt about the truth of something, for example, whether a war is just or unjust; whether painting on a feast-day is servile work or not; whether baptism conferred with distilled water is valid or not, and so on' (Liguori, *De Consc.*, c. 2, n. 21). But such doubt has no relationship to conscience. First, it is not concerned with a particular action to be done here and now. Second, it is a doubt pertaining to what theologians call *synderesis*, that is, the whole complex of moral principles in our spirit. However, the definition of practical doubt given by moralists does concern a particular action to be done here and now. This definition alone has some relationship with conscience. Liguori states it as follows: 'Practical doubt is present when we doubt about the morality of something, for example, whether I can lawfully fight in such a doubtfully just war, or paint on this feast day; or baptize this child with distilled water' (Liguori, *ibid.*).

[467]

spirit uncertain?' The second question follows upon the first, but is not the first.

468. An example will illustrate the distinction I have made. I am uncertain whether I commit a sin by omitting to hear Mass today. My uncertainty can be produced by different reasons, some of which may be true and hence a solid basis for my uncertainty, and some false and weak and hence not a solid basis for uncertainty in my spirit. In fact I am asking two distinct questions: 1. 'What must I do when I am uncertain of the morality of an action?' 2. 'How can I distinguish valid from invalid motives for my uncertainty?' In the second question, I want to know whether my uncertainty is reasonable or whether it can be set aside as unreasonable. As we said, the questions, although interconnected, are distinct, and will be dealt with separately.

Article 3.
The question concerns the state of our spirit after, not before, reflection upon the morality of an action

469. We have to simplify our question still further. When we ask: 'Can we posit an action about which we have not yet formed a conscience?' we are not in any way asking if we can act morally before reflecting upon the morality of our action. In speaking about this problem (cf. 30–37), we showed that conscience is not an absolutely necessary element in morality. Two elements are sufficient for morality: *direct knowledge*, which holds the place of law, and *willed acknowledgement*, the basis of our moral act. A state exists therefore in which we can act morally or immorally prior to the higher level of reflection necessary for the formation of conscience within us. This *moral state of spirit* is anterior to *reflection on its morality*, and is not therefore a state of uncertainty similar to doubt or probability in which we falter between belief and disbelief in the lawfulness of an action. We are dealing with a *state of uncertainty*, strictly speaking, not with a *state of total absence of reflection* on the morality of our action. We are enquiring about the state in which we actually reflect on the morality of an action, but without forming a judgment or

conscience about it. Our state is one in which reflection, because it does not find sufficient reason or motive for pronouncing definitively, remains suspended.

Article 4.
The doubt under discussion is about the lawfulness or unlawfulness of an action, not about its advisability

470. Finally, the doubt of which we are speaking is about commands, not counsels. We are not asking which of two actions I propose to do is better in itself, or which can be counselled in preference to the other. We ask simply: 'What must I do when I doubt whether in doing a given action I sin or not?'

2

THE SOLUTION TO THE FIRST QUESTION: 'WHAT MUST I DO WHEN I AM UNCERTAIN OF THE LAWFULNESS OF MY ACTION?'

Article 1.
We cannot carry out an action[326] as long as we are unsure whether it is free from sin

471. When the first question has been reduced to these simple terms it is answered easily and without controversy. St. Alphonsus says clearly: 'It is never lawful to act with a practically doubtful conscience,' (as theologians commonly call the state of uncertainty we have described). 'If a person does act in this case, he sins. The gravity of the sin corresponds to the species and gravity of the sin about which he doubts.' St. Alphonsus gives the reason: 'If someone exposes himself to the danger of sinning, he already sins, as scripture

[326] The same must be said of an omission if our doubt concerns a precept commanding some action.

[470-1]

says: "Whoever loves danger will perish by it."[327] If therefore
he doubts whether the sin is mortal he sins mortally.'[328] He
concludes: 'If a person has a practical doubt about an action,
he must certainly first remove the doubt through some certain
or reflective principle assuring him of the morality of that
action.'[329] No Catholic theologian disputes this.[330] We therefore take it as an undoubted source of light from which to
continue our study. It only remains to explain it and draw the
necessary conclusions.

Article 2.
Continuation

472. We begin by reaffirming that we can posit an act
lawfully only if its morality or lawfulness is *certain* for us; it is
not sufficient for its lawfulness or uprightness to be *probable*.
We have to avoid every willed danger of sin. If any little
doubt remains about sin in our act, we willingly expose
ourselves to the danger of offending against the law. Our
spirit can never rightly intend this, and should flee from it
absolutely.

473. This conclusion, however, has nothing to do with the
question of probable opinion which is not connected with
practical doubt but with what theologians call *speculative
doubt*. Practical doubt is concerned with the final dictate
arising from the application of probable opinion to the
particular act that we wish to perform. The proposition
condemned by Alexander VIII: 'It is not lawful to follow
even the most probable of probable opinions', is not applicable in the least, therefore, to the general teaching of theologians which states: 'To do something sinlessly, it is not

[327] Sir 3: 27 [26].
[328] Liguori, *De Consc.*, c. 2, n. 22 [*App.* no. 5].
[329] Liguori, *De Consc.*, c. 2, n. 24.
[330] Fogarini in his *Tractatus Theologicus de certitudine honestatis in
actibus humanis* (part 1, p. 8) lists certain authors who maintain that it is
lawful to act 'while fearful of possible malice in an action to be carried out
immediately.' But Father Steidel, from the district of Trent, says that these
authors 'differ only verbally from the very general teaching about the
necessity of moral certainty relative to the morality of an action.'

enough to hold that the action's lawfulness is highly *probable*; we must be *certain* that it is lawful.' In other words, we must be certain that our act does not offend God.

This unshakeable, universal teaching common to Catholic moralists cannot be expressed in all its clarity unless we begin by defining what we mean by the word *certain*, and by understanding how the certainty of which we are speaking differs from *probability*. What, therefore, is certainty?

Article 3.
Certainty, and how it differs from probability

474. We have defined certainty as 'a firm and reasonable persuasion that conforms to the truth.'[331] As a persuasion, certainty is a state of the spirit. We have defined persuasion as 'our understanding resting in the assent we give to a proposition.'[332] But the *assent* in which our understanding rests, if it is to constitute certainty (as the definition of certainty affirms) must be *reasonable*. This means that assent must be generated *according to reason*.[333]

475. The *reasonable motives* producing a *state of certainty* in our spirit can vary. As a result, different kinds of certainty can be distinguished.

First, I have already noted two general kinds of certainty. One of them is generated when we see the necessity of the proposition to which we assent simply as part of the proposition itself. For example, I say: 'I am certain that at every instant a body must either move or be still.' I have no need to appeal to anything extraneous to the proposition in order to see its necessity. As soon as the proposition is present to my spirit, I see its *necessity*, the foundation of its *certainty*.[334]

The other kind of certainty is founded in certainty about a fact. In this case, the proposition is not itself necessary, but depends on a contingent fact for its necessity. For example, the proposition 'I am moving' contains nothing necessary,

---

[331] *Certainty*, 1044.   [332] *Certainty*, 1336.   [333] *Certainty*, 1052–1053.

[334] The *certainty* of necessary facts can be reduced to *logical certainty*: I can know their certainty only if I know their necessity. But knowledge of their necessity is always reduced to the intuition of a necessary proposition.

but expresses a fact which, if granted, makes the proposition certain.

These two supreme kinds of certainty can be called *logical* and *physical certainty*. The former is contained in *ideal being*; the latter consists in the relationship of equality between *ideal* and *real being*.

476. We can also distinguish a third kind of certainty which depends on *authority*. We shall call it *didactic certainty*.

The first two kinds of certainty are distinguished from one another by the objects with which their certainty is concerned. These are either ideal and necessary objects, or contingent-real objects made known and certain through their relationship with ideal objects. The third kind of certainty, however, is not distinguished from the others by the nature of its objects, but simply by the channel which transmits the certainty to us. By means of authority we can obtain certainty about both purely ideal objects and mixed objects provided that what another teaches us is not simply a stimulus to our own thought on the matter but a communication of their own certainty. In this case, the *teacher* or *witness* does no more than communicate his own certain knowledge of things. In so far as his act communicates *knowledge* it is called *teaching*; in so far as it communicates *certainty*, especially certainty about facts, it is properly called *witnessing*. Hence, *didactic* certainty is always reduced to one of the first two kinds of certainty according to the quality of its objects (whether these are ideal, or real as well as ideal) and only adds a new means of communicating.

477. This means of communication is itself a fact. From this point of view *didactic* certainty is reduced to *physical* certainty, or rather needs *physical* certainty as its condition and support.

478. Because of this diversity of its general objects, *didactic* certainty differs from the other two kinds of certainty. Hence we have: 1. certainty proper to ideal or necessary objects; 2. certainty proper to contingent-real objects; 3. certainty extending both to ideal and to real objects.

479. Just as didactic certainty is reduced to physical certainty from one point of view, so physical certainty is reduced to logical certainty. Certainty about facts (the object

of physical certainty) is founded on a preceding logical principle, as I have shown.[335] For example, the certainty of the proposition 'I am moving' springs from the principle: 'Given the fact of intellectual perception of movement, movement itself is undeniable because it forms an element of that fact. If my movement could not exist at the moment I perceive it, it would be, and not be, at the same time. Through the fact of perception, therefore, a proposition which of itself is contingent becomes necessary and is reduced to a particular case of the principle of contradiction.'[336]

480. This argument, in which the certainty of movement is deduced from the purely logical principle of contradiction, is undeniable provided only that the fact of movement is an element in the *perception* of the movement (I have shown at length that this is so), and provided that the fact of perception is certain. But the certainty of the perception, although pertaining to the order of real things, is rooted in ideal being, the seat of logical certainty, because what is perceived intellectively is perceived in ideal being as in its term or end whose truth it thus shares.

481. Didactic certainty is reduced therefore to physical certainty, and physical certainty to logical certainty. Nevertheless, these three kinds of certainty have to be distinguished: logical certainty, which bestows its own evidence on physical certainty, does not always and necessarily contain the physical fact to which it communicates certainty, nor is physical certainty always and necessarily received on the authority of another.

482. We can now subdivide into species the three supreme genera of certainty.

Physical certainty can primarily be divided into *conditioned* and *unconditioned certainty* or, to use Greek terms, *apodictic* and *hypothetical certainty*. *Apodictic* certainty is absolute, *hypothetical* certainty is conditional, and because it depends upon a condition, can exist only when its condition is certain. For example, if a physical cause really subsists, some real effect must follow; but the effect is certain only on condition that the cause subsists. Certainty is present, therefore, only if the condition has been realised.

[335] *Certainty*, 1342–1345.   [336] *Certainty*, 1342–1345.

483. We may note here that many authors who seem to admit some kind of hypothetical certainty even in the simple order of ideas, are misled by their own way of speaking. They say: 'If there is a human being, this person must have a body and soul', and go on to conclude that the proposition, which expresses simple possibility alone, is conditioned. But the notion of human being necessarily includes, without any exception whatsoever, body and soul. Hence we necessarily think of a possible body and possible soul in the human being, without any condition. Consequently we do not need to posit the conditional phrase: 'If there is a human being'; a possible human being must necessarily be possible, and cannot not be. On the other hand, in saying: 'If there is a human being, this person must have a body and soul' we simply affirm: 'If there is a human being, there must be a human being.' The body and soul in question are precisely the human being. Hence, 'human being' is not a necessary condition for 'body-and-soul-being' — it is the same as 'body-and-soul-being'. Purely logical certainty, therefore, contains nothing hypothetical although, granted human limitation, one thing always precedes another relative to us.

484. Finally we must add that our limited mode of understanding explains why we introduce suppositions or hypotheses in the order of logical truths, although these suppositions or hypotheses are often simple absurdities. For example, given an absurd supposition, we draw absurd consequences which seem to possess hypothetical truth, that is, truth conditioned by the initial absurdity. In fact, because the initial supposition was absurd, the consequences possess neither truth nor certainty. It is clear that on this basis there is no authority for affirming the presence of hypothetical certainty in the order of purely logical truths.

We can, therefore, disregard all ideal, hypothetical certainty because it lacks all the characteristics of certainty, and hence cannot be called certainty in the strict, absolute sense. We shall confine our attention to apodictic, demonstrative, unconditioned certainty.

485. What are the specific divisions of logical certainty, physical certainty and didactic certainty?

Logical certainty is divided into *intuitive* and *rational*.

Intuitive certainty, as I understand it, is that certainty in which I see immediately the necessity of ideal being. *Logical-rational* certainty, again as I understand it, is that by which I deduce many truths through analysis of, and by reasoning from, the *intuition* of possible being and the *perception of necessary real*, or *moral facts*. That is, I see these truths one within another, and finally behold them together, contained in the splendour of first being. Logical-rational certainty is derived, therefore, from intuitive certainty, its source and first seat. Consequently, logical-rational certainty is divided into the *certainty of ideas* and the *certainty of necessary real*, or *moral facts*.

486. The species, 'physical certainty', that is, certainty relative to subsistent things, is also twofold: *perceptive certainty* and *physical-rational certainty*. *Perceptive certainty* is proper to intellective perception. This certainty does not differ in grade from logical, intuitive certainty; it differs only in so far as its object does not contain in itself any intrinsic necessity. *Physical-rational certainty* is deduced from perceptive certainty by means of right reasoning.

487. *Perceptive certainty* is divided also into two classes according to its objects. In our present state we have two objects of intellective perception: 1. corporeal feeling (extrasubjective) and 2. feeling of ourselves (subjective). The first of these feelings provides our understanding with the matter required in the perception of bodies; the second provides our understanding with the matter required for its self-perception. These two classes of certainty can therefore be called *esthetic* and *psychic certainty*.

488. At this point we may ask whether any certainty is founded on the law of *analogy* and, if so, to which of the above-mentioned genera it belongs.

It is clear that analogical certainty, if it exists, can never belong to the genus 'logical certainty' but only to physical or didactic certainty. Analogy is never used for argument in the order of ideas, where the sole basis of reasoning is the necessity connecting the ideas.

489. But does analogical certainty exist? This can be decided only on knowledge of the law of analogy and of the principle on which this law depends. We must therefore examine the nature and principle of analogy.

The law of analogy embraces *time* and *space*.

When something has occurred frequently and periodically we judge that it will take place again when the same interval has elapsed. For example, we judge that the sun will rise tomorrow because it always has risen at daily intervals. From analogy with the past, we judge what will happen in the future.

What we say of time can also be said of space. A Tyrolese peasant who has spent his whole life in some remote mountain valley will be very surprised at what he sees when he has to go out into the world at large. His surprise springs from reasoning according to the law of analogy: accustomed only to what he has known in his own isolated community, he reasons that the rest of the world lives in the same way.

490. The law of analogy includes substances and accidents and, in general, every *connection* between things. When I hear a voice calling my name, although I see no one, I reason by analogy that there must be someone unseen nearby. Experience has taught me that every time I hear a word articulated, a person must be present to pronounce it. Nevertheless, I may be deceived; perhaps a parrot has been taught to pronounce my name.

491. The law of analogy leads us therefore either from an effect to a cause, or from a cause to an effect, or from a sign to what is signified, or from one property to another experienced as normally connected with it.

492. But what is the final foundation for this law of analogy, which we use so often, on which we continually base our reasoning, and without which it would perhaps be impossible to live? This question is twofold: either we are asking about the nature of the principle within us which *moves us* to rely so confidently on this form of argument, or we are asking about the foundation of analogy in nature which leads us *in fact* to make few mistakes when our reasoning depends upon analogy.

493. In answering the first question we begin by recalling that we are reasonable beings. Clearly, therefore, we rely on analogy largely because a principle of reason persuades us to do so. This reason may be hidden within us and not reflected upon, but it must nevertheless be intuited by us in the depth of our spirit where we behold many things unexpressed even

to ourselves. This principle of reason must also provide the explanation for our making few mistakes when we argue from analogy. The answer to the second question, therefore, contains at least in part the answer to the first. I say 'at least in part' because reasoning from analogy must depend not only upon a *principle of reason*, but also upon our being moved by an *habitual principle* which accustoms us to reason at least formally in a consistent fashion.[337]

494. But this need detain us no longer. We now have to seek the reason which, rooted in the nature of things, enables us to avoid frequent mistakes in our use of analogy. This reason provides us with the secret assurance that our way of arguing by analogy is sound. It may be stated as follows: 'The value of analogy is based on the constancy proper to substances, things and the properties of things.'

For example, when we see an effect reproduced every twenty-four hours, we begin to be persuaded that there is in nature a suitable cause for producing that effect every twenty-four hours. It is clear therefore that *the concept of cause involves the concept of constancy, just as it does the concept of substance*. We conclude, therefore, that the periodic effect will continue in the future as it has in the past because we are certain that its cause, which of its nature is firm and consistent relative to the effect, will continue to exist. For the same reason, we presume that the order of the universe will always be stable. This order is the result of a complex of effects that depend upon *substances* which, as *permanent causes*, produce transitory effects that either occur periodically or are renewed according to certain laws proper to the nature of these substances.

495. We must note, however, that the argument from analogy should not be confused with that of cause and effect, although both are founded on the principle of cause as follows.

If we can prove that a cause subsists at the present moment, we can certainly conclude as a direct consequence that all the

---

[337] One general principle governing instinctive human behaviour is: 'From all the actions in which activity can be expressed, the human being always chooses for himself the one which causes the least fatigue,' that is, the easiest — other things being equal.

effects necessarily springing from it also exist. This is the *argument from cause and effect*, not from *analogy*; it is self-evident and leads to full certainty.

On the other hand, it may be that we cannot prove the existence of a cause at the present moment. We know only of its previous existence through the effects, seen by us, which it constantly produced. We argue from this knowledge that the cause still exists, that it will exist tomorrow, and that its effects will come about. Granted the stability of the cause as a substance, or as rooted in a substance, we argue from the past existence of the cause to its present and future existence.

496. If however we are dealing with a contingent cause, it would not be absurd for a substance which has existed at length in the past to cease to exist in the future, through annihilation or destruction. The same can be said about any special power in the substance which makes the substance cause the observed effects. The cause would cease if this particular power ceased, although the substance in which it existed might continue.

The argument from cause and effect, therefore, always produces certainty because the existence of the cause is proved in the instant in which the effect is produced.

On the other hand, the argument from analogy is not always certain because the existence of the cause is not proved, but presupposed in the argument. The cause is conjectured in virtue of its constant existence as a substance. In this way we affirm tomorrow's sunrise as a consequence of the implicit supposition that the substance of the sun continues to endure with the same laws with which it has lasted until now. This supposition is not proved, however, but only conjectured from the principle of duration of order in the universe, which itself is founded on the duration of the substances composing the universe.

The argument from analogy is not such, therefore, that it can, of its own nature, bring about *certainty*. At most, it can offer *probability* which, although it may be very strong, can never compel free assent.

497. Moreover, just as the strongest probability can be induced by analogy, in some cases the probability can be weak or nil. This occurs when our argument arbitrarily

presupposes a non-existent stability of order, as we have seen in our example of our Tyrolese peasant. Supposing that everyone dresses in Tyrolese costume, our peasant may think he will find the same dress everywhere he goes. But the only foundation for this constant, universal supposition is his own limited perception of what people wear. In his case, the argument from analogy fails.

498. Analogy has to be used cautiously, in accordance with the qualifications provided by sound logic. If it is employed in this way our conclusions have some probability, which may vary from very weak to very strong. When probability is at its strongest, it may even possess enough force to capture the assent of our spirit, and only with difficulty be distinguished from certainty. Nevertheless, it never passes the bounds of probability; it is not certainty.

499. We must now examine the species composing what we have called *didactic* certainty.

500. As I said, didactic certainty is reduced to physical certainty (cf. 471) because the teaching or witness of others is normally received through *perception* (the seat of physical certainty). However, we have to distinguish in this species of certainty *absolute didactic* certainty and *normal didactic* certainty.

501. Didactic certainty is *absolute* when its teacher or witness is infallible, especially if the master or witness has the power (and this is the case with God) to enable his hearer, into whom he infuses evidence and persuasion, to receive with conviction what is communicated.

502. Didactic certainty is *normal* only when the authority of the master or witness is such that the moral law authorises us to take this authority as a *norm* for acting. This occurs, for example, in the case of direction from a confessor or religious superior, or in the case of belief about factual matters when we depend for our knowledge upon persons worthy of credence.

503. This kind of normal certainty presupposes that the person communicating it is himself in possession of it. If his knowledge were only probable, not certain, he could communicate his probability, but not the certainty which he lacks.

How then does a human being come to possess certainty? If it has been communicated to him by his own teacher, how does that teacher come to possess it? The problem must eventually be grounded in the first person to possess certainty, which will have been acquired not on the basis of teaching or witness but through logical or physical means (according to the kind of certainty possessed). Physical means enable a person to acquire physical certainty, which always refers to some *subsistent* being or to some *fact*, on condition that he is willing to use 'fact' as synonymous with 'subsistent.' Logical means enable him to acquire logical certainty. Didactic certainty, therefore, must ultimately be subdivided into physical and logical certainty.

504. Generally speaking, if we come to know facts through didactic certainty, we possess *historical certainty*; if we come to know various rational teachings in the same way, we possess *doctrinal* or *dogmatic certainty*.[338]

505. For a *witness* of facts to be authoritative, there must be no exception which allows reasonable doubt about the *certainty* of what he says, or about his *willingness* and *capacity* for communicating the certainty. If no exception is present, any person must be considered a suitable channel for communicating certainty.

506. In order to communicate doctrinal certainty, however, a *teacher* must not only possess it himself, but also show certain proof that he possesses it. More is required of a teacher than of a witness, as a channel of certainty. Although every human being must be presumed *truthful* when there is no reasonable doubt to the contrary, not everyone can be presumed *learned*. Positive proof of his teaching is needed if others are to believe in his learning.

507. However, when counsel is needed on moral matters, the teaching of a churchman is sufficiently proven if he is universally respected for his wisdom and above all for his

---

[338] We may first *believe* a teaching on the authority of another, but then go on *to understand* the reasons for the teaching. But if the reasons persuade us that the teaching is true, we can be said to possess *doctrinal teaching* (in so far as we believe the teaching on authority) and *logical teaching* (in so far as through logical argument we reach certainty about the teaching).

uprightness which will prevent his giving moral advice with complete certainty if he himself is not certain of what he teaches. His *uprightness* is a proof of his *truthfulness*, and his truthfulness is evidence that he possesses *sufficient sound doctrine* to give advice when he is asked.

508. If a witness to a fact is open to exception, his statements can induce probability only. If other witnesses concur with him but themselves are open to exception, the conclusion can only be more probable, but never certain until at least one witness is found who is completely sound and consequently worthy of credence. Agreement on the part of witnesses who are not altogether worthy of credence gives rise only to a calculation of probability.

509. The same must be said about knowledge of any fact communicated by a series of intermediate witnesses. If an immediate witness is worthy of credence, his word alone gives rise to certainty, provided his testimony has been securely documented. If the first testimony has been lost, certainty can arise in the case of a mediate witness only when he himself and those from whom he has received the testimony and the documents containing it are all proved worthy of credence. In such cases, the means by which we attain certainty are the *witnesses taken in conjunction with reasoning*. This is *critical* certainty, which itself is subdivided into *historical* or *perceptive-historical* certainty, and *rational-historical* certainty.

510. The schema on the following page will help summarize what we have said about the different species of certainty.

SCHEMA OF CERTAINTY

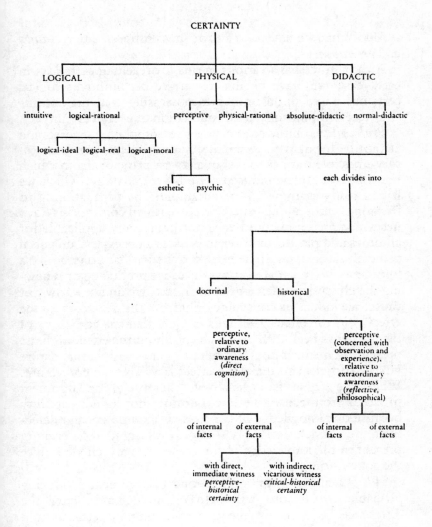

Article 4.
Continuation

511. What we have said allows us to differentiate *certainty* and *probability*.

Although we have various means for reaching certainty, in each case we have finally to arrive at intuitive, logical certainty based upon principles possessing evident, immutable necessity, the only solid foundation of every certainty.

Probability, on the contrary, is present when our reasoning cannot be brought to terminate in any evident, *per se* necessary principle but has to rest in a law or principle from which necessity cannot be induced. The law of analogy, which we have already examined, is one example. The affirmation 'This has gone on for a long time, therefore it will continue' is not a necessary principle, and hence not universally applicable for all times and places. In order to possess a necessary, universal principle, it is not sufficient to know what has gone on for a long time. We must also know the cause producing or renewing the effect over such a period. In fact, we do not know this cause; we induce its constancy only from the constancy of the effect. But the effect itself tells us only that the constancy of the cause has been sufficient to bring about the effect until the present moment; it does not tell us in any way that its nature will be sufficient to make the effect last. This we conjecture. When we argue from analogy, therefore, the argument proceeds from cause to effect, but does not induce certainty because our knowledge of the cause is incomplete and defective. Our conclusion possesses only the grade of certainty present in the knowledge of the cause from which we induce the conclusion.

512. Examination of another kind of argument producing probable conclusions will help us understand better the difference between arguments terminating in certainty and those terminating in probability.

Imagine a bag containing ninety marbles, ten red and eighty yellow. The probability of my extracting a yellow marble is obvious, but this is not certainty: I could take out a red marble. In foreseeing that I will take out a yellow marble, I depend upon probability, not certainty, for the simple reason that we lack full, perfect knowledge of the cause of what is happening. If I knew all the circumstances present in determining the extraction of the marble, I could foresee with certainty the colour which would emerge. If, for instance, all the marbles were yellow, I could be sure that whenever I put my hand in the bag, a yellow marble would be extracted. The effect is determined by the colour of the marbles which, in this case, are all yellow. In the case of different coloured marbles, my hand is not predetermined to a single colour. I mean that it is not determined as far as I am concerned, as far as my knowledge is concerned. In fact (leaving aside the question of free will) it is always determined by definite, hidden causes and reasons, but these are unknown to me. I do not know the efficacious, physical causes determining the action of my hand, nor do I know the relationship of these causes with the colour of the marbles. I am forced to reason simply on the basis of data known to me. In the present case, this means that I am limited to arguing to the determining cause (that is, the movements of my hand) from the proportion of yellow to red marbles. And this is insufficient for providing me with full information of the cause determining me to extract the particular marble that emerges from the bag.

513. On the same basis we can see why agreement between witnesses all of whom are open to exception can induce probability only, never certainty, whatever the number of the available witnesses. Although I am aware of the agreement present in the various depositions, I also know that I can be fully certain of what is said only if each of the depositions has a single cause, that is, the truth. In such a case, I can with full certainty induce from the effect, that is, the agreement between the witnesses, the truth of their depositions. But if their agreement can be produced by a cause different from the truth of their deposition, this possible cause is sufficient to show that I may not fully know the cause or the complex of causes which induced the witnesses to give common testimony. This defective knowledge of the total cause means that I can never reach full certainty about the matter, but only probability which is greater in so far as the deficiencies in my knowledge of the cause are smaller.

[513]

Article 5.
Continuation

514. What I have said about the different kinds of certainty may have led my readers to think I have broadened the field of certainty more than is necessary. Such an objection could be stated as follows.

It is agreed that there are truths given by nature about which we cannot fall into error. This is easily grasped on the basis of what has been shown in the *Nuovo Saggio* [vol. 3].[339] It is also clear that everything deduced by right reasoning from the first truths, or reduced to the first truths as principles, is immune from error. But how can we be sure that we have reasoned correctly? Granted our fallibility, is it not possible for us to err even in the first deductions we make from the sensations we have received. For example, we sometimes judge that a body is moving, although it is in fact motionless, and are led to make this mistake by the appearance of movement arising from the spatial relationship of the body with others that are moving. We must conclude, it would seem, that we can have *certainty* only about the small sphere of truths in which nature protects us from error. In other cases, we possess only various degrees of *probability*.

515. This difficulty, although it has a basis of truth, is false if taken too far, as it has been in modern times.[340]

First, the human spirit can sometimes be found in a state in which the truth of certain consequences is clearly grounded in principles, with the result that our persuasion is felt to be as free from error as it is in the intuition of the very first truths.

516. Second, we have to distinguish certainty which excludes the *possibility of error* from certainty which excludes *error* but not its abstract possibility. The second kind, although it does not totally eliminate all abstract possibility of error, is certainty no less than the first kind because 1. the means bringing it about are *per se* infallible; 2. the possibility of error arises from the general knowledge of our *fallibility* without any particular reason causing us to doubt the certainty we possess.

[339] *Certainty*, 1061.
[340] Lamennais' troubles began in this way.

If it is considered desirable to grade the simple, general possibility of error and fallibility I would be happy to distinguish *rigorous* from *normal certainty*. The former would be certainty related to matters about which nature protects us from all error; the latter, certainty about things we come to know through *per se* infallible means, although the mere general possibility that we may have erred in using them still remains. It is always true that this *normal certainty* is sufficient to allow us to act decisively without any reasonable fear of damage or sin, and for this reason it is called *moral certainty*. It is also true, and this must be noted carefully, that it has to be distinguished from even the highest *probability*.

517. What we call *normal certainty* differs from *probability* in so far as it is attained with means that are *per se* infallible; probability, on the contrary, depends upon the use of means that are not *per se* infallible.

518. Any doubt remaining in conjunction with *normal certainty* is *negative doubt*. It offers no particular reason for fear of error except the universal possibility we have of erring in the use of the means producing certainty, even when we do not appear to have made any mistake whatever. In *probability*, however, a *positive doubt* is present, that is, a special reason for fearing that our conclusion may be mistaken.

519. Fr. Valperga di Caluso puts the matter very well, and we may use his authority to confirm our own observations. He says: 'We must not confuse the issue. We can ask if there are truths that must be known and if there are mistakes so gross that neither erroneous reasoning nor madness can attain them. But this is not in question here. We are not trying to restrict the matter to a small number of incontrovertible principles (such as existence for the individual, or the universal principle that a thing is unable to be and not to be at the same time). We are speaking about certainty in contested matters. If certainty has to be present where facts all too often prove our fallibility, certainty can scarcely be infallible.

'The adjective *doubtful* must add something to its noun, but would signify nothing if it indicated only the simple possibility of doubt. Careful attention to the way we speak will show that something is said to be doubtful only when a particular reason for doubt is applicable to the case. The reason may not have much weight, but it will be specifically applicable to the case in question. It is true that we can doubt about everything, and that our fallibility is an ever-present reason, good or bad, for this doubt. But our question' (how to know whether something is doubtful) 'is not concerned with this doubt. When we say that something is doubtful, we never think about this general reason which is foreign to what we are talking about, and completely absent from our minds and intention. The reason for universal doubt, that is, our fallibility, is present in us; the reason for saying that one thing is doubtful rather than another must be found in the thing itself. Something will be *doubtful* if there is a particular reason for doubt; it will be *certain* if no particular doubt is present in its regard.'

Shortly after he adds: 'The attention we should give to this reason for doubt, in so far as it is applied to particular cases, is altogether different from the knowledge that we have about our fallibility in general. In the first case we are concerned with reflective knowledge which, springing from an exact, detailed examination of a question which we consider from all sides, can indeed provide us with unassailable, if not infallible, certainty. Sometimes our sensation of certainty is so vivid, our memory of it so firm and positive, and our reasoning so clear and conclusive, that we could not doubt even if we wished to.

'However, only *direct doubt* is impossible when we examine a question in itself. But an *indirect doubt*, extraneous to the question, cannot be in contradiction with the evidence offered by the question, precisely because the doubt is indirect and irrelevant. We often say: "As certain as two and two are four", and all arithmetic is equally certain to those who know it. But at the end of a long calculation, carried out and verified with all possible attention, we write *errors excepted*.'[341]

---

[341] *Principes de Philosophie pour des initiés aux mathématiques*, by M. Valperga di Caluso, member of the *Légion d'honneur*, etc. Turin 1811. *Au palais de l'Académie*, Vincent Bianco.

Article 6.
Continuation

520. A further answer is required, however, if the difficulty we have broached is to be entirely overcome. First, we have to reflect on the great difference between the *direct* and *indirect doubt* referred to by Caluso.

Indirect doubt rises from our *reflection* on the solution to a question; direct doubt arises within the question itself. But if the solution to the question is examined on all sides, and no foundation is discovered for doubting the correctness of the solution, the indirect doubt must be considered an idle fear rather than a true doubt.

521. It is certain that while human beings are in the first stages of their development and do not exceed first-level reflection, they think and act with conviction, free of any disturbance whatsoever from indirect doubt. Either they see what is true and enjoy it, or they do not see it and they remain ignorant, but without any doubt.

522. When, however, the mind rises to higher levels of reflection, indirect doubt is stimulated, that is, fear of having erred even in those acts in which no error exists. This indirect doubt or fear cannot provide sufficient reason for causing us to lose the completely firm certainty we previously possessed.

523. Nevertheless, we can see more clearly how *practical, normal* certainty has as much claim as *rigorous* certainty to the title *certainty* if we ponder once more our definition of certainty: 'a firm and reasonable persuasion that conforms to the truth.'

This definition shows that true certainty can be present in a great deal of knowledge not protected from error by nature. Even here it can and does happen that we 'assent firmly and reasonably' precisely because we assent as a consequence of using *per se* infallible means of certainty, and that 'our assent conforms to the truth.' Given this assent, all the conditions necessary for constituting certainty are present within us.

524. It may be objected that we are not infallible, and that our assent can therefore be deceptive. That is true, but the *possibility of deception* does not destroy certainty, provided we are not in fact deceived. Saying that we can be deceived is

equivalent to saying that we are able not to be certain. But if in fact we are certain, being able not to be certain expresses nothing. What is in question is whether we possess certainty or not, not whether it is possible to possess it or not. Whoever we are, we possess certainty in fact when, using one of the means of certainty which we have called 'infallible', we give our assent simply and firmly. Simple, upright people always do this, especially if, as we suggested, they have not attained high-level reflection.

525. We exaggerate if we allow the possibility of human self-deception to affect us in such a way that we become restless and lose the quiet and peace of truth as it offers itself to our gaze. In such a state, assent to truth begins to vacillate. This kind of exaggeration and idle fear paves the way to scepticism for many.

We are made for truth; we possess and use *per se* infallible means for knowing the truth. All that remains is that, whenever we are in possession of these means, we adhere to them simply and tranquilly without cavilling: then certainty is formed. 'But one can deceive oneself!' Yes, we can deceive ourselves in general, but in very many cases we do not do so, and here lies certainty. We can deceive ourselves, but only when we let ourselves be overly dominated by fear of deceiving ourselves. It is this fear which removes the the firmness of assent that we must give and would give to the truth standing before us if we were not afraid. We can deceive ourselves, but only when, instead of giving our assent to the means of certainty we possess, we *willingly* create errors, or confuse the means providing probability with those offering us full certainty.[342]

Article 7.
Continuation

526. Our final reflection enables us to overcome the difficulty entirely. We have already distinguished *willed* from

[342] This is why St. Augustine does not hesitate to say that there is no error in what the intellect sees: 'But he (the human being) does not err in what is seen by his intellect: either he understands, and it is true; or if it is not true, he does not understand. It is one thing to err in what he sees; it is another to err because he does not see' (*De Genesis ad litt.*, bk. 12, c. 25, 52).

unwilled error, and we saw the almost unlimited field open to the efficacy of our will in generating error.[343] We noticed that we cannot deceive ourselves through formal error if we have an upright will. In such a case we can only fall into material error, which is not error, properly speaking. Human fallibility, so exaggerated by sceptics and abusively turned to their own advantage, proves on careful examination to be simply the *fallibility of the human will*. If, therefore, we are in possession of an upright will, which is without love of any sort for error or for self, but full of love for naked truth, we will easily reach certainty — just as, if we want to be virtuous, we will attain virtue. And as the power we have of making ourselves virtuous does not remove our possibility of being vicious, if that is what we want, so having certainty within our grasp does not render us infallible in such a way that we cannot deceive ourselves, if that is what we want. In a word, we can deceive ourselves because we are able to love something other than truth. Disorder can gain entrance to our affections, but only on condition that our will consents to its entry. Without the deleterious action of our will, our powers are upright, and each of them in relationship to its object is infallible.

527. Drawing together all that we have said about certainty in our endeavour to clarify the moral rule we have set out, we may conclude as follows.

If we are intimately persuaded of our certainty about the lawfulness of an action, and this persuasion is not an error dependent upon our evil affections, we can safely act. But if we are doubtful that an action is lawful, although its lawfulness may seem probable to us, we cannot act until we are sure that it is lawful. We note, however, that the degree of doubt telling us that we are less than fully certain of the lawfulness of our action is something more than the simple, general thought of human fallibility, which is not sufficient to make any judgment of ours uncertain. Nor is it simple fear devoid of rational motives. Such fear is powerless to weaken our certainty and diminish the rational assent in the depths of our spirit unless the assent of our will moves the faculty of

[343] *Certainty*, 1245.

judgment to act according to the fear. We saw that this often happens with scrupulous people.

528. If a person gives way to irrational fear (and this usually occurs when a state of nerves takes hold of the person at the mere thought of the *possibility* of evil which through his overheated imagination he has changed into *probability*) and changes shadow into solid body, he adds another judgment and persuades himself of fault where none exists and, as we saw, develops the scrupulous conscience that must be eliminated before he acts.

Article 8.
If we act when in doubt about the lawfulness of our action,
the gravity of our sin is in proportion
to the degree of probability to which we give assent
in the doubtfully lawful action

529. We cannot act without sin if we are uncertain about the lawfulness or unlawfulness of our action. But what is the nature of the sin we commit?

Its *species* is determined by the quality of the action, considered from the moral point of view; its *gravity* and malice is calculated relative to the degree of probability of its unlawfulness as understood and assented to by us — although other circumstances may also have to be considered. First, it is certain that in positing an action which we certainly know to be unlawful we sin more seriously than in doing something which we know to be doubtfully unlawful. In the same way, it is clear that the higher our degree of probability about the unlawfulness of an action, the greater our sin when we do it, and vice-versa. If therefore the probable degree of unlawfulness is slight, our sin will be slight (although truly sin).

530. If the degree of probability is so slight that we fail to consider it, and give full assent to the lawfulness of the action as though it were undoubtedly certain, we commit a venial sin of lack of attention and nothing more.

3

THE SECOND QUESTION:
'HOW CAN I ELIMINATE UNCERTAINTY
ABOUT THE LAWFULNESS OF AN ACTION,
AND FORM A CONSCIENCE IF MY DOUBT
CONCERNS THE INTRINSIC UNLAWFULNESS
OF THE ACTION?'

Article 1.
New proofs of what was affirmed in the preceding chapter

531. As long as we are uncertain whether our action is lawful or unlawful, we cannot do it. This proposition follows from the principle that we are obliged to preserve due order in the objects of our esteem and affection. Indeed moral good is truly the only good, the true good, the essential, perfect good; and the best of all objects is the moral object. As a result, we have to say that whatever the cost we must never expose ourselves to the *danger* of losing what is morally good for the sake of attaining some other good which relative to moral good is false, illusory and truly evil. Only when moral probity has been safeguarded have we the right to act.

532. We read in the psalms:

'You have commanded your precepts to be kept diligently,'[344]
and in the book of Wisdom:

'I preferred her (wisdom) to sceptres and thrones,
and I accounted wealth as nothing in comparison with her.
Neither did I liken her to any precious gem,
because all gold is a little sand in her sight,
and silver will be accounted as clay before her.
I loved her more than wealth and beauty,
and I chose to have her rather than light,
because her radiance never ceases.'[345]

[344] Ps 118: [4 (Douai)].
[345] Wis 7: [8–10].

[531-2]

The sacred author insists that this wisdom, which is uprightness and virtue, *went before him*, that is, he considered
innocence as the chief characteristic of all his actions, and did
nothing before finding wisdom in accord with what he
intended. An abundance of other good things followed from
this way of acting.[346]

Article 2.
A clearer exposition of the second question

533. I cannot posit any action if I am uncertain about its
rectitude. Before acting, therefore, I must have formed for
myself a conscience declaring that in acting I neither sin nor
expose myself to the danger of sinning. We must now ask
how such a conscience can be formed, and how uncertainty
eliminated.

Here we have to deal with the famous teaching on *reflective
principles*, a matter of great importance scientifically speaking. As I have noted, this teaching indicated a great step
forward by the human spirit as it advanced from a lower to a
higher level of reflection. It is not surprising that such
progress produced a kind of moral-scientific crisis in
mankind, so that the names MEDINA and TIRILLO ought to
stand in any philosophical history of moral sciences as
marking the beginning of a new scientific epoch. However,
this has not been done; and as moralists, Medina and Tirillo
are no more than two amongst many.[347]

---

[346] 'Now all good things came to me together with her, and I rejoiced in
all these: for THIS WISDOM WENT BEFORE ME' (Wis 7: [11–12]).

[347] A grave objection against the adversaries of probabilism is the facility
with which, according to them, the question can be solved. Ignatius
Camargo (*Praef.*) maintains: 'This difficulty requires no study on the one
hand, and a certain degree of cunning on the other; it requires no study . . .
to attain the truth provided that the question is regarded with a straightforward and simple spirit; it requires a certain degree of cunning to convince
others entangled in the specious, inextricable bonds of probabilism.'
Patuzzi (*Trattato della Regola prossima delle azioni umane nella scelta delle
opinioni*, t. 1, p. 1, c. 1) agrees wholeheartedly with this opinion. But if a
question, difficult in itself, is said to be very easy, we can affirm without
rash judgment that it has not been understood. However, probabilists are

534. This extremely important teaching on *reflective principles* aims at making us certain of the morality of an action where first we were uncertain. We must consider the problem carefully. It can be expressed as follows: 'Is it possible for one who hesitates between two opinions, and does not know whether a proposed action is lawful or not, to reassure and persuade himself completely through a reflective principle that his action is certainly lawful?'

We cannot answer such a serious question without first indicating some undoubted, evident truths which will serve as the starting point for what we have to say.

535. First, it is certain that if I doubt whether I sin in doing an action, I can always lawfully examine my doubt to see 'if it has been produced by valid or invalid reasons, and is therefore reasonable or unreasonable.' And we have already proposed the question in this form.

Second, it is equally certain that I can and must abandon my doubt if a reflective examination shows that I have no valid motive for it, and that it arises from useless fear or false reasoning. And having abandoned my doubt, I can freely do the action because my new reflection has changed my doubt about it into certainty.

Third, it is clear I cannot do the action without sinning if my reflection resolves the doubt by showing that the action is certainly unlawful.

Fourth, it is also clear that I cannot lawfully act if further

emphatic about the difficulties it presents. Esparza calls it 'the most difficult and complicated amongst all moral questions, whether speculative or practical'; Cardenas speaks of it as 'an obscure and extremely metaphysical matter that calls for much mental reflection.' Tirillo does not hesitate to declare it an impenetrable mystery to all except the finest intelligences. These affirmations show that the *knot* of the matter was well taken by the probabilists. We cannot conclude, however, that they unravelled it. It is one thing to see the difficulty of a question, and another to solve it. Usually, the person who takes the first step by proposing a new, difficult question is not the one who solves it. Often centuries elapse before the solution, the second step, is reached. Very frequently important questions arise in one century, only to be solved in future centuries. Progress is made, but only at the cost of many errors, repeated efforts and false or imperfect solutions before a true or complete answer is given. But let us do justice to the probabilists by acknowledging their scientific merit in proposing such a new, important question to the world.

[534-5]

reflection simply confirms my spirit in its doubt without clarifying the situation.

536. An unassailable conclusion from these simple principles is: 'Any reflective principle which is able to change my state of spirit from doubt to certainty about the morality of an action must render my doubt insubsistent and baseless because founded on a false, useless presupposition of my own.'

The problem has now been stated much more clearly, as far as I can see. It is easy to understand that reflective principles will be available to remove uncertainty of spirit if we can find 'reflective principles enabling me to see that my doubt about the sinfulness of my own action is useless and insubsistent,' that is, founded on motives that cannot reasonably bring me to such uncertainty.

Do such principles really exist? Let us first be clear that there are cases 'in which even to suppose their existence would imply contradiction.'

Article 3.
The first step towards answering the second question:
we prove that any doubt about the lawfulness of an action
arising from the intrinsic nature of the action itself
can be eliminated only through persuasion
of the action's intrinsic morality

537. We note that the motive for my doubt about the lawfulness of a given action may have two sources, that is, the *intrinsic nature of the action itself* or *some exterior cause*.

538. But it is clear that I can resolve my doubt in the first case only if I show that the intrinsic nature of my action does not contain the blameworthiness that I presupposed or feared. In the second case, I must show that the exterior cause making me doubtful about the action's lawfulness has no power to produce this effect in me. In other words, my reflection must resolve the doubt at its foundations, either in the very nature of the action or outside it.

539. An evident, beautiful corollary of this principle can, I think, be stated thus: 'Where doubt falls on the intrinsic

lawfulness of an action, none of the principles concerned with causes of the doubt exterior to the action can resolve it.'

540. Laws are causes exterior to the action. Principles drawn from the state of laws cannot therefore resolve a doubt intrinsic to the action.

541. The following principles, proposed by noted moralists, are extrinsic to actions:

1. A doubtful law does not oblige; or, an uncertain law does not produce a certain obligation.

2. A person's actual condition is presumed better than its opposite. If he is presently acting freely, freedom must maintain its right against the law; if he is presently following the law, the law rightly prevails.

These two principles can be reduced to a single principle because actual freedom[348] would not exist if the law were certain and therefore restricted freedom.

These principles, although applicable in other cases, are certainly not applicable where doubt falls on the *intrinsic malice of an action*. They presuppose a law distinct from the action; but law, considered as *extrinsic to an action*, prohibits and hence renders unlawful an action not evil in itself (which is contrary to our hypothesis).

542. When I say 'Law which is certain obliges; law which is uncertain does not oblige', I mean 'Law which is certain makes an action unlawful for me; uncertain law does not render it unlawful, but leaves it lawful for me.' The subject of discussion therefore are actions which can sometimes be lawful and sometimes unlawful. We are not discussing actions unlawful in themselves; we are presuming that the actions are lawful when not forbidden by some law whose existence is doubted, but unlawful when forbidden by the law. In this

[348] Some theologians have found fault with the use of the word *freedom* in questions about probable opinion. This is an unreasonable objection because the use of the word has been authenticated by scripture. St. Paul says: 'But if someone says to you, "This has been offered in sacrifice," then out of consideration for the man who informed you, and for conscience' sake — I mean his conscience, not yours — do not eat it. For why should my LIBERTY be determined by another man's scruples?' (1 Cor 10: 28–29). Here, in contradistinction to *liberty* or *freedom*, *conscience* is used for *consciousness of the law* that forms the bond of conscience (cf. 1 Cor 7: 37; Jas 2: 2).

case the law is a principle completely distinct from and
extraneous to the action, giving the action a quality it does
not of itself possess. This principle, therefore, will be valid
only for those actions which, although lawful in themselves,
may be rendered unlawful by some law. It will be valid only
in the case of a positive, external law. But when the doubt
falls on the intrinsic evil of an action, and not in relationship
to knowledge of a law which renders a good action immoral
by forbidding it, this principle has no force. The very enunci-
ation of such a principle shows that the action is certainly
moral in itself.

543. The same can be said about the second principle, or
rather about the second way of stating the same principle. We
ask whether freedom or the law holds sway. If we say 'freedom', there is no obligation to stand by the law. This is clear.
But we are presupposing that freedom holds sway ante-
cedently to the law, and this can be true only in the case of
actions moral in themselves, and in the case of positive laws.
Our concern, on the contrary, is not with a law prohibiting
an action, but with the intrinsic morality of an action. We
want to know whether freedom, prescinding from the law,
holds sway or not. If in fact the action is intrinsically evil,
freedom cannot hold sway even in the absence of any
contrary positive law. In moral matters, freedom means
simply freedom to act lawfully, and acting lawfully means
doing what is lawful. The presupposition in our present case
is that the action is lawful until the law renders it otherwise.
If, however, we doubt whether the action is unlawful
independently of a law distinct from it, our presupposition is
no longer valid. The intrinsic lawfulness of the action, and
hence the possession of freedom, is now uncertain. The
principle of *possession* is no longer applicable.

544. It follows that I cannot act as long as I doubt whether I
am free. If I were to act in such a case, I would be in danger of
using a right I do not possess. Uncertain freedom is not
freedom; the uncertainty destroys the freedom to act if I am
uncertain whether in acting I may not be exceeding the limit
of my right. This must be granted by every upholder of
reflective principles, each of whom in recent times has
reaffirmed the proposition: 'A person in *practical* doubt

about any action must, before acting, definitely resolve the doubt about the morality of that action by means of a CERTAIN or reflective principle.'[349] All modern defenders of reflective principles are also agreed in deploring the laxity arising from their predecessors' support of the principle 'He who acts probably, acts prudently.'[350] A reflective principle which leaves in doubt both my freedom to act and the blameworthiness of my action is definitely not one of these *certain* principles capable of eliminating doubt about the morality of an action. And as long as doubt remains, it is not lawful for me to act.

Article 4.
An answer to an objection dependent upon the obscurity of the natural law

545. Some, however, may be hesitant about accepting what we have said so far. Their objection would be: 'In speaking about intrinsically evil actions can you indicate which they are? Is weak, fallacious reason capable of knowing the internal malice of actions in such a way as to produce obligation in human beings?' We are dealing obviously with the celebrated controversy between Father Giovan Vincenzo Patuzzi and the famous bishop of Sant'Agata de'Goti [St. Alphonsus de Liguori] about the promulgation of the natural law.

546. Patuzzi maintained that the natural law obliges us independently of the divine positive law because it is sufficiently promulgated by the light of reason. Liguori denied this and concluded — arguing that a doubtfully promulgated law is doubtful and does not therefore oblige — that it cannot

---

[349] Liguori, *De Consc.*, c. 2, n. 24.

[350] 'Probability is not sufficient for lawful action; moral certainty about the uprightness of the action is also needed, as St. Paul says (Rom. 14: 23): "For whatever does not proceed from faith is sin." He says: *from faith* meaning from a SURE dictate of conscience which persuades us in our conscience that we are acting rightly. This is the explanation of *from faith* given by Sts. Chrysostom, Ambrose and others together with St. Thomas (*De Verit.*, q. 17, 3). For this reason I noted in the dissertation mentioned previously the falsity of the probabilists' tag: "Acting probably means acting prudently"' (Liguori, *De Conscientia, morale systema, etc.*, n. 55).

oblige without the addition of the divine law. 'Natural reason arising from the nature of the human being,' says the Saint, 'is obscure, deceitful and fallible. This is especially true in the present condition of *human nature corrupted by sin* which blinds our understanding. Natural reason springing from human nature cannot be the rule for human moral actions. God must illuminate us with a particular, certain and infallible light if we are to be sure of what we must do and what we must avoid. He impresses this light upon us, and promulgates it as his law.'[351] This *particular light* of which St. Alphonsus speaks is different from natural reason, and can only be the light of revelation and the internal light of grace. If St. Alphonsus were referring to *natural reason itself* as the *particular light*, his argument would have been inconclusive, and would have simply stated that 'natural reason does not oblige without the particular light of natural reason.'

547. In some places, St. Alphonsus seems to maintain that even in the state of pure nature human beings would have no moral obligation! 'I reply that if God had not raised this (natural) law to be his law, human beings in another state, that is, in the state of pure nature (which was certainly a possibility, as the Church affirmed against Baius, who denied it), would have remained without any strictly obliging law. But in such a hypothesis would we not be obliged to live according to the law of human nature? This is not the case, because natural law, unsustained by authority, could never have been a law of obligation for human beings, as we showed above; we would have remained without law. I find it impossible to maintain that in the state of pure nature we would have had to obey reason and its natural dictates. As Finetti says so well, reason is a faculty proper to human beings, and obeying it would make them simultaneously subjects and superiors to themselves.[352] Therefore, the natural law, which

[351] *Appendice alla IV Apologia*, n. 3.

[352] Finetti's false reasoning is a consequence of the *subjectivism* which has ruined a great part of modern philosophy. I have shown that although the reason 'is a faculty proper to human beings', the *light* of reason is not something pertaining to, but distinct from human beings, infinitely superior to them, and wholly divine. This light is the source of moral obligation imposed upon human beings. We are not simultaneously

results from human nature, can never impose true obligation on us. Finetti himself says several times that the natural law originating from nature is not true law. If therefore the law of nature is not true law, it cannot induce true obligation.'[353]

548. In my opinion, this is definitely erroneous.

Certainly, there is no difficulty in admitting that *natural law*, prescinding from every supernatural revelation, is not *positive* law. We call it natural law precisely because it is not *positive*, that is, not promulgated with external signs but through the internal light of reason which shows and induces in the nature of perceived beings the esteem proper to each of them.

We could also admit that *natural law* without positive revelation does not merit the title 'law' if the meaning of this word is restricted to external, positive law alone, and has no significant reference to obligatory principles in general (cf. 143).

Again, St. Alphonsus could mean that *natural law* is not always known through a manifestation of the divine will, and that what is known as obligatory by the simple light of reason can be distinguished conceptually from that which is willed by God. This could be granted to those who take the will of God as a principle of arbitrary divine decrees without realising that the word *God* not only signifies an omnipotent being as efficient cause of the universe, but also eternal, subsistent truth.

It could also mean that transgressors of the natural law would be punished (in the supposed state of pure nature) by natural penalties, or at most by penalties much less severe than those destined for offenders against God when he is known as legislator in the supernatural order. In scriptural language this second kind of punishment is rightly called *loss of one's own soul*. This also could be granted.

549. But outside these qualifications it is certainly an extremely serious error to maintain that the *natural law* contains

'subject to and superior to ourselves', but subject to the light shining before us that 'enlightens every man coming into the world', a light other than ourselves (cf. *PE*, 13–19).

[353] *Appendice alla IV Apologia*, n. 12.

no intrinsic obligating force independently of a positive revelation.

550. It would also be an extremely grave error to imply that *natural law* shows no trace of the divine, if this meant that it is not a manifestation of the will of God as *nature* but only as *decision*, or that it is not a manifestation of God as *eternal truth* and unchangeable order but only as *free will*. In this case natural law would not be a *participation in eternal law*, as the Fathers rightly call it.

It is an error to deny, in opposition to the constant teaching of the Fathers, the qualities and divine authority proper to the principles of natural law. As I have shown in several places, natural law is reduced in its entirety to the respect given to truth, to the *acknowledgement of being*. And truth and being are immutable and eternal. *Ideal being* or truth, the supreme principle of both natural and positive law, is infinitely superior to human beings and to all natures. It is universal, and as necessary as God himself, because it is truly an appurtenance of God himself.

551. It is also erroneous to say that without the addition of a positive law, TRUTH, to which all law is reduced, contains no obligation requiring our esteem, love and obedience. Finetti's argument attempting to prove that no obligation exists where there is no superior, and that natural reason is not superior to human beings, is absurd and contradictory.[354] In the first place it is false (this needs repeating) that there is in us no light superior to us. Reason (as a faculty) is indeed an element in human nature, but *we* are not the the light of reason or truth which shines before us; rather, we are commanded by it.[355]

---

[354] 'Reason lacks the authority proper to a superior, and can therefore only stimulate but not oblige action or limit freedom. It seems perfectly clear that only a superior can impose obligation. No one would say that reason is superior to human beings since freedom is a faculty proper to us' (*De principiis univ. nat. et gent.* t. 2, c. 10, c. 6). What incredible confusion between reason, in which an eternal light shines, and freedom, which has to conform to that light!

[355] Church tradition distinguishes the power of reason from the principle illuminating it, as a lamp is distinguished from the light which makes it shine. 'A lamp,' says one writer, 'does not shine of itself but receives its light from elsewhere. So the interior intellect sees what is right only in your light' (Remigius Antisoderensis *in Ps 17*, t. 16 of the *Biblioteca Maxima*).

On the other hand, if some superior has to show us his will in order for us to be truly under obligation, what obliges us to conform to this will? We could simply try to explain that this is the will of a superior, and it is of course true that we must respect and obey the will of the superior. But it is only the light of reason that tells us that the superior merits respect and that his will must be an inviolable law for us. If we do not first believe in and obey the light of reason, we cannot believe in or obey any superior, not even God. We cannot respect the positive law if we do not first respect the rational law; we submit to the positive law only because it draws its force from a preceding dictate of the rational law.

552. Nevertheless, the saintly bishop would certainly not wish to sustain the consequences of his principles relative to the natural law in so far as they deny obligation to the natural law separated from revelation. As a result he is often inconsistent in what he says. For instance, there is certainly inconsistency in speaking of *natural law* which does not oblige. A *law* which does not induce obligation is both law and not law; law and obligation are interdependent.

553. Again, as St. Alphonsus acknowledges, there are indeed *intrinsically good* and *evil* actions. Given the existence of human beings and the present order, therefore, the natural law could not be other than it is.[356] But why are some actions intrinsically good and others intrinsically evil? Is it because God had *necessarily* to command or permit the former, and forbid the latter? Given human nature and the present order of things, why is the natural law, as willed by God, not arbitrary? But if the law does not depend upon God's *arbitrary*

---

[356] 'Actions commanded or forbidden by the divine, natural law are intrinsically good or evil because they are *necessarily* commanded or forbidden by God. Let me explain: human existence first depends upon the will of God the Creator. But granted that God wanted us to exist, he must *necessarily* have given us laws *suitable* to our nature. God created us as rational beings so that we might serve him on earth and thus merit eternal life. Necessarily, therefore, he had to give us the rule according to which we might serve him — a rule in conformity with his divine holiness and adapted to human nature. Because the law is *necessarily* in conformity with the holiness of God, it is not arbitrary, but intrinsically just. Hence our actions are intrinsically good or evil in so far as they conform to, or differ from, what is prescribed by divine law' (*Appendice alla IV Apologia*, n. 10).

will, it can spring only from the *intrinsic order* of beings which of its nature requires respect and observance by us because it is the truth rooted in divine nature and shining *per se* before the reason, obliging its consent. As St. Alphonsus himself acknowledges, an obligation, if it does not come from an *arbitrary decree* of God, must arise from a *principle of reason*, that is, from the natural order itself which, while it is conceived mentally, manifests itself as requiring the service of our will.

554. St. Alphonsus also quotes St. Thomas: 'Human reason is not of itself the rule of things, but the principles NATURALLY inserted in reason are so many general rules and measures of all that is to be done by us.'[357] These words express exactly what we are saying, that is, obligation does not come from *reason* as a human faculty, but from the *light* inherent in reason by nature — a light which, as we have shown, takes the name and form of *principles* as a result of its various applications.[358] Without this light, reason itself would not be. But the text from Aquinas certainly does not prove that the natural light of human reason needs another light of revelation or grace in order to induce obligation. On the contrary, it shows clearly that this light, that is, the natural principles known *per se*, 'are rules and measures of everything to be done by us'. St. Alphonsus' attempt to use these words to support his own opinion is therefore misguided. He says: 'The rule of moral actions is not the natural law that springs from human nature or human reason and is dictated to us by nature. It is the law impressed by God in the human heart. God, in creating angelic and human nature, gave these creatures a law suitable for each nature. The law, therefore, does not originate from the nature itself, independently of the will of God, but arises from the will of God who has given to human beings and angels laws in keeping with their natures.'[359]

As I have said, this comment is irrelevant. The principles of law impressed in human reason are precisely the essential constitutents of human reason which sees order amongst

---

[357] *S.T.*, I-II, q. 91, art. 3, ad 2.
[358] *OT*, 558 ss.
[359] *Appendice alla IV Apologia*, n. 9.

natures and immediately knows that it is to be safeguarded, not destroyed. The law comes both from *natures* and at the same time from the *will of God* who has made and ordered natures, giving to reason the light to know the order of the natures he has created. This order is indubitably eternal, and the natural law is certainly of itself 'a participation in the eternal law', as St. Thomas elegantly defines it.[360] Indeed it does not differ essentially from the eternal law itself.[361] It therefore obliges of itself alone, without the addition of any other law. The question 'Does the natural law oblige?' (without any other external revelation, or the help of interior grace) is solved affirmatively by saying, as St. Alphonsus does, that it obliges because it is impressed by God. This question does not ask: 'Why does the natural law oblige?', but 'Does it oblige?' It is one thing to ask: 'Does the natural law oblige of itself?', and another to ask: 'Does this obligation come from human nature or is it impressed divinely?' Let us grant, with St. Alphonsus, that it is divinely impressed (although there is a certain ambiguity even here); we still conclude that for this very reason 'the natural law obliges without the addition of any other particular light different from the law.' It even obliges those who have no knowledge of positive revelation, and those who might have been created in a state of pure nature. It obliges because truth, the law from the hand of God himself, or rather an appurtenance of God himself, is written into natural reason. St. Alphonsus, in trying to prove that the natural law obliges only because it comes from God, unwittingly changes the whole question and, at the same time, concedes to his adversaries all they want because he grants that 'the natural law obliges of itself alone', thus contradicting what he had formerly said relative to the hypothesis that human beings had been constituted in a state of pure nature.

555. According to St. Alphonsus himself, therefore, there

---

[360] 'The participation of the eternal law in a rational nature' (*S.T.*, I-II, q. 91, art. 2).

[361] St. Thomas puts the following difficulty: if there is an eternal law, the natural law appears useless. He replies: 'This would be true if the natural law were different from the eternal law, but in fact it is only a participation in the eternal law' (*S.T.*, I-II, q. 91, art. 2, ad 1).

are intrinsically good and intrinsically evil actions; the moral law is not abitrarily imposed by God, but depends upon his eternal reason and the exigency, resplendent in that reason, of created natures; God has impressed in us the moral rules of life which together form the natural law; the natural law obliges us because of its relationship with the divine nature. But if this is so, why is the natural law ineffective and without authority for us?

556. St. Alphonsus maintains that if we are speaking about 'the true, natural law itself, we agree. It is certain that we are bound to live according to the natural law which, without doubt, is divine law and depends upon the divine will. According to St. Thomas, the natural law made known to us by the light God impresses upon us is the divine law according to which we must order our actions. But he' (St. Alphonsus is referring to Fr. Patuzzi, his opponent) 'is mistaken if in speaking about reason he means the human dictate coming from natural reason by way of the mind . . . Natural reason as it originates in human nature is (as we have said) obscure, ambiguous and fallible.'[362]

These words are unintelligible unless they mean: 'Human dictates have no force without relationship to the light impressed on us by God. Without this light, they are obscure, ambiguous and fallible.' And the Saint seems to say this shortly afterwards.[363] If this is his meaning, then all agree that the *natural dictate* obliges *per se* without need of any other light. It would in fact be strange to suppose that God had impressed in us a light of justice which either did not enlighten us in any way or had need of some other light to enlighten us.

What is 'the human dictate which comes from natural

[362] *Appendice all'Apologia IV*, n. 3.

[363] 'Because our reason is so ambiguous and subject to error, it cannot oblige our adhesion WITHOUT the support of divine law' (*Append. all'Apolog. IV*, n. 9). If by divine law Liguori means the natural law itself (which as he says is 'certainly divine law'), the passage would show: 1. that the natural law obliges of itself because it is divine; 2. that it has to be well understood and interpreted, and clearly known by us if it is to oblige. We shall show that the natural law obliges even when its dictate seems obscure and doubtful.

[556]

reason by way of the mind'? What is the mind? What is reason? The 'human dictate' is only the intuition of the very light impressed upon us by God. If it were not, it could not be a *dictate*; the mind, the reason, is simply our faculty for intuiting that light. If reason errs in consulting the light that illumines it, it loses all its authority — no one doubts this.

But it is not always mistaken. Principles are present to it about which reason cannot err: for instance, it is impossible to prefer a lie to the truth; it is impossible, as Saint Augustine says, to prefer an irrational to a rational being; it is impossible to prefer to do evil rather than good to another human being. These and other dictates of human reason are perfectly clear to us independently of divine revelation. If they are clear, as St. Alphonsus himself confesses, they oblige. But the only explanation given by him in arguing that the natural law does not oblige is that reason manifests it to us obscurely. If, therefore, reason does manifest the natural law clearly and evidently, it does indeed oblige. Moreover, if the natural law were in no way evident, we would not know that respect is due to a superior, that we have to obey the positive laws that express his will, and that we have to keep the divine law (cf. 175–187). It is certain, therefore, that at least some part of the natural law is evident.

It seems utterly clear therefore: 1. that the natural law obliges *per se* without the addition of any special light to the light already impressed in our rational nature by God; 2. that this law is extremely clear in its principal points, and is proposed by our reason with complete certainty; 3. that we have a true moral obligation, at least in these evident points of the natural law, in such a way that there can be no discussion about the non-promulgation of this law; 4. that in St. Alphonsus' hypothesis about human creation in a state of pure nature, free from the darkness of sin, human beings would have known the natural law fully and certainly in all the consequences they could have drawn from it. In such a condition, we would have found ourselves fully bound to conform to this law.

But does the natural law oblige us when our imperfect reason leaves us in doubt about it?

Article 5.
Continuation

557. The problem has now been reduced to its minimum terms.

First we note that in considering St. Alphonsus' order of ideas we can see clearly that he focused his attention on remote, uncertain and doubtful consequences of natural principles and then, from the obscurity of such consequences, generalised about the natural law in its entirety. The obscurity and uncertainty he presupposed in the law enabled him to deduce as a consequence that it has no obligating force because it is not sufficiently promulgated by human reason alone without the addition of an extraordinary light from divine revelation.

We then observed that the natural law is not entirely obscure. At least its supreme principles are very clear, and even clearer than the divine positive law which is itself founded on a principle of natural reason. And we proved at length the clarity of the natural law on the authority of scripture.

Nevertheless, we granted that the dictate of the natural law remained doubtful in some of its remote conclusions. We now have to see, as we said above, whether St. Alphonsus is right in maintaining that the law is not sufficiently promulgated in this case, and does not oblige us.

558. We have already seen that no fault or sin is present if through mental limitation, and without any wish on our part, we fail to draw certain remote conclusions from the natural law and, without knowing them in any way, act contrary to them. As we showed, the notion of fault and sin are absent if the two elements of knowledge and will are lacking (cf. 74). But we are not at the moment dealing with totally unknown dictates of the natural law; the real object of our present discussion is the case in which we are doubtful about a dictate of the natural law and in particular about whether an action is intrinsically lawful or unlawful.

In this case, speaking of the natural law as insufficiently promulgated and hence as not obligating entails an invalid application to the natural law of an argument applicable to

[557-8]

positive law. In the case of positive law, the law itself and the action to which the law applies are different things. The action, which is not blameworthy of itself, becomes such from outside, that is, from the positive decision of the legislator: the law is external to and distinct from the action under consideration. An intrinsically evil action, however, is forbidden of its very nature because of the disorder and malice that it bears deep within itself. This disorder is an obligating principle to which the word 'law' is applied through a mental abstraction that considers the exigency and obligating force of the action as separate from the action itself (cf. 46–48). In this case, the action is not rendered evil by prohibition from some external law, but is evil in its mere existence.

In matters forbidden by positive law, the law must exist if evil is to be present; in intrinsically evil matters, evil exists along with the action. The action and disorder exist together; and the natural law prohibiting the action is one with the disorder itself. The concept of disorder is then formulated in an imperative which expresses the concept in the form of law. But no external promulgation of the law is necessary to tell us such actions are forbidden; it is sufficient for them to be present to our minds for us to know that we must avoid them.[364]

559. It may be urged that we should be certain of the intrinsic immorality of actions before we need to avoid them. But as we have seen, all theologians, including Liguori himself, agree that the danger of moral evil, as well as its certainty, is to be avoided. There is a real difference between an action which I know with certainty to be lawful, although I doubt whether the external law forbids it, and an action about

---

[364] Patuzzi objected to Liguori that favouring human freedom in doubt about the natural law entails favouring the flesh. Liguori answered: 'It cannot be denied that disorder and sin are present when we choose vice and the flesh. But following vice and the flesh when this is equivalent to licence is one thing: it is quite different from following lawful freedom permitted by God when we see no law prohibiting it' (*Append. alla IV Apol.*, n. 4, 19). This passage shows that the Saint always supposes that freedom remains lawful if positive law is removed. But this is precisely what does not happen in the case of intrinsically evil actions which contain in themselves their prohibiting law.

whose lawfulness I am in doubt. In the first case, my doubt
does not fall on the morality of the action, but on the
existence of the law; in the second case, my doubt falls
properly speaking on the morality of the action. And it is the
morality or immorality of our actions which constitutes the
natural law itself. Here the law does not precede, but follows
upon, the quality of the actions; a law exists when the morality of the action or actions has been formulated. In the second
case, we have what the theologians call *practical doubt* which
renders action unlawful; in the first case, we have what the
theologians call *speculative doubt*, with which it is lawful to
act (cf. 465).

560. We can now state the teaching in exact terms and
conclude: when the judgment of conscience remains
suspended and unformed because there is doubt about the
morality of an action, as happens in the second case, it is
unlawful to act except by following the safest path and avoiding any danger of committing an intrinsically evil action.

Article 6.
Contradiction in the opposing teaching

561. Liguori, whose heart was set on the truth and on the
salvation of souls, could not rest altogether content with his
teaching. This can be seen clearly not only in the corrections
he felt necessary as he matured,[365] but also in the incomplete,
not altogether coherent, condition of his final teaching.

562. After laying down several general principles, he either
does not apply them universally or offers many exceptions in
particular cases. This alone is sufficient to prove that the

---

[365] Liguori's fourth Italian *Apologia* begins: 'I am accused of being a
probabilist. I want to repeat in this short work that I am not a probabilist,
and do not follow probabilist teachings which, in fact, I reject. It is true
that in my first books on morals, written when I was still young, I
sometimes accepted rather more liberal opinions than I should. But further
reflection allowed me to repudiate them, which I did even in print.' The
Saint says the same thing in the declaration first published in *Regola de'
costumi*, Naples 1780, and reprinted by Fr. Jacopo Basso, CSSR, in his
Riflessioni critiche on the booklet *Pedante* by Fr. Andrea Tingello. In the
last editions of his moral works, St. Alphonsus corrected 120 statements.

theory is deficient and unable to embrace all cases. For example, he establishes the principle: 'Because obligation imposed by the law has to be certain, it is not sufficient that the promulgation of the law be probable. But granted the certainty of the obligation, the law and its promulgation must also be certain.'[366] According to this principle, obligation would exist only when both the law and its promulgation were certain.

But the Saint could not stomach this consequence, and substitutes other principles that cannot in any way be made to harmonise with his starting point. 'First, I affirm that we have to follow the opinion in favour of the law when it is certainly more probable. The chief reason for this is our obligation, when we have moral doubts, to follow the truth. If we cannot find the truth clearly we must at least follow the opinion nearest the truth which is, of course, the opinion we think more probable. The truth itself obliges us to follow the opinion in favour of the law when this opinion is nearest the truth.

'Second, when the opinion in favour of freedom is equally as probable as the opinion in favour of the law, we cannot follow it on the ground that it is probable. Probability alone is not sufficient for us to be able to act lawfully. We need moral certainty about the probity of our action, *as all probabilists will unhesitatingly agree.*'[367] And he says elsewhere that the law obliges even if it is probably promulgated.[368]

It is clear that this teaching is inaccurate and riddled with contradictions.

[366] *Append. alla IV Apologia*, n. 20.

[367] *Apolog. IV*, n. 3.

[368] 'Thirdly, a strict, rigorous doubt is present when two opinions are equally probable, because the opinion in favour of freedom is of equal weight with that in favour of the law (although any less certain opinion cannot of itself be followed because probability alone is not sufficient ground for acting lawfully). In this case we suspend our judgment about the existence or non-existence of the law, and consequently ignore the existence of the law forbidding the action because the law cannot be said to be sufficiently promulgated. What has been sufficiently promulgated is doubt about the existence of the law, not the law. And since the law is not promulgated, there can be no certain obligation to observe it' (*Apolog. IV*, n. 4).

563. First, St. Alphonsus asserts the principle that an *uncertain* law cannot produce a certain obligation, but then goes on to say that if the law is *probable*, it obliges. Again he first establishes that the promulgation of the law has to be *certain*, and then draws the conclusion that the law, if it is *probable*, obliges. Another principle is that *certain truth* has to be followed, but this is substituted by the assertion that when the truth cannot clearly be found, we must at least follow the opinion nearest the truth, that is, the opinion that seems to us the *more probable*. Again, one principle states that if the opinion in favour of the law is *equally probable* with that in favour of freedom, we must follow the law because an *equally probable* as well as a *probable* law obliges. But then we find that if the opinion in favour of the law is equally probable with that in favour of freedom, *doubt* is present and the law does not oblige.[369] Finally, St. Alphonsus lays down that we cannot follow the opinion in favour of freedom if it is *equally probable* with that in favour of the law, but immediately goes on to deny that the law is *probable* if freedom is *equally probable*. In a word, in order to be probable the opinion in favour of the law has to be *more probable* than the opinion in favour of freedom. These are all absurd contradictions when understood according to the strict sense of the words used.

It is clear that the law and its promulgation have to be *certain* in order to oblige: it is not sufficent for them to be *probable*.

It is clear that if truth is necessary, it is not sufficient to be near truth; what is near truth is not truth.

It is clear that if it is sufficient to follow a probable opinion, we cannot require a *more probable* opinion.

It is clear that if we suppose that two opinions in favour of the law and of freedom are *equally probable* and then go on to claim that we must follow the law, it is contradictory to add

---

[369] 'In conclusion, if the opinion in favour of the law were more probable, I would grant that the law is probably promulgated. But if the two opinions are of equal weight, the opinion in favour of the law is not even probable, as we have seen. But if the opinion in favour of the law is not even probable, how can the law be said to be probably promulgated? Only the doubt is promulgated, not the law' (*Appendice all'Apolog. IV*, n. 21).

[563]

that in the same case no doubt exists and that consequently the law does not oblige.

It is clear that if we say the law can sometimes be as probable as freedom in a given case, it is contradictory to add that the law, in order to be *probable*, must be *more probable* than freedom in the same case.

In each of these assertions one half of the proposition is at odds with the other. It is impossible to accept both, although St. Alphonsus is forced to do so because of the defective principles from which he sets out.

Article 7.
Continuation of our proof
that doubt about the intrinsic unlawfulness of an action
cannot be resolved by any reflective principle,
but only by showing
that the action is not intrinsically unlawful
although falsely supposed to be so

564. It would be possible to illustrate other departures from principle in St. Alphonsus. Often, in particular cases, he states the opposite of what his principles seem to require. Sometimes he is unaware of this; sometimes, although aware of the difficulty, he is content to say that these are *exceptions to the rule* he has given, as for instance in the case of the validity of the sacraments, the choice of religion and the danger of harming our neighbour. But it is certain that principles must be *universal*. Principles allowing exceptions are not true, complete principles. However, I do not wish to insist on this difficulty in St. Alphonsus which I shall have the opportunity of discussing elsewhere.

565. I want to insist, with further proof of the solution I have adopted, that when 'there is doubt about the intrinsic unlawfulness of an action, no reflective principle can prove it lawful without showing with certainty that the action is not intrinsically unlawful, and consequently without dissolving the doubt directly.'

If I doubt that an action is intrinsically unlawful, what reflective principle can authorise me to act as long as this doubt remains? There is an obvious contradiction in maintaining that my doubt about the intrinsic unlawfulness of an action can be resolved by the principle 'What is doubtfully unlawful is not unlawful.' The simple affirmation of the principle demonstrates its obvious contradiction.

566. The contradiction can be avoided only by taking a different approach and arguing correctly as follows.

Doubt exists about the intrinsic unlawfulness of an action.

Knowing this, and acting notwithstanding, I expose myself to the danger of doing something intrinsically unlawful.

But my love for uprightness and moral good must make me hold back from the least danger of losing uprightness and moral good.

I err therefore if I expose myself to such danger.

567. In his great wisdom St. Alphonsus softened and tempered the mistaken principle by introducing many *ad hoc* exceptions. This however was not the case with a number of other moralists. In particular, one very sharp mind tried, prior to Alphonsus, to subject the most unyielding cases to the same principle. Fr. Segneri, well known for his acute arguments, requires our utmost respect, and it is in this spirit that we shall consider what he says.

568. According to Segneri, it is calumny to maintain that probabilists affirm the universal lawfulness of following probable opinion. 'This is not the case. The same reason which makes the probable opinion lawful for some renders it unlawful for others. The chief reason in its favour is that noted at the start: if it is not certain that the law places us under an obligation to do something onerous, such as give alms, make a legacy, undertake more rigorous fasts,[370] it is not just that we should have the same duty to carry out this obligation as we would if the law were certain.[371] The same

[370] These examples are irrelevant because they are not concerned with cases where doubt falls on the intrinsic evil of actions.

[371] We do not want to maintain that a person carrying out an action which he knows with certainty is intrinsically unlawful has the *same degree of culpability* as another person who does the same action while doubting its lawfulness, as we showed (cf. 630, 631). The reason given here has been inserted oratorically in the middle of the argument without any regard to philosophical criteria.

reason proves that some persons cannot follow a less probable opinion because certain law forbids them to do so.'[372]

We notice that this brilliant man, who sees that exceptions would ruin the authority of the principle, feels the need to defend his view by excluding exceptions, and wishes to show that 'the same reason which makes it (the probable opinion) lawful for some renders it unlawful for others.' But how does he demonstrate this?

His argument runs as follows:

'It is lawful to follow probable opinion because an uncertain law cannot oblige.

'But sometimes the law is certain.

'For the same reason, therefore, it is not lawful to follow probable opinion.'

This is an attractive-looking argument, but careful examination will show that it has no internal force whatsoever. It presupposes the existence of less probable, but nevertheless probable, opinions condemned by a certain law. But this is absurd. What kind of probable lawfulness is enjoyed by an action which is certainly forbidden? The argument has changed: it is no longer true that the less probable opinion can sometimes be followed, and sometimes not. According to Segneri's argument, it has either to be followed in all cases or not at all, because an opinion opposed to certain law is no longer probable, but certainly erroneous.

569. But what law is Segneri speaking about? He cannot intend to speak about any certain natural law. If an action were certainly condemned by natural law it would not have even a relative and hypothetical probability in its favour. He must intend speaking, therefore, about positive law, and must mean: 'A less probable opinion in natural law cannot be followed if a positive law forbids it.'

In the first place I repeat that if a positive law forbids the action, the question is resolved on the ground that the probability which once existed no longer does so. In the second place, why has the positive law forbidden this action which according to natural law was probably unlawful? What

[372] *Letters on probabilism*, Fr. Paolo Segneri, letter 1, §8.

is positive law? Where does it get its force if not from natural law?[373]

We are dealing with cases in which the human legislator sees that doubtfully lawful actions would be harmful to the public good and decides to forbid them under human sanctions. But in forbidding them, he has not changed their nature; he has simply decided that they cannot be done. The positive law intervenes therefore to declare solemnly that it is not lawful to carry out actions which are supposedly doubtful. Relative to such laws, therefore, we have to conclude that the weight of public authority has declared the probabilists' opinion mistaken at least in this matter. Positive laws, and certainly those cited by Segneri, have condemned this teaching of probabilists by condemning the actions they defend.

570. Other examples given by Segneri support this criticism: 'Without doubt, a judge cannot follow a less probable opinion because he is faced with a certain, contrary law established by the state. The state puts the scales of justice in his hands so that after he has weighed the case he may let them settle of their own accord. Moreover, it is certain that the litigants themselves have legislated for him by offering witnesses, arguments and proofs to show that they are probably in the right. But what is the point of such information if he could value it as though it did not exist? And again the law says: "Laws always presume in the judge's favour."[374] But a similar presumption would be unjust if he were not always bound to follow the better-founded amongst two contrary judgments.'[375] There is confusion here between *probability relative to the parties in a case*, and *probability relative to the probity of the judge's action* in passing sentence. The question under discussion is concerned only with the second difficulty: 'Is it possible for a person to act while he doubts about the intrinsic morality of his action?' The example proffered by Segneri is irrelevant.

571. In fact, his argument presupposes as probable (although less probable than its contrary) that 'the judge can

---

[373] St. Thomas says: 'Every law springing from human action shares in the notion of law in so far as it is derived from the law of nature' (*S.T.*, I-II, q. 95, art. 2).

[374] *Digest.*, bk. 47, t. 8, 1, §2, 20; *Decretal.*, bk. 1, t. 9, c. 6.

[375] *Letters*, 1, §8, n. 41.

[570-1]

find in favour of the party less favoured in the balance of justice.' But this probable opinion cannot be followed, says Segneri, because it is opposed by a certain law established by the state — and he cites instances in the law of Justinian.[376] But has it been established by the state, or by the nature of things? Does this mean that the scales of justice could be tipped in the less favourable direction if the Justinian Codex had perished in the Dark Ages along with the works of so many other authors? Is a positive law needed for us to know that it is unlawful and unjust to favour the side with the less favourable arguments? I cannot bring myself to think that until the formation of positive laws, judges could for centuries have passed sentence against parties with more favourable arguments and ruled for those with less favourable arguments. Segneri could never have meant this.

He does in fact feel the weakness of his position and goes on to add reasons drawn from the intimate nature of things, not from the existence of positive law. These reasons, such as the motive for establishing judges and enhancing the trust shown by the litigating parties, provide a foundation for the positive law itself but show that even without it the judge must favour the party on whose side the scales of justice incline of their own accord. In other words, the *intrinsic probity* of the action requires that the judge act in this way. In saying: 'It is certain that the litigants themselves have legislated for the judge', Segneri is speaking rhetorically. The litigants do not legislate for the judge, nor can they forbid him to do what his own judgment allows him to do. The judge cannot find in favour of the less probable party, even though there is a real doubt about the matter, without exposing himself to the danger of committing an injustice (something intrinsically unlawful) by exchanging the more probable for the less probable side. He must not only act justly when he sees clearly where justice lies, but also avoid the least danger of offending justice. Doing the contrary would imply dis-esteem and lack of love for the virtue of justice which has to be cultivated and safeguarded without limit, whatever the cost.

---

[376] VI *Decretal.*, bk. 5, t. 12; *Reg. juris*, 12 and 45; *Digest.*, bk. 22, t. 5, l. 21, §3; *Cod.*, bk. 3, t. 1, l. 14; *et alia ap. Tiraqual, ad l. si unquam* (*Cod.*, bk. 8, t. 56, l. 8).

572. But then Segneri offers another example: 'If the government makes war it cannot follow the less probable opinion in raising taxes and similar matters because of the existence of the certain law of commutative justice which demands that it attribute to the citizenry the same right which it seeks from them. The government wants the people, when they doubt, to tip the balance of reason in its own favour and bear patiently all the burdens it prescribes for the prosecution of the war; the people want the government, when in doubt, to tip the balance of reason in their favour by burdening them as little as possible: "Where both sides have equal reason, equal rights are indicated."[377] And, we must add, the government is not only the higher, but the supreme judge. Hence while "the presumptions of law are always in the judge's favour, they always presume" much more "in the government's favour". If, however, in order to establish presumption in favour of the judge, the judge himself is always bound to pass sentence in favour of the more probable party in controversies before the tribunal, the government is *a fortiori* bound to do the same in the much graver disputes concerning its own rights. We can appeal against the judge, but not against the government.'[378]

First, the final reason ('The presumption is in favour of the government') is very weak. And the same may be said of 'The presumption is in favour of the judge'. If the government could lawfully use even the less probable opinion, it would never lose the right of presumption in its favour, but always act morally and lawfully. In this case, we would constantly have to presume good, not evil of it. To say that the government would lose the presumption in its favour if it were to follow the less probable opinion indicates an implicit confession that the government cannot in any way follow the less favourable opinion when there is danger of damaging others (danger, that is, of something intrinsically evil) who as a people would resent this and believe their rights to be offended; common sense also condemns it.

[377] *Cod.*, bk. 37, t. 50, l. 19; *Decretal.*, bk. 2, t. 30, c. 4.
[378] 'There can be no appeal against judgments in the Senate' (*Dig.*, bk. 1, t. 11, l. 1).

[572]

573. But how does Fr. Segneri know that the government wishes the presumption to be in its own favour, and that the people are prepared to grant this provided the government keeps to the more probable opinion in burdening its citizens? I doubt that he has found it in Roman law, or amongst the dictates of natural equity. Such a presumption has never been the subject of positive law as far as I know, but even if it were it would need support based on the very nature of things. Presumption in favour of the government originates from public persuasion, which is neither created nor imposed upon anyone by decree. But if reason and the nature of things provide a *certain law* which obliges the government to act considerately towards its citizens, as Segneri affirms, can he also affirm that there is any opinion with some degree of probability which disobliges the government from care and circumspection in burdening the people? But if this is not even amongst the less probable opinions, it must be altogether false and wrong. Segneri's example provides no support for his theory.

574. Again, although Segneri mentions more probable opinions, he makes no mention at all of opinions more favourable to the people.

A burden laid upon the people could *more* probably be just; it could *less* probably but still probably be unjust. Would the people be happy if in our present case the government were to follow the more probable opinion? Would they not prefer the government to forget more or less probable opinions for the sake of choosing to avoid the opinion in which there is danger, however slight, of offending against justice (all things being considered), that is, the opinion which would burden the people excessively. This is the reasonable way of acting which would enable the government to say with Samuel: 'Testify against me before the Lord and before his anointed.'[379]

575. Moreover, the principal reason impelling the government to use every care in not burdening the people unjustly is not in order that the citizens may presume in favour of the government. The government's sacred and inalienable

[379] 1 Sam 12: 3.

[573-5]

responsibility when faced with an intrinsically evil action is to avoid all danger of evil and every taint of injustice. And, we have to repeat, it is intrinsically evil to injure a people by requiring from them more than the laws of equity and justice demand. If, therefore, all things being considered, it is feared that a tax or fiscal obligation is unjust, a just government cannot in any way impose it.

576. Segneri offers as his third example the distribution of care-of-soul benefices by a bishop. 'He cannot follow the less probable opinion because there is a contrary, certain law which obliges him to choose the most worthy candidate, all things being considered, especially when the most worthy candidate is in direct competition with one less worthy and is obviously superior to him. A natural, certain law relevant to vacant churches also dictates this: the flock does not exist for the benefit of the shepherd, but the shepherd for the flock.' But if both positive and natural law are certain on this point, probable opinions can be disregarded.

577. Moreover, if it is certain according to natural law that a bishop must confer care-of-soul benefices on the most worthy candidate, the source of this law can only be the principle 'In the case of intrinsically evil actions, the safest choice is to be made.' What is at stake, of course, is harm to souls. If the bishop were to choose as beneficiary the less worthy candidate, he would expose himself to the danger of harming his flock by giving it a worthy, but not the most worthy person available. But depriving those souls of the best available pastor is an action containing an intrinsic evil, the very suspicion or shadow of which must be avoided. It is clear, therefore, that this example also proves and confirms the principle we wish to establish.

578. Fr. Segneri's fourth and last example is equally unhappy. 'A doctor cannot follow the less probable opinion in treating his patients because of the certain law of charity which demands the greatest possible caution in safeguarding their lives. This obligation is strengthened by the patient's desire to be cured (that is why he calls the doctor), and by the fee paid for treatment. The patient wants to receive the best possible attention.'

Segneri again confuses the *more or less probable opinion*

[576-8]

about the efficacy of the medicine with the *probable opinion about the morality of an action* in this case. The problem of so-called *probable conscience* is concerned solely with the second, not the first probability. Here, too, it is clear that the opinion dispensing the doctor from employing what are thought to be the best medicines is altogether false, not simply less probable.

579. But the example does support *our argument*. If the doctor gives the less suitable treatment to his patient, he exposes himself to damaging the sick person, or depriving the patient of his due. But this would be intrinsically immoral. Even if the sick person did not suffer as a result, the doctor would not be free from fault. Against all charity and faith he has chosen the less secure method, and inflicted probable, if not certain harm on his patient. This is sufficient for the act to be imputed to him as blame.

580. But Segneri goes on: 'In all these cases we are dealing with law that is certain. Hence the principle "An uncertain law does not oblige" remains unshaken.' But no one is attacking this principle which may indeed be true. What we are insisting is that an action whose intrinsic morality is doubtful can never be rendered lawful by such a principle without certainty that the action has no intrinsic evil. This principle does in fact support my supposition: 'It is most certain in natural law that I cannot expose myself to the slightest doubt I may have about doing something intrinsically evil.'

Clearer and stronger light will be thrown on the subject, however, if we explain the nature of intrinsically evil actions. This we shall do immediately.

Article 8.
The intrinsic guilt of actions

581. We have to return to the supreme principle of morality, formulated and analysed by us,[380] if we wish to discover what constitutes the intrinsic guilt and evil of human actions. This principle, in setting out the *essence of morality* free from every other element, also indicates what offends against the

[380] *PE*, cf. 13 ss., and elsewhere.

[579-81]

essence of morality. But that which offends against the essence of morality must be essentially immoral. We could go so far as to establish the following definition: 'The intrinsic evil of actions is that quality by which they offend the very essence of morality, or (and it amounts to the same thing) offend the supreme principle of morality.'

582. The supreme principle is the first law from which all other laws are derived as consequences. Hence, 'an intrinsically evil action is that which is conceived not only as contrary to one of the lower, deduced laws, but as directly contrary to the first in the hierarchy of laws, and therefore to the principle and explanation of all others.'

583. This definition of the intrinsic evil of human actions may at first be difficult to understand, but it is true and such that it easily confirms the principle we have laid down: 'In dealing with intrinsically evil actions the smallest doubt about their morality must restrain us from acting.' It is surely evident that actions which could perhaps damage the essence of morality cannot be authorised by any reflective principle incapable of resolving the doubt in question.

Article 9.
Continuation

584. We must analyse the intrinsic evil of human actions a little more carefully. As we have said, the supreme principle of morality consists in 'our acknowledging intelligent beings in the way that we know them.' According to this principle, *knowledge* must precede morality. Ac*knowledge*ment cannot be present where *knowledge* is lacking.

As we have often said, therefore, we have no duties towards any being of which we are altogether ignorant. In the same way, if we are ignorant, without any fault of our own, of some circumstance or relationship relevant to a being we know, we are free of the duties which would be present if we knew these circumstances and relationships. We have to insist upon this in order to avoid the absurdity of imagining that we could be under some obligation towards something unknown. As we have said, the different weight of moral duties incumbent upon various individuals depends upon and is derived from their different levels of ignorance and the limitations constituting personal characteristics — what we may call their moral 'identikit' in the natural order, and evident diversity of spirits in the supernatural order.

585. The second element necessary to the essence of morality, according to the same principle, is *will*. Practical acknowledgement, the principle of every moral act, is willed.

586. But this is still not sufficient to constitute the essence of morality which in the moral act requires, besides knowledge and will, a movement towards some *intelligent being* serving as the final object of the act. In other words, the act, in order to be moral, must have its beginning and end in a being endowed with intelligence. It is posited by an intelligent being and directed towards an intelligent being.[381]

587. The intelligent beings in which all morality must of its nature terminate are, for our present purpose, *God* and *human beings*. These are also the two beings to which it would seem our divine Master has, through the two precepts of charity, reduced all moral virtue.

It is therefore morally necessary, once we have mentally conceived the beings, to acknowledge God for what he is, and the human being for what he is. Viceversa, it is intrinsically evil to refuse to acknowledge God for what we know him to be, and the human being for what we know him to be. What is needed morally speaking, therefore, is that we avoid the least danger of willed disavowal of these beings. Such a willed danger already constitutes an injustice by which we do injury to one or other of them.

At this point, we could descend immediately to particular cases, but better progress will be made if we arrive at them step by step.

Article 10.
Continuation

588. We have already seen that a stimulus to the formation of conscience is found in our evil will and the remorse which

---

[381] *PE*, 91–100.

accompanies it (cf. 116, 117). Although this would seem to indicate that human waywardness serves to facilitate and hasten the moral development of humanity,[382] progress is made in this case only in so far as we form a conscience about our actions. Only moral goodness gives us the impetus needed to discover the more detailed formulas relative to our duties; negligence and malice impede and obstruct this work.

589. How does the upright person proceed as he gathers greater knowledge about his own particular duties? Let us examine first his duties related to God. To begin with, this person has a concept of God as the almighty Being, the creator and preserver of things, the wise and supremely good one. This concept will be confused to some extent in so far as the divine attributes are conceived more or less implicitly within one another, but the particular degree of clarity and light in the concept will not prevent its being true. When the upright person makes his first *practical judgment* in accordance with his concept, he will *acknowledge* the God whom he *knows*, and express his acknowledgement in a formula like this: 'I want to honour God as the supreme, infinitely powerful and wise Being which he is.' This practical judgment is a general decree of his will, generated necessarily within him and perfected in the depths of his spirit.

Let us imagine that an evil person acts in the same circumstances. He would not formulate such a decree, but would either act as though God did not exist, or form a contrary decree belittling God himself. In either case he would never deduce his other particular duties towards God because he would have failed to form that first, general decree in which all particular duties are contained. For such an evil person the religious part of moral science would not develop, but from the beginning remain stunted and sterile.

The upright person, however, who elicits the first practical judgment and general decree accepting God as the infinitely perfect and supreme Being that he truly is and upon whom all

[382] By 'the moral development of mankind' I do not mean 'the moral perfecting of mankind', but only the development of understanding in the moral sphere, which is brought about as we discover different moral formulas and show their natural, hierarchical relationship. For a long description of this cf. *supra*, Book 2

depends, sows in his heart the seed and root of the great branch of morals which has God as its object and which we call religion. Every particular duty towards God is contained in the first duty, supreme of its kind. Acts of reverence, love, adoration, thanksgiving and prayer are simply applications and consequences of the first decision with which the spirit decides to regard God and esteem him as he merits.

590. Another important question can now be formulated: 'Do these particular acts of reverence for God flow of themselves from the first practical judgment in such a way that they arise spontaneously, without need of other decrees, from the first interior decree with which the upright person resolves to give God all the esteem he deserves?'

If the first judgment is brought about emphatically with the practical force that causes us to act as a result of what we know, I am convinced that even our bodies would move instinctively to actuate that first decree externally; movements indicating reverence and external worship of the supreme Being would be forthcoming. These instinctive movements, with their roots in the first, universal, practical judgment, would however be natural tendencies of this most general acknowledgement rather than the fulfilment of particular duties, and would not, therefore, help to expand moral teaching about duties towards God.

591. This teaching develops only by the deduction of particular decrees and practical moral judgments from the first, universal decree. These particular moral judgments are the link between the first, universal, practical judgment and the particular actions honouring the divinity. When a person has decided to esteem God for the supreme Being he is, he soon tries to harmonise his affections and external operations, that is, all his powers, with this decree. His powers themselves are bound together in such a way that external actions result from affections, and affections proceed inevitably from the practical judgment.

592. The movement from the initial judgment is made as soon as the person realises and judges that some particular affections and acts are included in the first judgment. When he decides to take God as his supreme Good, he also decrees the affections and acts without which the decree of his will

would be false and inconclusive. Human knowledge, in grasping the relationship between these particular, special acts and the initial general decree, formulates a judgment about each special, particular act seen as a consequence, effect and necessary expression of the first decree recognising God as Lord and infinite Good. By means of the judgments he brings to bear on his affections and special acts (judgments that determine the connection between affections or acts and the first practical judgment) he makes these particular affections and actions into duties for himself. The piety of a good, upright person gives rise to many responsibilities towards God and to the great reverence God receives as the human spirit turns towards him internally by its affective acts, or externally in words and outward actions. All that the upright person does in this respect springs from his first *general duty* and the first *decision* by which he determines to execute the duty. But we need an example showing us how our *acts of exterior worship* towards the divine Majesty rise from our *supreme, practical judgment* by means of *particular judgments*. Through these judgments we affirm and establish for ourselves the connection between particular acts of worship and the supreme judgment of which we have spoken.

593. Bowing our head when we say God's name, and genuflecting, are considered acts of external worship, and are indeed such. How do they originate? Of itself, bowing is a sign that we wish to subject ourselves to the one before whom we bow; a genuflection is likewise a clear sign of adoration by which we show our desire to annihilate ourselves before the majesty and greatness of the one whom we adore. In order to be obliged to these acts, or to consider them as good, we must have:

      1. decided to consider God as a supreme being — the universal, *first judgment*;

      2. judged that in our decision to hold God as the great, supreme Being are contained all particular decisions about the particular affections of respect, adoration and self-abasement we offer in his sight, i.e. the particular *second judgments* by which we apply the first judgment and decide on the *ontic connection* linking the effects with the first judgment and enabling them to be contained in that judgment;

[593]

3. judged finally that the will and deliberation to carry out the external actions of bowing and genuflecting are contained in the decrees by which we decide to exercise these acts of respect, adoration and humility before God. In a word, by deciding on our internal acts, we implicitly decide on the consequent, spontaneous external acts — the more particular, *third judgments* which indicate the natural connection between external acts and internal affections.

In this way we activate the first, universal decree of our spirit in all our powers, and apply it through practical judgments to particular internal and external acts. These *practical judgments*, which always include *ethical judgments*, thus contribute to the development of moral science and the discovery of new, more determined, moral formulas. But I must explain this in another way.

594. If I really want to honour God, I desire to find the means by which to do so and I want to know the special acts with which I can truly honour him. I ask myself therefore about the special *internal affections* and *external actions* through which to activate and best fulfil the reverence I owe the supreme Being, and I decide which affections and actions are needed. So far I have only enunciated *ethical judgments*, found moral formulas, and decided how God is best honoured. But I now wish to make affective acts, to offer sacrifices and to put into practice all the external acts that render praise to God. I have now formed, in union with the ethical judgments, the *practical judgments* which were my aim in the formation of the ethical judgments themselves.

595. We have to note that as we come to know more explicitly the relationships between things and God, or the rise of new relationships, or changes in circumstances, so the first norm 'You must desire to appreciate God for the great Being he is' enables us to decide many questions that face us. Take, for example, the question of ritual both in divine worship and in ordinary human intercourse (decency, or common civility, as Monsignor Della Casa calls it). As society progresses, our external way of honouring God and human beings takes new forms dependent upon the various stages in which society finds itself; this is particularly true in the case of a society's state of intellectual culture. Tribunals

even are instituted to decide difficult questions of ritual. The norm or supreme law governing such decisions is the first judgment or decision by which we resolve to esteem and honour the persons concerned. The grade of honour we give them will be in proportion to what we know of them, and we will want to know what external acts correspond to the honour they deserve. In other words, we have to choose only those external acts which are suitable for indicating the honour we wish to pay. We are trying to judge the *connection* between these *external signs* and the *interior reverence* to which the signs should conform.

596. The same can be said in general about all particular duties of affection, about what we say, and about how we act externally when we try to express and actuate, as it were, the supreme decision by which we decide to revere God as the great Being that he is. While these decisions vary according to relationships, circumstances, materials at hand, common opinions and customs, and according to the increase we experience in more particular fields of knowledge, our basic judgment is always concerned equally with the dynamic connection between the act about which we are judging and the first decision by which we take God as God. This first decision, therefore, is the supreme norm or decree of the other judgments which after all are simply an analysis of the initial decision.

Article 11.
Continuation

597. I have discussed this matter at length because I want to remove any possible ambiguity in my use of the phrase 'an intrinsically evil action'.

For an action to be intrinsically evil, and hence included amongst those which we have to avoid even in the case of a slight probability of doubt, it is necessary:

1. that we effectively doubt about it. If we have no suspicion whatsoever about the act because of our lack of development, the act would not, of course, be known as evil either certainly or doubtfully, and would lie outside our present study.

2. that the doubt fall on the connection of our action with the first law[383] containing the essence of morality. In this case doubt about the action means doubt that in doing it or omitting it we are in danger of detracting from the essence of morality.

598. In a word, we have to distinguish carefully between the *material* and *formal* elements in moral goodness. We can never harm the latter, nor ever expose ourselves to the danger of harming it.

599. Because these important distinctions can never be sufficiently clarified, we need to sum up the whole matter once more and present it in a new way. Three objects, therefore, have to be distinguished in moral actions:

1. the physical object;
2. the intellectual object;
3. the moral object.

Let us take church law on abstinence as our example. Meat is simply the *material object* of this precept. But meat is also an *intellectual object* conceived in different ways. For example, one person may consider as meat an animal not normally thought of as such. In this case, the person concerned will have as part of his false or at least extraordinary opinion an intellective object different from the real object and the object understood by other people. The truly *moral object*, however, is neither meat nor the concept people have formed of it, but the legislator, mentally conceived as such, towards whom we desire to show due reverence by obeying his will through abstinence. When we abstain from meat, therefore, the objects we have called 'physical' and 'intellectual' are simply occasions for the moral object, which is reverence given to the legislator. They are not themselves objects forming morality, but mere conditions for morality. Taken together the physical and intellectual objects are called the *material* part of morality; the *formal* element is constituted by the truly moral object.

600. When our action is defective materially speaking, it is called 'material sin.' We must note, however, that such an expression does not mean sin at all. If we eat meat on a day of abstinence without realising that this is forbidden, we say that

---

[383] The connection must be necessary so that in desiring the action and the first law together no one may be in contradiction with himself.

we sin materially but mean that we have offended against the physical and intellectual object without offending in any way against the moral object (respect for the legislator); in a word, we have not sinned [*App.* no. 6].

Article 12.
Continuation

601. It will now be easier for us to determine accurately the kinds of action that are intrinsically evil. As we have said, they include all those actions which offend against the *first law*, the *moral object* of which is every intellective being, God and humans (cf. 586, 587). Every time that we refuse to *respect* God and human beings according to their superior nature, our action is intrinsically evil because it offends the moral object. As we know, God and human beings are, for us, essentially moral beings[384] in so far as they are intelligent beings presented by our mind to our will so that we may acknowledge them for what they are.

602. We can offend God and human beings by detracting from their dignity in our *thoughts*, *affections* and *external works*. Consequently intrinsically evil actions can be any one of these three kinds of actions. We must note, however, that although we can harm our neighbour, we can do no harm to God with our actions.

603. Intrinsically evil actions, therefore, are those with which:

    1. we do some willed *outrage*, and

    2. we do some willed *harm* to an intelligent nature [*App.* no. 7].

604. These kinds of actions must be avoided, therefore, both when they are certain and when they are doubtful. In our actions we have to shun every danger involving *outrage* or *harm* to natures which merit our respect and benevolence.

605. This principle is equally true whether the *outrage* or

---

[384] The *moral object* is always:
    1. an intelligent being;
    2. an intelligent being known to us,
    3. and placed before our will to be acknowledged or disavowed.

harm comes from our *thoughts*, *affections* or *external actions*. Every outrage and harm must be avoided *absolutely*. We must not leave ourselves open to such evil in any way, and even slight danger of such an evil must be shunned completely.

Article 13.
Continuation

606. Intrinsic moral evils can therefore be opposed either to God or human beings. Other things which we refer to God are what I call God's *appurtenances*, that is:

    1. *truth*, and

    2. *moral goodness* or justice abstractly considered.

Truth, certainly, cannot appertain to the order of creatures; creatures can be *true*, but not *truth*.[385] The same must be said about *goodness* or justice: creatures can be *good*, but cannot be goodness. Hence all that is done in opposition to universal *truth* and *goodness* is done against God himself. *Truth* and *goodness* therefore must be loved even to the extent of avoiding all danger of acting against them.

607. According to this teaching, St. Thomas says that intellectual good is the truth not of contingent, but of universal, necessary things.[386] What is contingent is *true*, but not *truth*;

---

[385] One of the proofs of the divinity of Jesus Christ used against the Arians by the Fathers of the Church (and an excellent proof, I think) lay in their noting that Jesus is called TRUTH in the scriptures. This term was never applied to human beings or to angels. The famous Vulgate MS of the Benedictine monastery of Cava, between Naples and Salerno (according to Cardinal Mai a 7th century document at the latest, which Leo XII was very careful to have re-copied), contains the following gloss at 1 John 5: 6. 'It is the Spirit who witnesses that Jesus is the TRUTH' (according to the Cardinal's reading): 'If he is TRUTH, how can he be a creature? A creature can only be *true*. Again, we do not read that any of the angels is truth.' The reader will remember as a direct consequence of our system that creatures can be said to be *true*, but not *truth* (cf. *Saggio sull'Idillio e sulla nuova letteratura italiana* in *Opusc. Filosof.*, vol. 1, p. 303 ss.).

[386] St. Thomas, in teaching that no one must be thought guilty until he is proved guilty, answers the objection that in such a case we could offend against the truth: 'In such a judgment, we should rather tend to consider a person good unless there is some obvious contrary reason for not doing so. If in judging well of another we judge falsely, we are not committing evil

universals are truth, because truth consists, as we have
shown, in the ideas of things, which are universal and necessary.[387]

608. Goodness is that to which St. Augustine would have
us turn our heart's affection even when we believe, mistakenly, that evil persons are good, and love them. He writes to
Antoninus: 'You should love *goodness* itself. That is what we
truly love when we love a person we believe good, whether he
is good in fact or not. We have to avoid only one error in such
a situation: we must not feel differently from that which truth
requires us to feel about that person's good — the person
himself however requires another approach. Beloved brother,
you certainly make no mistake in believing and knowing that
it is a great good to serve God willingly and chastely. And
you profit by this when you love a person because you
believe he shares this good, even though he may not be what
you believe him to be.'[388]

609. We should therefore always be on the side of *truth* and
goodness because these are essentially moral objects and
everything opposed to them is intrinsic, formal evil. This is
the principle governing all that St. Augustine and other
theologians say against lying as opposed to *truth*.

610. This also explains what the gospel says about the sin
against the Holy Spirit who is *essential, personal goodness*,
manifested to us supernaturally.

611. It also explains what theologians and holy people say
about willed rejection of interior inspirations[389] and about
secret antipathies opposed to public promotion of moral
good, especially supernatural good.

with our understanding, just as we do not perfect our intellect through
knowing the truth about individual contingent matters. In judging well of
someone, our good affection is at issue, not our understanding' (*S.T.*, II-II,
q. 60, art. 4, ad 2). For the rest, we should not pass judgment when we
doubt, but preserve our trust in, or supposition of, another's goodness
until something has been proved for or against it. This *trust* or *hypothetical
credence* is, I think, what St. Thomas has in mind when he speaks about
judgment.

[387] *Certainty*, 1112 ss.   [388] Ep. 20, 2.
[389] St. John's words: 'The light shines in darkness, and the darkness did
not comprehend it' (1: [5]) could refer to this kind of rejection, when
inspiration calls us to abandon a sinful life.

[608-11]

Article 14.
Continuation

612. The other object of our moral duties is the *human being*, whose dignity we must respect in ourselves and others. In the first place we violate and damage ourselves when we refuse obedience to the *truth* and enslave ourselves to *sensation*.

613. In particular:

1. The first harm we can do ourselves consists in damaging our soul by exposing ourselves to the danger of formal sin.[390] All theologians, including St. Alphonsus, teach that we must flee the *proximate occasions* of sin. How do we explain this most certain truth? The reason, as we know, is that it does not suffice to flee what is certainly sin; we also have to avoid probable and doubtful sin. We cannot excuse ourselves by saying that the sin is doubtful if the law is doubtful, because it is certain that no one may lawfully expose himself to the danger of sinning. This is the very law we are upholding.

614. 2. The same must be said about a choice of religion. If in making our choice we do not keep to the safest path, we leave ourselves open to the danger 1. of offending God; 2. of offending ourselves. This is one of those points, therefore, at which St. Alphonsus completely abandons his own system in favour of very wise exceptions. He says: 'Hence we can conclude that it is not lawful in matters of faith, and in everything touching upon the means of eternal salvation to follow either *the less probable opinion* (according to the fourth

---

[390] St. Thomas makes the same point in *Quodlib.*, 8, art 13: 'Anyone placing himself at risk in matters relative to salvation, sins'; and in *Quodlib.*, 9, art. 15: 'Anyone placing himself at risk or in danger of committing mortal sin, sins mortally.' In the canons we find: 'In matters relative to eternal salvation, the safer way is to be taken if serious remorse of conscience is to be avoided' (Clement., bk. 5, t. 11, c. 1, § *Item quia praeter ea*). Scotus also declares: 'If there is an easier way, that is, one over which we have greater power and which is a more sure way of re-acquiring grace, we must take it. To attempt a more difficult and less sure way when the easy one is open is equivalent to endangering and despising our own salvation' (in *4 Distinc. 17*, quaest. unica).

proposition condemned by Innocent XI),[391] or the *more probable*. We are bound to hold the *safer opinion* and consequently to choose the safest religion, that is, the Catholic religion.' He adds: 'Because any other religion is false, even if one of them appears more probable to someone, he cannot accept it in place of the safer religion without placing in jeopardy his eternal salvation.'[392]

615. 3. The same danger makes it unlawful for a person to put his life at risk without necessity.

Article 15.
Continuation

616. Moreover, St. Alphonsus makes exceptions of all cases in general where there is doubt about actual harm. 'We maintain that it is never lawful to follow a probable opinion, relevant to probability in actual fact, where *harm could be done to another or to oneself*. Such a probability does not remove harmful danger. If in fact the opinion were false, harm to one's neighbour or to oneself would not be avoided.'[393]

617. The Saint realises that here he is dealing with an intrinsic evil because the harm to our neighbour or ourself comes about *ex opere operato* (if I may use that expression), and not intentionally on our part. Knowing that this harm cannot be avoided on the basis of good intention, we effectively desire such harm if we desire to act when there is some probability of harming our neighbour. Wanting such an act in any way at all makes it an intrinsically evil moral object.

Article 16.
Continuation

618. Hence, when there is danger of harming our neighbour, we have to follow the safest path. No reflective principle can disoblige us in such cases.

[391] The condemned proposition states: 'A non-believer following a less probable opinion will be excused.' Such was the extent to which moralists were prepared to go!

[392] *Th. M. De Consc.*, 43.   [393] *Th. M. De Consc.*, n. 42.

1. We apply this principle first to our thoughts. St. Thomas, along with the best theologians, teaches that we must not judge others when we have some doubt about their motives because we have to avoid any danger of harming them even in our thoughts. He says: 'My answer is that even if we think evil of someone with sufficient cause, we do them an injury by despising them. But we must not despise or harm another without some compelling cause. Therefore, unless there exist *obvious indications* of others' malice, we have to think well of them and interpret doubtful matters in the most favourable way.'[394]

619. 2. The principle can now be applied to our actions, and in the first place to actions that harm people spiritually. First, therefore, we must avoid giving scandal to little ones because our action, although good in itself, could at least put them in danger of falling. This alone makes our action, in these particular circumstances, intrinsically evil.[395]

620. 3. 'In conferring the sacraments,' says St. Alphonsus, 'a minister cannot make use of the probable or more probable opinion about their validity, but is obliged to keep to the safest opinion or to that which is morally certain. Innocent XI's condemnation of the first proposition makes this clear.'[396]

621. 4. Actions which cause bodily harm. According to St. Alphonsus 'if anyone when hunting doubts whether his target is an animal or a human being he cannot shoot, although he thinks it probable or more probable that it is an animal. If it were a human being, no probability or greater probability could save him from death.'[397]

622. 5. St. Alphonsus applies the same principle to doctors who prescribe medicines for their patients.[398]

---

[394] *S.T.*, II-II, q. 60, art. 4.

[395] We can never, therefore, place ourselves in a *proximate* occasion of sin, whatever the foreseeable temporal advantage.

[396] The proposition states: 'In conferring the sacraments it is not unlawful to use a probable opinion about the validity of the sacrament unless the law, custom, or grave danger of harm forbids this. Hence the probable opinion may be used, but not in conferring baptism and priestly or episcopal ordination.'   [397] Lig. *Th. M. De Cons.*, n. 52.

[398] 'A doctor is bound to use safer remedies for the sick. He cannot use less probable remedies, and neglect the more probable or safer remedy. In

623. 6. The same is true about a judge in the execution of his duty. It seems unbelievable that the following condemned proposition could have been taught by a Christian moralist: 'I think it probable that judges can pass judgment even in the light of less probable opinions.'[399] We conclude with St. Alphonsus: 'Universally speaking, therefore, it is never lawful to use a probable opinion about the probability of an actual fact where there is danger of harming or injuring one's neighbour.'[400]

624. 7. It is clear, therefore, that G. V. Bolgeni is wrong when he affirms that a doubtfully usurious contract can freely be drawn up.[401] If I doubt whether a contract is an act of usury, I also doubt whether I actually harm my neighbour with that contract. In such a case, I do much better to hold St. Thomas' view. He teaches in his brief work on usury that 'in doubt it is highly useful to examine the question from the point of view of truths known to be helpful to salvation, rather than from the point of view of what is unknown and could place human salvation in danger.' 'In modern times', he adds, 'serious controversies have arisen not only about natural sciences, but also in moral questions WHERE DIFFERENCES IN APPROACHES AND OPINION are dangerous, especially in cases of commutative justice, as the philosophers call it.'[402]

625. 8. St. Thomas' view on multiple holding of simple benefices without dispensation (that is, benefices not requiring the care of souls) depends upon the same principle. In doubt, he says, this must be rejected: 'By holding several benefices while remaining in a state of doubt, a person puts himself in danger and hence sins indubitably because he prefers a temporal benefice to his own salvation.'[403] And this is indeed a question of justice because 1, church temporalities can be enjoyed only according to the prescriptions of divine and ecclesiastical law; and 2, in holding several benefices the use of remedies, the more probable is what is safer for the health of the sick person' (Lig. *Th. M. De Cons.*, n. 44).

[399] 'A judge is bound to judge according to the more probable opinion; a divine and human precept obliges him to grant each person his rights in accordance with the greater weight of reason in the person's favour' (Lig. *Th. De Cons.*, n. 47).

[400] Lig. *Th. M. De Cons.*, n. 52.   [401] *Del Possesso*, c. 15, 115–117.

[402] Opusc. 73, *De Usuris, in proemio*.   [403] *Quodl.*, 8, q. 6, art. 13.

without any right to them, I may leave others without, and hence harmed.[404]

626. We conclude therefore: in the case of probability about factual harm, intrinsic evil is always present in the *moral object*, and must therefore be excluded at all costs. I emphasise *moral object* because simple harm done to an intelligent being is a material object. When such harm is *willed*, however, it becomes an intrinsically evil moral object relative to those who will it. But we must avoid every risk of falling into such moral evil. The same argument is valid in the case of injury done to God or human beings. As soon as it is willed, it is a moral object, and we must avoid all danger of falling into it [*App.* no. 8].

Article 17.
Continuation: on chastity

627. At this point, we can ask if the intrinsic evil of which we are speaking is present in actions against chastity. And we must answer affirmatively, granted that we doubt whether the action contains the *intrinsic evil* present in unchastity. Ambrogio Stapf puts the matter well in his *Etica Cristiana* when he states that we must follow the safer path in matters of chastity, truth and charity.

628. This intrinsic evil is present:

1. In sins against nature. Such sins are an outrage against humanity, and indicate the degraded human condition in which, as the Apostle says of the Gentiles, people are held in subjection to 'base feeling'.[405] The victory obtained by fleeting sensation is an outrage and mockery of truth. Damage is also inflicted on human nature. Tertullian's words are greatly to the point: 'Disallowing birth is murder right

---

[404] We note that St. Thomas himself considered this question in its relationship to natural and divine law, as well as to positive law. He says: 'This is a theological question in so far as it depends on divine law or NATURAL LAW, and a canonical question in so far as it depends on positive law. Hence contrary opinions are found in this matter amongst theologians, and amongst canon lawyers' (*Quod.*, 9, q. 7, art. 15).

[405] Rom 1: [28].

from the beginning, whoever it is that takes the baby's life or interferes with the as yet unborn child who is already what he will be, a human being. All fruit is present in its seed.'[406]

629. 2. In the use of sex by married people outside marriage. In such cases, marital fidelity suffers harm, injury and violation.

630. 3. In simple fornication, that is, between unmarried persons. Here again, injury is inflicted upon human nature by people who subject themselves to sense rather than to reason. Reason requires intelligent beings to unite physical love with permanent and lasting friendship, to be confirmed on oath and publicised. This, in the state of natural society, constitutes marriage.

631. 4. In the case of polygamy, the evil relative to natural law is less, and could indeed be non-existent in those born outside the Christian dispensation (who may not realise that love united with friendship, the foundation of marriage, has of its nature to be between two partners only). In the age of the patriarchs this relationship, although present in natural law, was unknown because explicit spirituality was defective. As a result, polygamy was permitted, and no doubt existed about its lawfulness. But anyone who did doubt about it could not have practised it.[407]

---

[406] *Apolog. pro Christ.*, c. 9. St. Augustine says: 'Any woman who acts in such a way that she cannot conceive as many children as she can bear should realise that she is guilty of murder each time she so acts' (Serm. 244, *de temp.*). Plato had already written: 'I insist that homosexuality should stop. Men who have sexual relationships with other men are deliberately slaying the human race. They sow their seed upon rock where it can never put down roots' (*De Legib.*, 8).

Once, when I was hearing confessions, a simple-minded person accused himself of a great number of murders. At first, I did not understand what he was trying to say; it did not seem possible that he could have killed so many people. But then I realised that this simple person was accusing himself of onanism. The natural light of his mind taught him to compare this foul sin with that of murder. Note, however, that for the [loss of seed] to be an intrinsic evil against chastity, the following conditions have to be present: 1. it must come about as a result of sexual impulses outside marriage; 2. these sexual impulses must be willed.

[407] Sexual pleasure resulting from fantasies is dealt with by St. Bonaventure, who says: 'In this case, the theologians maintain, he sins mortally. His

632. All this must be affirmed irrespective of any positive law against fornication. Such law does not *cause* intrinsic guilt in the actions under discussion.

633. It is true, and I acknowledge openly, that some dispositions of canon law seem at first sight to militate aginst this theory.

1. In doubt about the impotence of a married person, the spouses are granted three years in which to see if the impotence is true and permanent. If it is, the marriage is annulled, that is, the union is declared never to have been a marriage. Nevertheless, in the three years during which the couple were not married, they were permitted to remain together. It would seem that while the couple were doubtful of their marriage, their actions in matters of chastity were also doubtful. Nevertheless, they were permitted to cohabitate.

2. A partner who doubts the validity of the marriage, cannot ask for intercourse, but is permitted to render the debt. Being forbidden to ask for intercourse would seem in keeping with the principle: 'In the case of a doubtful marriage, intercourse is not permitted.' But this would lead to a contrary conclusion from that established in the preceding case of doubtful impotence. On the other hand, being permitted intercourse would seem a consequence of the opposite principle: 'In the case of doubtful marriage, intercourse is permissible.' It is not sufficient to say that intercourse can be rendered for the sake of not depriving the other partner of the right, but cannot be asked. If the marriage is doubtful, the right to intercourse is doubtful for both partners. In this case, even the non-doubting partner has no certain right because the marriage is not certain, or at least has no right to force the doubtful partner to undertake a doubtfully lawful act.

consent, although not true, can be interpreted as such . . . Nevertheless, this is not altogether certain. Some deny that mortal sin has been committed, even though the danger of sin has been adverted, where negligence in rejecting bad thoughts is combined with displeasure at their presence. Nevertheless, the safer way is to be followed whatever the truth of the matter' (*In Sent.* 2, d. 24, p. 2, art. 2, q. 2). Note, however, that St. Bonaventure is discussing the case of a person in whom pleasurable sexual fantasy is combined with knowledge of the danger present in entertaining it. We say this to avoid occasioning scruples in tender souls.

[632-3]

It would be possible to bring forward similar cases[408] of positive law relative to marriage. Some of these laws seem to derive from a principle of natural law, others from the opposite principle.

634. For our purposes, it is enough to observe:

1. If positive laws such as these seem to decline a little from the rigorous law of chastity, they always do so solely in favour of marriage, that is, as a necessary proof for establishing that the marriage exists. These laws do not exist in other married cases.[409] But what is done in favour of marriage, and with marital devotion, does not harm human dignity. Consequently, the intrinsic evil associated with unchastity is not present.

2. That those who make use of what the law permits do not doubt the lawfulness of their action.

3. That the Church herself, in permitting such a diminution of the normal rigour of the law in a matter as delicate as this, desires that chastity should prevail, and would be happy if spouses doubtful of their impotence lived together as brother and sister in all chastity.[410]

Article 18.
Continuation.
Cases in which some compromise must be reached because the mutual rights of the parties are doubtful

635. We have established the principle that an action cannot be done lawfully if we doubt whether it causes undue harm to our neighbour. This principle also resolves another question: what is to be done when there is danger of both parties causing harm whether the action takes place or not?

---

[408] For example, the decision of Lucius III (*Decretal.*, bk 4, t. 21, c. 2): 'No spouse doubting the death of a first partner, should deny the debt when asked by the present partner, although it cannot be required spontaneously by the one in doubt.'

[409] *Decretal.*, bk. 2, t. 27, c. 26. 'Lest damage be done to the law of marriage.'

[410] 'If they both consent to remain together, let the man take her at least as a sister, even if she is not his wife' (Celestine III in his reply: *Decretal.*, bk. 4, t. 15, c. 5).

We reply: the question must be solved according to rational law in favour of the least possible harm, or at least in favour of the solution where harm is divided equally amongst those who could suffer it — granted that no higher reason exists for favouring one party or the other when harm is inevitable. Let us consider some particular cases.

I

636. A deceased person leaves a legacy to John Smith. Two people bearing the name, John Smith, come forward to dispute the will, both of whom allege equal friendship, familiarity and service to the deceased. According to Roman law, the legacy is given to neither because the legatee is insufficiently determined by the will.[411] At this point, I do not want to decide the political end of these positive laws, which may indeed have been intended to make testators more careful in drawing up their wills.[412] I only wish to see how the question would be decided on the basis of rational law alone.

According to rational law, it seems clear that by depriving both John Smiths of the legacy, definite harm is being done to

---

[411] *Dig.*, bk. 34, t. 4, l. 3, §7, and t. 5, l. 10. See also: *Dig.*, bk. 43, t. 17, l. 3, and *Decretal.*, bk. 3, t. 5, c. 20. The laws found in canon law, which deprive both persons of a prebend if doubt cannot be resolved about the true holder (and similar cases) (*Decr. Greg.*, bk. 3, t. 5, c. 20; *Decr.*, p. 1, d. 39, c. 8) are not merely *juridical*, but principally *political* laws, that is, intended for the public good.

[412] It is certain that Roman laws do not always contain merely *juridical decisions* pertaining to commutative justice, but often include in addition a *political element* leading to a decision dependent upon advantage to society as a whole, even though damage could result to the rational right of individuals. The Institutes of Justinian, for instance, sometimes cite public benefit as their motive for deciding a case. For example, limits are set to the ill-treatment meted out by owners to their slaves not in order to defend the rights of the slaves, who have none, but for the public good: 'It is not in the interests of the good of the state' (this is the expressed motive) 'that anyone should misuse his possessions' (*Instit.*, bk. 1, tit. 8). Such a motive indicates the erroneous principles upon which a great part of Roman legislation is based. The motive presupposes that 'a person has the right to use badly what he possesses'. He is forbidden the bad use of his possessions only by the law providing for the public good. See also *La Società ed il suo fine*, bk. 1, c. 12.

[636]

a person designated by the testator. Moreover, the maximum harm is being done by depriving him totally of what the testator wished him to have.

In the second place, it seems equally clear that by giving the whole legacy to one of the two John Smiths, without a solid motive in favour of either of them, the judge acts arbitrarily and therefore unjustly. In doing so, he exposes himself to the danger of depriving the true legatee of the whole legacy and thus inflicting maximum harm upon him.

Because it is certain that the will of the testator does not fall outside the ambit of the two John Smiths, but on one or the other of them, all that remains is to make the least harmful choice, the terms of which the two persons themselves should decide. That is, they can either 1. decide to cast lots for the legacy (in which case, the stake equals half the value of the legacy, with which each gambles) or 2. take half each (and this is more reasonable).

If the two John Smiths, although obliged in general by natural law, do not wish to compromise, the judge can decide to give each of them half the legacy. He cannot, however, lawfully let the matter be decided by lot because he cannot be responsible for putting in danger the certain right each has to half the legacy.

This is how we see the matter according to natural equity, although positive laws view it differently.

637. Nevertheless, these principles of equity we have proposed were recognised and followed in other cases by public laws, and affirmed by jurists.

Baldo, for example. says that when there is no proof on either side, some mutual decision must be reached.[413] Others say that in such a case, the judge cannot arrive at a decision, but must leave the parties to reach agreement.[414] Julianus the jurist states that if the arguments brought forward by the two parties leave the difficulty unresolved, the judge can divide the difference.[415] Antonio de Butrio and Peter of Ancharano

[413] *Cons.* 352, in f., bk. 4. See also Boerio, *Dec.* 42, n. 39.

[414] The gloss in c. *Licet causam*, in ver. *Uti possidetis, de probat.* (*Decretal.*, bk. 2, t. 19, c. 9). Likewise Matth. Matthesil, *in opusc. electionis verioris opinionis (inter tractatus communes)*, n. 10.

[415] *Cod.*, bk. 6, t. 24, l. 4.

[637]

reply that the judge himself must do this, and end the case by
dividing the legacy if it is divisible.[416] Hence the laws
themselves state that in certain cases the judge has to arbit-
rate,[417] not however in any 'arbitrary', absolute sense, but
always on the basis of the equitable decision expected of an
upright, prudent person.[418]

II

638. If a person is uncertain whether he has paid a definite
debt, must he repay it?

If the doubt can be resolved by ascertaining whether the
payment has been made or not, this must be done. But if
nothing certain emerges, some say that the debt must be paid
because a debt that is certain, requires certain payment.

I think there is an equivocation here, however. If I am
doubtful about having paid a debt, it is false that the debt
remains certain. The debt was certain at the beginning, but as
soon as I doubt whether I have paid it, I necessarily doubt
about the debt which is then uncertain for me. What must be
done?

First, I must find the source of my doubt. If it has arisen
solely from my own fault or serious negligence, it should not
be allowed to cause possible harm to my creditor. It is fitting
in this case that I should take the safest step and pay the debt.

639. If the doubt arises through no fault of mine, I then run

[416] *Cons.*, 110, *Inter Cons. Anchar. incipien. Inter contraria* (See also,
Felinus in c. 1, n. 55, cf. second note, *Super eod.*; and Boer. decis. 155, n.
24. See also *In tanto discrimine opinionum*). Antonio de Butrio and Peter of
Ancharano use the judgment of Solomom as an example. They observe that
although Solomon had proposed the division of the child only as a test, that
judgment nevertheless was based on a true principle: where the rights of the
parties are equally doubtful, it is equitable to divide the thing in contention.

[417] *Decretal.*, bk. 1, t. 29, c. 4, §1; *Dig.*, bk. 28, t. 8, l. 1, §2.

[418] Baldo (in c. 2, § *Indices*, n. 5. *De pace juram. firma.*) says that the will
of the judge must be 'according to the mind of the law, of right and of
reason, and finally according to equity.' Thus the best jurists explain how
the judge's decision is never left wholly dependent upon his will, but has to
be guided by laws. See Aret. in l. *Videamus*, § *Deferre* n. 7, ff. *de in litem.
jur.*; in Jas. in d. 1. *Si sic legatum*, n. 10. de l. 1; in Felinus, col. 7, *circ. med.
sup. eod*; and in Menoch. *de arbitr. Judic.* bk. 1, q. 8.

the risk of harming myself if I pay, and harming the creditor if I do not pay. It seems altogether fitting that in this case I should pay 'proportionally to the doubt',[419] dividing the danger of harm in two as equity requires.

III

640. If a person doubts whether he is in debt, must he pay the debt?

It is always necessary to begin by making every effort to remove the doubt. If, however, it cannot be solved, some distinctions have to be made:

1. The difficulty may occur relative to the *nature of the title* to the debt, that is, the validity of the title itself may be in doubt. But if the title has not yet been established, no one can have any right and I do no harm to anyone by not paying.

641. 2. My difficulty is extraneous to the title, and arises from mere doubt about my having paid. The conclusion is the same as in the previous case.

642. 3. The doubt occurs about the existence of the *title*. I am uncertain if there is a title (although if there were, that title would be valid), and once more the doubt either arises from

[419] Layman (bk. 1, tr. 1. c. 2), Diana (p. 4, tr. 3, v. 35). Sporer (*De Cons.*, c. 1, n. 83) and Taralusino, all cited by St. Alphonsus (*Th. M. De Cons.*, n. 34), hold that one should pay *proportionally to the doubt* only when the creditor doubts whether he has been paid. If the creditor holds for certain that he has not been paid, the debtor must pay the whole sum.

But the creditor's affirmation is only valid as an authority certifying doubt about the payment of the debt. This authority is applicable in conscience only when declared such by *suitable discernment*; it alone can constitute moral certainty in some cases. In fact, if the creditor affirms that he has been paid, the debtor's doubt is resolved totally unless he has some proof that the creditor's affirmation is mistaken. We have to say, therefore, that the debtor who doubts has to discern, with the help of the creditor, if the debt was paid or not, or at what *level* the doubt stands. This level of doubt determines simultaneously the creditor's right and the debtor's duty.

This removes any difficulty about one party having a right greater than the other's obligation, and vice-versa. It is true that the creditor's and the debtor's reasons for doubt may be very different, but in this case they are bound by a law of nature to search for a compromise. There will be a sound basis for the compromise if they fuse their arguments in a single calculation and arrive at a single result.

my own fault or not. In the first case, I must avoid the danger of causing harm to another through my own fault, and must therefore pay the debt in full — if my fault was the full cause of the doubt. In the second case, I must pay only 'proportionally to the doubt'.

IV

643. Must the possessor in good faith make restitution if he begins to doubt? St. Alphonsus replies: 'If the doubt is equally balanced for and against, it is the common opinion,[420] with few dissenting, that the possessor has no obligations, according to rule 65[421] where we read: "When the case favours both sides equally, the possessor is in the stronger position", and in rule 128: "When the plea favours both sides equally, the possessor must be considered to have the stronger case."'[422]

But has this rule of law been well applied? Surely there is a great difference between the pronouncement made by a judge in the external forum in favour of another, and the pronouncement to be made by individuals in their own cause in the forum of conscience?

644. As far as I can see, we need to distinguish with the utmost care:

    1. the *external, public forum*,

    2. the *external, private forum* of the sacrament of confession,

    3. the *internal forum of conscience*, and finally,

    4. the *divine forum*.

Here we want to speak solely about the *external, public forum*, in which a society's positive laws are made, and about the *internal forum of conscience*.

645. First, let us examine the determining factor for societal laws in the case where one person possesses something, and another person maintains that the object is his own and

---

[420] He cites Sanchez, in *Dec.*, bk. 1, c. 10, n. 9.
[421] *De Reg. jur in 6 Decretal.*, bk. 5, t. 12.
[422] *Dig.*, bk. 50, t. 18; *Th. M. De Cons.*, n. 35.

unlawfully possessed by the other. We have to consider the possible circumstances of the case.

Two people litigate about dominion over some property. One of them is the *de facto* possessor. Both go to the judge declaring that they are certain they have a right over the thing. Both want to be in the right: the defendant maintains he lawfully possesses the thing, the plaintiff maintains that the *de facto* possession is unlawful. On his part, the judge directs his attention to the plaintiff who, he says, has to prove, for the sake of the *public good*, that the present peaceful possession of the thing is unlawful. The judge acknowledges the distinction between *de facto* and *de jure* possession, and the possibility that the former may not be sustained by the latter. But because no one must be disturbed in his possession without cause, the plaintiff must prove his case. Until this is done adequately, the judge must pronounce in favour of the *status quo*, and prohibit any disturbance of possession. This is the simple interpretation of the juridical rule: *When the case favours both sides equally, the possessor is in the better position.*

646. It is now clear

1. that the judgment in favour of the actual possessor is *summary*,[423] *temporary*,[424] and *preparatory* to the principal judgment,[425] as the jurists say. The judgment is not concerned, properly speaking, with the *right* of the parties, but with *a presumption of right*. That is, it does not decide that the *de facto* possessor has the right to the thing, but *presumes* that he has it until the contrary has been proved.[426] When the jurists say that 'possession in good faith produces a definite right', they are speaking about the *de facto* possession which cannot be proved to be held in bad faith. In such a case, possession must be maintained in the external forum as indicating a definite right, until the contrary can be proved. Clearly, we are dealing with 'a definite *right* relative to positive law and subject to human judgment, but nothing more.'

[423] *Rota Divers. decis.* 641, n. 8, p. 1.
[424] Cagnol., in C. *In pari num* 6 ff. *de reg. jur.*, Caesar. de Grassis etc.
[425] Bk. *Interim. Rota* etc., Covarruvias.
[426] See Wig., exam. 3, *De Consc.*, and Lugo, *De Justitia*, d. 17, n. 94.

647. 2. that the reason which serves as a foundation for the temporary judgment, if I may call it that, in favour of the possessor (the judgment made by applying the rule, *when the case favours both sides equally, the possessor is in the better position*), is the *public good*, peace in society, the defence of tranquil enjoyment of their possessions by individual citizens, discouragement of harmful litigation, and other political ends.[427] These are not matters belonging to the order of interior justice, nor to the forum of individual conscience.

648. 3. Nevertheless, I should add that if peaceful possession in good faith has been maintained for a very lengthy period, prescription equivalent to a proof of one's right would arise even in natural law provided there were no indications of weakness in the original title granting possession, but only ignorance of the title. The jurists' tag 'Better no title than a bad title' would be applicable here. If there is total ignorance about the original title, it must be taken for granted that it did exist, but has been forgotten after such a length of time. Later exceptions prove nothing unless one can show, as I said, the weakness of the original title.

649. But can the rule, *the possessor is in the better position*, be applied also in the forum of conscience? Are the circumstances the same?

A number of theologians think it is possible to apply the principle in this case, but I take my stand with those — and they are many — who find the circumstances present in the exterior, public forum to be non-existent in the forum of conscience. Lack of these circumstances changes the very nature of the case.

In the external forum the human judge has to judge 'in accordance with allegations and proofs'. He does not know

---

[427] According to the law *Aequissimum*, § *de usufructu*, the reason for the law about *de facto* possession is to prevent the use of armed violence on the part of litigants. And Prospero Fagnani (In *Decret.*, bk. 1, c. 5) says: 'Moreover, in the interdict *Uti possidetis* or *Retinendae*, the praetor safeguards the possessor from violent ejection on the part of the litigator (*Dig.*, bk. 43, t. 17, leg. 1 *in princip.*), and issues his interdict when the *de facto* possessor is disturbed by someone (*Cod.*, bk. 8, t. 6, l. 1 . . . *Lap. allegat.* 73, in q. n. 3, vers. *Iste videtur*, et n. 4, vers. *Tertiam Probat.*), or when two parties contend possession (Bartol. *in dict. leg.* 1, §. *Hujus autem interdicti*; Anchar. cons. 274, *ad declarationem in princ.*).

everything about the case, nor is he aware of interior convictions. Two litigants present themselves before him, both of whom appear to believe totally in their contrary claims to possession or for dispossession. The forum of conscience is very different. The possessor in good faith has now become uncertain about the legitimacy of his possession; he doubts, and has reasons for doubting about his title. He begins to think that his possession may be a mere fact, and that the right to the possession may belong to the other party. Whether the thing is in his possession, or that of another, is a material accident that neither makes nor destroys the moral right.

As soon as I doubt the lawfulness of my possession, therefore, I am certainly obliged to examine with all available means whether my *de facto* possession is indeed my possession, or whether I ought to restore it because it belongs to someone else. God-fearing Tobit offers us a good example of such a case. He was blind, and hearing the bleating of a kid in his house, wanted to know if it had been stolen: 'It is not stolen, is it? Return it to the owners; for it is not right to eat what is stolen.'[428] But what is to be done if the doubt remains?

650. I can offer no simple answer. As far as I can see, the nature and circumstances of each doubt, which differ from those producing baseless, despicable fear, are to be examined carefully.

First, if the *doubt* is merely *negative*, in the sense that it arises from ignorance about the original title to possession and not from any positive indication that the possession is insecure, no obligation is present because there is in fact no doubt (cf. 518–528).

651. The same must be said if peaceful possession has lasted for a considerable period, as we already noted. Forgetfulness of the primitive title after a long period can reasonably be attributed to the title's antiquity, unless there is some clear evidence to the contrary.[429]

---

[428] Tobit 2: [13]. Saintly Tobit was putting into practice, as everyone should, the divine teaching: 'Keep my commandments and live, keep my teachings as the APPLE of your eye' (Prov 7: [2]).

[429] This is *prescription* as understood in natural and civil law. When prescription is applied to chattels by positive law after a short period, the

652. Actual possession, however, may not have lasted for long, and there may exist positive motives for doubting the title to possession. In this case, the *de facto* possessor must try to clarify the matter, and if necessary consult the person whom he thinks may have the right to possession. Finally, he should come to some compromise with the other party 'proportionally to the doubt' on the basis of *proof* — not purely *legal* proof, but proof founded on thorough *discernment*, and on true love and study of truth. In moral matters each of us should be as careful or even more careful of the rights of others as of his own.[430]

653. St. Alphonsus seems to favour this opinion somewhat when qualifying his own decision: 'The first opinion says that the actual possessor must make restitution when general assent is totally against him. This must be understood when possession is weak through doubt or initial doubtful faith, and does not seem to allow any legitimate presumption in favour of the possessor' (I also admit a *presumption of right* found in natural law. If St. Alphonsus has this in mind, we agree). 'In this case, the possessor is not sustained by a probability, and general assent holds that the thing in question is the other person's.'[431]

---

aim seems to be a political disposition relative to public good. It seeks 1. to eliminate difficulties as soon as possible; 2. to stimulate people to care for their own belongings. But if in such a case the law does not support the right in the person who holds it, it does not justify the other party if independently of the law he acts unjustly. Hence, as far as I can see, this *short prescription* alone gives no one any true right.

[430] Some moralists, not content with applying to conscience the rule, 'When the case favours both sides equally, the possessor is in the better position', which is valid only for the external forum, enlarge and extend it to every *de facto* possessor, even when more positive, valid reasons are opposed to this. St. Alphonsus says: 'The principal reason for this opinion is that a true right is acquired through possession in good faith' (*Th. M. De Cons.*, n. 36). But this is false. Possession of something not free gives a legal *presumption of right*, but not the *right* itself. The possessor acquires only a merely *legal* and *provisory* right which entitles him not to be disturbed in his possession by force. This is true even to the extent that any betterment in what is held in good faith belongs to the true owner to whom an account must be rendered as soon as he is discovered and recognised as the owner.

[431] *Th. M. De Cons.*, n. 36.

V

654. What is to be done if the possessor in good faith culpably neglects to clarify the matter after some positive doubt has arisen about the justice of his possession, and then finds that he can no longer identify the true owner of the thing in question?

St. Alphonsus says: 'I think it more likely to be true that such a *de facto* possesor is obliged to restore something either to the owner (doubt), or to the poor if the ownership is uncertain. The reason is that the actual possessor has culpably deprived the owner of the *hope* that he could have of what belonged to him. That hope can be valued at a price, and hence some damage has already been inflicted on the owner who held that hope with certainty. Nevertheless, I do not think that restitution should be made according to the quantity of the doubt in such a way that equal reasons would give the contendants half each. Less, and perhaps much less, should be available because the owner's hope could never be said to equal half the value of the thing in question. Equal probability of reasons on the one hand, and on the other the certain right of possession which favoured and still favours the possessor, indicates that much less than half should be given to compensate the possession of the hope which is obviously less valuable than the actual possession of the thing itself.'[432]

The last reason would have some weight if the word 'possession' were not used in two different senses. If we speak about the *possession of a hope* (although such a phrase contains a certain impropriety), we are dealing with the possession of some right, a possession which is unexceptionally just. But the *possession of the thing in question*, to which the possession of hope is opposed, is *certain in fact*, and *dubious by right*. The doubt exists precisely because it is uncertain whether *de facto* possession of the thing is just or unlawful and vitiated. This is what has to be clarified.

Hence, if my doubt about the lawful possession is equal relative to the two parties in contention, I must, all things considered, pay half, as in the case of insoluble doubt. Only

[432] *Th. M. De Cons.*, n. 37.

thus, in cases of culpable neglect, can I be said not to have harmed more than assisted, granted that the right could have been verified as much in the other's favour as in mine.

4

SOLVING A DOUBT ABOUT THE EXTRINSIC UNLAWFULNESS OF AN ACTION

Article 1.
Connection with the preceding chapter

655. Before continuing, it will be useful to summarise what we have said and see its connection with the present chapter.

The first question was: 'How must we act when we doubt about the unlawfulness of an action?', that is, when a conscience has not yet been formed about the lawfulness of our action. Our general reply followed the common opinion of theologians: 'No action may be performed unless a conscience has been formed about its lawfulness' (cf. 471, 472).

This pointed to a more practical question: 'How do we form this conscience?', and again we answered generally that: 'The *cause* of the doubt must be carefully examined. If investigation and counsel show the *cause* to be ineffective and baseless, the doubt is immediately dissolved and we can act freely' (cf. 537–544). If, however, we cannot dispel from our mind and spirit the doubt about the action's *unlawfulness*, but find it well founded, we cannot act for the very clear reason mentioned by St. Thomas: 'Anyone who neglects dangers, seems to spurn the harm that can be caused by the dangers.'[433]

After answering the question in general, we descended to particulars. We saw that for an action to be lawful, a doubt about its unlawfulness had to be resolved absolutely. This required careful examination to see whether the *cause* could in fact produce a true doubt about the unlawfulness. Next, in order to investigate some *rules* for carefully making the

[433] *Quodl.*, 3, art. 9, ad 3.

examination, we sought the *causes* which can render actions either really or apparently unlawful. This was the most difficult and important question we proposed.

Causes rendering actions unlawful, we said, are divided into two classes, which produce their effect either through an *intrinsic disorder* inherent in the action, or through some reason extrinsic to the action.[434] In the second case the action is lawful considered in itself; the unlawfulness comes from an external, accidental cause. If the doubtful unlawfulness is *intrinsic* to an action, the only way to remove the unlawfulness and the doubt is to show that the suspected intrinsic unlawfulness does not exist. But as long as we have a well founded doubt about the intrinsic evil of an action, we must follow the principle given initially: 'We must never expose ourselves to doing something unlawful.'

We concluded, therefore, that no reflective principle of any kind exists allowing us to perform lawfully an action whose intrinsic evil is justly doubted. Indeed, there are principles which can be called reflective, certain and evident, which indicate that what is *doubtfully* unlawful because of intrinsic unlawfulness is *certainly* unlawful (cf. 564–580).

These certain, evident principles are:

1. Moral evil must be avoided absolutely, totally and before every other evil. Every possibility of moral evil must be excluded by absolute will.

2. No human being may expose himself to *harming* an intelligent nature, and must therefore avoid every danger of doing so (a consequence of the first principle).

---

[434] Here 'action' means a single action of logical, not material unity, so that the action can in fact be composed of a series of material actions. This logical unity is the object of the moral case under discussion, and therefore when we ask if such and such an action is intrinsically unlawful, our reply must be relative to the action as described in the question. But as we have seen, this action, depending on the different ways it is presented, can be either material or intellectual or moral. If the action, in its nature or the way it is proposed, is only a material or intellectual object, it clearly cannot be classed as intrinsically evil. But if it is a *moral object*, it can be intrinsically evil. Moreover, the action can be a moral object because of some circumstance or relationship. For example, causing a person's death is in itself a material object, but relative to the will of the perpetrator it is a moral object. When a question presented for discussion, therefore, concerns an action, we must carefully consider what kind of action is meant, and what elements and circumstances govern it.

3. Likewise, no human being may expose himself to the danger of causing any *harm* to an intelligent nature (another consequence of the first principle).

These laws are certain, natural and immutable.

656. Consequently we must note that the question is not a matter of *counsel*, as some think,[435] but of *duty*.

657. Nor is it a matter of simple *prudence*, as others hold who seek, among various means available to obtain an end, only the means best suited to the end. We are dealing with *justice*, in which one path alone may be chosen; probability is insufficient — there must be *certainty*.

Whenever, therefore, the *cause* of unlawfulness is intrinsic to an action, the cause, even if doubtful, certainly and effectively renders the action unlawful. Conscience is formed on this reflective principle, and by means of it must judge the action unlawful.

This is the point our discussion had reached. We must now examine the *extrinsic causes* of the unlawfulness of actions. The question we will discuss is: do doubtful, uncertain,

---

[435] Fr. Segneri's words cannot, therefore, be used against me. He says: 'For this reason St. Antoninus, Humbert, Nider and other important authors subscribe to the rule given by Albert the Great: "An uneducated brother or any person whatsoever can, in matters of counsel, safely follow any opinion, provided it is the opinion of some great teacher." However, this must exclude anything the Church has declared to the contrary. Hence, Nider, in order to explain himself better, uses the words of Bernard of Clairvaux, and adds (*in cons. timor. cons.* 3, p c. 12): "When opinions are found amongst the great teachers, and the Church has not determined which is correct, anyone may hold what opinion he wishes, provided judgment in the matter is founded on the statements of those he considers expert." This was the ancient rule, and is the true rule to be followed perpetually; all other rules cause confusion. The basic reason for the rule is that in order to act correctly in all things it is sufficient to act prudently. And this is precisely how a person acts who follows truly probable opinions still in use. It may be objected that still greater prudence would be used by following the more probable opinion. And this is true. But it only proves that it is right to encourage, exhort and strengthen the person to act in this way. It does not show that it is right to command him.' (*Lettere sulla Materia del Probabile*, Lett. 1, n. 23). Nothing can be gainsaid about this argument of Fr. Segneri, provided all sides agree that we are dealing with *matters of counsel* only. With this proviso, the problem disappears. But we must respectfully question whether it is in fact 'a matter of *counsel* or of *precept*'. Consequently, while Fr. Segneri's observation is correct in itself, it has no value at all in solving a doubt 'about the unlawfulness of an action'.

extrinsic causes bind us and render an action certainly unlawful?

Article 2.
Two extrinsic causes that make an action unlawful

658. There are two extrinsic causes that can render unlawful an action in itself lawful:

    1. Positive law which forbids the action.

    2. The physical connection between what is essentially moral and what is not moral.

659. When *positive law* forbids an action, the action is unlawful; when positive law commands an action, omission of the action is unlawful. There is no difficulty here.

660. We must explain rather how an action is rendered unlawful by means of its *physical connection* with what is essentially moral. To understand this, we must recall our proposition that the essence of morality consists in the *practical acknowledgement of intelligent being*; in our view, nothing else is essentially moral.

But this acknowledgement and practical esteem has a physical bond with human *affections*, which have a physical bond with *external actions*. Therefore, just as the acknowledgement is determined and required by the law, so are the *affections*[436] which are connected with the acknowledgement. In the same way the external actions are determined by the law because they are physical consequences of the affections.

661. If the human being were in a perfectly constituted state, without any disorder, the physical connection between *affections* and *practical esteem*, and between *actions* and affections, would be so reliable and effective that a just, upright practical esteem would be followed by spontaneous affections

---

[436] *Acknowledgement* is an act of the will and, if upright, allows and furthers the natural action of the acknowledged object upon us. This action gives rise to spontaneous *affections*, which in turn can be assented to by *actual volitions*. The affections are followed by *external actions*, which also can be assented to, and accompanied or preceded by, actual volitions, which are all virtually included in the first, general volition of the acknowledgement.

which in turn would be followed by spontaneous actions. We would recognise at once which *affections* belong to the just evaluation we make of things, and which actions belong to just affections. We would necessarily want the affections and their consequent actions to be whatever our esteem wanted them to be, because we would want everything to be ordered and all our faculties to serve the truth we mentally conceive.

662. But in our present disordered state this does not always happen. The emotions we feel do not obey the practical esteem, and our external actions do not always correspond exactly to our emotions. It is very often difficult to know what degree and kind of emotions, if any, should follow practical esteem, and what words and external actions should correspond to emotions and esteem. We remain uncertain and harbour many doubts about the uprightness of some external actions, because we do not clearly see their connection with the intimate moral disposition of our spirit, which consists precisely in our practical esteem. We must therefore ask: 'In this kind of doubt are we under any kind of moral obligation?'

Article 3.
The formation of conscience
when doubt about the unlawfulness of an action
arises from doubt about the correspondence
between the action and the required PRACTICAL ESTEEM

663. I will deal with this question first, and then with the question of unlawfulness.

It is my opinion that when external actions inflict unjust harm on intelligent natures, the unlawfulness of the actions is no longer doubtful but certain, because it comes from an evil *practical esteem*. But if the *acknowledgement*, or *practical esteem*, is just and upright, a doubt whether an external action corresponds to it or not does not seem a valid cause for rendering unlawful an action which in itself is harmless and innocent.

I believe that such actions, even when they do not correspond by their nature to an upright *practical esteem*, can be *material sins* only, as long as they are not the effects of a sinful *interior esteem*. At most they are an imperfection or defect of our human condition, sometimes accompanied by venial offence. External, material actions do not have their own morality but receive it from the intention with which they are done, from the willed principle producing them. Hence, their morality, whether good or blameworthy, is entirely derivative, so that whatever real moral value or goodness they have comes from the goodness of the interior *evaluation* or esteem, and any blameworthiness from the malice of the interior esteem or evaluation. Thus, when the estimation is sound and unbiased, whatever else is human is never formal but only material sin, or at most venial sin.

664. This explains the difference between Mosaic and Christian law. Mosaic law, which sought to establish *legal* justice as a figure of true justice, tried hard to govern external actions by precepts (another purpose, of course, was to instruct the Hebrew nation about the relationship between external things and internal morality. This instruction was necessary for their progress, and they could never have gained it of themselves). Christian law, on the other hand, whose purpose is not *figurative* but *true justice*, that is, morality properly understood, summed up the whole law in the *evaluative love* of the two precepts of charity, and thus completely forsook the great mass of Mosaic commandments, which concerned external actions.

665. Consequently, a doubt whether an external action is obligatory because connected with an obligatory act — for example, whether the obligation to genuflect is connected with the spiritual act of adoration — is not a sufficient cause for making the action obligatory or its omission unlawful, provided the evaluative affection is entirely internal, as it must be. The non-correspondence of the external action, or even of our emotions, is a deficiency and imperfection of damaged nature, but not actual sin. We are not obliged to know this connection (this is very often impossible), but we are obliged to safeguard entirely and always the *evaluative love*, which the Fathers called the 'abbreviated word'[437]

[437] 'What is therefore the word which embraces and sums up all that can be said? You shall love the Lord your God with all your heart, etc.' (St. Aug., *Sermo. De disciplina christ.*, c. 3).

[664-5]

because it is truly the summing-up of the whole law, and the essence of morality.

Article 4.
The formation of conscience
when doubt about the unlawfulness of an action
is CAUSED by doubt about the positive law

666. The other external cause of the unlawfulness of an action is positive law. When the *cause* of doubt about unlawfulness has its roots in whether a positive law forbids the action, is the doubt about the action's unlawfulness sufficient to render the action certainly unlawful?

We must distinguish two very different cases. Doubt about the existence or binding force of a law arises either from the *essential conditions of the law itself* or solely from our lack of *information about the law*. On the one hand, I can have perfect knowledge of everything concerning the nature of the law, yet be doubtful about its existence or obligation. On the other hand, my imperfect knowledge of the nature of the law could cause me to doubt its existence and binding force. I will deal with each case separately, starting with the second.

Article 5.
Continuation: doubt arising from the law

667. The following are the cases when, because of the law's intrinsic defects, a doubt arises about its existence or binding force:

1. if the acts by which the law was formed are doubtful;

2. if the doubt is about some defect in the sense of the law so that, in a particular case, the law ceases or does not obligate;

3. if the exposition of the law is so defective that some cases are not seen to be clearly covered by it;

4. finally, if there is cause for doubting that a previously binding law continues to exist or bind.

[666-7]

668. Each case is different and can be subdivided, and all the subdivisions involve a doubt 'about the existence or binding force of a law'. Is it possible then, without examining each case individually, to give a safe answer to our question: 'How must conscience be formed when doubt about a positive law is the *cause* of doubt about the unlawfulness of an action'?

For myself I feel unable to reply; I could neither affirm nor deny that there is a general solution for so vast and complex a problem without first examining and solving each particular case and comparing the solutions. This is the only safe path to find a general solution, and in my opinion moralists have never taken it. Here, perhaps, lies the origin of so many differences of opinion: each thinker seeks a universal solution without using a rigorous method to obtain it by comparing the particular solutions. Whatever the explanation, I will attempt to answer the four questions individually, and then, by comparing the results, seek a general solution.

§1. Doubt about the existence of a law arising from doubt about how it was instituted

669. Positive law comes into existence by the following acts:

1. an act of will by the legislator;
2. the exposition of the law;
3. promulgation of the law;

If one of these acts is lacking, the law does not exist and therefore does not bind. But if we doubt about any of them, does the law still bind?

670. In the first place, if the will of the legislator is certain, neither the *exposition* nor the *promulgation* of the law can be doubted. Hence, when the *promulgation* is certain, no other indication is generally needed of the *will* of the legislator — the promulgation itself is the authentic proof.

But there could be proof that the law had been extorted from the legislator by violence, or fear, or deception — 'obreptitiously' or 'subreptitiously', in legal language. If the proof were certain, the law would not be law because the will

[668-70]

of the legislator is lacking. But if, after full consideration of the case, a real, positive doubt remains about the will of the legislator, the law has no standing, because the legislator's will, which is the law, is unknown.

671. But we must be careful not to err. I said that if doubt about the will of the legislator is to be effective in removing the obligating force of the law, the doubt must still persist after full consideration of the case. Due weight must also be been given to whether the law has been correctly promulgated. Only after this can we establish for certain the principle that 'the will of the legislator must be known with practical certainty, or at least with sufficient probability to produce in us a reasonable, firm opinionative asssent.' Without the legislator's will, the law lacks the first of its essential constitutives; only the material part remains, without the obligating force which gives it vitality.

672. We turn now to consider doubt about the *promulgation* of a law. Authors who doubt whether promulgation belongs to the essence of law,[438] have evidently not understood how *natural law*, founded on the natural order, differs from *positive law*, founded on the will of a legislator. The *natural order* is *per se* an obligating principle, since the necessity to observe it is contained within it. Hence, St. Thomas says the common precepts of nature do not need

---

[438] G. A. Alasia says: 'Although promulgation is understood to be included in the definition of law, it does not belong to the essence of law. Many great thinkers have followed the opposite opinion, but we think that promulgation is more probably only a condition of law. Nevertheless it is an essential, necessary condition in order that the law may actually oblige' (*De Lege generatim*, Diss. 1, c. 2, n. 15). Alasia then falsely claims to confirm his opinion with the authority of St. Thomas. But Aquinas does not say that promulgation is only necessary for law 'in order that it actually oblige', but that it is necessary 'in order that it may have the force of obligation'. Law can easily be conceived without its actually obliging but not without having the force of obligation. Hence, St. Thomas states that this force of obligation 'is proper to law'. His opinion is clearly that *promulgation* is 'of the nature of law', as can be seen from the objections in the article where he deals with the matter (*S.T.*, I-II, q. 90, a. 4), beginning: 'It seems that promulgation does not belong to the nature of law'. Nor is it correct to say that he compares law to a *standard*. He says in fact that law does not become a *standard* of actions until it is promulgated.

promulgation:[439] of themselves they produce obligation in all those who *have been informed* about them.

673. On the other hand the *will* of the legislator does not oblige *per se*, but through the *act of command* by which it is communicated. The legislator could not wish his will to be done before he has communicated it. If he did, he would be acting absurdly. The *act of command* is itself the promulgation instituting the law. Thus Gratian correctly says: 'Laws are instituted when they are promulgated.'[440]

674. We must therefore distinguish *being informed* of a law from *promulgation* of the law. Once informed of the natural law, I am necessarily subject to obligation because the natural order is law *per se*. If, however, I am informed that the ruler has conceived, drafted and signed a law, I am not obliged by it until it has been intimated to me, that is, promulgated to the community for which it is made. The concept alone has no force of obligation, and cannot therefore be law. It becomes law by the declarative act called *promulgation*.[441] This declaration or promulgation is therefore necessarily intrinsic to positive law.

675. But we must also note that human legislators have clothed the act of *intimation* required by the nature of the matter in certain formalities and have declared that the law is promulgated and binding only when accompanied by them. For example, according to Roman legislation, a law had no force in the provinces unless promulgated in each of them. Moreover, the law did not apply until two months after its publication.[442] In some states a law must be registered in the

---

[439] 'The first general precepts of the natural law . . . do not need promulgation' (*S.T.*,, I-II, c. 4, ad 1) [q. 100, art. 4, ad 1].

[440] *Decr. Grat.*, p. 1, dist. 4, ad can. 3.

[441] 'Hence, if Titius certainly knows that a law has been drawn up and will be promulgated in three days by order of the government, he is not obliged by it until it is in fact promulgated. The law is a general precept enacted for the whole community and cannot therefore oblige an individual member independently of the community. But the community is not obliged unless the law is publicly announced and thus promulgated (Antoine, *De Legib.*, cap. 2, quaest. 6).

[442] *Constitutiones* Authent. At the end of the Council of Trent, in the Bull beginning *Sicut*, Pius IV says: 'Common law establishes that new constitutions have no force except after a certain period of time.'

senate before it has binding force. Thus, everything necessary for the promulgation of a law to be binding is also necessary for the existence of the law.

676. Consequently, if publication is for some reason doubtful, the law is also doubtful. If the law is doubtful, the act of command on the part of the legislator is doubtful, and carries no obligation. We must also bear in mind that if the law is to be binding, certainty, or at least sufficient probability, is required to persuade us reasonably and intimately of the *correctness of the promulgation*. Lacking this, no law has been constituted. Our conclusion therefore is: 'A law must be constituted in order to be valid.'

677. Clearly the same principle governing positive laws also governs every kind of *mandate*. A *mandate*, by which a person receives authority and power, must allow no reasonable exception to its necessary observance. It is not sufficient for a mandate to be probable or very probable. If it is to have binding force, it must be fully *certain*, as canon law explicitly lays down. To the following question (asked about a man pretending to be a delegate of the Apostolic See): 'When you are uncertain about the validity of another's apostolic mandate, must you execute the mandate?', the Pope replied: 'Unless you consider the mandate of the Apostolic See to be CERTAIN, you are not obliged to carry out what is commanded.'[443]

§2. The doubtful existence of a law arising from doubt about an intrinsic defect in the matter of the law

678. If on sound evidence we doubt whether a positive law opposes a higher law — for instance, the natural law, or positive divine law, or even a church law concerned with faith and morals — the doubt is solved by one of the ordinary rules applicable when laws *clash*.

The law that binds us in such a doubt is solely the higher law, because we must not expose ourselves to offending the greater law by observing the lesser. Nor can we say that we

---

[443] *Decretal.*, bk. 1, t. 29, c. 31.

would *certainly* transgress the lesser law simply by *doubt* about not transgressing the greater. If it is doubtful that a positive law offends against a higher law, it is equally doubtful that it has binding force. The positive law, therefore, is doubtfully, not certainly transgressed, just as it doubtfully exists.

679. Nevertheless, we must do all we can without passion to solve the doubt before we set the law aside, and we must consider all the consequences of not obeying the law.

680. If, however, we have no doubt about a law clashing with a higher law, we may still doubt its usefulness.[444] In this case, we must presume in favour of the legislator whose responsibility it is to judge the usefulness of laws, as we said. We must act in the same way in all cases where judgment about the justice of a matter is the responsibility of the person in command, as, for instance, in judging the justice of a war.

§3. Doubt about the cases included in a defectively stated law

681. Another weakness of positive laws is the obscurity of their exposition. It is extremely difficult to draft a law so that it covers all the cases envisaged by the legislator, and excludes all others. When there is doubt whether a case is included in the exposition of a law and it is not possible to consult the legislator, the existence of the law is doubtful and has no binding force. It is not sufficient for the law to probably cover the case. We must be certain that it does so, or at least that its probability must be great enough to produce complete *opinionative assent*. Thus, if a law forbids the eating of meat, and we are faced with an animal or food without being able to decide from the words of the law or from authoritative explanations whether it falls under the law, it is not forbidden by the law.

[444] Everybody accepts the principle that 'the law never obliges anything unreasonable or harmful to the common good' (Antoine, *De Legib.*, c. 5, q. 3).

§4. Doubt whether a law has been abrogated or has ceased, for any reason

682. If, all things considered, doubt about the abrogation or cessation of a law (for any reason whatsoever) renders the actual existence of the law uncertain, then the law has lost its binding force. We cannot say that the law is in possession, and therefore that certainty is required to dispossess it, because from the moment we can firmly doubt its existence or actual obligation, the law is not truly in possession.[445]

§5. General solution of the problem

683. From what has been said we can draw the following general conclusion:

'Every time the existence of a law is not CERTAIN, the law has no binding force. Doubt about its existence, however, must not come from our ignorance but from a defect in the law itself. This defect must be present either 1. in the acts by which the law is instituted; or 2. in its own content; or 3. in its exposition; or 4. it must come from one of the causes that make the law cease, so that the law is uncertain in itself, not relative to us. Hence:

'When we doubt the unlawfulness of an action solely because of a doubtful positive law, we can form our conscience by means of the *reflective principle* mentioned above, and act freely.'

---

[445] In some cases, positive laws do not oblige where *serious harm* may result, but in others they do. In treatises on law, the two cases must be distinguished. The *serious harm* we *fear* (granted it is serious and we have not imagined it as such through our own weakness), can apparently free us from observance of the law, even when the serious harm is *doubtful*. The goodwill of a legislator who dispenses us from the law because he does not wish us *serious harm*, clearly does not intend to expose us to the *excessive danger* of harming ourselves.

§6. Limits to the solution

684. We must remember that many positive laws are not only positive but also a *mixture* of positive and natural law, which they explain.

685. To solve any doubt in this case, we have to separate the *positive* from the *natural* element, applying to the *natural* element the rule we have given for natural laws, and to the *positive*, the rules above, which appertain solely to positive laws.

§7. Explanation of some well-known rules on conscience

686. We can now understand the truth, and the limits, of many of those time-honoured rules used by scholars or in canon law to solve cases of doubtful obligation. For example:

1. 'A doubtful law does not oblige', 'An uncertain law does not impose a certain obligation', 'A doubtful law is not a law'. These principles, which all express the same thing, seem clear and evident, but are valid only for positive law. They do not cover uncertainty about the law relative to us, which comes from our ignorance. This uncertainty, strictly speaking, is not *uncertainty about the law* but *our* uncertainty about the law, a subject we shall discuss in a moment.

2. 'What is disadvantageous must be restricted, what is favourable, extended.'[446] This principle is developed from what has been said, and presupposes that a law is doubtful in itself. If a law does not in fact bind in its doubtful part, it cannot impose a burden on anyone.

3. 'A less strict interpretation is to be given where a penalty is attached.'[447] This rule is a specific case of the previous rule, and comes from the same principle that the doubtful part of a law does not oblige nor impose a burden.

687. All these rules were applied without dispute, and received the support of the Fathers. But they have to be applied strictly within the limits I have given, that is, when they refer to 'a positive law doubtful in itself.' Exceeding this

---

[446] *Reg. jur.*, 15, in 6 *Decretal.*, bk. 5, t. 12.
[447] *Reg. jur.*, 49, *ibid*.

limit has engendered new controversies, and good sense has reacted against it, despite the claim that the broader extension given to the question was due only to new conclusions reached by logical necessity.

688. I conclude by quoting two ancient authorities who support these rules.

Lactantius says: 'Only a very foolish person wants to obey commands whose truth or falsehood is doubted.'[448] This passage refers to the moral teachings of philosophers, but its meaning includes the truth expressed in the first of the rules above.

St. Gregory Nazianzen, replying to a claim that St. Paul prohibited the remarriage of widows after baptism, says: 'What argument do you use to support your claim? You must prove that the case is so, or if you cannot, do not condemn. If the matter is doubtful, humanity and gentleness must prevail.'[449] This principle is contained in the second rule above.

§8. Injustice towards probabilism

689. From all we have said it is clear that many theologians, in their praiseworthy effort to avoid a harmful laxism, were unjust to *probabilism* by condemning it totally. Probabilism, however, is partly true; if it were not, it would not have attracted the attention of so many moralists [*App.* no. 9]. The important thing is to distinguish the true from the false.

690. One cause of the confusion is the too extended meaning of the word 'opinion', the use of which does not determine the object of the opinion. Does a doubtful or probable opinion concern the *unlawfulness of an action*, the *existence of the law*, the *application of the law* or something else? The broad, indetermined meaning of 'probable opinion' is not fixed by accurate distinctions; instead it produces an incredible mixture of conclusions and a labyrinthine series of arguments which cannot be reconciled and from which it is totally impossible to extricate oneself.

---

[448] *Instit.*, 3, 27. And Lambertini, in Notif. 13, says: 'No bond must be imposed when no evident law imposes it.'   [449] *Orat.*, 39.

691. Consequently, we deemed it necessary first to distinguish *opinion about the unlawfulness* of an action. We agreed with the majority of scholars that opinion in this case, whether probable or more probable, cannot be followed, because certainty, not opinion, is required. We also said that if the doubt or the probability of an action concerns the *intrinsic unlawfulness* of the action, no reflective principle can solve the doubt and remove the uncertainty; the doubt must be overcome by direct reasons, or the action omitted.

We then examined *opinion about the existence of a positive law*, and said that such opinion, whether doubtful, probable or more probable, has no binding force. Only a certain positive law can produce a certain obligation.

In this way we found the true part of probabilism, which we were able to separate from the rest of the system by asking: 'Which opinion in favour of freedom can be followed?', and defining this opinion as 'that whose object is the uncertainty of a law in itself, an uncertainty caused by an intrinsic defect in the law.'

692. We thus obtained our final conclusion: we are not obliged to follow an equally probable opinion in favour of the law, or a more probable opinion. As long as we have a firm doubt 'about the intrinsic defect of the law, the law neither exists nor obliges.' This is true even if the defect nullifying the law more probably does not exist — no amount of probability can bind us; we must know for certain that the defect does not exist.

693. To my mind, this teaching was always followed in practice by the truly great teachers. I quote for example the opinion of Benedict XIV advanced by probabilists as proof of their system: 'Where scholars vary greatly in their opinions, it is safe to follow the more favourable opinion.' Benedict expresses this opinion in his *De Synodo Diocesana*, bk. 7, c. 11, n. 3, where he discusses the question: 'Can viaticum be given to a dying person who out of devotion received communion in the morning?' It is clear that disagreement among scholars is a reason for concluding that church law is not certain about the refusal of viaticum to a person who out of devotion has received the Eucharist the same day. The Pope does not prescribe the observance of the more probable

opinion in the matter. He allows complete freedom to choose the opinion that seems more pleasing, whether it is less probable or, because of the number and authority of scholars, more probable. The existence of the law remains seriously doubtful and therefore has no force of obligation. If the action is lawful, we are free to do it or omit it. If the action is good, doing it is laudable but not obligatory. If it seems better to omit it, it will be laudable but not obligatory to refrain from the action.

Article 6.
The formation of conscience
when doubt about the unlawfulness of an action
is caused by doubt about the positive law
arising not from the law but from our ignorance

§1. *Legal* and *moral* effects of positive law

694. We have distinguished *promulgation* of positive law from *information* about the law (cf. 674). They produce different effects. *Promulgation* and innocent lack of *information* produce *legal* effects; *information about promulgated law* produces *moral* effects.

695. If the positive law is *promulgated*, the judge passes sentence as if it were known to all, because a term has to be established beyond which *ignorance of the law* cannot be pleaded. Without this term, anyone could excuse himself in this way from observance of the law. Hence, *public order* required that promulgation be made according to certain forms and fixed periods of time, based on the principle that 'everyone must be able to know the law', a natural condition of just promulgation. Later, the maxim was established that 'ignorance of the law does not excuse', in order to preclude false excuses and to pressure people into being well instructed about laws as the laws were promulgated. Thus, the need for instruction became a social duty.

696. We clearly see, therefore, that the principle 'Ignorance of the law does not excuse' appertains to *external* and purely legal rights (unless, as I have said, the ignorance is culpable),

and was often inappropriately applied by moralists to settle
questions in the forum of conscience.

697. Thus, the *legal* effects of a law legitimately promulgated but unknown are penalties and punitive factors, such as
invalidation of contracts, disqualification of persons, and so
on. They are decided by the legislator, as we see in impediments to marriage, irregularities, etc., and, despite ignorance,
are real effects of the law although they do not necessarily
presuppose fault.

§2.

698. We can omit the discussion of *legal effects* because
they do not come within the scope of our question. Our
concern is conscience, a purely *moral* question.

699. We asked: 'If through ignorance we doubt the *lawfulness* of an action, not in itself but because forbidden by a
positive law, can we use the principle we have stated to judge
the action lawful and form our conscience accordingly?'

In this state of mind, we must first of all take every care to
remove the doubt and seek the truth 'with all the means in our
power'. We must note, however, that because we are dealing
with a law that does not oblige in *serious difficulty*, we are not
obliged to carry out the examination if it imposes serious
difficulty.

What is to be done however if, after making this examination, the matter is still not clear? What judgment of conscience should we make?

§3. Culpable and inculpable ignorance: solving a doubt caused by culpable ignorance of the positive law

700. The ignorance which makes us doubtful whether an
action under consideration, or its omission, is prohibited by a
positive law must be classified as culpable and inculpable. I
say *culpable* or *inculpable* and not *vincible* or *invincible*
because ignorance could be invincible here and now but

vincible and culpable when we neglected to inform ourselves. In our case the ignorance is considered invincible at present because everything possible had been done (unsuccessfully) to dispel it.

701. It is my opinion that when a definite doubt persists arising from ignorance we certainly know is culpable, we must first repent of negligence in knowing our duties.

702. If the law concerns the public good in such a way that the performance or omission of the doubtful action could apparently damage this good, we must follow the *safer* action. In this way we avoid defrauding the public (through our own fault) of what, as a result of the law, they may have a right to.

703. If the positive law in question, however, concerns our private good (such as the duty to hear Mass or to fast) rather than public order and good, it would be enough, in my opinion, to follow the *more probable* action. Hence, if the existence of the law is more probable, the law must be carried out; if the non-existence of the law is more probable, we can act. However, if the probability were equal for both sides, we would have to take the *safer* action, and fulfil as much of the law as we could.

704. The reason explaining this last opinion is as follows. If we know that we ourselves are responsible for our uncertainty about the prohibition of an action or its omission, we must do all we can to prevent our fault producing an effect contrary to the law, because we should not gain any advantage or right from the fault. Sorrow for our past negligence, or care taken to overcome the doubt is not enough; they are only a part of our duty, not the total amendment we must and can make.

If we are truly sorrow for our first fault, we will use every means in our power not to break the law. And the means available to us for avoiding this danger is to perform the safer action. In this way we avoid the possibility of doing something against the law, and fully redress the initial evil. It seems to me an obvious principle that if sorrow is sincere, 'anyone who has sinned culpably, must not only oppose the evil he has done but also all consequent evils, which he should prevent with all his might.'

705. Nor is it true to say that in such a case the infringement of the positive law would be only material. The infringement would be willed and therefore culpable, because its cause is culpable ignorance and an *accommodating will* which freely allows culpable ignorance to produce non-observance of the law.

706. It seems to me St. Thomas confirms this solution when he says: 'An erroneous conscience will not serve to absolve us if its sin is present in the error itself, as for example when it errs about the things it is required to know.'⁴⁵⁰ Two sins are clearly distinguished here: ignorance ('if its sin is present in the error itself') and the action done in ignorance ('will not serve to absolve us'). This second sin can obviously be avoided by following the safer action. We are obliged to do this in order to nullify the first error which, although it cannot be nullified in itself, can at least be nullified in its consequences.⁴⁵¹

707. It will be helpful to note that properly speaking the object of the sacrifices required by the Mosaic law for sins of ignorance⁴⁵² was not ignorance but the consequences or actual transgression of Mosaic positive laws due to ignorance. This shows that both the cause and the effect are imputed when the effect can be, but is not, avoided; and it can be avoided every time we suspect it.

708. It may be objected that if this reasoning applies whenever the existence of a law is of equal doubt with the non-existence of the law, it must also apply when the existence is less probable. If we do not execute the law, we willingly expose ourselves to the risk of falling short of what is

⁴⁵⁰ *De verit.*, 17; *De conscientia*, 3, ad 4.

⁴⁵¹ We must distinguish *harm*, which I have already discussed, from *scorn*, which is a lack of respect for law. I said *harm* must be compensated *proportionally to the doubt*, but because lack of respect is indivisible, we must follow the safer way.

⁴⁵² The following are the places where the Mosaic law prescribes sacrifices for transgressions arising from ignorance: Lev 5. [17, 18], 'If anyone sin through ignorance . . . he shall offer . . . a ram without blemish' [Douai]; c. 4. [27, 28], 'If anyone of the people of the land shall sin through ignorance . . . he shall offer a she-goat without blemish' [Douai]; and Num 15. [27, 28], 'If one soul shall sin ignorantly . . . the priest shall pray for him'. Thus, if there was *ignorance*, but no resulting *transgression* of the law, external sacrifice was not enjoined.

commanded. The following reasons will show that in my opinion this is not true.

If I observe a positive law whenever my ignorance makes me uncertain about its existence (whatever the degree of probability of its existence), I will certainly bring upon myself more obligations than the law imposes. I am definitely not obliged to do that. On the other hand, if I observe the law every time its existence is more probable, and consider myself not obliged by it whenever it is less probable, there will be occasions when I will not be doing what the law commands, but also occasions when, out of respect for the legislator, I will be doing more, because I will be doing what is not commanded. It seems that equity would allow this balance between the duties I do not undertake and the non-duties I do undertake. In this way, I would make up fully for what I owe to the law and out of respect for the legislator's will. Moreover, this would seem a reasonable interpretation of the intention of a good legislator, who wishes his intention be carried out according to my ability, but does not intend me to burden myself more than the other members of the community for whom the law is made. If I had to observe a law every time I were uncertain about its existence (even if the existence were less probable), an uncertain law would oblige equally with a certain law, which is absurd.

709. I conclude with an observation that seems to me of the greatest practical importance. If the fault I committed by not informing myself at the appropriate time about the positive law were a minor fault and not seriously imputable, any resulting obligation to observe the law could only be minor. But this must be noted in conjunction with what is said in the next section about inculpable ignorance.

§4. Solving a doubt arising from inculpable ignorance about a positive law

710. An insoluble doubt arising from inculpable ignorance concerns:
    1. the existence of a law; or
    2. some fact which is a necessary condition for the law's existence and obligation.

711. Doubt about the existence of a law can be present either before or after our action.

712. In the case of doubt after the action, it is clear that the law either determines a fixed time for its observance, or not.

If the law determines a period of time, as in the case of fasting for a fixed number of days, then clearly, once the period is completed, the law no longer exists.

If the law has no fixed period for its observance, what we did in the past was not sinful because we acted in good faith, without any doubt about the existence of the law. For any future action, the doubt must be solved by the rule which governs the case of doubt arising before action.

713. If this doubt remains, despite our every effort to resolve it, we can apply all I have said about uncertain positive law in itself. To oblige in conscience, positive law must be: 1. promulgated, and 2. known. If knowledge of the law is lacking, without our fault, the law does not exist for us, although it obliges others who do know it. The knowledge must be *certain* or *so probable* that it gives us a reasonable *opinionative assent*. But if a contrary doubt remains, the law has no force to oblige; it does not yet exist for us, even though greater probability supports the law. Here too, we can lawfully take as guide of our action the *less probable opinion about the existence of the law*.

§5. Doubt about a fact which is a condition of a positive law

714. Sometimes our doubt is not really about the *existence* of a positive law but about the existence of some *fact which is a condition of the law's obligation*. Perhaps there is no positive law whose obligating force is not conditioned by the verification of some fact.

The problem is: if I doubt and cannot verify the facts on which the obligation of a law depends, am I obliged to the safer action? We take for granted that the law contains no invalidating defect, and also that we know it fully — I simply doubt the truth of the facts conditioning the law, and am totally unable to solve the doubt. What am I to do?

715. These facts or conditions principally concern place,

time, persons and actions. Some actions themselves constitute the title of obligation, for example, a vow; others do not, but are the *object*, or *matter*, or *occasion of the law*. A crime, for example, is the occasion by which a penal law comes into force.

716. These facts, or conditions, which actuate the law also give rise to another classification more directly concerned with our problem. Some facts, unless they are verified before the application of the law, would or could harm or disconcert third parties; other facts are such that even without their verification, the execution of the law neither harms nor troubles others, but rather produces good. Verification is needed if, for example, a person is accused of a crime, or claims some authority, dignity, merit or right to recompense. It is not needed relative to the time or *place* of an obligatory good work. For example, the time or place for fasting, which is always good, need not be verified.

717. It is clear therefore that I cannot apply a law as long as I lack certainty and reliability about the first kind of such facts. This solution is contained in what we have said about natural law. In the case of the second kind, I *may* or *may not* observe the law.

718. But if I *may* or *may not*, *must* I observe it?

We must distinguish: the fact is either 1. a circumstance prescribed in order that we *may* lawfully carry out some action, or 2. a circumstance that merely occasions the application of a positive law, activating the law or not. In the first case, we cannot use the freedom to act given by the law, unless the certainty of the circumstance is at least *opinionative certainty*, precisely because without this certainty the action is forbidden. For example, reception of Communion is permitted on condition that we are fasting from midnight [as the old law stated]. We must be certain that we have not broken our fast after midnight.[453]

---

[453] Some authors say that the law requiring fasting before reception of the Eucharist is *prohibitive*, not *positive*; the law *prohibits* anyone who has broken the fast. Hence they deduce that reception of the Eucharist, which is a free act, is always free as long as its prohibition by the law is not *certain*. A person who doubts about having fasted has no certain knowledge that the law forbids him to communicate, and therefore he may do so (Liguori, *Th.*

719. However I must point out that in prescribing these circumstances and conditions, positive law does not always require the strictest interpretation. Approved custom and other indications must reveal the intention of the law or of the legislator. Sometimes a strict interpretation is clearly indicated by the law itself; often the nature of the case is such that the circumstances clearly belong to the substance of the precept. In this case we must strictly adhere to it. An example would be the death of the first spouse as a condition imposed by the law on anyone wishing to enter a second marriage.

720. If the fact is a circumstance which only occasions the application of the law, it either directly posits a title of obligation, as we saw in the case of a vow, or posits no title but only a determination and occasion for the application of the law, without being the title itself. For example, whether I know the day and place of a fast, whether midnight on Wednesday or Friday has passed, or whether someone has turned 21 years of age and is obliged to fast, and similar circumstances.

In the case of circumstances which constitute a true title of obligation, uncertainty about the title, in my opinion, removes the law. For example, I have no obligation to observe a vow I have not made; if I, without fault, doubt I have made the vow, the vow is null because the law is not yet

---

M. De Consc., n. 38). This seems to me to be a subtle and feeble reason. If I do not know the law with certainty, I can never say my action is free; to know that an action is free, I must know what the action concerns. In the present case I truly do not know the action concerned because my doubt is precisely about the quality of the action. To communicate while fasting or not fasting are two different actions, and I have no doubt that one of them is either free from or bound by the law. In fact I know for certain that the first is free, and the second is bound and prohibited by the law. 'he question therefore does not concern my knowing 'whether an action is certainly or doubtfully prohibited', but knowing 'whether the action I am about to do is free or prohibited'. This second case is very different from the first, and in my opinion must be solved in favour of the law in order not to expose oneself to doing an action certainly prohibited by the law. Indeed, it seems to me the Church desires each person to approach the Eucharist fasting, or else abstain from Communion. Anyone, therefore, who seriously doubts whether he is fasting cannot be disposed for Communion in the way the Church desires. If certainty is lacking about his right dispositions, he must abstain. Communion is always possible the next day.

in being, as St. Alphonsus and others teach.[454] We must note that in this case, the fact itself (the *vow*) furnishes the obligation of the law, which is true of any *title* whatever — it is not simply a fact occasioning the application of a law which already binds of itself.

721. The other circumstances, the doubt, for example, whether Thursday midnight has passed with the consequence that I cannot eat meat, do not, as I have said constitute a title of obligation. It is the law that obliges me to abstain from meat. I know that it will soon be Friday and that the law definitely holds. It is not a question of knowing whether there is an obligation or not, because the obligation is or will be certain; it is solely a question of knowing whether the obligation begins sooner rather than later. This circumstance does not make or remove an obligation; it only anticipates or delays it. In these circumstances, application of the rule of possession seems gratuitous and out of place. The rule applies to the external forum, and solely for things we own, as many respected theologians teach.[455]

722. I think we go too far in applying the rule of possession to every moral case, as Bolgeni does. We complicate the matter by speaking metaphorically. This must be avoided at all costs if we wish to proceed with precise ideas. To say that *freedom possesses* and *has dominion*, and similar things, means applying to freedom the words devised by civil laws and applied to quite different things, that is, to real possessions.

723. Furthermore, the words *dominion* and *possession* are sometimes applied with a false, culpable change of meaning. *Dominion* relative to freedom is made to consist 'in the physical power to do what we please'. Yet laws never give this

---

[454] *Th. M. De Consc.*, n. 28. We should note, however, that generally speaking there is an obligation to remember our vows, like all other obligations, in so far as human weakness permits.

[455] The case could be defined even by positive law, in which event the question would no longer be valid. Moreover, when we say that the principle is valid only in the external forum, it does not follow that we affirm all principles contained in canon law to be valid only for the external forum. Many of these principles can decide cases of conscience. Bolgeni, in order to refute the teaching, expounds it far too generally. Cf. his dissertation, *Del Possesso*, n. 94.

[721-3]

meaning to *dominion*; they indicate something moral not physical. There is no *dominion* without *right*. In fact, *dominion* over a thing is only the *right* to use it as we please. Right is not founded in simple physical power but in justice. Hence it is totally mistaken to imagine some kind of freedom without any right but with dominion of its own. It is a mistake to couple a right with *possession* alone, because *de facto possession* can clearly exist without a *right*, and one must not be confused with the other. Once these ambiguities are removed, the universality claimed for the rule about possession collapses [*App*. no. 10].

To settle the question under discussion, it would seem necessary, if certainty is impossible, to follow *what is more probable*, but if the doubt is equal, to follow the *safer* course, from respect for the law. In my opinion we do not have to contend with the law as though its dominion became a burden by *perhaps* being initiated a few minutes early (I say 'perhaps' because it could indeed have begun already). The law is certain, the obligation is certain. But does it begin a little sooner or a little later? Here *equity* should be the rule. If it is more probable that the law is not yet in force, let freedom prevail; if it is more probable that it is in force, let the law prevail; if the doubt is equal, freedom should respectfully give way to the law.[456]

724. The same decision, it seems to me, should be made in the case of doubt about our having fulfilled the demands of the law. For example, have I heard Mass on a day which is certainly a feastday, or given the alms I had promised God to give? Hearing Mass or giving alms are facts which remove or occasion the application of the law, refining its actual obligating force. If I have heard Mass or given the money to the poor, the law no longer obliges me in any way; it obliges me only if I have not done those things.

As in the previous cases, therefore, we must distinguish here between a law's undoubted *existence* and its actual *obligation*, which alone we doubt. We are not asking about the law's existence but its obligation and actual binding force

---

[456] If we act otherwise, I do not think the sin would be equal to a sin committed with the certainty that the time has passed. But I do not see how we could completely excuse ourselves.

[724]

when we have good but uncertain reasons for believing we have fully satisfied all it requires. The meaning of 'the law *possesses*' is that the law *obliges* (otherwise the expression has no meaning). But we cannot assert that it obliges because this is precisely what we want to know; if the obligation is uncertain, possession is also uncertain — granted we can speak in this way. It is my belief that only *equity* can be used in this kind of uncertainty, because we are dealing with an unculpable and insoluble doubt and with merely positive law. We conclude therefore that if what ought to be done is naturally divisible, we divide it 'proportionally to the doubt'. For example, we give £50 to the poor if there is equal probability of our having given or not given the £100 we bound ourselves to give. If it is not divisible, we should follow the *more probable* course and thus compensate the acts in favour of both the law and freedom: when we doubt, we should, out of respect for the law, follow the *safer* course.

5
REMOVING DOUBT ABOUT
THE UNLAWFULNESS OF AN ACTION
WHEN WE HAVE ONLY FALLIBLE AUTHORITY
TO GUIDE US

Article 1.
The question at issue

§1. Summary

725. We have travelled a long way, and it is now time to review our journey.

We have examined the rules needed for the formation of a sure conscience by persons who are undecided about the unlawfulness of an action because of their *proximate moral doubt*.

Such doubt concerns either the *intrinsic* unlawfulness of an action, or arises from some other relatively *remote* doubt unconnected with the intrinsic nature of the action.

[725]

These *remote doubts* fall either on the law, or on facts and conditions related to the obligating force of the law.

If they fall on the law, they are founded either on an inherent defect in the law itself or on our ignorance.

If they arise from our ignorance, the ignorance itself is either culpable or inculpable, vincible or invincible.

All these distinctions were taken into consideration when we indicated the different rules of conscience which can be summarised as follows:

1. When we doubt about intrinsic unlawfulness, we cannot act because we must be *certain* (morally certain) that the action we are about to do is not intrinsically evil. Otherwise, we expose ourselves to the danger of formal evil.

2. Positive law does not oblige if it is uncertain in itself or in its conditions. In order to impose obligation upon us it must either be *certain* or so probable that it produces a *reasonable, opinionative assent* in us.

3. If the law is uncertain only for us as a result of our culpable, vincible ignorance, we must remove our ignorance by careful enquiry and research into the truth.

4. When the law or fact is uncertain either because of our culpable, but presently invincible ignorance, we have to act in the *safer way* (that is, observe the law) if the doubt is evenly balanced or the public good is endangered. When the existence of the law is more or less probable, the safer way will be that which is *more probable*.

5. If our doubt about the positive law is without fault on our part, we are not obliged to follow the law because it does not yet exist for us.

6. Finally if an inculpable doubt is concerned with a fact as a condition of the law or of its application

a) either the fact cannot be verified, and following the law without verifying the fact would lead to moral impropriety; in this case the law cannot be followed;

b) or the fact cannot be verified, but following the law would not lead to moral impropriety; in this case the law *can* be followed. But:

i) if the fact itself constitutes a *title* of obligation, the uncertainty about the fact is equivalent to uncertainty about the law in itself, and does not therefore oblige;

ii) if the fact does not constitute a title of obligation, and the law and obligation are certain so that the fact determines only the *limits* of the obligation itself (as in cases of time, space, and so on), we should follow the *more probable* indication because certainty is lacking.

§2. A new question

726. These are the rules we have proposed, and we submit them very willingly not only to the infallible authority of the Church, but also to discussion by moralists, which we have always thought extremely useful. Nevertheless, it is clear that even if these carefully thought out but complicated rules were true, they would not provide much help for people in general. The reader may well have asked himself already how ordinary people could be expected to make such distinctions, or learn to classify and solve their doubts with the rules we have offered. Is there no easier way for ordinary people to solve their doubts safely than this complicated system? There is, of course, a sure way for all, and it is that of *authority*.

727. Certainly not everyone can be obliged to know how to arrive, theoretically and reflectively at least, at the distinctions we have indicated. This is the responsibility of the masters in Israel whose duty it is to distinguish one kind of leprosy from another, and to throw light on these matters.

728. But at this point, a new, captivating question arises: how and up to what limit can we use *fallible authority* to resolve our moral doubts and to form a conscience for ourselves? We have to give this complex question the most careful consideration on account of its difficulty and because its importance and universal use have made it the source of endless arguments amongst moralists about *probable opinion*, as detailed investigation shows. It is clear, in fact, that these arguments are finally reduced to weighing up the moralists' authority.

729. The early Fathers, who first wrote on Christian morality, had only reason, scripture and the oral deposit of faith as the sources of their moral teaching. But as time went on, the number of authors necessarily multiplied while the

problems they discussed dealt with increasingly particular applications of moral principles to special, detailed circumstances. The inevitable result was a multitude of differing opinions and the foreseeable — and fearful — consequence summed up in the phrase 'There are as many opinions as people'.

There was another danger. Detailed conclusions, and minute distinctions expressed in appropriate language, were not to be found in scripture nor in the Fathers of the Church, the early commentators on scripture. Consequently it was easier in practice to use modern authors, who treated matters in detail and resolved difficulties by considering their obvious circumstances. In the end these authors became the most used and consulted by the majority of confessors and spiritual directors, and provided the textbooks for the education of young men for the priesthood. It is clear that the number of authors, the variety and difficulty of the individual cases they considered, and the distance separating their conclusions from basic principles would lead to an immense quantity of solutions in which opinions would range from extreme laxity to extreme rigidity. Support could in fact be found for every kind of conclusion, and even the most evidently true and sound opinions would have their adversaries. The diversity and contradictions found in priests educated in different schools of thought naturally led in practice to fearful, confused consciences amongst people who did not know where to turn for certainty.

This was the inevitable state of affairs in Christian society when the great question arose: 'How can and must we choose the safe way amongst so many opinions?' This was the tremendous question that the memorable system of *probabilism*, which will always remain famous in the Church, set out to solve. Its enemies, its allies and those who tried to mediate between the parties were all intensely concerned with this problem, the subject of the present chapter.

§3. Continuation: the limits of the question

730. Is it true that we no longer need to direct ourselves with our reason, but on the sole authority of moralists? As far

as I can see, the question has been proposed too broadly and its natural limits removed. When multitudes of moralists acquired more renown than they merited and gathered favourable groups around them, it was thought that everything should be decided on their authority. It seemed rash to use one's own reason in considering moral problems.

731. This is the accusation levelled by Segneri against Tirso Gonzalez, his Father General. Segneri reproves his superior in rather intemperate language for wanting to decide moral cases by reasoning rather than on the contradictory authority of the moralists: 'The law (which the compiler attributes to Father Tirso) seems hard and impracticable. According to him, you should judge the judges themselves (that is, the moralists) who decide in your case. It is you who have to see if their judgment accords with the truth contained in the saying: "The law always presumes in favour of the judges".'[457]

If this reasoning were valid — that is, if it were true that moralists are our *judges* against whom there could be no appeal — we could never without rashness reject any of their contrary decisions. Moreover, if it were presumptuous to rely upon ourselves rather than upon more learned and more pious people, we would have to conclude:

1. That all moral questions have to be decided on the *authority* of moralists, without reference to our own reason and to the early authorities whom the moralists would have already examined.

2. That it would not be lawful to condemn contrary opinions upheld by any of the so-called expert moralists. Segneri himself does in fact say: 'The following supremely safe principle is all that is needed for the direction of consciences: "Anything can be done prudently, piously and laudably which the experts commonly think can be done".'[458] With these words Segneri reduces the *sole moral principle* to the authority of experts, that is, moralists whose conclusions are so often contrary to one another. And these conclusions are good precisely because they are contrary to one another. Rejecting them would be rash in the extreme, and would mean setting up our tiny selves against publicly attested experts whose knowledgeable work we should respect.

[457] Lett. 2, §7.   [458] Lett. 2, §7.

[731]

732. Another motive for taking only the authority of moralists as our rule of conduct (on the basis of humble disregard for our own reason) is the possibility that we may misuse our reason. According to Segneri: 'We are not able to judge dispassionately.[459] We have to listen to others who are well-known for their knowledge, good sense and faithfulness. It would be very dangerous to want to judge those (*the moralists*) who understand so much more than we do.[460] . . . It is no longer possible to pretend that subjective probability is safer for mankind than objective probability. The former entails individual probability on the part of the person who does the action; the latter is universal,[461] formed by persons different from the individual. In whose favour does the presumption lie? In favour of the person judging his own cause, or in favour of the person judged by others?'[462]

Finally Segneri says expressly that the question of probabilism consists in following authorities without reference to one's own reason.

[459] Is there any guarantee that we will be dispassionate in choosing to follow one moralist's opinion rather than that of another? Even if we choose to follow the opinion of the most noted moralist, we can still be led by our feelings. It would be foolish to deny this.

[460] *Who understand so much more than we do.* Who are *we*? Fr. Segneri is describing himself, and although I admire his act of humility, he seems to exaggerate. I consider Segneri far more intelligent than the moralists whom he praises so highly. But Segneri cannot be the only one included in that *we*. Fr. Tirso, Segneri's superior general, is also included and *judged*, together with the teaching of the great moralists. We can go further. If the argument is to have any weight, that *we* must mean many others besides Segneri and Gonzalez. It must embrace all those who have cases of conscience to resolve. How then does Segneri know that the moralists he quotes *understand so much more* than those who still have cases to resolve? Here Segneri not only plays the judge, but the prophet.

[461] This is rhetoric. The opinion of some accredited moralists *other than ourselves* is not *universal*. It often happens that 'the will's tendency is to seek AUTHORITY for wrongdoing; it persuades us either that evil is good or nearly good.' Because of this tendency, St. Augustine wants Christians to be as vigilant as possible: 'And not TO BE DECEIVED BY OPINIONS THAT APPEAR TRUE, nor misled by clever words, nor blinded by the darkness of error. For good is not to be thought evil, nor evil good' (*De Civ. Dei*, 22, 23).

[462] Lett. 2, §7. We are not dealing with *presumption* but with *conscience*. A judge cannot see into the heart, and often has to pronounce sentence on the basis of presumption. But God does not act like that. When he judges, 'presumption has to give way to truth'. Two very dissimilar matters are confused here, and as usual the reader's mind is being led astray.

[732]

'Until now the question has been: can I follow an opinion which, according to the moralists, is less probable than another? The question has never been: can I follow the opinion I think more probable, although the majority think it less probable?'[463]

'The benign opinion does not follow this line. Without hesitation, it requires a person not to act, whatever his attitude, when the reasons brought forward by a number of experts against a contract are so powerful that *in the common estimation of moralists*[464] the reasons adduced in its favour by half that number of experts have no probability. This is because the person concerned is definitely required to believe one who knows more than he[465] does; he is not permitted to rely on his own opinion, however safe or dangerous it may appear.'[466]

What a humiliation! The only worthwhile opinions are those found in the books of dead moralists. Reason has ceased to command.[467]

[463] Letter 2, §7.

[464] The *common estimation of moralists* is always a powerful argument, but probabilists follow the *less common*, not the *common opinion* because, according to them, even the less common opinion is often *very probable*.

[465] Once more, who is this *he*? Is Segneri rashly judging people whom he does not know? Throughout his work he demonstrates a very low regard for his contemporaries, and a very high regard for dead moralists. He seems to think that reason, which previously existed in the world, even in recent times, had altogether vanished.

Segneri's views on the value of moralists' opinions are very different from those of another Jesuit, Fr. Giovan Vincenzo Bolgeni, who wrote more than a century later. History had had time to pass judgment on highly-praised moralists, and Bolgeni uses stronger language than we would in criticising them. 'There are very few amongst them who can be called *classical moralists*. Most copy from one another without attempting a thorough, careful examination of the problems involved. This can be seen in the way moralists constantly bring forward reasons with the same inherent contradictions, false premises and so on, while using the same authorities with the same misunderstandings, irrelevancies, etc . . . Such authors cannot be relied upon. We have to examine the principles and reasons supporting their opinions and decisions without paying attention to the authority of the moralists' (*Il Possesso, principio fondamentale* etc., c. 7, n. 30).

[466] Lett. 2, §7.

[467] Segneri's view that the best of living moralists are greatly inferior to their predecessors and should give way to them is clearly shown in the following quotation: 'There are many moralists either incapable of

733. Nevertheless, I have to say that I do not believe our present generation to be less human than those who preceded us. Before our present crowd of moralists existed, there were no *experts* to whose word we could refer every difficulty. But scripture and natural reason existed, and little by little the Fathers and teachers appeared. Segneri's moralists became *expert* only by studying divine revelation, the scriptures, the decisions of the Church and the Fathers. These beacons have not gone out, and I do not see why they can no longer enlighten us directly just as they illuminated the moralists, nor why we have to content ourselves with reflected light when the sun shines upon us.

This does not diminish the worth of those of whom Segneri thought so highly. It simply prevents our reducing all moral norms to their authority as Segneri would have us do, and allows us, long after Sanchez and Macado, to consider the human race as something more than sheep.

We now have to examine the exaggerations of such a daring opinion which requires us to depend entirely for a moral norm of life on the *opinions of modern moralists*. When the exaggerations become clear, we shall also be aware of the limitations present in the question we have proposed: 'What part is to be played by authority in the removal of doubt and the formation of conscience?' The 'authority of recent authors' will no longer be the universal principle in the application of laws, but a special principle to be associated with other principles such as that of the light of reason which is impressed upon us by the Lord in the very act of our creation.[468]

examining, discussing and weighing reasons in their own field or, if they are capable, have insufficient time to do this! — as we have already said. And if they did have time, would they do it as well as St. Antoninus, Suarez, Sanchez, Macado and other illustrious writers? Why do they not rely on these much wiser moralists?' (Lett. 1, §5). This kind of argument effectively disallows all opposition. And Segneri, in considering himself capable of *judging* the moralists of his own and the preceding century, does not cut too good a figure.

[468] This desire to resolve every problem solely according to the opinions of moralists is the true foundation of *probabilism*. If every solution to difficulties has to depend upon the simple authority of moralists, it becomes impossible to find what is *certain* in many questions, and even

§4. Continuation

734. What we have said in this work is already sufficient to put limits to our question about authority. We have seen that

1. Intelligent human beings cannot make use of authority without first using their reason. How does Segneri know that authority must suffice unless his reason tells him so? How can we recognise authority for what it is, and distinguish one authority from another, unless we *necessarily* judge authority? The individual *reason* (and there is no other kind of reason) is not acting rashly when it judges authority. It cannot do otherwise. It could not go on to subject itself to authority without first making a judgment about the situation.

735. 2. The first norm governing moral duties is the idea of things.

It would, for example, be impossible for me to value a human being for what he is unless I had the idea of 'human being'. I could not know that human beings are not subject to animals unless I could evaluate human dignity through the idea I have of it. My reason, therefore, clearly indicates my duty to me. With regard to the first principles of what we call *natural* and *rational* law — because nature and reason reveal them to me — I have no need of express *authority*, provided my reason has been developed in some way. I know these principles for myself, just as I know the proximate consequences of these principles.

---

what is *more probable*. Segneri uses this argument to defend probabilism. If we grant him his major proposition, the argument is of course valid and convincing. He writes: 'Only in very rare cases, therefore, do we find moralists in agreement about the more probable of two truly probable opinions. In the majority of cases each of the contending authors claims greater probability for his own view. Granted this, how can a scarcely probable opinion be declared improbable when it is so like the most probable opinion that it is taken for such by some people? (Lett. 1, n. 9). In n. 18 he shows even more clearly that in many cases it is impossible to distinguish the more from the less probable opinion. And this is what I meant when I objected that Segneri judged opinions good precisely because they are contrary to one another. Such *scepticism* in moral science, accompanied as always by scepticism in the study of law, was the prelude to *universal scepticism*.

736. Indeed, authority often does nothing relative to these first duties except obfuscate the clear light of reason through false maxims developed by human weakness. Only God can judge if this frequently deceptive use of authority excuses human beings from their sin. It is surely very difficult to be altogether free from guilt when we carry this law in our hearts and can know it simply by looking at it.

737. The confines of authority are therefore already restricted by these principles. The first place in human moral government belongs to the *light of human reason*; and all duties enclosed in the *practical acknowledgement* of individual beings perceived by us are so clear (at least where evil authority does not vitiate our vision) that we cannot ignore them even if we want to do so.

Obscurity begins when we need to deduce duties from *relationships* between several entities, not when we deduce duties from *individual beings*. Amongst these relationships, some are more difficult to know, and demand different powers and levels of reflection.

738. We must use every possible means to overcome this obscurity, and call in aid: a) our own effort at reflection, and b) the authority of others. Our aim is not only to know how something must be done but, if possible, to see the clear reason for it by deducing it from its principles.

739. *Authority* helps us not only as authority, but also as a guide to reflection. It is obvious that the precepts of the natural law became clearer to human understanding after the declaration of the ten commandments when God acted as *teacher* as well as *legislator* of his Israel.

740. It is true we cannot always attain *rational knowledge* of our duties. Sometimes the nature of the duties themselves prevents this, as for example in the case of certain positive obligations which depend upon information about strictly factual matters that must be obtained in the way we gain knowledge of all facts. Sometimes we do not succeed in discovering, understanding and applying even rational laws for ourselves. In all these instances we have necessarily to depend upon authority but not unrestrictedly.

Either we are totally ignorant of the duties in question, or we have doubts about them. Only in the first case do we rely fully on the help of authority, which however we should choose with care.

741. In the second case, where we possess doubtful knowledge about our duties, the role of authority is severely limited. We have recourse to it for resolving only the essential element of our doubt.

As we have seen, doubt does not always affect the same point in moral questions. It can be concerned with the intrinsic unlawfulness of an action, or with some external cause. The latter can be either the *material aspect* of an action or any aspect of law *as positive law*. Again, relative to the positive law, doubt can fall on its existence, on our knowledge of the law, on a fact which serves as a condition for the application of the law, or on our knowledge of a fact. These distinctions, and others which result from them, constitute doubtful elements which can be solved by use of the rules already given. If, however, we are unsure of the kind of doubt we are dealing with, or which rule should be applied in resolving it, recourse to authority is necessary.

742. The authority we consult can answer in two ways. It can resolve the doubt either directly if this is possible, or indirectly by applying the reflective principles we have set out. If, for example, we doubt about the existence of a law, it is sufficient that the authority to which we submit the question reply in one of the two ways we have indicated. Nothing more is needed because the rest is clear. With this light alone, our reason can now proceed to solve the doubt.

It is not always necessary, therefore, to ask our authority for a definitive answer to the question: 'Must I do this action or not?' It is sufficient to enquire about the doubtful points in my series of thoughts. If we rely on authority beyond these limits, it will either simply confirm what we are thinking, or be accepted on our part as a teacher freely leading our thought forward without imposing blind obedience on the will, which has no need of it. In this way, limits are placed on the *necessary* use of mere authority and we, as intelligent beings, are not in danger of becoming autonoma, as some would have us. We must not be deprived of the great merit bestowed upon us by our prompt, careful and unhesitating obedience to the light of reason and of grace given to us by God.

[741-2]

§5. Objections by those who wish to decide all moral cases on the sole authority of modern moralists

743. According to us, therefore, the authority of moralists is always useful, and their opinions more or less acceptable. But we have to insist that it cannot exstinguish *reason* in intelligent beings, and that it cannot oblige anyone to take as guide 'only and all the opinions of the most noted moral theologians of a given period.' It is not right to accuse of open pride those who refuse to accept this rule as a guide when they think it lawful or even obligatory to make good use of their own reasoning. Nor does Segneri's accusation of *lèse majesté* — against those wishing to examine the moralists' opinions — have any validity. It is not a question of people wanting to judge their judges, but of fallible human beings who mutually wish to discuss certain problems [*App*. no. 11].

744. As far as I can see, we are dealing here with an abuse of a good principle, that is, our need to be diffident in our own regard. This sublime attitude is a principle of logic and of religious humility, but it has sometimes taken material forms and what I call conventional expressions. We are led to believe that we are humble only if we think we know nothing, and firmly hold (or at least say we hold) that others know more than we do in every case. These 'conventions' were changed into maxims, and the new precept of humility was preached to the letter. Each person thought he had the right, without injuring his own humility, to accuse others of pride and presumption if they used the light shining within them. This talent had to be hidden, and the opinions of modern theologians accepted. The good people who shamed others by arguing in this way imagined they had won the battle before it had started.

745. Something has to be said against taking the praiseworthy feeling of self-abasement to such extremes and, may we add, against such falsification of true, holy humility. We need to reply to the objection that 'it is rash to bring one's own reason, in addition to the opinions of theologians, into decisions about moral cases.' If this prejudice is not overcome, the teaching we have developed will not be accepted, nor produce its hoped-for benefits, whatever its truth.

[743-5]

I wish to state, therefore, that when we see any truth whatsoever by means of the light of reason, we are obliged to acknowledge it. But we can see the truth with the light of reason in two ways: either by receiving knowledge on another's authority, or by conceiving it of ourselves. We must therefore respect not only the truth communicated on the authority of others, but also that which we may find for ourselves.

This obligation becomes clear when we consider that truth must always be respected, obeyed and kept before each and every one of us as the light of all we do. It is not rash to follow the truth when we see it directly, nor can it be said that doing so means believing in ourselves. It is absurd and false to maintain that we believe in ourselves in adhering to the truth which shines before us; we do *not* of ourselves produce true opinions. Whenever we adhere to the light of our reason, we follow a principle altogether different from ourselves. In this case we certainly have no human being as a teacher, but we do have the truth which is in God himself, 'your sole master'. Why instead are we so attached to what Christ calls 'human precepts and commands'?

We have to insist that there is no rashness or pride in the submission we give to the truth itself and to the Word of God rather than to human beings. We simply defer to the greater not the lesser authority. I suspect that secret human pride, disguised as humility, is present in the totally gratuitous assertion that 'every moral rule must be reduced to the opinion of moralists (who are themselves human).' The aim of this pride is to substitute what is divine with what is human, and to extinguish the sole light from which all good opinions are drawn by moralists, and with which all errors can be overcome.

746. 'You suppose that we see the truth directly.' That is the obvious objection to what has been said, and it goes on: 'And even if we do at times see it, how can we be certain that we see it? How do we know that we are not deceiving ourselves? Isn't it simpler and safer to rely on the judgment of others, and safer to let others judge in our own case?'

At first sight, this appears a very serious difficulty. In fact, it has no weight, although I will reply to it fully. First, however, I would like to recall certain statements of good,

[746]

holy people which confirm our right and duty not to pull down the shutters on the light God himself places and shines in us through the window of our reason.

The author of the *Imitation of Christ* certainly cannot be accused of favouring rashness. Yet he writes: 'The teaching of Christ precedes the teaching of all saints. He who possesses the spirit finds hidden manna within it.'[469] The writer sends us directly to the source without scorning the authority of saints. He simply says that there is more to be found in the teaching of Christ than in that of others. And he would not have hesitated to assert his diffidence about the teaching of moralists who are not holy, or at least not yet sanctified. He adds: 'Happy is he whom the truth itself teaches not through passing examples and words, but as it is in itself.'[470] Once more the author rises above human authorities, and invites us to hear the truth which itself teaches us. He goes on: 'The one to whom the Word speaks frees himself from many *opinions* . . . No one understands or judges correctly without the Word . . . O God, you who are the truth, make me one with you in everlasting love! So often I tire of reading and hearing many things. All I want and desire is in you. Let all teachers be silent, and every creature be dumb in your presence. You speak to me, you alone.'[471] If this is rashness and presumption, it is holy and highly desirable!

747. We can see the same teaching reduced to practice by the most celebrated writers in the Church's history. For example, St. Augustine, after speaking of the infallibility of the sacred scriptures in a letter to St. Jerome, goes on to describe the degree of reverence he has for other writers: 'When I read others, I do not think that what they say is true, however holy and learned they are, simply because they feel it is true, but because they have succeeded in persuading me of its truth on the authority of canonical authors or on the basis of a good reason which reflects the truth.'[472] No moralist

---

[469] Bk. 1, c. 1.   [470] Bk. 1, c. 3.   [471] Bk. 1, c. 3.

[472] *Ep.* 82 (al. 19), c. 1, §3. Note that the word *probable* does not bear the meaning commonly given to it by probabilists. We shall speak elsewhere of the ambiguity in this word, which has been grossly misused to the growing detriment of the question under discussion. St. Augustine himself, whose immense knowledge was no bar to deep humility, considered this very

could turn these words of St. Augustine against him by accusing him of wanting to trust in himself, or make himself judge over the judges. And St. Augustine certainly does not want to rely upon himself in preference to others cleverer than himself. What he says is true, modest and humble. And it clearly shows more humility than that demonstrated by persons who continually insist upon humility in their fellows.

St. Augustine was not guilty of pride in following the rules he had laid down for himself, nor in wanting others to use the same rules when they examined his own works. And he did not accuse others of pride when they did so. In holding to his rule for judging non-inspired writers, and stating that he desired others to do the same with him, he showed himself equally just and prudent to all and manifested a supreme love of truth. It gives me great consolation to be able to quote his beautiful words in favour of my own opinion: 'I do not want anyone to accept everything I say for the sake of following me. Let him accept those opinions in which he recognises clearly that I have not erred. This is why I am presently engaged in writing books which provide corrections to my previous works. It will be seen that I have not even followed myself in everything.'[473]

748. St. Gregory of Nazianzen also, in refusing to impose on others the yoke of probable, fallible human authority, declares they have a *duty* to use their own reason. We will be judged, he says, on the good or evil use we have made of our reason. 'You will say that others think differently. But how does that affect me who love the truth more? It is the truth that will condemn or absolve me.'[474] St. Gregory clearly affirms that although the truth may be contrary to what

important matter in another passage: 'We must not consider the arguments of other authors, although holy and praiseworthy people, as on a par with the sacred scriptures. While we duly respect these writers, it is always lawful to object to or reject anything in their works which we find inconsistent with the truth which, with God's help, has been understood by ourselves or others. This is my attitude to the writings of other authors, and that which I hope others have towards mine' (*Ep. 148 (al. 111), ad Fortunatianum*, c. 6, §15).

[473] *De Dono persev.*, 21.
[474] *Orat.*, 27.

others teach, it can nevertheless shine before our minds in such a way as to judge us.[475]

749. St. John Chrysostom speaks with the same good sense, balance and far-sightedness. He does not think that we should make obeisance to vague, probable opinions, but instead offers us the following extremely wise rule: 'Let us not be content with the *opinions* of many, but investigate things themselves, that is, the effective truth. If we are dealing with money, we do not think it absurd to count it ourselves rather than rely on what others say. Surely we should act in the same way in more important matters and not simply be content with what others decide, especially if we have for our norm, measure and rule what the divine laws assert? I beg you all, therefore, to put aside human opinions and seek your answers in the study of the holy scriptures.[476]

750. The early Church and its great teachers never committed the indiscretion of *obliging* its members to abandon their own reason and allow themselves to be led blindly and exclusively by the probabilist authority of 'moralists' (an indeterminate name with no precise meaning). It was commonly held in the great centuries that human beings have in themselves a clear light which they can see if they want to, especially in the

[475] This, however, must not in any way diminish the esteem which we should have for others. It does not follow from our seeing some truth overlooked by many others that we are superior to them (although we could be, without any reason for vanity — it is God who endows our nature with its gifts; we do not merit them). Sometimes one who knows less can see further than a more knowledgeable person; a child is perfectly capable of noting a philosopher's error. St. Augustine, the humblest of men, shows us why in words of great wisdom: 'In very obscure questions it is not impossible for an individual or a few people to be nearer the truth than the majority. Nevertheless, without considering the matter deeply and forcefully, we ought not to decide in favour of the individual or the few against the overwhelming majority of erudite, extremely intelligent men who hold the same religion and unity' (bk. 3, *De Bapt. contra Donat.*, c. 4, n. 6). St. Augustine means: 1. that an individual can see a truth that cannot be seen by many great people; 2. that seeing it, he can uphold it against many; 3. but that he can do this only after great consideration and mature study of the matter in question. If we were all content with this moderation and wisdom, things would go well. Difficulties arise when lesser men than St. Augustine are prevented from recognising such moderation and wisdom in their anxiety to say what they think. They see good only in exaggeration.

[476] *Hom. 13 in Ep. 2 ad Corinth.* n. 4.

case of the natural precepts. If they do not want to, they *sin*. Moreover, supernatural light will be given to the individual in proportion to his desire for it.

St. Cyprian says: 'Your written law should not depart in any way from the natural law. Condemnation of evil and right choice is divinely impressed in the rational soul in such a way that no reasonable person can offer lack of knowledge or of strength as an excuse for ignoring it. We know very well what has to be done, and we can do it.'

St. Thomas certainly does not restrict the sources of our light to the miserable rule of probabilist modern authorities. He maintains that everyone with an upright heart can have enough light to know what is true if he asks for it. 'Unless we are degenerate, we all love the truth and desire to know it above all things. And truth reveals itself to those who desire it with a sincere heart, and seek it in simplicity of heart. God, who has promised it, is faithful and gives it to those who love it, as we read: Wisdom "hastens to make herself known to those who desire her,"[477] and: "Son,[478] if you desire wisdom, keep justice; and God will give her to you".'[479]

751. It is not zeal for the gospel but childish pedantry that wishes to subject the human race to instruction from the probabilist authority of moralists. But treating mature people as children will not make them remain in the schoolroom. Careful observers of human affairs, who can discern the roots of distant events in causes that normally go undetected, will

---

[477] Wisdom 6: [13].   [478] Sir 1: [13].

[479] *Opusc. 73, de Usuris, in Proemio*. Henry of Ghent's comment on the duties of those who write on moral questions is applicable and useful here. He not only provides further confirmation of the *obligatory* moderate and prudent use of one's own reason that we have urged, but also indicates the kind of feeling for moral duty that has led me to express in this study openly and frankly (as my temperament and custom normally require me to do) what I think conforms to the truth. Henry says: 'A teacher sometimes does not clarify the truth as he knows it when this seems opportune, that is, when he realises it would be useful and advantageous for his hearers. He talks around the subject instead, proposing what OTHERS hold, not what he feels himself. In concealing the truth (perhaps as a result of fear or hatred), he SINS MORTALLY, I think, both against the truth and against his responsibilities as a teacher . . . This is particularly the case in difficult and dangerous questions where arguments for and against open an abyss which, by not revealing the truth, he fails to close' (*Quodl.*, 10, q. 16).

have noted that the immense leap of human ingenuity which took place from the middle of the last century with such harm to piety was, in great part, the natural outcome of the yoke imposed upon mankind especially in the 17th century. Human beings were arbitrarily subjected to every kind of confusion emanating from teachers who were neither infallible nor masters of their material, although public opinion acknowledged them as such. They had no exclusive right to command others, nor to pronounce juridical or even authoritative decisions. Reason, despised and abandoned, took its revenge. It rose forcefully from its degrading humiliation and chose the opposite extreme. Not everyone will agree with this, but those who see its truth will find in it a very salutary lesson.

752. But we must return to the great objection: if we act as judges in our own cause, we will be led by passion. Segneri maintains: 'When an educated person hesitates between two sides of a question, he will easily find reasons for persuading himself that the truth is more likely to favour his inclination: "We easily believe what we desire," as St. Thomas says.'[480] The objection seems to support the *rigid* rather than the *benign* opinion, and appears at odds with Segneri's fear of imposing over-heavy burdens upon people.

But we have to remember that we are discussing a matter of moral conscience, in which only God and the individual play a part. It is not sufficient, for example, for a person to be persuaded that a contract is untainted with usury if his persuasion springs from blind love of money rather than the light of truth.

We have to insist that passion can only blind, not convince the intellect. Truth alone can guide us. Those who judge on the basis of passion will be punished although they neither know nor realise how blind they are. As we have said so often, our first moral duty is to judge uprightly, which is certainly *possible* for us. We are not excused if through culpable passion we deceive ourselves about the probity of our judgment. We simply need to keep in mind:

1. that the truth about very many things shines in each of us;

[480] Lett. 2, §6, n. 17.

[752]

2. that we are *obliged* to follow this truth loyally, promptly and courageously, without renouncing it.

753. 'When it is evening,' Christ said to the Pharisees and Sadducees, 'you say, "It will be fair weather; for the sky is red." And in the morning, "It will be stormy today, for the sky is red and theatening." You know how to interpret the appearance of the sky, but you cannot interpret the signs of the times.'[481]

Christ thus declared:

1. that the Hebrews were capable of knowing many things about the kingdom of God by using the light of reason with which they judged the facts of nature;

2. that they were obliged, under pain of sin as an *evil and adulterous* generation,[482] to hear the voice of their natural reason, although they excused themselves on the pretext of observing the traditions of their fathers.

754. Our divine Master goes further in clarifying the command about using our own reason in matters of salvation, and using it well — which is not impossible (if it were, not using it would cease to be a fault). He says: 'When you see a cloud rising in the west, you say at once, "A shower is coming"; and so it happens. And when you see the south wind blowing, you say, "There will be scorching heat"; and it happens. You hypocrites! You know how to interpret the appearance of earth and sky; but why do you not know how to interpret the present time?' He means that by considering the signs, they would understand that the time for salvation had come. He concludes: 'And why do you not judge for yourselves what is just?'[483] Christ says that they could and should have been able to judge with their own reason ('for yourselves') what was just; and they sinned gravely in not doing so. He adds that they should indeed have freed themselves from the *passion* which led their judgment into error, and themselves to the edge of the abyss. He compares this passion to an accuser who brings a guilty person before the law: 'As you go with your accuser before the magistrate, make an effort to settle with him on the way, lest he drag you to the judge, and the judge hand you over to the officer, and

---

[481] Matt 16: [2, 3].   [482] *ibid.*   [483] Lk 12: 54–58.

[753-4]

the officer put you in prison. I tell you, you will never get out until you have paid the very last copper.'[484]

Christ does not dispense us from using our reason and good judgment. Indeed he commands us to do so, and to shrug off the affections perverting our reason and judgment. He demands just judgments, so often commanded of reasonable human beings in the Old Testament. Zechariah proclaims: 'Thus says the Lord of hosts, Render just judgments, show kindness and mercy each to his brother.'[485] Despite being subject to the obscurity of passion, we cannot say to the Lord that he has commanded the impossible, nor complain about his wanting us to trust our own judgment. If passions themselves are not removed, any other rules, including all the opinions of the most highly regarded moralists, are useless.

755. We are not in fact asking whether it is difficult to follow reason, but only whether a precept exists in those cases when truth presents itself to our reason. 'But how can we ourselves discern when the truth speaks to us and when it does not?' This is the usual sophistry, the normal reply. But even if we cannot distinguish, God can, and it is he who will judge us. 'But if we cannot distinguish between truth and passion when they speak to us, how can we be obliged to listen to the truth, and turn a deaf ear to passion?' Let me repeat the divine command about subduing our passions, intimated long before modern moralists appeared: 'But desire shall be under you, and you shall have dominion over it.'[486] Cain had no schools of theology to consult, but he was able to distinguish the voice of passion from that of reason. If not, how could he have been obliged to do the impossible? Such an absurdity shows that we can, if we wish, distinguish passion and its raucous cry from reason and from the divine word. Confusion between the chaotic roar of passion and the gentle attraction of reason and grace arises only from the faults which blind us. Remove the faults with the means at hand, and the cataract that obscures our vision is eliminated. The light-filled sky is unveiled to us in all its beauty.

[484] Lk 12: 58, 59. John 7: 24 is similar: 'Do not judge by appearances' (this is what is forbidden), 'but JUDGE WITH JUST JUDGMENT': this is what is commanded.
[485] Zech 7: [9].   [486] Gen 4: 7.

756. But besides destroying our *passions*, we must also defend ourselves against *opinions* which would destroy our hold on truth. These opinions may be eminently authoritative, but if we discover of ourselves that they deceive us and combine with our passions to detach us from truth, we must abandon them by following the light we have been accorded. There is no excuse for not doing this.

757. Amongst the Hebrews, those exercising the office of doctors of the law possessed the most authoritative voices. Nonetheless Christ called them blind guides who led others into the pit with themselves: 'If a blind man leads a blind man, both will fall into a pit.'[487] Christ imposes upon us all the duty of guarding against direction from blind guides. Their authority will not save those who fall into the pit with them. Christ wants his disciples to keep their eyes open, not to walk in darkness, nor to sleep, but to watch. It is not the one who leads who needs to see, but the one who is led; and in the kingdom of Christ all is light. We must not allow ourselves to imagine that we can pick and choose opinions from well-known moralists. Our duty is to choose the best opinions with the greatest possible care and diligence in order to avoid the kind of sin which, as St. Bonaventure says, 'is more dangerous than open transgressions. If a person knows that he falls, he can correct himself easily enough. But if he does not know, and goes so far as to persuade himself that what he does is lawful, he has no real change of heart even at death. Holding to the false hope that what he had done was permitted, or at most was a small sin, he finds himself clinging to a broken reed.'[488]

Article 2.
The question answered

§1. The order to be followed in the use of sources employed for deciding moral cases and forming one's conscience

758. The principal duty of every human being is to love and seek moral truth, as scripture says, 'that he may understand

[487] Matt 15: [14].   [488] St. Bonaventure, *Opusc. de process.*, 5, §3).

[756-8]

what he does.'⁴⁸⁹ It follows, therefore, from all we have said that we must not neglect any means that provide the knowledge which serves to direct our life.

759. The natural order of these means, or sources, which enable us to decide doubtful cases of conscience is as follows:

1. *Reason, with its natural light.* This is of considerable help because it enables us to know the first moral principles and their immediate consequences. Knowledge of remote, moral consequences varies from individual to individual.⁴⁹⁰

2. Reason assisted by the light of revelation and the infallible decisions of the Church. This assistance brings strength and vital persuasion of the truth to reason, and also helps it to understand previously unknown, remote consequences of the principles of the natural law. It also indicates many positive precepts.

3. Reason assisted by the interior light of grace. Grace helps reason to understand better what it already sees, and puts it on the road to discovering other moral matters.⁴⁹¹

---

⁴⁸⁹ Deut 29: 9.

⁴⁹⁰ St. Antoninus rightly distinguishes *positive* precepts known on authority from *natural* precepts known through reason. He writes: 'Ulricus says that a person who doubts about what is lawful or unlawful in relationship to some possible fact, and by consulting EXPERTS' (the experts spoken about by Segneri, whom St. Antoninus finds unsatisfactory, as we shall see) 'does what is in his power to discover the truth, is excused if, on the basis of what he is told, he follows what is contrary to truth. He labours under invincible ignorance, as for instance in a schism when he doubts about whom he should accept as pope, or as in the case of subjects faced with a doubtful war, and so on '(these are remote consequences of the natural law, dependent upon positive facts). 'But if in his ignorance he follows even the BEST ADVICE contrary to the truth about natural or divine law he is not excused from sin when he acts because there cannot be invincible ignorance about these matters in one who has the use of reason' (P. 2, tit. 5, c. 9, §2).

⁴⁹¹ St. Augustine says that this light, united with the previous two, provides the surest way of acting uprightly: 'More than anything else, we need judgment and discernment so that Satan may not draw us to evil when he transforms himself into an angel of light . . . But who is capable of avoiding the devil's mortal deceits except by God's rule and help? Such a difficulty is useful, however, in preventing us from trusting in ourselves or IN ONE ANOTHER and in leading us to place all our hope in God. No devout person would hesitate to assert that this is our greatest need' (*Enchir. ad Laurent.*, c. 60).

[759]

4. Finally reason, already supported by the lights indicated under 1. and 2., is also helped by the *fallible authority* of other people, which varies considerably.

760. It is clear that this final aid, although useful, is subservient to those preceding it, and that any solution obtained with certainty by use of the first three sources eliminates any need for the fourth, which has a role only when our own defects and weakness frustrate the work of the first three.

761. We have now determined exactly the question we set out to answer in this chapter. When natural light, aided by revelation, the authority of the Church and grace shows human beings their duties, they have to adhere to it without hesitation. In this case, there is no need to search for other teachers who could at most only confirm the known truth, and at worst muddle it. But when we do not know or we doubt about what to do in given circumstances, how are we to rely on the authority of others? What kind of authority can offer us sure consciences? This is our question.

§2. Continuation: the fallible authority of experts must not render doubtful any sure decision dependent upon the first three sources

762. Our question has two parts, as we have seen, because we seek assistance about our rule of life from experts when we are either in *doubt* or in *ignorance*.

763. Let us deal first with doubt: how must a person who doubts make use of expert opinion? We begin by removing the fairly common, false opinion that we must make use of the opinions of experts to produce doubt, not to solve it. Such an attitude would render authority dangerous, not helpful; it would distance us from certainty rather than bring us closer to it.[492] Unfortunately, when we assert that one

---

[492] St. Thomas says that the many differing opinions of moralists are dangerous: 'In moral matters differences in attitudes and OPINIONS are dangerous (*De Usuris, opsuc. 73 in proemio*). Elsewhere he says that anyone 'led into doubt by CONTRASTING OPINIONS, and holding multiple benefices while the doubt persists, puts himself in danger and certainly sins . . . ; or he is not led into doubt by CONTRASTING OPINIONS, and so avoids danger and

opinion is held by Thomas and another by Bonaventure, we tend to conclude that the matter is doubtful. It is, of course, for anyone who acknowledges no other source than expert opinion for solving doubt; in this case there must be doubt when authorities differ. But let us imagine that someone, without knowing the opinions of Thomas and Bonaventure, has resolved the question with the light of reason and with some of the aids we have described above, and only then comes to know what Thomas and Bonaventure have said. Is he obliged to relinquish his firm, certain persuasion and begin to doubt before he has examined the reasons for the differing opinions? Those who want to reduce everything to expert opinion answer with a definite affirmative. In this way, and in this way alone, mankind, faced with the innumerable opinions of so many authors, finds itself adrift in an ocean of moral scepticism, bereft of all knowledge and certainty. Mankind is thus well prepared for *indifference* and *modern scepticism*.

764. The inevitable outcome of such universal and desolate uncertainty, in which human beings lose every trace of firm, certain persuasion, is the necessary substitution of a *probable* norm, such as the decisions of experts,[493] for the norm of *certainty* which emanates naturally from the light and sense of reason, and especially from the light and sense of reason when it is infused supernaturally.

765. This hesitant, unstable reign of fallible authority

does NOT SIN' (*Quodl.*, 8, q. 6, a. 13). St. Thomas supposes therefore that a person can have firm certainty despite the discordant authorities of others, and in following it does not sin.

[493] Many people who found *probabilism* repugnant from this point of view vigorously protested against it. Antonio Merenda in his treatise on probable opinion (*Praef.* n. 14) says: 'The use of probable opinions is the devil's own way of relaxing the power of the commandments.' Alexander VII and other popes complained for the same reason. The decree of September 7th 1665 states: 'His Holiness (Alexander VII) has heard with sorrow of a great number of opinions, some old and some new, which circulate to the detriment of Christian discipline and cause harm to souls. He is also disturbed by the daily increasing licence of dissolute, clever people whose OPINIONS, altogether foreign to gospel simplicity and the teaching of the holy Fathers, have found a place in matters pertaining to conscience. Christian life would be greatly corrupted if the faithful were to use such licence as a safe rule.'

[764-5]

produces characterless, cowardly individuals, incapable of straightforward action. The inevitable result is the extraordinary discord which causes different voices to affirm: 1. that the most probable opinion has to be followed; 2. that the safest opinion (the one most favourable to the law) has to be followed; 3. that all opinions, however contradictory, are good provided they have the support of at least one serious teacher.[494] The last affirmation is the most coherent although it is ultimately self-defeating.

766. Why is the third affirmation the most coherent? On the one hand (the argument runs), divided expert opinion causes doubt in such a way that if, in the face of some contrary opinion, we did not doubt, we would commit a sin of rashness; on the other hand, only expert opinion can remove that doubt because it alone is the sure criterion of the differing opinions about a moral case. The probabilists hold the only coherent view, therefore, because they alone are completely right in asserting that all opinions are good provided they have some support from a respectable teacher. In fact, because expert opinion exists simply to resolve the doubt it fabricates, the so-called principle of fallible authority cannot do more than give rise to doubt.

It is also clear that if one serious moralist is sufficient as a guide to my moral conduct, another serious moralist dissenting from the first can himself be my guide. But in this case I am necessarily left in doubt because, although there are two opinions, there can be only one truth. In such a doubt, however, there is no reason except my own well-being[495] for

[494] This conclusion was taken further when some maintained that any opinion could be taken as probable provided it had the support of at least one modern author. The proposition was condemned, however, by Alexander VII in the decree of September 24th 1665 (7th proposition). 'An opinion must be thought probable if contained in any book of a minor modern author, provided there is no proof that it has been rejected as improbable by the Apostolic See'.

[495] But what if one or several of these *serious* teachers say that this is not sufficient? Scotus, for example, writes: 'There are many doubtful matters in human affairs which may be mortal sin even after the teachers and commentators have said all they can about such subjects' (In f. 2, Q. *Prol. Sent.*). This assertion, coming from such a respected authority, must also be probable. If it is probable, the opinion that following every opinion of serious teachers is not sufficient for salvation is at least less probable. In this

[766]

choosing the opinion of one expert rather than another. To say that I should hold the more probable opinion is gratuitous because the more probable opinion is not certain if it is opposed by one or more serious moralists. By adhering to the more probable opinion in this circumstance, I would be rashly despising their opinions as insufficient, and putting myself forward as a judge of people cleverer than myself. Moreover, it is impossible to know which is the *more probable opinion*. No one can be familiar with all the authors, but even if it were possible to know them all, it would still be extremely difficult to work out and compare their various degrees of authority. In fact, it would be better simply to take the easy way and use our God-given criterion.

767. 'Choosing the safest way' provides no securer principle because following this path, too, is gratuitous when we are dealing with precepts rather than counsels. Use of this principle entails implicit condemnation of all moralists, however famous, who hold opinions favouring freedom. But if they are wrong, they have erred, and the suppositions — that every dissent about opinions amongst serious moralists must leave us in doubt, or that we should resolve all questions on their authority — is untrue. It is not authority, but reason, that leads us to knowledge of the safest path.

768. The probabilism, therefore, that we oppose — what we may call the 'system of false humility' — offers no thread of hope in the labyrinth where we find ourselves. It may seem consistent with the great principle of authority when it accepts as good all the contrary opinions of reputable authors, but its internal contradictions inevitably destroy it, as we said. There are reputable authors who maintain that probable opinions are not sufficient in every case but sometimes need to be replaced by more probable or safer opinions. Such assertions undermine and throw into doubt even the reflective principle 'All opinions are good provided they emanate from reputable authors', with which we are supposed to eliminate doubts and find certainty. Let us look at the problem once more.

case I am not only doubtful which amongst several opinions is true, but also whether I can lawfully pick and choose amongst opinions, all of which are doubtful.

[767-8]

If Thomas reaches one decision and Bonaventure another, what brings them to their decisions? Neither author is doubtful: their decisions show that. Each of them believes that he has to reach his conclusion by the light of reason shining in him unsullied by passion.[496] We, however, if we have only their authority to rely on, are left in doubt. But besides their authority we have available all the sources they themselves made use of; we can also examine their arguments rather than accept their naked authority. There is nothing to prevent our profiting by the light they have diffused and adding our own tiny rational contribution to the work of their genius; a pigmy standing on the shoulders of a giant sees further than the giant. We ourselves are able to use the sources that enabled our authors to reach their firm persuasion of certainty and through these sources to reach certainty about one or other of their decisions. All that remains is for us to accept and follow this decision. If, however, we cannot arrive at any certainty, we have necessarily to depend upon expert opinion. And this is the subject of the present chapter.[497]

Our problem, therefore, has been considerably restricted: we depend upon expert opinion only in those cases where reason, despite the different kinds of assistance available, cannot resolve our difficulties. But if we have in fact reached the firm persuasion of certainty, we should on no account allow the confused authority of muddled, solemnly academic moralists to disturb our tranquillity.

§3. Continuation

769. Nevertheless, this can happen either through our own fault or not. We can abandon the truth shining clearly in our spirit for the sake of some expert opinion that appeals to our passions. In this case we act with despicable hypocrisy by

---

[496] As we said, inculpable self-deception is not morally harmful.

[497] St. Thomas himself restricts the necessity of expert authority to cases in which a person cannot follow the argument for himself: 'A person with little knowledge is more certain of what he hears from a knowledgeable person than of what his own reason seems to present' (*S.T.*, II-II, q. 4, art. 8, ad 2). He says 'a person with little knowledge', not 'all persons'.

submitting our own judgment to that of another. We bury the talent of our reason, and God will give us what we deserve.

Sometimes, however, it is not our evil *passion* that impedes our assent to the truth we see and to which we are in duty bound, but some *weakness* that excuses us, at least from grave sin.

770. Although the truth shines before us, we, the *subject*, are free to give it our assent and, as subject, have more or less power to do so. The degree of power available, which gives a certain level of decisiveness and greatness to what we call a person's *character*, may be so weak that our assent to the truth before us is shaken and disturbed by the ulterior *reflection* we make on authors who disagree with our conclusion (we note that the degree of power also corresponds partially but not completely to the grade of light imparted to our intellect by the truth). It is not surprising to find authors' 'respectability' leading us to doubt and vacillate about our previous, firm certainty. More elevated reflection, if it becomes a principle of action, is then rendered personal to such an extent that it alone is considered the source of good or evil. That is, the good or evil of an action is attributed to us in so far as we reflect and act on the basis of that reflection.[498]

At this point, in order to find certainty once more, the doubter has to make use of the authority which by eliminating the reason for his certainty roused his doubt. He takes his place amongst those for whom we wish to provide a sure norm of action.

§4. Is there a safe way provided by authority, and what is it, for a person who lacks knowledge or cannot eliminate doubt for himself?

771. A necessary, safe norm for a good moral life is not and cannot be absent in the Church of Jesus Christ which is the 'pillar and bulwark of truth.' But where does each of the faithful find it?

The Church is divided into the *Church teaching* and the *Church taught*. The former consists of the bishops, masters in

[498] Cf. *AMS*, 854–864.

Israel, who teach and guide souls personally or by means of priests whom they appoint as parish priests and confessors. Any Christian, although he cannot have recourse to the bishop in every case, can choose as guide a priest approved for confessions. The choice must be made maturely. After invoking the Holy Spirit, the Christian must choose, according to his own ability and knowledge, the most holy, learned and prudent priest available. The choice must be made without secondary motives, and solely for the sake of having the surest guide on the road to salvation. If the choice is made in this way, I am sure that the Christian will never err in cases of ignorance and doubt (this is the limit to which we have confined our problem) by following the authority disinterestedly. The confessor thus resolves the *doubt* in the subject, if it is a case of doubt, or supplies for the *ignorance* of the penitent, if it is a case of ignorance.

772. Without being dispensed from our obligation to listen to, and obey the voice of our own reason, we are thus securely helped by the authority of the priest when there is need for assistance. At the same time, we avoid appealing to this assistance under the disguise of false humility rooted tenaciously in a secret refusal to face up to our passions and vices.

773. On the other hand, we must not believe that this teaching gives us licence to think just as we please by weaving for ourselves a web of sophistries entangling us in disobedience and evil. This would merit the severest condemnation by God because the holy voice of reason and grace would have been shouted down in our heart by the unreasoning bellow of evil desire. Doubt about such possible deceit should be sufficient to make us submit the case frankly to judgment and instruction from our master.

774. The reason enabling us to affirm that we follow the surest authority in opening uprightly to our confessor the matter of our doubtful duties or ignorance is that we are not following *probability* but what we have called *normal* and *moral certainty*. This is sufficient as a rule of life and moral behaviour. We have already seen that *authority* is of itself a source of normal *certainty* because it is nothing more than the communication to us of another's certainty. I assume that the

[722-4]

confessor, in telling me that something is lawful, is himself *certain* of what he is saying. I am not asking here and now how he has obtained his certainty; but I am obliged to believe that he would not have declared the action lawful unless he himself was sure of its lawfulness. Because I cannot ascertain the matter for myself, I seek the assistance of someone who possesses the *certainty* I lack, and I make use of it. The only difference between the certainty I have gained for myself and that obtained on the authority of the confessor is that in the former case I use my *certainty* and in the latter the *certainty* of someone else. In both cases, I have *certainty* as my rule. I cannot and must not believe that the confessor is telling a lie in communicating his own certainty to me; and if he did, it would be his fault, not mine.

775. The intrinsic reason for our conclusion is as follows. In seeking advice finally from the confessor, we have left nothing undone in our search for the truth. First, we consulted the interior light of reason and of grace. Where this has shown no clear direction, we sought the assistance of the Church and chose the minister whom we thought best suited to us; we were ready to accept whatever this divine minister prescribed for us, and to obey him promptly in our desire to do what is right; we did what we should have done. Errors which may then occur do no harm to our soul because they are at most material. As St. Thomas, the 'Angelic Doctor', says: 'The *truth* of the practical understanding is found in its conformity with upright desire,'[499] not in the conformity between the understanding and the thing. We were looking for moral good, and we found it; and having found it, we found the *truth* for our practical, if not always for our speculative, understanding.

§5. An objection resolved

776. A possible objection, which we shall refute, is that by entrusting ourselves to a confessor's fallible authority, we place ourselves in danger of positing some intrinsically evil act.

[499] *S.T.*,, I-II, q. 57, art. 5, ad 3.

As we have said, we are either *ignorant* of, or have some *doubt* about, the moral implications of a situation. If our doubt is concerned with the natural law and consequently places us in danger of performing an intrinsically evil act, we must do all we can to guard against the danger. No one can be ignorant of this obligation which the natural light of reason reveals even to the least educated;[500] no one need depend on authority to be sure of this. But in all other cases, I must insist, lawful authority can do us no harm even if it deceives us.

The danger of which we are speaking has already been excluded in the case of *ignorance* relative to remote consequences that we ourselves cannot deduce from the principles of natural law. It is also excluded relative to positive legislation, and to the facts upon which the application of positive law depends, as well as the way in which it should be applied. Even the consequences of natural law, if unknown to us and available only by means of information from others, have lost their rational characteristic as far as we are concerned, and are entirely on a par with positive laws.

In all other cases, the director's reply is straightforward: he passes judgment on the lawfulness of our actions and says: 'You can do this; you cannot do that.'

§6. Is the authority of a single moralist sufficient as a rule of life?

777. Because we distinguish between *authors* of moral works on the one hand, and *confessors* and spiritual directors

---

[500] In fact, the simple-minded normally believe themselves obliged to follow the safer path even in the case of positive laws. We need to consider carefully this phenomenon whose explanation is found in the intimate, clear conviction present in all human beings that 'we must never place ourselves in danger of willingly breaking the law.' The simple-minded are unable to make the explicit, obvious distinction between rational and positive law, and consequently lack the distinction between material and formal violation of the law. Lacking this distinction, they generalise excessively the tutiorist principle originating from the natural light. This principle is good, as we shall see, relative to the state of their spirit. We should not be surprised at the absence of this distinction amongst the simple-minded. Theologians themselves avoided it for a long time in solving cases of conscience, and tutiorists (or a very close equivalent of tutiorists) still exist.

on the other, nothing that has been said so far is related to our previous question 'Does the authority of a single reputable moralist make a decision probable?'. The Church of God has absolute need of confessors, but not of authors.

When we wanted to indicate how each of us could work out his salvation, we spoke of directors or confessors as the sure means of avoiding harm that might result from any ignorance or doubt on our part. We insisted that a single director or confessor was sufficient when we approached him in good faith and with an upright intention. Although he is never infallible, speculatively speaking, he is infallible in practice because 1. he is the lawful minister of the Church, our natural teacher, and as such is amongst those to whom it was said: 'He who hears you, hears me'; and 2. he was the best we could find amongst the Church's ministers.

778. This is outside controversy unless serious, positive doubts arise in the penitent's spirit about the veracity of the confessor's decisions. If these doubts are well-founded, and not useless fantasies, they should first be put to the confessor himself. Then, if his replies still leave room for well-founded doubt in the penitent's mind about his being deceived by the confessor, or about positive self-deception on the part of the confessor in important matters, the penitent may ask someone else or even change his confessor. But if more than one of those asked agrees with what has already been said, and those questioned have a reputation for learning and holiness, the doubtful penitent can and must trust their decision and take what he has been told as certain.

779. The problem about obtaining certainty through guidance by a confessor must not be confused with the other question: 'Is the authority of a single reputable moralist sufficient guarantee that we are not misled?' because:

1. The written works of moralists, who are not essential ministers in the Church, lack the *practical certainty* present in confessors who are.

2. Living confessors decide cases which occur in our daily lives according to the circumstances in which they occur. Authors are concerned with theoretical cases only.

3. It is possible to think and talk at length about the case with a confessor who can also be informed about all the

relevant circumstances, including the state of our spirit. This is impossible with books.

4. Above all, there is a world of difference between choosing a single confessor, whom we prudently believe is the best available, and upon whom we rely in all our doubts, and taking *en bloc* as guide, or claiming to do so, innumerable 'reputable' authors amongst whom we can pick and choose as we please and, in doing so, mock truth, virtue, God, and reality.

Article 3.
The knowledge appropriate to a confessor

§1. Knowledge of probable opinions is not sufficient for a confessor

780. At this point it will be useful to consider more fully the authority proper to moralists in helping us form firm persuasions about moral matters. This can be done conveniently through our examination of the knowledge proper to a confessor or spiritual director. It soon becomes clear that the question: 'Does a single reputable moralist suffice to render an opinion probable?' is totally useless. It would not be useless, of course, if it were true that in order to accept an opinion immediately it were sufficient to show that the opinion was *probable*. In this case the entire question would be reduced to knowing when an opinion was probable.

This was Fr. Segneri's view (I consistently take Segneri as my target because of his outstanding reputation, which I hold in great respect): 'The whole point consists in determining which opinions can be called *probable* and which not. This is the real difficulty. Provided we are dealing with truly *probable* opinions, it is indifferent whether they are more or less probable. All probable opinions fall under our consideration.'[501] And this is undeniable because the word *probable* has already been defined by Segneri as *approvable* or worthy of the assent of a wise person. 'The term *probable* in our present discussion means an opinion which has proved itself such by

[501] Lett. 1, §1.

[780]

meriting the assent of a prudent person.' (Segneri leads us into a vicious circle here. He has already established that 'a person acts prudently if he follows a probable opinion', but now defines probable opinion as one meriting the assent of a prudent person). Segneri continues:[502] 'The foundation of moral theology consists in agreeing about the constitutive elements of probable opinion, that is, opinion worthy of acceptance (as previous writers thought); moral theology cannot be based on squabbles about the lawful use of what by comparison may be a less probable opinion.'[503] He thinks that this is sufficient to win the field for probabilism, and continues: 'The term *probable* can undoubtedly be accepted in an upright sense. Just as 'lovable' is that which is worthy of love, and 'estimable' that which is worthy of esteem, so 'probable' is that which is worthy of being approved. It is clearly contradictory to declare an opinion probable in practice, and then go on to deny that it may lawfully be followed.'[504]

This is indeed obvious, and its clarity should have enabled Segneri to see that the meaning he gave to the word 'probable' was not that normally given in the question under discussion. If it were, the whole problem could be reduced to this ridiculous query: 'In practice, can we follow a decision worthy of approval?' Segneri is playing games, as orators often do, by juggling with the twofold meaning of the word *probable*. It is of course true that in Latin this word also means 'worthy of approval',[505] but that is not the meaning it bears in theological and philosophical schools, as we shall show.

[502] Lett. 2, §2.
[503] Lett. 2, §3. Fr. Segneri requires the authority of several moralists for declaring an opinion probable. He writes: 'No one thinks it unlawful to undertake it (the contract) if its justice is rightly thought probable, that is, worthy of approval not only by himself but also by several learned moralists who have examined it carefully. This is what the more benign opinion demands of each of its followers' (Lett. 2, n. 24).
[504] Lett. 1, n. 6.
[505] St. Leo, for example, forbids turning to the sun in adoration so that converts might not think their old idolatrous practice *probable*, that is, *worthy of approval*. But this is very different (obviously different, we may add) from the use of the word *probable* as contrary to *certain* in the discussion about probabilism.

781. Segneri himself defines its meaning in the probabilist dispute: 'Probability is that semblance of truth which *any* uncertain *opinion whatsoever* possesses in its favour.'[506] He does not say 'the probability of a proposition is that which renders it worthy of approval.' He now wisely abandons that meaning which certainly cannot be proper to *any opinion whatsoever which has a semblance of truth in its favour*.

782. This also explains Segneri's contradiction when he wishes to defend himself against accusations of following the proposition condemned by Innocent XI: 'Generally speaking, we always act prudently when we do something in doubt provided that the intrinsic or extrinsic probability of the case, however slight it may be, does not exceed the bounds of probability.'[507] If *probability* means that which renders an opinion worthy of approval so that it may be accepted and followed, any probability whatsoever, however slight, is sufficient for action, 'provided it does not exceed the bounds of probability', because we are then following an opinion worthy of approval by a prudent person. And this is indeed how Segneri defends less probable opinions: 'Simply because they are less probable, such opinions never cease to be probable. They are probable in the way more probable opinions are, but not to the same extent.'[508] But if this is sufficient, the proposition requiring any probable opinion, however tenuous, for action, has been wrongly condemned. Segneri is now forced to contradict himself, as I said, in order to avoid the censure attached to the condemned proposition. He says: 'The condemned proposition would allow any probability, however slight; the common view (that of the probabilists) excludes slight probability, and allows the less probable opinion which, considered in itself, is sometimes the most probable . . . Generally speaking, it is not sufficient for wine to be wine if it is going to be put on the tables of the nobility. It has to be the kind that meets with the approval of connoisseurs as soon as they put it to their lips.'[509] This is the opposite of what Segneri has so often maintained in insisting that

[506] Lett. 1, n. 8.
[507] Pr. 3 of the condemned propositions.
[508] Lett. 1, n. 8.
[509] Lett. 1, n. 46.

probable opinion 'has only to be probable' in order to be worthy of approval. It is not necessary to ask whether that probability is great or small.

783. But if, on Segneri's own admission, it is not sufficient to know that 'an opinion is probable' in order to follow it in practice, it is clear, as we said at the beginning, that the question: 'Does the authority of a single reputable moralist suffice to make an opinion probable?', is altogether useless. It also follows with equal truth that a confessor who is conversant only 'with probable opinions in moral matters' would not have sufficient knowledge to direct souls: 'probable opinions alone are not a safe, infallible norm of upright living.'

§2. Confessors have to form firm, certain persuasions for themselves; how they can do this

784. St. Alphonsus rightly rejects as false, therefore, the generally accepted rule: 'A person acts prudently if he follows a probable opinion.'[510] The saintly bishop also says: 'Before accepting any opinion, the confessor has to weigh its intrinsic reasons. If he finds some convincing reason in favour of the safer opinion for which he has no reply, he cannot accept the less safe opinion, despite the favourable authority of the majority of the moralists, provided the authority is not of such weight that it seems to require more respect than the reason which he has seen . . . But this happens very rarely.'[511]

St. Alphonsus, a holy moralist, is not happy that confessors should be content with knowing the opinions of particular authors, and he does not think that he is encouraging pride by urging them to extend their knowledge beyond these authors. It is not enough for confessors to count opinions and

---

[510] 'Hence, in the above-mentioned study I concluded that the common affirmation of probabilists: "A person acts prudently if he follows a probable opinion", was false' (*Morale systema etc.*, after n. 55 of the *Tract. de Consc. in Th. M.*).

[511] 'The confessor must weigh the INTRINSIC REASONS before accepting any opinion, etc.' (*Th. M. de Consc., Syst. Mor.*).

weigh authorities (which is perhaps more dificult than trying to solve the question directly[512]). Purely historical knowledge of moralists' opinions cannot provide the clear ideas and firm persuasion of certainty required in the spirit of a priest as teacher of the Christian people. It leaves priests hesitant over probabilities; what little persuasion they have is often about misunderstood formulas.

785. Priests who represent the Church, on whose behalf they act as teachers and judges, must make every effort to obtain *certainty*, or at least *certain persuasion*, which enables them to set aside infinite, contradictory and more or less equally weighty opinions for the sake of taking a safe road along which they can walk confidently and securely.

786. St. Bernard distinguishes clearly between the founts of *certainty* from which a spiritual guide must draw and the sources of mere *opinions* which leave the soul hesitant and unsure. '*Understanding* is founded on reason; *faith* on authority; *opinion* is safeguarded only by its probability of truth. The first two (reason and faith) possess certain truth, but opinion, which expresses no certainty, prefers to search for the probability of truth rather than affirm truth . . . Many people think their *own opinion* is *understanding*, but they are mistaken. Opinion can, of course, be taken for understanding, but understanding cannot be taken for opinion. Why? Without doubt because opinion can be deceived, and can deceive itself. But if it can deceive itself, it is opinion, not understanding. True understanding not only possesses certain truth, but is informed of truth.'[513]

787. The confessor must, therefore, acquire the knowledge that can render him a light for the people whom he directs.

---

[512] Bolgeni puts the matter well: 'Educated persons who are capable of understanding intrinsic reasons clearly and profoundly will not find moral certainty by depending solely on the number and authority of people who think differently from them. Note the words: solely on the *number and authority*, that is, separately from intrinsic reasons. Error generally has its first source in a single reputable author. It spreads both orally and in the written works of followers, who accept it either because of their little knowledge or because of blind reverence for authority or laziness in examining the matter in depth, or finally through passion or *esprit de corps*. A little stream will flow on to become a great river' (*Del Possesso*, c. 7, n. 31).   [513] *De Consid. ad Eug.*, bk. 5, c. 3.

He should not seek authorities alone, but the intimate understanding of moral questions that comes as he makes good use
of his reason to reach firm, sure decisions. He can achieve this
by doing what we have already indicated, that is, by drawing
the truth from sources which are available to everyone. They
are 1. the natural light of reason; 2. the light of revelation; 3.
the light of grace; 4. the decisions of the Church. To these he
must add his own study and meditation which, as Liguori
says, will enable him to weigh together intrinsic reasons and
moralists' authority. He should often ask advice, and attend
conferences of more learned confessors; he should have
recourse to bishops themselves if this is necessary; he must
leave nothing undone that will help him find the truth and
attain the wisdom that should be his.[514]

Finally, if he still has doubts that he cannot overcome, he
will be able to resolve his difficulties and be sure of avoiding
error by means of the rules we have set out in this book [*App.*
no. 12].

Article 4.
The difference to be observed in applying
to oneself and others the rules we have set out

788. But we have to point out here the great difference that
exists between applying to oneself and applying to others the
rules we have set out.

789. This diversity depends upon 'our knowing the state of
spirit of another in a way different from that in which we
know our own.' We know the state of our own spirit — our
knowledge, our persuasions and our doubts — by means of
the internal awareness that we have, or can have, as a result of
reflection. The internal state and persuasions of others,
however, can be known only through external signs and
through what people tell us of themselves. It is this very
important difference which obliges us to modify these rules

---

[514] The confessor, therefore, should not rely only on his own or another's
judgment, but should in good faith try to unite both in an all-out effort to
obtain a firm conclusion that will serve as a safe guide. On certainty as a
guide to practice, and on its constitutive elements, cf. *Certainty*, 1351–
1353.

considerably in applying them to others rather than to ourselves.

790. The point at issue will be clearer if we first note that the rules we have given are all founded on the interior state of the person who must act according to them. This may be a state of doubt or certainty; if a state of doubt, the doubt may be close to or remote from action. We can now express the question as follows: 'Are these rules to be applied according to the penitent's persuasions and dispositions of spirit, or according to the confessor's persuasions and dispositions of spirit?'

791. A careful examination of the problem shows immediately that, in dealing directly with the salvation of the soul of the penitent, the rules must not be applied *merely* according to the confessor's persuasions, but *at least in great part* according to those of the penitent in such a way that they become fruitful to salvation. It is not unreasonable, therefore, nor repugnant (as many would like us to believe), that 'the confessor should at times adhere to the persuasion manifested by the penitent', provided this statement is rightly understood.

792. We take as our premise, therefore, the following principle: 'The confessor must always seek the moral good of the penitent', and the assumption: 'The moral good of the penitent is often attained by applying our rules (with the qualifications we shall describe later) according to the state of his spirit.' Such principles allow us to understand correctly St. Alphonsus' declaration: 'I do not know how one can teach in good conscience that generally speaking (this qualification must be noted carefully) the penitent, who has already acquired a definite right to absolution by confessing his sins, can be denied absolution because he refuses to follow the safer of two equally weighty opinions.'[515]

The saint supports his statement with the authority of other moralists. He quotes:

1. Pontas: 'Nevertheless, the confessor who is convinced of the probability of the opinion held by the penitent, can give him absolution because in this case he would not be acting against his own conscience.'[516]

[515] *Th. M. De Consc., Morale Systema.*
[516] Pontas, at: *Confessarius*, c. 2.

2. Cabassuzio: 'All confessors must absolve penitents who do not want to abstain from something declared lawful on the authority (not reproved by the Church) of several pious, learned moralists, even if the probable authority of others followed by the confessor declares the same act less probable.[517] This is the opinion of Navarrus, Silvius, etc., and is founded upon the fact that the confessor, although acting against *his own opinion*, does not act against *his own conscience*. Rather, he is bound to absolve any well-disposed person.'[518]

3. Vittoria: 'If both opinions are probable and upheld by moralists the confessor is bound to absolve the penitent whether he is the penitent's regular confessor or not.'[519] And he cites Paludanus in his favour.[520]

4. Adrian: 'If several moralists of greater or equal authority hold a contrary opinion, the priest must not presume that he can restrict matters to the limits of his own opinion which perhaps is mistaken.'[521]

He continues with quotations from other authorities: Navarrus,[522] Angelo, Silvestro, St. Antoninus,[523] Gerson[524] and Soto.[525]

---

[517] Here St. Alphonsus himself moderates this statement by noting that the phrase 'less probable' is to be understood as 'not noticeably less probable'.

[518] *Theol. jur.*, bk. 3, c. 13, n. 13.

[519] *De Confess.*, n. 109.

[520] 4, §17, q. 2, a. 1.

[521] *De Confess.*, q. 5, dub. 7.

[522] 'If moralists' opinions differ, and the confessor believes that he has a clear text or evident reason on his side, and the penitent a doubtful opinion, he must not absolve him' (this merits careful attention); 'but if the penitent depends upon a reason equal or nearly equal with that of the confessor, and has a reputable moralist in his favour, he can absolve him . . . If, however, there is any doubt whether the penitent must indeed rely upon, or give such a reason, the confessor must choose what is more favourable to the penitent' (Nav., *Manual.*, c. 26, n. 4).

[523] 'Godfrey of Fontaines seems to agree where contrary opinions are tolerated by the Church, as we have said; he also thinks that the confessor should require the penitent to study the matter well in order to form an opinion for himself by consulting prudent authorities if others hold a contrary opinion. This is especially the case when the penitent confesses to someone not his ordinary confessor. He can then be absolved. Richard is very clearly of the same opinion, and makes no distinction between the

793. However, the saintly moralist adds that this theory holds only in general. We now have to try to outline its necessary limitations as carefully as possible, indicating the cases where it is or is not applicable. In this way, we shall provide confessors with some guidelines in what appear to be very complex circumstances.

First, 'The confessor must resolve the penitent's doubts with the rules we have given by applying them to the state of persuasion in which the penitent finds himself.' The confessor's immediate responsibility, therefore, is to discover the state of those persuasions of the penitent to which the rules must be applied. In this case the general principle of verification is: 'The confessor, unless he has suspicions to the contrary, must give credence to what the penitent says.' He must presume that the penitent is speaking the truth, and be careful not to form rash, harmful judgments about him.

794. Nevertheless, he must proceed with great caution, and prudently ask the penitent questions that help to elicit enough information about the state of his persuasions.

795. When this has come to light, the confessor should note whether the penitent is suffering from any mental *blindness* or *obscurity* produced by passions or vicious affections which confuse or distort his judgment, or whether his persuasions

---

normal confessor and others' (St. Antoninus, part 1, tit. 6, c. 10, §10). 'If anyone refuses such advice . . . let him freely hold his own opinion and be granted absolution' (*Idem*, part 2, tit. 1, c. 11, §29). 'If, however, he (the confessor) is not sure whether mortal sin is present, he should not, as a result, immediately rush, as William says, to deny absolution, or to make the penitent aware that it is a question of mortal sin. If the penitent were later to offend in this way, even though the sin were not mortal, it would be mortal for him because everything which offends in conscience is worthy of hell (28, q. 1, § *Ex his*). Laws are more ready to absolve than bind . . . It would seem, therefore, that he should be absolved and left to divine judgment' (*Idem* p. 2, tit. 4, c. 5, § *In quantum*).

[524] 'Doctors of theology must not be over-eager to assert that mortal sin is present unless they are completely certain that such is the case' (Gerson, *De Vita Spirituali*, less. 4).

[525] 'If the penitent's opinion is probable, it excuses him from fault; and therefore he has a right to ask absolution which the chaplain is bound to give' (Soto, in 4, d. 18, q. 2, art. 5, ad 5). 'And when reputable moralists have different opinions, you may follow one or the other in good conscience' (*Idem*, bk. 6, *de Just. et jur.*, q. 1, a. 6, towards the end).

are completely sincere and upright, free from artifice and illusion. If his persuasions were the result of passion, the penitent would be in a dangerous position, and the confessor would have to enlighten him about his bad state in order to help him secure salvation.

796. But apart from this case, and granted that the penitent's state of persuasion is altogether sincere, the confessor must apply to him the rules we have already given.

If the penitent doubts about the intrinsic unlawfulness of an action, and the confessor can resolve the doubt by showing that the action is not unlawful and persuading the penitent of this, the penitent may be given permission to act. But if the penitent thinks that something is lawful which the confessor judges or doubts is intrinsically unlawful, the confessor must explain his reasons to the penitent, listen to those of the penitent and only permit the action if he is convinced that there is nothing immoral in it. If 'it is certain that no one can expose himself to the danger of doing what is intrinsically evil, it is equally certain that he cannot give another permission to do so.' This is, perhaps, the only case in which the confessor cannot follow the penitent's persuasion. Nevertheless, if the penitent has already operated in accordance with his persuasion, and the confessor thinks that guilt was neither seen, nor understood, nor feared by this agent, he can give him absolution because such a case can be concerned only with remote consequences of the natural law. These consequences may be totally ignored or virtually non-existent either because they are so remote from the principles, or because they require more reflection than the penitent is capable of (cf. 279–331). Outside this case, the confessor cannot expose the penitent to the danger of doing what the confessor himself thinks or doubts is intrinsically unlawful. This is the exception indicated by St. Alphonsus when he said that the confessor can rest in the opinion of the penitent *generally speaking*, although not always.

797. If the penitent's doubts about the lawfulness of an action are not proximate but remote — such as those concerned with the existence of positive law, and others previously listed by us — the confessor who thinks differently can again dialogue with the penitent in a mutual,

reasonable search for what appears nearer the truth. If, however, the penitent maintains his own opinion in all sincerity (not out of evil affection), the prudent confessor can rely upon this opinion in applying the rules already given.

Let us imagine that the confessor holds that a positive law is completely certain and reliable, but that the penitent, even after hearing the confessor's explanation, continues to think it doubtful for apparently good reasons. In this case, the confessor can apply the rule connected with doubtful positive law to the penitent's doubt, although he cannot apply it to himself in his state of certainty.

798. This explains why it is commonly said of holy people that they are 'austere with themselves, but gentle with others';[526] it also confirms the saying that moralists should not too easily affirm the presence of mortal sin if they are not totally certain of it.[527]

6

HOW DOUBTS ARE TO BE SOLVED BY THOSE UNABLE TO USE THE PRECEDING RULES

799. We must now deal with a particular case which, although not commonly found among civilised, Catholic nations, is present in the human race. We have indicated two ways of removing doubts about the lawfulness of our actions. The first is to apply the various rules we have given; these rules require a great deal of instruction and considerable precision of mind. The second is by means of any priest constituted by God as a teacher in Israel.

However, some simple-minded people are incapable of solving moral doubts by applying the right rules and, because of a lack of confessors or other competent authority, have no one to turn to for a decision. We need think only of ancient

[526] 'Be austere in your own life; but gentle with others' (St. John Chrysostom in can. *Alligant.*; *Decret. Grat.*, p. 2, caus. 26, q. 6, c. 12).
[527] 'Doctors of theology must not be over-eager to assert that mortal sin is present unless they are completely certain that such is the case' (Gerson, *De Vita Spirituali*, less. 4).

and primitive peoples to convince ourselves that many human beings can find themselves in this state. At the same time we must remember that morality applies to all human beings without exception, and that whatever our mental state and condition, a subjective moral norm must always be available to answer our need. This norm must be relative to and adapted to our condition, enabling us to avoid sin and live innocently. What form of rule therefore must be followed by those who have no light or help to solve their doubt about the lawfulness of an action?

The reader will notice that the case takes us back to the first of the two questions we proposed concerning unformed conscience. We leave the second question, which we have just discussed, on how to solve a doubt about the unlawfulness of an action, to return to the first question which concerns what we must do while in doubt. We have supposed that simple-minded people are devoid of all means for solving their moral doubts, and are therefore like people who have to act while still in doubt about the lawfulness of their action. In this state, as we have said, the safer way must be followed (cf. 471–473).

800. This accounts for the *tutiorism* of primitive peoples. We find it consistently in simple-minded people, who are incapable of distinguishing between a case of natural law forbidding something intrinsically evil and a case of positive law which by prohibiting something makes it evil although it is not intrinsically evil. Because of this inability, these peoples' doubts are complex and total; they doubt the general unlawfulness of an action without identifying the source of its unlawfulness. In this situation the simple-minded are always doubting whether the action is opposed to the natural or positive law, or whether it is intrinsically evil or not. They have no means of applying the law governing their action, and therefore, in order to act correctly, must keep to the safer way.[528]

[528] This *tutiorism*, suggested to the simple-minded by their natural light, comes under the rules for solving cases of *perplexed* conscience, which is apprehensive about evil in acting and not acting. In doubts of this kind, we must distinguish the *degrees of probability* and the *amount of evil* that is possible. The distinction allows us to formulate the following rules:

1. If the amount and probability of evil are the same on either side, *nothing new must be done;*

[800]

801. Observation shows that this mode of action is suggested to the simple-minded by the light natural to them all. We should not be surprised therefore that *tutiorism* is the first system in history for judging the morality of human acts. It remained the only reliable system and rule of conscience until humanity advanced to another stage where tutiorism was first set aside and then rejected and condemned as false. Hence, the older a moral system is, the more rigid it appears. *Rules* of conscience are not so absolute that they can always remain the same relative to different states of individuals and the human race. They have a *subjective* truth which changes in keeping with the change of the state and condition of the subject. This observation has been neglected, which explains why the opinions of moralists are too universal.

7

A COMPARISON BETWEEN OUR SYSTEM AND BETTER KNOWN SYSTEMS

Article 1.
Systems rejecting all reflective principles

802. At the end of this study, I want to make a few observations on the more common systems dealing with solutions

2. If the evil is less on one side that on the other, but the probability is the same, *we must choose the lesser evil*;

3. If the evil is the same on both sides but the probability less on one side, *the less probable evil is to be chosen*;

4. If the evil is greater on one side but the probability less, *the probability must be multiplied by the evil, and the lower result chosen*. For example, suppose the evil on one side is 10 and the probability 1%, and on the other side the evil is 2 and the probability 40%. If we multiply the evil by the probability, we have 10% in the first case, and 80% in the second. This difference requires us to choose the 10% evil rather than the 80% evil. In other words, we must prefer the danger of a greater evil, because the small amount of this danger renders it relatively much more improbable.

These rules are found in the natural tutiorism under discussion. Obviously, a simple-minded person cannot state them explicitly; if he were able to distinguish them, he would have developed beyond the tutiorist stage of human moral behaviour. On the other hand, it is no less true that all the rules are virtually contained in the conscience formed at different times by a simple-minded person.

[801-2]

to doubts of conscience. This will allow the reader to see the advantage of this system over preceding systems.

Some authors clearly condemn *reflective principles* indiscriminately, but we need not discuss writers who obviously do not understand their subject or the nature of reflective principles, although they unwittingly employ one of these principles (which they abhor) when they say (as they do) that 'a person in doubt must follow the safer path'. In this case, they are actually laying down a reflective principle suitable for solving the quandary.

Article 2.
All reflective principles enunciated up to now are right and true,
but insufficient to solve moral cases

803. We can pass from considering those who deny the need for reflective principles, to considering whether the well-known reflective principles are true or false.

While there is no doubt that they are true, their weakness lies in their universality and indeterminateness, which is too extensive, and therefore very difficult to apply. They do not go sufficiently to the heart of the matter and consequently extend much further than the very small, indivisible point of truth which is at issue. However, we must admit that if the principles are proposed more universally than necessary, theologians do in fact restrict their sense and render them more particular with use. But this procedure itself becomes the source of insoluble equivocations and endless disputes, because the principles are not understood by all in the same way.

804. In order to understand better what we are saying and to show how too extensive a meaning renders the principles unsuited for their purpose, we will make some short observations on four of the most well-known:

1. 'Amongst probable opinions the more probable is to be followed.'

This is obvious. To follow the less probable opinion would be contrary to reason and therefore unworthy of human beings. Pagan philosophers acknowledged this: 'Where certainty is lacking in any matter, we must, all things considered, follow what is more probable and direct our life accordingly. The wise person must act in this way.'[529] This was the teaching of the Academicians, who used the more probable way as their rule because they despaired of directing themselves with certainty.

But if the rule is so clear, why is it contested so strongly? Because it is too extensive in meaning, and unsuitable for practice. Once applied, its meaning is indeed restricted, but its clear, obvious universal sense is lost when it is arbitrarily restricted or given a meaning it does not have. Consequently the proposition can easily be manipulated by two opponents, each laying claim to it. For example, among the theses upheld at Lavis we see: 'Our probabilism upholding freedom is clearly more probable than the probabiliorism upholding the law.'[530] Hence probabilists quote the very principle of probabiliorism in their favour and by so doing declare it in contradiction with itself. This was inevitable!

All defenders of probabilism maintain that their system is *true*, and the contrary system necessarily false. Obviously they believe that when they think they are following the true opinion, they are *a fortiori* following the more probable opinion. If both sides rely on the same principle taken in its universal sense, a sophisticated reasoning can be put forward by either side to invalidate the opposite system. The *probabiliorists* argue against the *probabilists* as follows: the *more probable* opinion must be followed; but probabilists allow the less probable to be followed; therefore they err badly. The *probabilists* argue from the same principle but say the opposite of the *probabiliorists*. The more probable opinion must be followed; but probabilism is certainly the more probable of all the systems of morality; therefore probabilism must be followed, and opponents err.

These two arguments indicate that the principle 'The more

[529] In *Phaedo*.
[530] These theses were publicly defended on the 10th June 1760 in the Church of Lavis by Fr. Agostino Bonora, priest of the Canons Regular of S. Michele all'Adige. They were condemned by Rome on the 26th February 1761 [. . .].

probable opinion must be followed', considered solely as an abstract, logical proposition, is entirely acceptable. But it does not favour one system more than the other, nor solve any problems. Every system, whether probabiliorism or probabilism, is proposed and defended by its authors as the only true system, and therefore necessarily much more probable than all the others. We must therefore find another principle that cannot be applied and defended by either side in its own favour.

805. To understand the matter more clearly let us see how the division between the two parties arises not so much from the rule itself as from arbitrary restriction in its use. The probabiliorists maintain that when the opinion upholding the law is *more probable* it must be followed. The probabilists say, on the contrary, that even the less probable opinion (provided it is probable) can be followed in favour of freedom. Either side maintains that its proposition is certain and therefore more probable than the other. Thus, both admit that the more probable opinion must be upheld when the principle of the more probable opinion is understood without any restriction. But the probabiliorists arbitrarily restrict the principle to the *greater probability of the law*. Whether the existence of the law is more probable or not is only a part of the general proposition 'The more probable opinion must be upheld'; it is simply a reason that must be taken into account without excluding other reasons which can all be used for verifying whether the complete proposition *is more probable*. The complete proposition is either 'We cannot act in favour of freedom when the law is more probable' or its opposite 'We can act'. Logically, the probabilists win against the probabiliorists who claim that the mere statement of their principle precludes the difficulties.

806. The inefficacy, due to excessive indeterminateness, of the principle of the more probable opinion, is proved in another way. Segneri makes the following very acute and true observation: 'However, this shows all the more clearly the uselessness of the remedy (against laxism) we are discussing. If those who profess broad-minded teachings in their books said on each occasion that their teachings were less probable compared with others, I grant I could easily protect myself

against these teachings, according to the rule I have established of not following less probable opinions. But unfortunately they often say their opinions are more probable. In this case the rule about not following less probable opinions is meaningless, and another rule is required to teach me what is broad or not. And so we start again to untangle the skein.'[531]

2. 'In the case of doubt the safer way must be followed.'

807. This is also clear; no one can doubt its truth. Cicero saw and noted it in his *De Officiis*. His opinion, taken from earlier philosophers, runs: 'They command well who forbid anything to be done when there is doubt whether the action is good or bad.'[532] But this does not solve the problem. There is nothing less safe than the system of *tutiorism*, condemned by the Church. Anyone wishing always to follow the safer way is certainly following an unsafe path. This contradiction arises because 'the safer way' is understood in a narrow sense and is not synonymous with 'safe' taken in its simple, universal sense. Settle the difference of meaning and the contradiction ceases to exist.

The probabilists therefore claim the safer way equally with the probabiliorists, and so we read again among the theses of Lavis: 'The use of probabilism is very safe. The use of probabiliorism is very dangerous.' The followers of probabilism seem to find in St. Alphonsus the reason why probabiliorism is less safe than simple probabilism: 'Opponents insist that anyone who follows safer opinions acts more safely. I reply that it is certainly unlawful to relax the observance of divine laws more than is possible. But it is no less evil to make the divine yoke heavier than is necessary. Cabassuzio writes that excessive severity, by urging human beings to an excessively difficult task, closes the way to salvation';[533] thus the safer way is not safe. Segneri maintains that 'any truly probable opinion is always safe, otherwise it would be improbable and not probable. If the more probable opinion is safer (which is not always true), what evil is there in deciding to follow only safe opinion?'[534] Indeed, simply saying that an

[531] Lett. 1, n. 12.   [532] Bk. 1.
[533] *Th. M., De Consc., Morale Systema.*
[534] Lett. 1, n. 23.

[807]

opinion is *safe* means much more than saying it is *safer*. The latter is relative safety; the former is absolute.

808. The word 'safe' therefore indicates of itself a way of acting in which there is no error. All theologians agree that we must act in this way, and this is why the various systems are proposed. But the general meaning of the word is neglected in the proposition: 'In the case of doubt we must follow the safer way.' Here, *all things considered*, it no longer means the safer way in practice, because we are judging the action safer by only one element of the assessment, that is, whether the action is more favourable to the law in question. This does not make our action safe; it offers only one circumstance among many to be evaluated for discovering the safe action.

This rule therefore is also insufficiently determined to help us as a clear guide in our hesitation.

3. 'A doubtful law does not oblige.'

809. This rule, like the first two, is undeniable, but solves no problems because it is too indeterminate.

In order to determine it, we would have to know first what is meant by doubtful law. *Tutiorists* say that from the natural law 'comes a certain law that we must always follow the safer opinion'. *Probabiliorists* say the same about 'following the more probable opinion'. *Probabilists* strenuously reject both, but maintain the principle that a doubtful law does not oblige, and deny that the natural law is certain in the way arbitrarily established by its two opponents.

For the principle to be effective, therefore, other principles must be added. On its own, it solves nothing.

4. 'Whoever is in possession has the stronger case.'

810. This is accepted by everybody, but within limits. As a *juridical*, not a *moral* rule, it cannot be denied. If we wish to use the same expression metaphorically in deciding cases of conscience, there is no difficulty, provided we understand it in its full universal sense. Without restriction of meaning, it adapts easily to all systems. Whichever system we follow, if we define the law as obliging, we simultaneously define it as in legitimate possession, and freedom without possession. Antoine rightly refutes this: 'When we doubt whether a prohibitive law exists, we thereby doubt whether we can

lawfully act, and hence whether we are in possession of our freedom. But this is to beg the question; the very thing we are questioning is offered as a principle.'[535] This rule, like the others, is not Ariadne's thread, and cannot lead us out of the labyrinth.

811. We conclude therefore that all the reflective principles proposed so far for solving the difficulties are right and true in themselves, but used alone they are too indeterminate and equivocal to help us with our problems. The reader will be able to judge whether the argument we presented earlier has succeeded in determining the principles so that not only is all misunderstanding removed about their use, but also each has had assigned to it its previously indeterminate object. We tried to do this by accurately distinguishing the objects into their naturally different classes.

Article 3.
Reflective principles must be certain;
probable or more probable reflective principles
are not sufficient

812. A reflective principle is established as *true* only by this precise determination of the sphere of the objects it governs. A principle not established as completely true is a mixture of truth and falsehood, and cannot be *certain*. Certainty is something true which, accepted by the human mind, produces a reasonable persuasion of its truth. A reflective principle which is not *certain* is completely meaningless, because its sole use is to remove doubts and reach a definite answer. What is uncertain can only produce equally uncertain consequences. In this respect we must recognise that the opponents of reflective principles are right when, in order to eliminate them, they attack them as uncertain and therefore useless, like all other opinions.

813. No one can deny that this reasoning carries much weight against those who accept the principle of probabilism in all its extension and affirm that all truly probable opinions can be followed, and that probable opinions are those given

[535] *De Consc.*, c. 4, quaest. 3, resp. 2, ad ob. 1.

by respected authorities. Such probabilists accept all this as
certain, and willingly grant that if it were not completely
certain, there would be no safe principle capable of saving us
in practice from the hesitations of probability and doubt.

We can now see how the probabilists are justly accused of
contradiction by the anti-probabilists.

Reflective principles proposed for solving doubtful cases of
conscience must be certain. This is agreed by everybody and
is self-evident. But the probabilists maintain that any opinion
supported by many authoritative teachers is probable. Yet it
is an irrefutable fact that many teachers of great authority
deny reflective principles or at least their effectiveness. Therefore it is probable that the principles are false, and
consequently not certain. Probabilism is thus torn apart by its
own principles. This argument is definitive, and unanswer-
able.

814. The subtle error always lies in the arbitrary proposition that 'everything must be decided on the authority of
experts, and that if some of them deny the certainty of an
opinion, the opinion is not certain.' It seems to me that the
moral system has to be restated in the way I have suggested,
and reduced to the following propositions:

1. The most reflective of all reflective principles used
by human beings for judging the lawfulness of their actions[536]
must be *certain*.

2. This certainty must not be obtained solely by
consulting the authority of experts, but by examining all the
sources of human certainty available for judging the actions
we are about to do.

3. More probable or less probable *opinions* are
possible, but they are subject to this principle of *highest
reflection*, which is the measure and judge of their moral
force. Hence, their uncertainty does not make the final
decision of our conscience less certain and less safe [*App*. no.
13].

815. Let us conclude. When we act uprightly, certainty is

---

[536] Careful attention must be paid to the teaching we gave in *AMS*, 859–
863: the action of a person (who is the subject of the *imputability of
actions*), always stems from the highest of the reflections he makes when
acting.

always present at both ends of the sequence of persuasions and opinions that occupy our spirit. It is present in the *supreme principle*, which is the highest principle directing our reflection at the moment of our judgment, and in the *final judgment* which constitutes conscience. Between the supreme principle and the particular judgment derived from it uncertain opinions of greater or lesser probability can exist without the least prejudice to the moral safety of our actions.

8

A COMMENT ON THE PROBABILISTS' BOAST THAT THEIR SYSTEM HAS REMOVED SIN WHERE SIN ONCE EXISTED

816. We must add a few more words about probabilists who have undoubtedly made the extraordinary boast that their system has made 'sin no longer exist where sin once existed'. Such a proposition has also undoubtedly offended many people and caused great scandal. But is the proposition as false and absurd as it seems? Only now, I think, after our long discussion, can we make a balanced judgment about the proposition. I shall therefore add a few words on the matter.

817. First of all, we must note that the claim implicitly contains two things: the possibility that what formerly was truly sin may no longer be sin; that in many cases this has been brought about by the moral system called probabilism. The first point is theoretical, the second merely factual. I will comment on both.

818. Relative to the first, we accept as true, *if correctly understood*, that 'what is sin at one time can indeed be entirely lawful at another'. We say '*if correctly understood*' because the only immutable law is eternal law, and to maintain that this law can change would be blasphemy. But if we are asking whether the quality of an action can change from being sinful to being lawful, the immutability of the eternal law is not in question. The sinfulness of an action relative to human beings does not depend solely on eternal law but on many other circumstances. In the first place, the

lawfulness of an action sometimes depends on *positive law*, and positive laws change; new laws are promulgated, old laws abrogated, derogated, prescribed, abandoned. Therefore what was once forbidden can now be permitted, and vice versa.

819. In the second place, the lawfulness or unlawfulness of an action depends on the conditions of the *subject* on whom the law imposes an obligation. It is not sufficient for the law to exist in itself; it must also be applied to and bind a subject. Thus, in the case of the mentally handicapped, for example, although the law exists, it does not bind; the law cannot oblige them because they lack the necessary condition for being bound by it. A *law* does not in itself always produce the same *obligation* for everybody (cf. 667, 694–724). Its principles are fixed, but they *apply* only when the *title of the application* is present in a *fact*. Moreover, the applications, as corollaries of the abstract principles, are not clear to everybody, nor deducible by all (cf. 274–284). In fact the final corollaries are so difficult to know that even amongst the great teachers they cause irreconcilable disagreements. Thus we said with St. Thomas that relative to the remote consequences of the natural law invincible ignorance can be present in many people and excuse anyone who, because of inculpable ignorance, does not follow its dictate.

Furthermore, we expressly considered the successive progress of natural legislation in the human race, and saw how it developed and grew like other theories found in human understanding. We saw this development take place principally according to the law regarding the different levels of reflection to which the human race raises itself. The knowledge gained gave rise to *new duties*, and hence to new imperative formulas. These were successively clarified and classified into grades corresponding to the levels of reflection (cf. 145–194).

820. This development of moral teachings revealed duties not previously noted and, because unnoted, not obligatory. But is it possible that earlier duties ceased, and that some previous obligations no longer had any binding force? This was the real point at issue when we asked 'whether actions that were sinful in the past, can be sinful no longer.' And the

[819-20]

answer is still in the affirmative. Duties decrease just as much as they increase with the changing level and nature of human knowledge and of the reflections producing this knowledge. If higher reflection is absent, it is obvious that we may be obliged to something to which we would not be obliged if we had reflected at a higher level. This was precisely the situation of tutiorism in earlier times, and of the simple-minded, whom we have mentioned. If we consider ourselves obliged, then we are truly obliged, since our conscience is the proximate rule of our action which binds us.

In this book we have given not one but many examples of this situation. Amongst others, we observed that persons can believe themselves obliged, and therefore are obliged, to an exacting effort that destroys them. But all they need do is reflect on the result of their action to know that the effort is too much. If fulfilling the obligation would greatly damage their health, they may even be obliged not to undertake it. But they do not reflect on the matter; they think only of performing the duty as they see it, and that they sin if they do not do it. In this erroneous conscience they have a duty that ceases simply with further reflection.

Many judgments can be rectified in this way, that is, by a higher reflection which is therefore safer and more universal. However, as long as the reflections are not made, such consciences, even if erroneous, oblige fully. There are, therefore, undoubtedly, innumerable obligations that can cease.

821. More important, however, (and I have already pointed it out in describing the progress of moral formulas (cf. 145–194)), is that this does not occur only in individuals and by accident. It is a law applicable to mankind and human societies as they gradually progress from lower to higher levels of reflection. This progress takes place at different times and intervals by means of certain movements which are not accidental, despite appearances to the contrary. While humanity progresses from lower to higher reflection, the moral order obviously undergoes a noticeable modification, and writers of moral science announce new duties and declare others obsolete. This can only cause scandal to those who cannot keep pace with progress in the world, or are unable to explain the change.

[821]

822. We will apply these observations to the well-known system of probabilism, a system that has created as many enemies as it has attracted followers.

The question we proposed is: 'Is it true that since the arrival of the moral system of probabilism, some things which were formerly sins, have ceased to be sins?'.

If what is affirmed is true, then it could not have come about by a change in divine laws (as we said),[537] but only through some change in human beings, that is, in the subject to whom the laws are applied. This change can only result in a higher level of reflections which enables human beings to solve problems better than they could previously, and to deduce new moral consequences. In this way they form new consciences, or rectify and perfect older consciences. For example, a person at a certain level of reflection reasons as follows: 'I do not know if there is a law commanding abstinence from meat today. I doubt it, but I cannot verify it. If I eat meat I run the risk of breaking the Church's law, and I sin. Therefore, I will not eat meat.' This reasoning is natural and simple. People reasoning no further than this are certainly obliged to abstain because of their doubt about eating meat, so that if they do eat it, they undoubtedly sin because they are persuaded they sin.

If, however, a person rises to a higher level of reflection, the reasoning changes dramatically: 'I do not know if a law prescribes abstinence from meat on this day. I doubt it but I cannot verify it. If I eat meat, do I run the risk of breaking the Church's law? Does the Church's law (this is the higher reflection) have the force of obliging me in conscience while I am unable, through no fault of my own, to verify the existence of the law? The Church certainly does not wish to oblige me to that. Therefore, in this case, I am not obliged by the law. I can safely eat meat without sinning.'

At one time the world certainly found itself at these two intellectual levels of lower and higher reflection. When people reasoned in the first way, eating meat while in doubt was

---

[537] Fagnani, therefore, makes a great mistake when he argues: 'If probabilism has made what was once sin, no longer sin, opinions are above the law of God.' He says: 'If this is true, probable opinions are above the law of God and of nature' (*Dist. de op. prob.*, n. 332).

[822]

sinful. Later they reasoned in the second way, and it was no longer a sin. But we should not be surprised at this, if the fault is a subjective act which originates and changes according to the consciences of the subject.

823. These observations, or rather this history of the two intellective states of the world, explains many apparent contradictions in opinions amongst experts, and in laws themselves. When the world, in the first state, was persuaded of sin while acting against a doubtful law, experts used to decide and laws used to command what they had to decide and command, namely, that in doubt the safer way was to be followed, and that the opposite was sinful.

Thus, canon law often gives the general rule: 'In the case of doubt the safer way is to be followed.'[538] The rule was founded precisely on the *persuasion* that to act otherwise is to run the risk of breaking the law; the persuasion makes the rule true and necessary. Canon law itself shows the rule is founded on this *persuasion* common to all, when it says: 'What is harmless in one person must be feared as a great danger in another.'[539] Granted, therefore, that this danger of sin is removed, the rule itself need no longer be applied. It remains true, but doubt about it ceases because of further reflection.

824. It is clear therefore that when tutiorists or probabilists appeal to the writings of earlier experts, the writings, although true, prove nothing in their favour because the writings are valid only for those periods when it was supposed 'that a person had a certain or doubtful conscience that he was committing mortal sin by acting.' But when reflection at a higher level has removed the supposition and reformed conscience, the principle stated by the authors, although true, is no longer useful because the occasion for applying it has passed.

825. No one who examines the problem dispassionately

[538] *Decretal.*, bk. 5, t. 11 and 18.

[539] *Ibid.*, c. 18. *Decret. Grat.*, caus. 33, q. 3, dist. 7, c. 2 and 4. Calderini observes (*Cons.*, 147) that the canonical rule of following the safer path is founded on the *danger of sin*, that is, the case expressed in law means 'every time this *danger* is present'. Therefore, when the danger ceases, we may conclude differently.

can deny that the controversies caused by probabilism have raised the human mind to view the question from a higher level, and have dissipated and rectified erroneous consciences. This has happened in the case of doubtful positive law, which has been shown to have no obligation at all. Thus, where there is no longer doubt, there is no longer danger of sin, and we can proceed safely using our own judgment.

826. Although probabilism has certainly done much harm, it would be wrong to think that the system contains nothing true. To do so would be an injustice to all the good, intelligent people who followed it, and would demonstrate ignorance of human things. No human being has ever devised an entirely true system. To say the least, there is always something false as well as true in any new system. This gives rise to controversies and disputes amongst authors which continue without solution or reconciliation until time has separated the good from the bad, the true from the false, and both sides of the dispute are seen to be right and wrong. Only when reflection has moved to a third level can judgment be made about how much each side's argument is supported by reason. Agreement (always desired by the good) is now possible, and the system which was once a mixture of heterogeneous parts is refined into a homogeneous whole.

827. As long as the important demarcation was not drawn between things intrinsically unlawful and things lawful in themselves, the problem about doubt remained so complex and unrefined that it was impossible to note the difference between natural, essential law and positive law. Consequently it was necessary to adhere to the safer way in order to avoid the accusation of courting the danger of formal sin. Probabilist authors viewed the matter from the point of view of positive law, and to that extent were correct. But doubt remained because they failed to distinguish between doubt about something upright or about something intrinsically and essentially blameworthy. In this sense the system was false and opened the door to broad interpretations. Before it can be used to solve doubt, therefore, it has to be confined to its own limits. Different kinds of doubt must first be distinguished (in the way we have shown) and simplified.

We would then see where the probabilist principle could be applied or not, and where its truth and falsity lie.

828. This, it seems to me, outlines the whole history of probabilism. We have seen its errors: it went too far by applying to every obligation, even those derived from a natural, rational dictate, the reflection which is perfectly correct in the case of positive law. This distinction had to be made (as we said) at the *third level of reflection*, which had still to be achieved. It would result in a higher principle which, although common to all, had not yet been fully applied. We stated it thus: 'An action is certainly forbidden if we doubt its intrinsic unlawfulness.' If, on the one hand, we do not expose ourselves to this danger, we exclude *laxism*; if, on the other, we admit that doubtful positive law does not oblige, we avoid *rigorism*. Here then, expressed in a few words, is the total content of this long work.

829. I humbly submit it, like everything else I do, to the judgment of the Church and the Apostolic See. It contains the opinion of one man, a priest, who for love of truth and the salvation of souls expects his fellow priests, and perhaps others, not to approve the opinion simply because it is his own, but to examine and correct it carefully, and where necessary refute it. Only when they are satisfied that it is true, or have made it true by their own reflection and studies, does he expect them to accept it. In this way all of us will possess the truth and live in its unity.

Appendix

1. (26).

Catholic tradition teaches that the natural law is impressed in human beings by nature. According to St. Augustine the eternal law 'is transferred into the human heart not by passing from one place to another but by imprinting itself on the heart, as the image of a ring passes into the wax without abandoning the ring' (*De Trinit.*, bk. 14, c. 15). We note that this passage identifies the natural law with the eternal law, the former being simply a participation in the latter. This can impart much light to students of thought who wish to think as Christians. It shows how, according to the holy Fathers and Church teaching, the fundamental norm of human actions is present within us by the communication of the eternal law. In no way does it come to us from sensations. I say 'according to the holy Fathers' rather than 'according to St. Augustine' because the teaching is common to them all.

St. Thomas himself clearly says that the natural law is not different from the eternal law, but only a participation in that law: 'The natural law is simply the rational creature's participation in the eternal law' (*S.T.*, I-II, q. 91, art. 2). In reply to an objection he says: 'The argument would be acceptable if the natural law, which is only a participation in the eternal law, differed from the eternal law' (*ibid.*, ad primum). Nor must we think that St. Thomas understands the natural law to be some instinct, as some of his passages might indicate. He expressly says that human beings, as opposed to animals, share 'intellectually and rationally' in the eternal mind: this explains why 'participation in the eternal law on the part of the rational creature is properly called law, because law can belong only to reason. Thus in irrational creatures there is no law, except by similitude' (*S.T.*, I-II, q. 91, art. 2, ad 3).

Moreover, we must note how St. Thomas expressly supposes that, although children cannot make use of the natural law, it is nevertheless impressed as a habit in them, as the principle of knowledge is: 'Sometimes we cannot use what we possess habitually because of some impediment, just as we cannot use the habit of knowledge during sleep. In the same way, the very young child cannot make use of the habit of intelligence, of principles, or of natural law which is habitually present within it' (*S.T.*, I-II, q. 94, art. 1, ad 3). Clearly, then, St. Thomas maintains that the child possesses the moral law in the way that an educated man who is asleep, or not actually thinking, possesses knowledge. It is not possible, therefore, to hold that St. Thomas is a sensist.

To show that I am in complete agreement with St. Thomas and St. Augustine I will add two more observations.

First, I have supposed that the light of reason, inserted in us by nature, is the supreme moral rule, which is precisely what St. Thomas teaches. After referring to the passage of the Psalmist, 'The light of your face, O Lord, is signed upon us' (Ps 4, [7 (Douai)]), he adds: 'as if the LIGHT OF natural REASON, by which we discern good from evil, and which belongs to the natural law, is simply the impression of divine light in us. Hence it is clear that the natural law is simply the rational creature's participation in the eternal law' (*S.T.*, I-II, q. 91, art. 2).

Secondly, I call this light of reason *truth*, which *truth*, as I showed, is *being* as *intuited*. This is precisely what St. Augustine teaches. After asking how the wicked see the moral rules which even they use to reprove evil actions, he replies: 'In the book of that light called TRUTH which describes every just law' (*De Trin.*, bk. 14, c. 15). Cf. also *PE*, 8–12.

2. (fn. 177).

According to St. Thomas, sin is present in the human being if sluggishness of mind, debility and lack of consideration arise from affection for what is carnal and evil. We need to note this carefully: shallow-minded people easily persuade themselves that sin is never present when actual advertence is lacking. But all the most reliable writers on morality teach that inadvertence and lack of consideration, as the effect of an evil disposition prior to the will, can itself be sinful. The evil

disposition and carnal affection depends on our free will; it is
not *consented to* of necessity. Suarez and other serious
authors rightly distinguish between lack of consideration
produced by an *external* (and therefore unwilled and inculpable) *cause*, and lack of consideration produced by an *internal
cause*, that is, from an evil (and therefore culpable) disposition of will.

It will be helpful to cite the passage where Suarez uses
reason and authoritative sources to show that 'it is certain that
there is such a thing as willed lack of consideration: St.
Thomas taught this expressly in I-II, q. 6, a. 3, ad 3 and a. 7.
He says that we can will not to consider something just as we
can will not to will, and will not to act. And hence just as
something can be indirectly willed without an act of will, so it
can be willed without actual consideration on the part of the
intellect. In question 73, a. 7, ad 2 he says the same as in the
question just quoted, q. 6, a. 8: although pleasure may diminish actual consideration, nevertheless lack of consideration is
willed because we have the power either to prevent concupiscence, or to apply our intellect, notwithstanding concupiscence, to consider the matter. Scotus correctly demonstrates
this in 2, Distin, 42, q. 1; and ALL THEOLOGIANS AND WRITERS
OF 'SUMMAE' presuppose it . . . The same teaching is found
also in Aristotle, 2 *De Anim.*, c. 5, where he speaks about
human beings actually understanding when they exercise
their will, and in c. 4 repeats the same thing relative to the
intellect constituted in its first act. St. Augustine is of the
same opinion in 2 *De Trinit.*, c. 3, and in bk. 14, c. 27; often
in these books he expertly discusses and enquires what the
intellect must do so that the will can apply the intellect to the
consideration of some matter.'

After quoting authorities, Suarez gives the reasons. The
first is: 'The will can move the intellect to perform an act, and
for this reason not all actual lack of consideration is natural
and EXTRINSIC; some is INTRINSIC, dependent upon the
human will. This was correctly explained by Gabriel in 2,
Dist. 22, q. 2, a. 1. For the same reason lack of consideration
on the part of the intellect could sometimes be attributed to
the will as its true positive, or at least, deprivative cause. Just
as affirmation is the cause of affirmation, so privation is the

cause of privation.' The second reason — and this is beyond controversy — is that lack of consideration, in the opinion of the authors, is sometimes imprudent and culpable, and therefore willed.

We can add that we are able to do what Christ has commanded, namely, not let our reason sleep but keep it constantly alert to its duties. Hence, we can sin without consideration, and indeed through lack of consideration. Suarez continues: 'Finally, to pray without attention is wrong and culpable because mental distraction can be willed; non-attention is simply non-consideration. Therefore, lack of actual consideration can sometimes and perhaps often be willed.' (*Tract. de Volunt. et Involunt.*, Disp. 4, sect. 3, 8).

3. (305).

In his *De Volunt. et Involuntar.* (disp. 4, sect. 3) Suarez asks when lack of attention is willed and when unwilled. He replies that any answer has 'to avoid two extremes' (n. 17). The second extreme — the only one we need to consider here — consists in thinking that 'inattention is unwilled simply because it is not adverted to, that is, in so far as a person does not reflect upon his inattention and consequently does not form any consciousness of it. The other extreme is present when we say that lack of attention is willed only when it is reflected upon formally in some way, and WE EXPRESSLY NOTICE THAT THE MATTER IN HAND, WHICH HAS NOT BEEN CONSIDERED SUFFICIENTLY, REQUIRES MORE CAREFUL ATTEN-TION or we at least doubt whether sufficient thought has been given to it, and consider that we are obliged to pay it more attention.' (n. 21). Suarez agrees that if this teaching were true, many difficulties would be solved easily, and many sins excused. But it is precisely this that makes him very suspicious of the opinion: 'But this makes me very SUSPICIOUS OF SUCH A MORALLY DIFFICULT opinion' (n. 21).

He goes on to note three absurdities which would arise if such lax teaching were accepted. First, no one would sin mortally who did not actually advert that his act was a grave offence against God. 'One EXTREMELY ABSURD consequence is that no one would sin mortally except the person who actually thinks that his act is a serious offence against God. Very few think in this way when they sin. They are preoccupied instead with their own pleasure, revenge or utility, etc.' (n. 14).

Second, all those who are on the whole perfect would never commit venial sins because they would never wish any evil to which they adverted. 'Secondly, it follows in the same way that no one would sin venially without actually pondering the malice and depravity of the venial sin and discovering it in the particular act he performs . . . The result of this can scarcely be believed. Many people in a normal state of perfection would rarely or never sin venially — yet the falsity of this is apparent from what we know on the subject of grace. The conclusion is obvious: there are many who would never commit an evil act for any reason whatsoever if they ACTUALLY ADVERTED even to its venial malice. But IS THERE EVER ANY ACTUAL ATTENTION IN VENIAL SINS WHICH COME ABOUT ON THE SPUR OF THE MOMENT?. When actual attention is present, the sin has already been deliberated with at least the IMPERCEPTIBLE DELIBERATION (hence without conscience) SUFFICIENT FOR MORTAL SIN. This applies to actually carrying out the sin, as Cajetan noted above (II-II, q. 88, art. 1) and we shall consider when we come to the section on sins' (n. 15).

Finally, the third absurdity, noted by Suarez (n. 16) as a consequence of the opinion that inadverted lack of attention is never willed, is that in such a case there could be no imputation to fault without some actual reproof on the part of one's conscience. 'Thirdly, it follows that an act is never imputed to fault unless it is done WITH SOME ACTUAL REPROOF ON THE PART OF CONSCIENCE. If there were no reproof, there would be some lack of attention.' This would appear contrary to scripture in the first place. 'This consequence appears contrary to Paul's saying (2 [1] Cor 4): "I am not aware of anything against myself, but I am not thereby acquitted", words used almost in our context by St. Jerome in his *Second Dialogue against Pelagius* where he reproves Pelagius for saying that no sin is committed through ignorance. "Often enough," he says, "THERE IS SOME HIDDEN MALICE WHERE WE THINK WE HAVE

ACTED WELL. This explains why the Apostle expresses himself cautiously: he may have sinned through ignorance." Certainly this ignorance in Paul could only consist in lack of actual attention . . . We also have the words of sacred scripture WHICH SEVERELY REPROVE THOSE WHO OFFEND WITHOUT ANY REPROOF ON THE PART OF CONSCIENCE BECAUSE THEY ARE SO ACCUSTOMED TO SINNING, and drink in sin like water.' The Fathers agree with this: 'The Fathers can be quoted as witnesses to this when they warn us that even words of virtue are to be done with great discretion "LEST WHAT IS THOUGHT TO BE A CAUSE OF VIRTUE BE IN FACT A GUILTY OFFENCE", as Gregory said (*Moral.*, bk. 1, c. 19, *alias* 39; and bk. 5, c. 22, *alias* 23; and bk. 9, c. 16 *seu* 25 ss.), and Cassian (*Collat.*, 1, c. 20–22).'

A little later (n. 23) Suarez considers the case of a person who in sinning adverts to what he does, but not to the species or gravity of the evil he commits. Suarez reproves those who say that such a person always sins venially simply because he does not advert in particular to the gravity of his sin. He says: 'This kind of moral teaching is FALSE AND HIGHLY DANGEROUS. If it were true, practically all sins would be venial, especially in the uneducated . . . Again, who would say that a person harming his neighbour, and actually thinking of doing evil and causing him harm — great harm, in fact — would sin only venially because he did not actually consider the gravity of the harm done?' He confirms this with another observation: 'This can be confirmed in another way. If two people commit a theft with exactly the same advertence, thinking only that the theft is evil but without considering the matter further, and one steals 100 and the other 10, the former sins more gravely although he does not advert formally to the more serious malice in the matter. If this were not the case, it would have to be said that sins done with simple, confused advertence to their malice, were equal and slight, which NO THEOLOGIAN WOULD HOLD.'

Suarez then brings forward (nn. 28–31) an intrinsic reason which shows undoubtedly that people can sin without conscience and without advertence to or reflection on the iniquity of their act. He begins with the principle obliging us to act prudently and with attention when our duties are in question. Such a precept can only be ignored through lack of attention and advertence. Now, let us suppose that this command would not oblige except when we reflect upon it. In this case, we have to go on to ask if this reflection on the command to reflect is obligatory or not. If it is not obligatory, there is no command to reflect on our duties. If it is obligatory, it either requires a further reflection on the obligation to reflect on the duty of reflection, or we have to say that there is an obligation to reflect without further reflection on the obligation. In the former case, we fall into the absurdity of requiring an infinite series of reflections before arriving at the precept of reflection on our duties. Because an infinite series of reflections can never be exhausted, this is equivalent to rendering this precept impossible. In the second case, our assumption is granted: a command to reflect can be required or not required without further reflection, that is to say, without advertence. 'The obligation (of considering this precept, and acting prudently), or rather of not excusing persons from it, does not require formal, actual reflection and ADVERTENCE ABOUT THE NECESSITY OF ACTING PRUDENTLY. If this were the case, there would be another obligation about the obligation to advert and reflect, which in turn would require MORE ADVERTENCE AND MORE REFLECTION, and so on ENDLESSLY' (n. 31). Nor can it be maintained that in the absence of this advertence and reflection, free will is lacking. 'By the very fact of considering something, we CAN WILL to consider it EVEN IF THERE IS NO OTHER ACT BY WHICH WE CONSIDER OURSELVES CONSIDERING IT. In the same way, we can set our understanding to consider, in itself and distinctly, either the term of such habit or what is contained there in a confused manner. Augustine is very clear about this in *De Trinitate*, bk. 10, c. 1 and 2) But we shall speak about this more at length in the proper place' (n. 28).

Nevertheless, Suarez agrees (n. 27) that it is difficult to conceive how inadvertence and lack of attention can be 'indirectly willed' not only 'by means of a positive act', but also 'when an act is lacking'. He writes: 'The latter is more difficult to explain, and IN MY OPINION IT IS OFTEN IMPOSSIBLE FOR US TO UNDERSTAND whether inadvertence is willed or not. This, perhaps, is why it is said that "the heart is deceitful above all things" (Jer 17), and "from my hidden sins cleanse me" (Ps 81 [18: 13]).'

But he notes that the difficulty in conceiving such an act of will is not sufficient to exclude it: 'Such a difficulty, however, does not provide sufficient reason for denying this kind of willed inattention.' He confirms this truth on the authority of St. Thomas and other teachers, 'St. Thomas (I-II, q. 6) undoubtedly presupposes this where he teaches . . . that an effect can be willed, although it may not be foreseen (he is speaking about direct, not about possible, indirect foresight) . . . The same truth can be gathered from other authors who say that VIRTUAL DELIBERATION, as Cajetan affirms, or INTER-PRETATIVE DELIBERATION, as Durandus affirms, is sufficient for a willed act. Others state that fault is present when the will neglects to apply the intellect sufficiently to learn what is required, as Gabriel says in 2, D. 12, and Cordova accepts with others whom he quotes, q. 17, dub. 1, *in fine*.'

I hope this extract from Suarez' teaching about inattention and inadvertence will be useful in pointing to a difficult moral question, which today is treated far too lightly. The extract shows: 1. that according to Suarez, St. Thomas, St. Augus-tine and the other doctors quoted, inadvertence itself is sometimes a sin, although the inadvertence is not adverted to; 2. that hence while *knowledge* of evil and *free will* are indeed necessary for a culpable sin, *advertence*, that is, reflection on one's knowledge and on one's free will, is not — hence neither advertence, nor conscience is involved; 3. that consequently an erroneous, malicious and blameworthy judgment is possible without reflection, attention or con-science on the part of the person who makes the judgment; 4. that this culpable error is not something *natural* and *neces-sary*, but *willed* and *free*, at least as a consequence of the bad disposition of will that precedes and determines it.

4. (360).

An apparently simple act is very often composite, that is, caused by many simultaneous acts, some good, some evil, which can differ in their morality. This union of good and evil in human actions is always possible in the case of venial sins which, because they do not drive grace away, do not prevent merit. It explains many otherwise inexplicable facts praised in divine scripture such as God's praise of the Hebrew nurses despite their untruthfulness. 'In saving children,' says St. Thomas, 'these nurses acted with a good will. Nevertheless their will was not upright when they lied' (*S.T.*, I-II, q. 114, last art., ad 2). The question of multiple good and bad moral acts existing in a single act is dealt with clearly by Cardinal Gerdil in his *De Actib. Hum.*, c. 4, prop. 3.

St. Bernard also recognises that it is possible, in the same act, to merit and to sin venially as a result of the complexity of the elementary acts constituting the action in its moral essence. After saying that if an act is evil, the intention cannot make it good, he adds: 'I maintain that a right intention alone also deserves praise. Clearly, a good will is not deprived of its worthy reward even in an act that is not good. However, simplicity is not deceived without some evil' (*De Praecepto et Dispens.*, c. 14). In my opinion St. Alphonsus does not use appropriately this passage of St. Bernard, and another of St. Thomas, in attempting to show that a good intention sanctifies an action in itself evil. He writes: 'The holy doctor (Aquinas) is speaking here of good understood simply and absolutely, not relatively and accidentally, that is, of good invincibly apprehended by conscience which is the proximate rule of our action' (*De Consc.*, c. 1, 7). This distinction does not seem to represent Aquinas' mind on the matter. St. Thomas speaks expressly about sin; he says: 'Whatever is done contrary to the law is always evil, and is not excused by the fact that it is done according to conscience' (*Quodlib.*, 8, 13).

Summarised, the different opinions may be expressed as follows:

    1. when we act contrary to the law, even if according to conscience, sin is always present;

    2. when we act according to conscience, even against the law, sin is never present;

    3. we must distinguish between a *vincible* and *invincible* conscience: we always act correctly with an invincible conscience but not with a vincible conscience. The majority follow this third opinion.

But the correct definition of an *invincible conscience* leads to further differences, or at least obscurity. An invincible conscience:

a) can be directly contrary to the rational law;

b) can never be contrary to the rational law;

c) cannot be contrary to the *principles* of natural law, but can be contrary to the *remote* consequences of the law.

I hold the third opinion, but I must add a distinction I consider important. Relative to the remote consequences of the natural law, an erroneous conscience can be formed:

1. through *inculpable ignorance*, in which case the dictate to be applied is absent and the conscience is indeed invincibly erroneous;

2. through *culpable ignorance*, that is, through neglect or hatred of the truth; in this case the dictate is again absent but such a conscience is seldom *sincere* (which means it is rarely conscience) and is always sinful. Nevertheless, if the *dictate* is absent and we have repented of our sin of ignorance (at least generally of all our sins, known or not), which we cannot dispel immediately, the *vincible* conscience becomes *invincible* for as long as we are not able to dispel the ignorance, and we do not sin by acting in accord with it;

3. through *error* in deducing or applying the proximate *dictate*. In this case:

either *A*, the *error* is due to *ignorance* of a fact or circumstance, and can be culpable or inculpable; or it is due to another's authority, which can be followed without fault, and sometimes must be.

or *B*, the *error* is *formal*; in which case moral defect and sin is always present; the conscience is no longer invincible, and it is sinful to follow it.

But this last sin can be *venial* or *mortal*. In the first case it is possible for the action, even if done with minor guilt, to be good, granted the good intention of the will. In the second case the action can never be good but can be accompanied by some good, natural disposition.

5. (fn. 328).

Impartiality, a duty imposed upon writers by the more general obligation of love for truth (cf. 443), obliges me to differ in this study from St. Alphonsus de Liguori, for whom I have the highest respect and devotion. Careful consideration will show, however, that if I criticise certain occasional, logical slips found in his works, I do not depart from the spirit of his basic teaching. If the Saint sometimes erred in his reasoning, his great holiness helped him to amend and abandon his unconscious mistake. An example will help to clarify the situation.

In the passage cited, St. Alphonsus teaches as certain and outside controversy that a person sins if he posits an act which he considers doubtfully sinful; he sins lightly if the doubtful act is lightly sinful; mortally if the doubtful act is mortally sinful.

If we keep this perfectly correct teaching firmly in mind, it soon becomes clear that what St. Alphonsus teaches immediately afterwards contradicts his premise. He asks: 'What sin is committed by a person who is certain, without doubt, that his action is evil, but doubts whether it is gravely or lightly evil?' It is clear that the moral condition of this person is worse than that of the one above who doubts whether his action is evil. The first does not desire a certain evil; the second wants to carry out an act which he knows is certainly evil. In the first case, an action which could be lawful is desired, although sin is present because the action could also be gravely sinful; in the second case, an action is done which could be as gravely sinful as in the first case, but which can never be lawful. In both cases, grave sin would be present if both persons exposed themselves to the danger of sinning gravely. In addition, there is also the certainty of at least venial sin in the second case, while the first case could, of itself, be immune from all sin.

Liguori, however, after deciding for mortal sin in the first case, seems almost to absolve the second person from sin. But his conclusion, which is so qualified that it falls within the bounds of sound teaching, lacks logical connection with what has already been said. He asks: 'What is the state of one who knows a thing is wrong but doubts whether it is mortally or venially wrong, and acts with such a doubt?.' He replies: 'Some . . . with Navarrus, Gregory of Valencia, Luis de Granada and many others, hold it sufficiently probable that he sins only venially.' This is the bare reply. But he then adds (and we should consider this carefully): 'Provided this person does not advert even confusedly to the danger of sinning gravely, nor to his obligation of examining the matter, and provided that the object is not certainly of itself grave sin.' Nor is Saint Alphonsus content with the qualifications of other theologians: 'And I might add, provided the person concerned has a delicate conscience' (*De Consc.* n. 23).

The qualifications surrounding the solution to the problem seem to destroy the very hypothesis which gave rise to the problem. In fact, if a person does not advert even confusedly to the danger of sinning gravely, nor to the obligation of examining the matter, how can he doubt whether his action is mortal or venial sin? If he doubts whether it is mortal sin, he must necessarily advert to the danger of sinning gravely. The other qualifications, 'provided the object is not certainly of itself grave sin' and 'provided the person concerned has a delicate conscience' have no connection with the question about serious sin in a person who is uncertain whether his action is grave or light sin. These qualifications are only prudential indications helpful to the confessor when he has to decide the state of his penitent.

In order to understand St. Alphonsus correctly we must remember that he is often writing for confessors. He does not intend to judge matters in themselves but, by means of the indications he offers, to help the prudent confessor form his own judgment. It is one thing to judge a matter when all the circumstances are known, it is another when only certain circumstances are known, as in the case of the confessor who cannot see his penitent's heart. The confessor's judgment has to be based on what the penitent tells him and on all he knows about the character of the penitent. Knowing that a person's conscience has been formed delicately, the confessor can prudently conjecture that if the penitent's confessed doubt about sinning gravely were truly doubt, he would not have committed that sin. In this case, the penitent would not in fact be doubtful whether a sin were grave or light, but at most would have a slight, idle fear about the gravity of the sin. This changes the question. The penitent is no longer one who doubts, but a person who fears without any foundation for fear.

6. (600).

St. Alphonsus has an excellent passage on practice in which he affirms that his sole desire is to help souls avoid *formal* sin. His words merit considerable attention, because this was also his motive in his teaching on probable opinion. *Formal sin* was his great anxiety, and through his teaching on probable opinion he thought he could best help people avoid it. This is another confirmation that our teaching, which differs somewhat from his on the theoretical side, is governed by the same intention and practice as that of St. Alphonsus. But even the theoretical part in which we differ is tempered and mitigated by this holy man through practical asides and exceptions, as we have said — in our theory these are an integral part of the teaching, not exceptions. Our system is amply confirmed by St. Alphonsus himself when his *theory* is brought into line with *practice*. After having set out his teaching on probable opinion he adds: 'So much for theory. In practice, the usual question is whether in choosing opinions we should decide for the rigid or the favourable side. My reply is that where there is question of shielding a penitent from the DANGER OF FORMAL SIN, the confessor must generally, and in so far as Christian prudence suggests, make use of the favourable opinions. But if the benign opinions make the DANGER OF FORMAL SIN GREATER — and this is the case with the opinions of some authors, for instance, opinions about avoiding occasions of sin and similar matters — it is ALWAYS right that the confessor should use the SAFER OPINIONS. Indeed the healer of souls IS BOUND to use the SAFER OPINIONS which help penitents to preserve their state of grace' (*Morale Systema*). This passage tells us all we wish to know. 1. The Saint confesses that his theory cannot always be followed in practice: 'So much for theory. In practice . . .'; we, on the other hand, are seeking 'what can and must be done in practice'. This is the only theory that we are trying to establish. 2. St. Alphonsus says that the confessor cannot always follow favourable opinions, although approved by his theory. He may do so only 'when these opinions help the penitent avoid the danger of formal sin.' This is exactly what we maintain when we distinguish the cases where formal sin is

present from those in which it is absent. And 3. If the favourable opinions 'bring closer the danger of formal sin' the
confessor *must* keep to the safer opinion.

In these examples we see how St. Alphonsus' *holiness*
always led him back to the *truth*.

7. (603).

More moderate and clearsighted probabilists hold back at
this point. They are afraid to press ahead coherently with
their system when they see that it could do harm or damage to
their neighbour. In cases of this kind, they prefer to deny
their own system, and abandon probabilism. Fr. Felice
Potestà writes: 'It is not lawful to abandon the more probable
and safer opinion, and follow the less probable, if the
consequence is certain damage or a danger of serious evil to
oneself or a third party' (t. 1, p. 1, n. 74, asser. 2). These
words do not explain, however, why we have to avoid the
danger of *serious* evil only, and not *light* evil as well; or why
we must avoid doing *certain* harm to others, and not *probable*
harm also. Fr. Domenico Viva agrees with Potestà's assertion, and explains it: 'because avoiding serious harm does not
depend often upon the probability of an opinion; for
although a given medicine probably serves as a cure, the
death, for example, of a sick person will not be avoided unless
the probability concurs with the truth of the matter' (*in Prop.
1, damn. ab Innoc. XI*). Fr. Segneri himself (letter 1, §3, n.
31, and letter 2, §9, n. 37) denies that the less probable
opinion can be followed 'when that opinion put into practice
results in harm to our neighbour from which he should be
protected.' Finally, Fr. Niccolò Ghezzi explains the limitation he believes necessary in the field of probable opinion:
'There is another very noticeable point in which the two
teachings under discussion concur absolutely, and must
concur. They are agreed in establishing those matters in
which the use of more and less probable opinions can be
employed. Both sides affirm that probability must be
restricted to opinions that directly regard moral questions
alone, that is, *questions relative to the law*, and cannot be

used in questions that regard the *nature* or *quality of things used as means to obtain an end to which a person has to tend.* Here too it is unlawful to prefer the less probable, the more probable or the most probable opinion to the safe opinion. For example, a doctor is bound to look after a patient as well as he can. If he has a choice between prescribing more or less effective medicines, he must use the most effective. The same can be said about the minister of a sacrament when he is doubtful about the matter or form of a sacrament; and about the government or minister of state in their decisions about how a country should be ruled; and again about a judge, or father, or tutor, or administrator of a sacred place, or about anyone in fact who has to choose the means necessary for obtaining the end to which he is obliged' (*Dialoghi sul Probabilismo, Notizia,* p. 23). According to this teaching, 'when a person is held to work for a given end, he must use the most probable means available.' But the great end to which every human being is obliged is at least that of not doing harm to anyone. He must therefore use the most probable means available to this end. In other words, he must to the furthest extent of his power avoid every danger in this matter.

8. (626).

St. Alphonsus himself asks: 'Must a subject obey his superior in matters which are doubtfully unlawful?' He replies affirmatively, but qualifies his answer in this way: 'Soto, Tournely, Lessius, Sanchez, the Salmaticensians and in general all theologians limit this: whenever what is commanded is extremely difficult or harmful, namely, if the subject in obeying had to expose himself or another person to danger of serious spiritual or temporal harm' (*Th. M. De Cons.,* n. 31).

St. Alphonsus reasons as follows: 'In doubt, the superior, who holds the power of command, is favoured. The doubt cannot rob him of his power to command.' He repeats this when he speaks of a doubtfully unjust war (*Morale Systema,* coroll. 1).

However, we have to ask ourselves in the first place if possession of the power to command — on which the argument relies — is the possession under consideration in moral cases. This kind of possession depends upon answering the question: 'Which actually prevails here and now: the law or freedom?'; it does not depend on the superior's actually holding the power to command, or upon any other person's holding it. Two principles, dissimilar in nature but similar in expression, have been confused.

In the second place, the reason why a subject must fight even in a doubtfully just war does not depend upon the ruler's possession of the power to command. In fact, if the ruler thought the war were doubtfully just, he could not put his subjects' lives in danger by waging it. The reason for obedience is that 'the right to judge if a war is just or not is the responsibility of the ruler', not of the subject. The subject has to consider it just on the *authority* of the ruler (as we saw, this is a principle of moral certainty) who declares it just, unless of course there are clear arguments to the contrary. If a ruler or government were to neglect morality and justice, and were to call on subjects to wage a doubtfully just war, the subjects would not be obliged to support what the governing authority has declared doubtfully just. This is true even though in general there is a definite right to command vested in the ruler or government. In this particular case, the right would not be certain, but altogether non-existent.

How then are we to solve our general question: 'Must the subject obey a superior who commands something doubtfully lawful?' We have to distinguish.

If the doubtful unlawfulness springs from positive laws, but in itself the action is certainly upright, the subject must obey.

If the doubt concerns the intrinsic uprightness of the action commanded, a further distinction is necessary.

If the person in command judges the action to be lawful (and we have to presuppose this, if he commands it), and his judgment is such that we *have to* abandon all doubt (either because of the right he has to make such a judgment or in general because he possesses magisterial authority), then we must obey.

If the judgment of the person in command is not such that we *must* obey it (granted, for instance, special circumstances), our first duty is to resolve the doubt. It will never be lawful for us to act while we are truly in doubt about the intrinsic lawfulness of an action.

9. (689).

We may have grave doubts about the opinions of the 150 probabilists cited by Fr. Tirillo, and of any 150 authors since Tirillo's time; we may reject the wide application of probabilism by Sanchez and Diana in their Catalogues, by De Champs in his famous *Quaestio facti*, and by Nicolò Ghezzi in his *Principi di Filosofia morale* — the last two authors would claim (absurdly) there was a time when every school in the Catholic world taught probabilism. Nevertheless, probabilism has been supported by a very large number of theologians and teachers, famous in their time, who were evidently persuaded they upheld the truth. It is no surprise therefore to note the great effort required by learned opponents of the system in answering Fr. Gagna, who challenged them to name 'a single Dominican theologian to oppose probabilism in the 80 years from Molina to the general chapter of 1656.' (This extraordinary controversy is found in *Risposta alle Lettere teologico-morali di Eusebio Eraniste in difesa dell' Istoria del Probabilismo del Concina*, Modena 1753, Lett. 1). Can a system supported by so many in the Catholic Church contain no element of truth? This would be difficult to believe.

If we admit that probabilism is a mixture of truth and false-hood (which, I believe, this book demonstrates), we also discover it does not stand alone; many disciplines in the history of knowledge are similar. The history of philosoph-ical and moral sciences is made up of such facts.

A person of authority propounds an insufficiently deter-mined principle, a principle which is partly true but too extensive, lacking the necessary limits. Some thinkers deduce true consequences from it, restricting themselves to the basis of truth in the principle; others, wishing to apply the principle to its fullest extent with a stricter, more coherent logic, deduce false consequences. At first, firm faith in the principle leads to the acceptance of the false consequences. They may indeed seem strange, but this is attributed to our ignorance, ingrained prejudices and our different habits of feeling. Finally a time comes when the errors and damage of the consequences attract the attention of alert people who are endowed with good sense and, in moral matters, possess a greater, more delicate moral feeling. The truth of the principle is doubted and there is a return to the beginning. The principle is now ferociously attacked and defended, but as long as good faith remains, both sides gain. Finally, the truth is reached, especially if the Church, by its decisions, gradually restricts the error. Such, briefly, has been the history of probabilism.

An attentive reading of the earliest authors to profess *probabilism* shows that at the beginning the principle was accepted without awareness of its consequences. The learned Veronese priest, Fr. Pietro Ballerini, in his *Risposta alla Lettera del Segneri*, c. 8, says: 'It is very difficult for me to understand the real feeling of those who wrote mainly before 1600. In some places we find them proposing what seem to be probabilist opinions; in other places we read what are apparently contrary principles.' A little further on he says: 'In the case of many of the early probabilists described in the lists above it is impossible to understand the probabilism they propounded and how they understood the words *more* and *less probable*. They speak so obscurely, so incoherently, with so many ambiguities and disparate meanings that obviously this new principle was not yet determined nor even understood by them in the way it is today. I also noticed among them a wide difference in the principles they used to establish their maxim, with the result that the basic principle admitted by one is denied by another.'

In this first stage, therefore, probabilists used the same principle in different ways, deducing different, incomplete consequences according to the wider or stricter meaning they gave to the principle. Only after many consequences had been deduced, was the importance of the principle acknowledged. At this stage, disagreement and discord broke out. Of the probabilists of this second period Ballerini says: 'The earlier notions of probability, which had been obscure and uncertain, were established and classified by the beginning of this century (1600). It immediately faced strong, continual opposition, which has prevented its total acceptance in good faith.' Next, in order to explain the position of those who on the basis of hearsay accuse the Jesuits of laxism, Ballerini, a great adversary of probabilism, continues: 'And it is to the everlasting glory of the Society of Jesus that they provided the first and most famous opponents of the system, who in turn were followed by others from every Order and nation.' Fr. Patuzzi says the same: 'In those dark days, the Society of Jesus truly provided the most outstanding anti-probabilists among private theologians' (*Trattato della Regola prossima delle azioni umane* etc., pt. 3, c. 3, §3).

Finally, after reaching its zenith, probabilism began to decline in the period following 1656, although it continued to be defended by the great Dominican school. Thus, the Dominican chapter held in the year 1656 when, as it were, the holy war was proclaimed, will always be memorable in the history of probabilism. The Church, in its divine wisdom, defended the freedom of both parties to debate the question, but at the same time fixed limits permissible to the experts. Subsequently it condemned any proposition infected with excessive laxism. Such propositions are the 28 condemned by Alexander VII with the decree of 7th September 1665, the 45 condemned by the same pope with the decree of 18th March 1666, the 65 condemned by Innocent XI with the decree of 2nd March 1679, and finally the two propositions condemned by Alexander VIII with the decree of 24th August 1690. They can all be found in *Damnatarum Thesium Theologica Trutina*, etc. by Dominic Viva.

These and other separate condemnations made by the popes at different times, together with their condemnation of Jansenist rigorism, restored moral science to the right path from which at times it seemed to stray. In the meantime the popes' own conduct showed that probabilism was not necessarily false in its entirety, because none of them ever condemned it totally. It is no surprise therefore that in our time we have seen a holy bishop use the work and thought of probabilists to render moral science as benign as the goodness of the divine legislator and as strict as his justice. This is clearly the spirit and intention of St. Alphonsus, and it is in the same spirit and with the same intention that we set out to write, and hope we have written, about those particular points in which we differ from the letter of the holy moralist, to whom Christian moral science owes so much.

10. (723).

Anyone who reads carefully chapter 4 of Gian Vincenzo Bolgeni's *Del Possesso* will have little trouble finding many obvious contradictions.

1. The author defines *dominion* relative to freedom as 'the *physical power* to do what we please' (c. 4, n. 14), although, as everybody knows, *physical power* is simply a fact, not a right. A few pages later (n. 18) we read: 'dominion is *quid juris*', which is a clear contradiction.

2. *Possession* is defined as 'the free exercise of dominion' (n. 15), and we are told that possession or free exercise relative to freedom consists in not being bound by *law*: 'Law places an impediment to the exercise of freedom' (*ibid.*); *possession* therefore is not only a *fact* but also a *right*, because human freedom unimpeded by law has a *right* to act. However, we subsequently read that 'possession is *quid facti*', which again is an obvious contradiction.

3. We recall that dominion to act freely was defined as 'the physical power to do what we please'. This definition must be related to what Bolgeni says shortly afterwards: 'The *dominion* to act freely and the dominion exercised by the law can be impeded and bound by some extrinsic obstacle . . . *Law* places an impediment to the exercise of freedom' (n. 15). But if *dominion* is the physical power to act freely, I cannot see how law can be an obstacle to this power. Even after the moral law has been announced, 'my previous physical power to do what I please' still remains with me. Bolgeni himself says this when he writes: 'Laws are contrary to freedom in one case only, namely, when they oppose *possession*. They cannot oppose the *dominion* to act freely, because freedom

subsists prior to all law, and can never be lacking or doubtful in its essence, that is, in its *dominion*' (c. 4, n. 17). If *dominion*, therefore, means physical power, it can be impeded by *penalties* but not by *laws, force*, or by *right*.

4. The words of Bolgeni just quoted indicate that in his opinion laws are never contrary to the *dominion to act freely* but only to *possession*; *dominion* is the physical power of freedom and as such will never be absent, whatever laws may be enacted. This allows us to understand his next words: 'If the law is probable, freedom becomes probable when . . . the law is cited as restricting freedom and removing the exercise of its dominion (*which is its possession*). It is not possible to have at the same time certainty in freedom and probability for the law; one necessarily destroys the other and both remain only probable. Likewise, when freedom opposes the law, and freedom is probable, the law also becomes probable, since there can be no probability contrary to certainty, and vice versa' (n. 18). These are reasonable, unambiguous words. When he says that doubtful laws make freedom doubtful, we must clearly understand that they make doubtful not the essence of freedom, which does not change, nor the physical power or *dominion* to act freely, which cannot be opposed by laws, but the (legitimate) exercise of the dominion; in a word, they make the *possession* of freedom doubtful. But if this is true, how can Bolgeni go on to say exactly the opposite (n. 18)? 'Although the law and freedom may be probable in some questions, one of them always has certain *possession*. Problems do not affect the certainty of *possession* (which alone is involved, in Bolgeni's view) but only the certainty of *dominion*. Dominion is *quid juris*; possession is *quid facti*. We are not dealing with matters of fact but of right.' Contradictory teachings like these are not expected in a man of such clarity of thought. The problem does indeed concern *right*, and for this very reason concerns *possession* and not *dominion*, according to the meaning given these words by Bolgeni. The essence of *dominion*, relative to freedom, consists in the *physical power* of freedom, a fact which can never be called into doubt nor opposed by the law, although the law can oppose *possession*. In his very example regarding the obligation to fast after 60 years of age, Bolgeni admits that

possession by the law is certain until 60 years, but begins to be doubtful after that. He says: 'The question concerns solely whether the law continues in *possession* and therefore in the exercise of dominion and obligating force' (n. 18). It is incorrect to say that despite doubt, possession is certain. Granted doubt, *possession* itself is doubtful (this differs from the case of real possessions, where the possession is physical not moral), and therefore the principle of possession cannot be applied to solve moral cases in general.

11. (743).

The obligation not to reject any so-called probable opinion, that is, an opinion supported by even a small number of moralists, was asserted so forcefully that 'refusing absolution to a pentient who acted according to a probable opinion' was considered 'a mortal sin by its very nature'. This was Fr. Bauny's very rigorous statement in favour of the lax view, and he cites Suarez, Vasquez and Sanchez. But such an absolute decision seems to me very strange on the lips of a probabilist. I have no doubt that many reputable authors would reject it and, in doing so, would approve as probable the opposite opinion affirming that 'the confessor does not sin if he refuses absolution to a penitent who refuses to accept an opinion supported by some contemporary moralists, but considered truly false and harmful by the confessor himself'. But if the second opinion (that the confessor does not sin) is as probable as the first, can Bauny accuse of mortal sin the confessor who follows it? The first opinion is indeed contradictory when affirmed by probabilists, and self-destructive.

I have defined *probable opinions* according to the mind of the authors I am refuting, that is, 'opinions sustained by a small number of moralists.' But the respect due to recent moralists was taken to extremes when their opinions were made an obligation of conscience according to the statement, supported by not a few authors, 'that a single reputable author is sufficient to make an opinion probable'. Amongst the moralists in favour of this assertion were Fagnani (*op.*

cit.), Gregory of Valencia (I, 2, dis. 2, q. 12, tract. 4, q. 4), Emmanuel Sà (*Summ. in 5 Dubium*, n. 1), Sanchez (*Decal*, tom. 1, bk. 1, c. 9, n. 6), Filliuccio (Tom. 2, tract. 21, c. 4, n. 134), and others referred to by Diana (*Resol. Moral.*, part. 4, tract. 4; *Miscell.*, resol. 30). Sanchez writes: 'You may doubt whether the authority of a single reputable author is sufficient to make an opinion probable. I reply, along with Angelo, Silvius, Navarrus, Emmanuel Sà, etc, that it can. The proof may be stated as follows. A probable opinion is one based on a solid foundation. But the authority of a pious, learned person is not a weak, but a truly strong foundation' (*Sum.*, bk. 1, c. 9). Therefore . . . Such teaching becomes repugnant when it is taken to the point of reducing all decisions simply to the *opinions* of theologians which then become an obligation in conscience *to confessors under pain of mortal sin*. And it is offered as *benign* teaching. On the other hand, there is some truth in it when its authority is viewed more moderately and accompanied by reason, which God has given to everyone. But we shall speak later about this aspect of the teaching.

12. (787).

The moralists' phrase *probable opinions* is concerned with *theory*; the phrase *the judgment on the probable lawfulness of an action I am about to do* is concerned with conscience. *Probable opinions*, which are so many different general theories, are found in books and in the minds of moralists; the *judgment on the probable lawfulness of an action I am about to do* is wholly particular, and is not found in books and in the minds of moralists but formed in an instant by a person about to act. It is therefore a spontaneous judgment on the probable lawfulness of the action which he is considering. *Probability* in this case falls immediately on the lawfulness of the action under consideration, and is therefore a *probability proximate to action*. In forming this judgment, use is sometimes made of a *probable opinion*, that is, a theory applied in judging the lawfulness of an action, but not the action itself. Relative *to the action*, therefore, we are dealing with a *remote probability*. For example, I could have a *firm, certain opinion*, and nevertheless remain uncertain about the lawfulness of my action if in applying this opinion I doubt whether I am applying it rightly. *Probable opinions* and what is normally called *probable conscience* are different things, giving rise to quite different questions. 'Is it lawful for me to follow probable opinions?' is not the same as 'Is it lawful for me to follow a probable conscience?' Considering the two questions as though they were the same is the cause of great confusion and harm, and my whole aim in writing this study on conscience has been to separate them clearly. Anyone wishing to act must first resolve the question 'What must I do if I am in doubt about the lawfulness of my action, or if the lawfulness of my act is only probable?' But the other question 'To what extent and how may I follow probable opinions?' has to be resolved principally by those directing others who act. It concerns the confessor's moral *science* especially, not the *conscience* of the person who acts. We have dealt with the first question throughout the book, with the latter only here at the end.

Nevertheless, these questions, so different in themselves, gradually develop towards one another. This takes place because theory in every science is always a complex of principles which of their nature form an order with different levels where the more general descend to the less, right down to the final species. The same occurs in moral science. The opinions (if I may speak like this) composing it are distributed of their nature in different orders: first, the most general, then the less general, and finally the most particular and deter-mined of all, that is, so-called *cases of conscience*. When these cases are solved, they come very close to the judgment of conscience which they help to form, although they must never be confused with it because:

1. Cases of conscience proposed in morals books usually lack innumerable determinations found in practice. The immense diversity of these determinations cannot be adequately catered for in a book.

2. Even if the cases proposed and resolved in books did in fact possess all the determinations and accidental qualities found in practice, the solutions given would still be

theoretical and general and, as such, applicable to an infinite number of equal cases.

The *real case* cannot therefore be resolved by means of the *theoretical case* until the latter is applied to the former. But this application also presents its own difficulties, and is subject to error if made inexpertly. For example, the theoretical case can be applied rightly to the real case only if the two are perfectly equal. And how easy it is to take two *similar* cases as though they were *equal*!

Although the most particular opinions, that is, those regarding the solution of cases presented in all their individual circumstances, do indeed come close to the real solutions found by the conscience of the person who acts, the two questions about *probable opinions* and *probable conscience* (to use the common phrase) remain distinct.

13. (814).

Probability is frequently mentioned in the rules of conscience that I have given in this book. Moral science will be helped, therefore, if in addition to the schema of *Certainty* referred to in 510, I classify *probability*.

I divide moral probability into seven classes:

First class: *maximum probability*. This kind of probability naturally produces a full *opinionative assent* whenever the opposite probability is so small as to be negligible, or, if not so small, escapes human attention, or, if observable, has no force to produce a significant fear of the contrary.

Second class: *legitimate probability*. This is required by those laws which allow a person to act when a condition prescribed by the law has been fulfilled. As we said (cf. 682, 684, 685), the probability varies according to the quality of the laws, and we should note that it is a *species* rather than a *degree* of probability.

Third class: *probability greater than its opposite*. This probability is seen by the *intellect* as greater than its contrary but lacks the power to give the *spirit* a full *opinionative assent*; it simply inclines the spirit. It is less than legitimate probability (which can make up for the lack of certainty), and provides only *opinion*.

Fourth class: *equal probability* on both sides. This is a case of perfect doubt, in which properly speaking we cannot have an *opinion*, because opposite opinions of equal probability incline the spirit to neither side. Opinion, according to its definition, is a 'consent given by the intellect to doubtful things for some apparent reason.'

Fifth class: *lesser probability*. This is the opposite of opinion, from which the spirit holds back. Here we should note the true sense of the moralists' words, 'more probable opinion, less probable opinion, equally probable opinion.' *Opinion*, relative to the person who has it, is always more probable than its opposite, otherwise he would not hold it. But when different opinions are present in different people, the person hearing them says one opinion is more probable than another, or less probable, or equally probable, according to the number of people who hold it and the weight of their authority. The person who classifies opinions in this way is not expressing his opinion, but judging the opinions of others; he believes he is making a judgment, not expressing an opinion.

Sixth class: *probability opposed to legitimate probability*. This is formed by the small degree of probability which legitimate probability lacks in order to be certainty.

Seventh class: *least probability*. This is that very small amount of probability which the greatest probability lacks in order to be certainty.

Fear is located in the spirit, not the mind. It can also come from the imaginary apprehension of a danger, although the mind clearly sees there is no reason for it. Consequently, fear has no place in a table of probability.

Index of Biblical References

Numbers in romans indicate paragraphs; numbers in italics indicate footnotes. Bible references are from RSV (Common Bible) unless marked †. In these cases, where the author's use of scripture is dependent solely upon the Vulgate, the Douai version is used.

Index of Persons

General Index

Numbers in roman indicate paragraphs or, where stated, the appendix (app.); numbers in italics indicate footnotes.

moral formulas as rules of, 222, 223

moral reason and, 23, 24

moral states before formation of, 104–107

most difficult part of ethics, 6

not necessary for moral acts, 40–48

obligation of, 112, 113, 366

order of means for solving cases of, 758, 759

origin of, 30, 31

perplexed, 391–396

pharisaical, 390

positive law and, 141

practical, 467, 468

practical judgment relative to, 18–20, 24

principal part of ethics, 5

principle of morality, 112, 140

probable, 464–466

probable opinion and probable, *app.* no. 12

proximate rule for human actions, 140

questions on, 220 ss.

reflection and, 15, 24, 25, 30, 57–71

rigid, 378–381

rules of, summarised, 725–727

scrupulous, 365, 391, 397–405

simultaneous, 274–278, 364

somnolent, 383, 385–388

speculative judgment and, 19, 22

states of, 201, 215

states of humanity and, 50–58, 62, 63

study of, 4, 5

subsequent, 17

true, 230

willed error and, 302

see also **Doubtful Conscience, Erroneous Conscience, Invincible Conscience, Less than Upright Conscience, Non-upright Conscience, True Conscience, Upright Conscience, Vincible Conscience**

Contract

morality of usurious, 624

Council of Trent

fomes defined by, 89

Custom

cause of ignorance, 354

Damned

sin and fault in, 79, 80

Debt

doubt about, 638–642

Direct Knowledge

principle of morality, 283, 284

Dominion

relative to freedom, 723; *app.* no. 10

Doubt

about a fact, 714–724

about abrogation of law, 682

about intrinsic lawfulness of action, 538 ss.

about meaning of law, 681

about opinion of confessor, 778

about positive law, 683

about promulgation of law, 672–677

about will of legislator, 670, 671

basic principles relative to solving, 535, 536

direct and indirect, 520–522

normal (moral) certainty and, 517, 518

of penitent about intrinsically evil act, 796

of penitent about remote lawfulness of actions, 797

practical and speculative, 473, 559; 325

use of authority in cases of, 763 ss.

when laws clash, 678–680

when natural and positive law are mixed, 684, 685

Doubtful Conscience

action and, 471–473

nature of, 464–466

not a conscience, 218, 398

speculatively and practically, 467, 468

Duties

knowledge about particular duties, 589–596

knowledge required for, 584

Erroneous Conscience

accidents affecting, 287–290

advertence to, 321–325

care needed to avoid, 459–462

existence of, 302

formation of, 412–416